SCI-FI SAVANT

SCI-FI SAVANT

GLENN ERICKSON

POINT/BLANK

To María Palacios, with love *Sin Fin.*

CONTENTS

INTRODUCTION

The DVD Savant column has been reviewing classic sci-fi DVDs on the Internet since 1998. Thirteen years later, nearly all of the genre's pre- *2001: A Space Odyssey* "Golden Age" is readily available on disc, a situation that only older consumers will appreciate. Before home video, fan curiosity was limited to the titles they could catch on late night television or see in revival screenings. Popular titles like *Forbidden Planet* were overexposed while others dropped out of sight. Val Guest's marvelous *Quatermass 2 (Enemy from Space)* remained unavailable for twenty years.

It is now easy to access titles once known only through listings in old film catalogs and film festival reviews. Roger Corman's *The Man with the X-Ray Eyes* was a big hit at 1963's Trieste Science Fiction film festival, but so was the superb Czechoslovak *Ikarie XB 1*, a film that waited forty years to be screened in the United States in its original version. Catching up with *Ikarie* and other Eastern Bloc films made during the Cold War is like discovering a new wing in a favorite museum. Some Soviet-influenced films politicize the conquest of space with anti-American messages that mirror our own anti-Communist bias.

I saw many of these pictures as a child or young adult and responded primarily to their special effects and fantastic content. Re-viewing the core films as an adult reveals a wealth of shared themes and active political agendas, more often than not conservative. This begins right at the start of the 1950s with *Destination Moon*. George Pal's speculative primer reveals a stifling climate of fear and aggression behind the dream of space exploration. In film after film, the bluntly stated motive for space research is to place nuclear weapons in orbit or on the Moon, to "seize the high ground" ahead of our international competitors. That Cold War thread continues right up through *2001: A Space Odyssey*, where politically opposed scientists engage in an uncomfortable, uncooperative meeting aboard a space station.

As has been done with the western, the tendency is to sort sci-fi films along ideological lines, creating an opposition between conservative and liberal fantasies. *The Thing from Another World* has been identified as right wing, while *It Came from Outer Space* is pacifist-leftist. Other films have been incorrectly categorized, such as the presumed pacifist classic *The Day the Earth Stood Still*. Some titles remain difficult to categorize, or are claimed by both camps. The brilliant *Invasion of the Body Snatchers* encourages an allegorical ambiguity that allows twin interpretations.

The anti-Communism of classic sci-fi is occasionally blended with religious themes that reflect the booming Revivalist movement of the early 1950s. The hysteria-driven *Red Planet Mars*, where God is revealed to be alive and living on our neighbor planet, is the most extreme of these naïve pictures. The apocalyptic subgenre frequently interprets the threat of nuclear weapons as a Biblical prophecy. Both *When Worlds Collide* and its French predecessor *La fin du monde* preach that higher powers are reacting to the sins of humanity by sending Old Testament fire and brimstone our way.

Fritz Lang's *Metropolis* takes place in a mythical future dominated by a technological elite. H.G.

Wells' epic rebuttal *Things to Come* predicts a century of war and ruin before a guild of engineers rebuilds civilization from the rubble. The bulk of 1950s sci-fi supplanted grand themes like these with amateur dramatics, rubber monsters and bland moralizing. But the visionary aspect of sci-fi was never entirely defeated, and many a juvenile programmer will suddenly surprise us with a minor revelation. No matter how cheaply mounted, Roger Corman's early films always entertained a strong concept. The humble *Attack of the Crab Monsters* sees human consciousness being harvested by super-evolved crustaceans; the lonely alien invader of *Not of This Earth* teleports life-giving human blood back to his home planet.

50s sci-fi films initiated a new kind of techno-fantasy that anticipates amazing but threatening futures – the "Imagination of Disaster" outlined by Susan Sontag. Exit dialogue inevitably doubted Man's readiness to accept the responsibility that comes with a Brave New World: "Your choice is simple: join us and live in peace, or pursue your present course and face obliteration." "When Man entered the atomic age, he opened a door into a new world. What he eventually finds in that new world, nobody can predict." "Why is it always, always so costly for Man to move from the present to the future?"

As with any genre, the overall appeal of sci-fi film can't be judged by its finest works alone. The early 1950s saw a boom in independent production, and the genre led the parade with cheap pictures that could be exploited for the newly perceived teen market. The makers of *Terror from the Year 5000* barely know where to put a camera; their key special effect appears to be achieved by pricking the film with a pin. But they manage to communicate a compelling idea, and their film works.

Casual writers often judge a sci-fi film on the basis of how well it predicts the future. Many details of the moon landing in *Destination Moon*, for instance, align impressively with the Apollo landing nineteen years later. But if prognostication is the only yardstick the classic films have failed miserably. The most celebrated film yet made in the genre, *2001: A Space Odyssey* doesn't realize that the pace of space exploration would slow after the initial moon landings. Stanley Kubrick also assumes that the (first?) Cold War would be a permanent political arrangement. *2001* still scores considerably better than the earlier classics. If history followed the timetable laid out by the 1956 *Forbidden Planet*, earthmen wouldn't land on the moon until "the final decade of the 21st century." But just a few years after that our futuristic militia will be using HyperDrive to propel flying saucers to the stars.

The exceptional *Forbidden Planet* jumps ahead 150 years. As a general rule, fifties sci-fi pictures are often set only ten or fifteen years into the future, so as to be able to get by with current fashions and customs. The extravagant space missions in the classic fifties titles rarely take place beyond the 1970s or 1980s.

Classic sci-fi often predicts the end of the world, which in *On The Beach* happened in 1964. The Ban-The-Bomb movement is given its strongest statement in Joseph Losey's *These are the Damned (The Damned):* asked if nuclear war is imminent, a government expert replies that it's an absolute certainty. But only in a few pictures does human life actually become extinct. As their companions die one by one, the forlorn couple of *Five* resolve to maintain hope for fertility and life. The post-apocalyptic Adam and Eve concept was almost a constant. Roger Corman returned to it at least three times, in *Day the World Ended*, *Teenage Caveman* and *Last Woman on Earth:* "This is The End – of The Beginning".

What has happened to the themes of fifties sci-fi? The Cold War has been supplanted by renewed global aggression, propaganda-based 'wars' on Crime and Drugs, and whatever else the public can be made to fear. Ed Neumeier's vitriolic satires *RoboCop* and *Starship Troopers* charge that cynical technocrats are already reshaping reality by controlling public perceptions. In Neumeier's view democracy is an illusion; a veritable anti-terrorism industry manufactures conflicts and villains for public consumption. Like the scapegoat Emmanuel Goldstein of George Orwell's *1984*, before one demonized foreign villain is captured or contained (Noriega, al-Gaddafi, Hussein), another has already been prepared to take his place.

The nuclear-powered Utopia predicted in the 1950s has since become unpopular with everyone except bomb makers. Global Warming has edged out radioactive doom as the greatest threat to the planet. Although cautionary anti-Nuke films remain a hardy perennial, sci-fi has found it difficult to translate the ecological threat into film terms, as witness the oddly irrelevant *The Day After Tomorrow*.

By far the biggest change to our lives has been the advent of personal computers, cell phones and the Internet, innovations that filmed sci-fi for the most part did not predict. The availability of convenient instantaneous communication has made the idea of being 'connected' a living constant; we're only a short step away from the Cerebrum Communicator implants lampooned in *The President's Analyst*. The fascination with computer-generated fantasy worlds is an outgrowth of the video game industry, an entertainment that drives technology and dwarfs the movies in terms of revenue.

The popular *Matrix* extended the 'enter the game' fantasy of *Tron* to speculate that a game environment might be the 'real' reality, and our visible world merely an illusion. Thus sci-fi has entered the province of intellectual puzzle films like *Last Year at Marienbad*, albeit through the back door of pulp fantasy. The subset of sci-fi fans overlaps broadly with the legions of young technophiles empowered by new technologies.

While the Establishment sees only new opportunities for commercial exploitation and political surveillance, those who have grown up computer-literate are potential pioneers on a New Frontier. The sinister interactive Telescreens of Orwell's *1984* watched those who were watching. With the erosion of privacy rights, governments and private entities can now monitor what we do, one keystroke at a time. Masters of cyber technology are now our society's most prized assets. Today's average sullen computer science major would surely qualify for recruitment by Exeter from Metaluna: "You have successfully completed your task … you've assembled an Interociter, a feat of which few men are capable." Do not pass Go, go directly to your new job at Pixar.

The selection of reviews collected in Savant Sci-Fi purposely concentrates on key films of the Classic Period. Most of the core fantasies are still relevant to the genre, and help us see where new ideas are going. The impressive *Children of Men* traces a line backwards through previous sci-fi pictures about dystopian futures and sinister conspiracies: *Soylent Green, No Blade of Grass, Quatermass 2.* The monster in South Korea's *The Host* persists as a menace because of callous and irresponsible politics, an echo that reverberates all the way back to Toho's *Gojira*, a film inspired by an incident in which irradiated fish were netted in an atomic test site. The nuclear test officials naturally denied any connection.

In the classic films, political themes begin as active subtext and graduate quickly to overt subject matter. When asked about flying saucers, a lady in *The Day the Earth Stood Still* assures us that they come from behind the Iron Curtain: "And you know where I mean!" Professor Deemer in *Tarantula* is convinced that mass starvation will bring civilization to a halt by 1975. The newspapermen in *The Day the Earth Caught Fire* learn that our global environment relies on a delicate balance of conditions. Some films see nothing wrong with the idea of a police state, as when federal agents in *Them!* order the covert detention of a citizen who 'knows too much' about classified secrets. A more universal fear is the loss of one's individual will, as seen in the many films in which aliens possess and control human bodies. In *Creation of the Humanoids* humanity is "phased out" when our organic bodies are surreptitiously replaced with robotic upgrades.

I hope that this political reading of Classic science fiction films communicates the excitement of finding 21st century themes and conflicts prophesized in an earlier era of speculative creativity. This reviewer first saw Nigel Kneale and Val Guest's 1957 *Quatermass 2* on television in the early 1960s and remembered it only as an exciting thriller about "Nazis from Space". The film now seems a veritable Rosetta Stone to the key themes of the anxiety-ridden present. Discovering that official secrecy masks a nefarious government project, Bernard Quatermass protests loudly: "Secret! You put a label like that on anything and law and order goes out the window!" That was only the beginning of a rediscovery of hidden treasures, such as the blatant anti-American messages that had been edited out of the East German *Der Schweigende Stern* when it was revised as *First Spaceship on Venus*. Much more important to genre history is the unexpected revelation that while Joseph Stalin was initiating his terror purges, his filmmakers produced an amazingly sophisticated film about a voyage to the moon. The 1936 *Kosmitcheskiy Reys* proves that Russia was just as keen on space science as the Germans, at a time when America still equated the subject with Buck Rogers comics.

-ķ- -ķ- -ķ-

Another reason that I've compiled these review essays is to counter a growing trend of cultural memory loss. Today's audiences consider filmed science fiction only in terms of the latest $200 million dollar blockbusters, most of which add little to the core ideas explored in the classics of the previous century. Hopefully this effort will inspire curiosity, and encourage a deeper look at the genre's social and philosophical messages. The dangerous ideas of filmed science fiction are a permanent record of society's fears and hopes at the dawn of the age of anxiety.

Glenn Erickson
July 14, 2011

METROPOLIS

Kino Blu-ray Reviewed: June 18, 2010
1927 / B&W / 1:33 flat / 145 min / *The Complete Metropolis*
Cinematography: Karl Freund, Günther Rittau.
Special Effects: Ernst Kunstmann, Eugen Schüfftan. Art Direction: Otto Hunte, Erich Kettelhut, Karl Vollbrecht. Music Gottfried Huppertz. Written by Fritz Lang and Thea von Harbou from her novel. Produced by Erich Pommer.
Directed by Fritz Lang

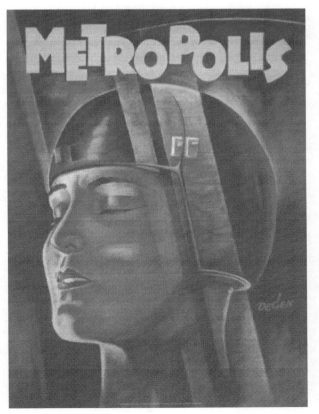

As this volume goes to print, its newest entry is James Cameron's *Avatar*, an enormously complex technical achievement that has been almost unanimously praised. It's ironic that the oldest entry herein is a wonder picture grossly under-appreciated when new. Fritz Lang and Thea von Harbou's **Metropolis** has undergone an unexpected restoration that rates as one of the biggest news events ever to involve silent cinema. The word first came in 2008, when the German archive Murnau Stiftung announced that a copy of the uncut initial version, believed lost soon after its premiere, had surfaced in a small film archive in Buenos Aires. Although of inferior quality, the South American print enabled the archivists to assemble a version missing only one scene and part of another. The 2010 re-premiere version adds a full half-hour to the now nearly full-length *Metropolis*. What was once a disjointed collection of impressive visuals is now a cinematic masterpiece of the first order.

Among Fritz Lang's many cinematic innovations is the mature science fiction film. *Metropolis* actually predates the use of the term "science fiction movie". Unlike various depictions of dystopian futures, Thea von Harbou's sociological epic is a bizarre mix of futurism and mysticism, faith and fate, an attempt to elaborate a modern myth from the contradictions of the 20th century. A machine is equated with an ancient god demanding sacrifice. A Tolkien-like house stands alone in the middle of a futuristic city. *Metropolis* is "quite a silly film" as H.G. Wells claimed and also "two films glued together by their bellies" as Luis Bunuel stated. It displays a giddy sense of awe at man's potential that no other film of its time even approaches. It is also constructed on a foundation of mawkish sentimentality and ponderous religious symbolism. A Prince of the City is fated to become a new Messiah, a mediator between opposed social classes. Brigitte Helm's Maria is a prophet whose heart beats with the conscience of the world. The working class is an ignorant and unworthy mob that acts and moves as an unthinking architectural mass. Always insightful and frequently simplistic, *Metropolis* sees the future as if gazing at poetic dream visions in a crystal ball.

2027. The all-powerful executive Joh Fredersen (Alfred Abel of *Dr. Mabuse the Gambler*) rules the spectacular city of Metropolis. Spoiled sons of the rich play with concubines in lush pleasure gardens. Fredersen's son Freder (Gustav Fröhlich) witnesses a mysterious woman gate-crashing the garden with a crowd of ragged children. When Fredersen cruelly dismisses his personal secretary Josaphat (Theodor Loos), Freder decides to investigate the workings of the city below. He finds a sub-class of worker-slaves maintaining vast underground power stations. Swapping identities with worker #11811, also known as Georgy (Erwin Biswanger), Freder attends a workers' prayer meeting in the catacombs. He falls in love with the prophet Maria (Brigitte Helm), the woman seen earlier in the garden. Interpreting the secret meetings as an uprising, Joh Fredersen conspires with his old rival, inventor/alchemist Rotwang (Rudolf Klein-Rogge, also of *Dr. Mabuse*) to instigate a premature revolt that Fredersen can suppress. Rotwang demonstrates his latest creation, a metallic Machine-Man (*Maschinen-Menschen*) robot in feminine form. Fredersen entreats Rotwang to kidnap Maria and transfer her likeness to the Robotrix, creating a 'False Maria' to be sent as an agent provocateur to agitate the workers. But Rotwang has never

forgiven Fredersen for stealing his wife, Hel, long ago. Rotwang orders the False Maria to instigate an apocalyptic revolt that will destroy everything Fredersen has made.

The Munich Filmmuseum's painstaking 2001 restoration had already determined precisely what was missing from *Metropolis*, through continuity records and inter-title logs kept with the Gottfried Huppertz music score. But the full-length Buenos Aires find enabled the digital restoration company Alpha-Omega to match existing edits exactly to this newly discovered copy. As the Argentine footage is a badly worn 16mm dupe of a scratched 35mm nitrate print, the "new" scenes are immediately apparent: the optical printer that made the 16mm copy cropped the left and top extremes of the silent-aperture frame.

The bulk of the new story material enlarges secondary roles and reinforces a pattern of complimentary characterizations. Maria and the robotic False Maria are no longer the film's only contrasting "twins". Freder and Georgy are comrades linked by fate across class boundaries. Freder takes Georgy's place and sends the worker to join Josaphat and wait for instructions. Georgy is instead seduced by advertising flyers for the exotic nightclub-brothel Yoshiwara.[1] The submissive Josaphat and the unyielding Thin Man (Fritz Rasp), both Fredersen's servants, are another study in contrast. The Thin Man fails to keep an eye on Freder, but Josephat succeeds in helping Freder save the workers' children.

Both Fredersen and Rotwang remain obsessed with Hel, Rotwang's unfaithful wife and the mother of Freder. Rotwang has created the robot to serve as her artificial replacement. But Hel has figuratively "split" into polarized good/bad opposites. Rotwang becomes deranged and projects his delusions onto the captive Maria, while Fredersen interacts with the robot in its guise as False Maria, the wicked harlot-provocateur. The true, virtuous Maria is continually in danger of losing her identity – only the "true hearted" Freder can recognize her.

Numerous short pieces of footage restore continuity to this new Metropolis, adding entrances and exits to previously ragged scene changes. Several minutes of action cuts and special effects augment the destruction sequence and the rescue of the children from the flooded worker's city. The additions make sense of the final wild chase in the streets, with the mob confusing the true and false Marias. Lang uses connective associations to transition between scenes, a technique elaborated in his later spy and crime thrillers. The Thin Man regards Georgy's work hat, printed with the number 11811. When Lang cuts directly to a wide shot of a figure exiting the Yoshiwara nightclub, we know instantly that it is Georgy.

The famous lab scene in which Rotwang gives his robot the appearance of Maria is still a main highlight, but the film's science fiction elements are now balanced by added sequences of occult mysticism. Freder's vision of a machine room disaster converted into an evil, devouring god ("Moloch!") is now only the first of several mystical revelations for Freder.

Economic calamities befell Ufa during production. New producers lost faith with Lang and von Harbou and severely edited the film almost immediately after its premiere. Even in its shortened version, Variety's critic dismissed the movie as incomprehensible. Average audiences almost certainly left the theater in confusion. Although the complete version allows us to marvel at Fritz Lang's cinematic achievement, the story still suffers from a major narrative disconnect. When rioting breaks out, the mastermind Fredersen unaccountably insists that the mob be allowed to

attack the key power plant, the all-important "Heart" machine. Ordering The Thin Man to do nothing, Joh watches calmly as the city's lights go out. He panics only when told that young Freder is lost somewhere in the flooded lower levels of the city.

The two scenes still missing are a sermon in the cathedral and a fight between Fredersen and Rotwang, neither of which would explain why Fredersen seems intent on destroying his life's work. The only possible answer is the absurd motivation given in Thea von Harbou's novelization of her script: Joh Fredersen wants Metropolis wiped out so that his son Freder can *build it back up again*.

The lapses in logic do not diminish the film's futuristic poetry. The most arresting restored sequence is Freder's fever vision of the False Maria's society debut. What was formerly an odd, disconnected erotic dance is now a supremely cinematic triumph. In a sickbed trance, Freder "experiences" the False Maria's dance as a series of mystical revelations. The collective lust of her audience becomes a literal forest of disembodied eyes. Freder's moral intuition also senses that the False Maria is a seductive demon. In his delirium Freder sees The Thin Man transform into the priest from the cathedral, who speaks of the Whore of Babylon, seen in a Bible illustration. The False Maria assumes an identical pose atop a platform borne by seven slaves. The cathedral's statues of the Seven Deadly Sins come to life and replace the slaves bearing the False Maria. As the men of Metropolis rush to worship this erotic wonder, Freder hallucinates a skeletal figure of Death advancing, slashing with its scythe. Fritz Lang has created a surreal religious vision in purely cinematic terms.

Too radical and visionary for audiences of 1927, *Metropolis* still dazzles the imagination. The re-beautified images allow a greater appreciation of the film's superlative designs – its montages, its surreal multiple exposures, its mastery of the illusion of scale. The cold beauty of the robotic "Maschinen-Menschen" is complemented by Brigitte Helm's ethereal face and silvery, staring eyes.

Even with its delirious mix of mythological magic and religious symbolism, Metropolis remains a science fiction film: its futuristic extrapolation of technology and social structures addresses core genre concerns. After their epics about the paranoid present (*Mabuse*) and the mythological past (*Siegfried*) Fritz Lang and Thea von Harbou envisioned *Metropolis* as a mystical spectacle of future anxieties. The grandiose tale resolves the conflict between capitalism and socialism with sentimental platitudes. Freder is an emotional Messiah, and the False Maria an Anti-Christ burned at the stake. A seemingly unlimited font of visual and thematic complexity, *Metropolis* is one of the greatest movies ever made.

Kino International's Blu-ray of *The Complete Metropolis* contains a beautiful encoding of the final restored assembly. Extras include a documentary about the restoration, *Voyage to Metropolis* and an interview with Paula Félix-Didier, the idealistic Buenos Aires curator who brought the uncut version to Germany. For viewers who have watched and wondered about *Metropolis* all their lives, taking in the new footage for the first time is like finding a lost book of the Bible.

1. Due to Argentine censorship, three short shots are missing from Georgy's limo ride to Yoshiwara. An erotic montage of the club's women is interrupted just before a cloaked figure can disrobe. And Georgy is fascinated when a beautiful woman in the car next door (apparently) entices him by pulling down the shoulder of her dress.

FRAU IM MOND
Kino Reviewed November 20, 2004
1929 / B&W / 1:33 flat / **169** 95 min. / *Woman in the Moon*
Cinematography: Curt Courant, Otto Kanturek. Art Direction: Joseph Danilowitz, Emil Hasler, Otto Hunte, Karl Vollbrecht, Prof. Gustav Wolff. Technical Advisors: Willy Ley, Hermann Oberth. Special Effects: Oskar Fischinger, Konstantin Irmen-Tschet. Written by Fritz Lang, Hermann Oberth, Thea von Harbou.
Produced and Directed by Fritz Lang

Fritz Lang's last silent film is the first scientifically accurate story of space travel. Lang and his scenarists (which included scientific experts later associated with Nazi and American rocket programs) invent a number of situations that would later become stock: The reverse countdown to launch, weightlessness humor and technical problems that force tough decisions about who will survive and who will not. Unfortunately, the film's impressive space hardware achievement takes up about forty minutes of screen time. The balance of **Frau im Mond** is an unusually unexciting (especially for Lang) tale of intrigue.

> Designer Wolf Helius (Willy Fritsch) discovers that criminals unknown have stolen his rocket plans, along with a confidential document from Professor Georg Manfeldt (Klaus Pohl). American con artist and master of disguises Walt Turner (Fritz Rasp) presents Helius with a unique extortion demand: unless Wolf and his partner, engineer Hans Windegger (Gustav von Wangenheim) allow an unnamed consortium of scientists and financiers to take over their planned moon mission, the colossal rocket will be sabotaged. Willy relents, and the moon shot goes forward with Turner as an unwanted passenger. Paperboy Gustav (Gustl Gstettenbaur) stows away as well. Nervous and indecisive on the ground, in flight Wolf shows the makings of a hero, resisting the temptation to embrace Hans' altruistic fiancée Friede Velten (Gerda Maurus). Meanwhile, Hans reacts to every outer-space danger with trembling cowardice and Professor Manfeldt goes batty in his search for gold on the moon.

Fritz Lang must have divided this film into halves, concentrating on the science fiction aspects and abandoning the schmaltzy story written by his wife, Thea von Harbou. Lang shows little interest in the laborious plot mechanics that establish the love triangle between the space partners and the stunning blonde Friede. With her bee-stung lips and silvery eyes, Gerda Maurus makes an impressive first woman in the moon. The scenario presents her as an ethereal, spiritual female not unlike Maria in *Metropolis*, complete with expressionistic gestures woefully out of place in this naturalistic story. Friede breathes heavily, grasps her bosom to represent emotional stress

and smiles beatifically at Wolf's every word.

The men don't fare well either. The handsome hero Wolf is a worrywart who frets over problems of romance and rocketry. Buddy Hans is all smiles until the launch and then transforms into a craven fool. The nutty professor is a consistent cliché and the beaming little boy scout Gustav is along for kid appeal. The only character for whom Lang seems to have an affinity is Fritz Rasp's bad guy Turner, who performs clever disguise quick-changes. Rasp played the grim security chief in *Metropolis* and is an arresting presence with his Hitler-like hairstyle. The characters and acting styles must have seemed dated, even by 1929 standards.

Von Harbou's story wastes an hour setting up a situation that we'd expect Lang to knock off in ten minutes. Big questions are left unexplored. We never learn where Hans and Wolf are getting the zillions of Reichmarks to build their colossal *Weltraumschiff*. The Al Capone-like project takeover (Turner is from Chicago) is the work of five civilized international types in a smoke filled room. One can't help but venture that these spy intrigues are modeled after Lang's previous experience in science fiction, which soured when American studios took financial control of Ufa and hacked his *Metropolis* to bits. Despite the interesting effects, *Woman in the Moon* isn't a tenth as impressive as that gigantic futuristic fantasy.

Space fans will be fascinated by the theoretically advanced view of space travel. British and American reviews from the original release admitted that the Germans had an obvious edge in space technology, and many details worked out by experts Oberth and Ley predict the American Apollo program. The giant two-stage rocket rolls out of a hangar on a gantry platform. It launches half-submerged from a giant tank of water that provides structural support, which begs the question, if the spaceship can't stand on its own, how could it hold together during the stress of launch? The astronauts rest in simple cots suspended on hammock springs. While crowds of onlookers and radio reporters wait anxiously, the launch is signaled by a clock that runs backwards to zero – the first Countdown.

The miniatures are beautifully done even if shallow focus betrays their small scale. Animator Oskar Fischinger handled some of the space scenes. In the launch the ship zips into space far too quickly, like a skyrocket. The details of the flight, the ship interior and the surface of the moon as seen from the rocket (named "Peace") are all well done. The failure of some retro rockets results in a crash landing so violent, everyone ought to be killed instantly.

The scientific realism ends when the explorers step onto the moon's sandy surface. The moon has no vegetation but enjoys mild temperatures and a conveniently rich, breathable atmosphere. The ship needs serious repair work but none ever gets done. Most of its vital water and oxygen are lost, but the ship can take off for the return flight anyway. Meanwhile, the professor and Turner walk through bubbling fumaroles and geysers to access a cave studded with solid gold nuggets. I suppose the cold bubbling liquids could be explained as due to low air pressure.

The professor finds a giant lunar gold piece in the shape of a human figure. Author Lotte Eisner has explained that Lang originally planned for the professor to view an archived projection-story left by an extinct race of moon people. Ancient Atlanteans had moved to the moon ages before and were unable to return. Eisner refers to several other 'lost' sequences that are now restored to this long version. [1]

The evil American Turner is responsible for a number of murders. Scenarist Von Harbou then lets us know that one crewmember must be left behind to conserve oxygen – I guess they just couldn't bottle up any of that excellent lunar atmosphere. Although the pat melodramat-

ics separate noble spacemen from the ignoble, it must be admitted that the final moments do contain an emotionally moving surprise, one that the movie never really properly resolves. [2]

Kino's DVD of **Frau im Mond** takes advantage of a sterling-quality German restoration. At 169 minutes it's a lo-ong picture; for a 1931 New York release as *Rocket to the Moon* it was pared to 95 minutes. The new score by John Mirsalis is quite good, especially around the big launch. A nice touch is Kino's retention of original German insert shots of letters, etc., with subtitles. At least one animated inter-title is included as well.

1. Sci-fi movies are forever delivering exposition through weird multi-media shows, like the magic rings in *The Time Machine* and the "montage of mankind's sins" cliché seen in several pictures including 1989's *The Abyss*. Is *Woman in the Moon* the source of this concept? Did Fritz Lang invent *every* new narrative idea in genre thrillers?

2. Caution – Big spoiler. The 'twist' ending is quite affecting. Coward Hans loses the lottery to see who stays behind, but the self-sacrificing Wolf tricks everyone by staying behind instead. After the space ship takes off Wolf has a moment to consider his suicidal decision. Then he discovers that Friede has elected to remain with him. The reveal of her standing imploringly by their little tent makes for a strong emotional surprise. It is interesting that some of the first 50s space epics heightened their conclusions with similar cosmic maroonings and doomed lovers.

Wolf and Friede can be seen as sexier versions of Fritz Lang and Thea von Harbou. Politically speaking, the ending places these Aryan heroes in a perfect, pure Nazi setting – they're rulers of a beautiful but dead world. It's a sterile suicide setting for their deliriously impossible romance, a Götterdämmerung for two.

LA FIN DU MONDE

Not Available on DVD Reviewed August 31, 2007
1931 / B&W / 1:20 flat / **105** 54 min. / *La fin du monde, vue, entendue, interprétée d'apres un théme de Camille Flamarion par Abel Gance; The End of the World.*
Cinematography Maurice Forster, Roger Hubert, Jules Kruger, Nikolas Roudakoff, Art Direction César Lacca, Lazare Meerson, Jean Perrier, Walter Ruttman, Matte Painter W. Percy Day, Original Music Arthur Honegger, Maurice Martenot, Michel Levine, R. Siohan, Vladimir Zederbaum, Written by Jean Boyer, H.S. Kraft, Abel Gance from a story by Camillle Flammarion. Produced by K. Ivanoff Directed by Abel Gance

Abel Gance's **La fin du monde (The End of the World)** is a difficult movie to see in its original version. The *Daily Variety* review from February 11, 1931 judged it an artistic and commercial disaster and placed the blame squarely at the feet of its 'overreaching' director. In production for almost two years, the movie cost five million francs and became the first all-talking French feature film. Gance spent a fortune developing a stereophonic sound system, hoping to expand the aural experience in the same way that he spread his masterpiece *Napoleon* across three screens. The film may never have been exhibited with a stereo track.

We don't know how long *La fin du monde* might have been had Gance been allowed to finish it, but it was taken away from him and cut to 105 intriguing minutes. The only version released in the United States is a drastically hacked 54-minute 1934 cut that eliminates most of the plot, including a major character played by Abel Gance. [1]

La fin du monde was the *Heaven's Gate* of its place and time. *Variety* implies that the financiers seized the film and released their own version because they thought Gance to be an irresponsible megalomaniac. Other sources say that upheavals in the French stock market forced the investors to pull the plug. Still, the image of Gance as an egotistical loose cannon is borne out by the film's original French title, which translates as *The End of the World, Seen, Heard and Rendered from an Idea by Camille Flammarion, by Abel Gance.* Everything about the film communicates Gance's conviction that the world is converging on a political and moral apocalypse, and that his artistic duty is to use cinema to redirect the hearts of the world toward spiritual values. The investors must have been shocked to see Gance cast himself in the role of a modern prophet pointing the way to humanity's salvation. The film initially lets us believe that the director is playing Jesus Christ, until the camera pulls back and reveals that he's an actor in a Passion Play within the film.

Abel Gance enthusiast and silent screen expert Kevin Brownlow used a few tantalizing excerpts from *La fin du monde* in his documentary on Silent European Cinema, *Cinema Europe:* interesting special effects of a bright heavenly body approaching Paris, and highlights of a wild orgy scene. It's been suggested that apocalyptic science fiction films relate to 20th-Century resurgences of Christian revivalism that accompanied the introduction of radio and television. *La fin du monde* not only supports that theory, it aids in understanding the religious-political hysteria behind later films like *Red Planet Mars*.

Because *La fin du monde* is at present so difficult to see, I've included a detailed breakdown of its highly melodramatic storyline, with spoilers:

Author, actor, poet and prophet Jean Novalic (Abel Gance) plays Jesus Christ in a church passion play. Socialite Isabelle Bolin (Sylvie Grenade) attends with her sweetheart, stock promoter Schomburg (Samson Fainsilber), who is entranced by the blonde actress playing Mary Magdalene, Genevieve de Murcie (Colette Darfeuil). Genevieve defies her astronomer father Monsieur de Murcie (Jean d'Yd) and proposes to the impoverished actor-poet. Jean tells her that they cannot marry because his destiny is to suffer for the redemption of mankind; Europe must be prevented from rushing into another war. Jean's wealthy brother Martial Novalic (Victor Francen) is a famous astronomer and Nobel Prizewinner. Martial offers to pay Jean to abandon his self-martyrdom and marry Genevieve, but the prophet refuses. Back home, Genevieve's father, jealous of Martial's success, accepts a grant from Schomburg to build an observatory superior to Novalic's. The money is an outright bribe: Schomburg announces his intention to court de Murcie's daughter.

Jean comes to the aid of a young woman being abused by her parents, who then falsely accuse him of rape. Jean is mobbed and critically wounded by a blow to the head. To Isabelle's displeasure, Schomburg accompanies Genevieve to a fancy party, takes her back to her apartment and rapes her. In his observatory high atop Pic du Midi, Martial detects the Lexell Comet in the constellation Gemini and computes that it is on a collision course with the Earth. The world will soon end.

Jean has already predicted the coming apocalypse, and prophesizes that the cataclysm has arrived to 'save the hearts of man.' Doves alight on Jean's bed as he asks Martial to swear to keep Lexell a secret, and to use the opportunity to teach men to love one another.

Martial confides to his colleagues that the comet will strike in 114 days. They confirm his findings and honor his pledge of secrecy. After Jean is taken to an asylum, Martial and a despondent Genevieve listen to the phonograph records he's left behind. They instruct Genevieve to abandon her worldly life and help Martial inaugurate a new World Government. Jean's voice tells them they must marry and become the shepherd and shepherdess of humanity. Genevieve then sees a vision of Jean as Christ.

With 92 days left, a major war scare develops. Schomburg invests heavily in armaments. Martial goes to the rich investor Werster and tells him that the world will end. Motivated to help, Werster pulls out of his stock market deals with Schomburg and gives Martial a fortune to buy a newspaper and a broadcast station. Genevieve stays single but helps to organize the "Radio Novalic" broadcasts of peace bulletins. Martial's loyal confederates jam official radio news, blocking warnings that war mobilization is imminent. Then Martial announces the coming End of the World. Stock markets plunge around the globe. The unbelieving Schomburg continues to buy; exhausted, Genevieve wishes she were back with Schomburg.

732 hours to go. De Murcie and Schomburg accuse Novalic of kidnapping Genevieve and using the Comet as a hoax to destroy the economy. A government minister orders the arrest of Martial and Werster. But Martial's agents learn of the arrest warrant with a hidden microphone. The newspaper is confiscated and the radio station destroyed, but Martial and Werster escape.

The government suppresses the truth and the stock market recovers. Schomberg holds a huge party on the night Martial claims that the Comet will become visible. The war profiteer tells a group of gangsters that he'll pay a million Francs if Martial and Werster are found dead before morning. Genevieve has returned to her father and joins Schomburg to neck in the garden; the jealous Isabelle runs to warn Martial. At the party, everyone sees the Comet!

Thanks to Isabelle, Martial escapes Schomburg's assassins and learns that full war mobilization will soon be announced. He and Werster rush to destroy the government's radio antenna in the Eiffel Tower. Schomburg and his gangsters arrive and trap the heroic saboteurs high above the city. Genevieve tips off Martial by telephone that Schomburg and his killers plan to ascend in an elevator. Werster warns Genevieve to stay on the ground. He uses a cutting torch to sever the elevator cable, not knowing that Genevieve has taken the elevator as well. She is killed with the rest.

All humanity can now see the Lexell Comet bright and large in the sky. Radio Novalic resumes broadcasting. Martial calls for the first convention of the "General States of the Universe" on August 5, the night before the collision. The world prays – Christians, Muslims, natives in Africa. The approach of the Comet triggers extreme weather: blizzards, storms, tidal waves. With 32 hours to go, riots and pandemonium break out. Wherever liquor is available, giant parties begin. A thousand elite revelers bring musicians into a great hall for a feast and orgy. Monks carrying candles interrupt the orgy and lead the group in prayer.

As the orbits of the Comet and the earth converge, Novalic addresses the One World Congress, which unanimously agrees (including the U.S.A.) to unite all governments into a single harmonious entity. The Lexell Comet narrowly misses the earth. Much of the world has been reduced to rubble, but life will go on.

La fin du monde is a delirious misfire. On the technical level, it has all the flaws of a first talkie effort. Most dialogue scenes are static setups interrupted by mismatched cutaways. Gance's action scenes have the feel of silent serials from the 'teens, with the hero Martial Novalic repeatedly escaping just before the authorities can arrest him. The film has a reasonable scientific attitude and the special effects are quite good. When the Lexell Comet is finally visible in broad daylight, the illusion is excellent.

Evidence of drastic cutting appears from the start. The title music cuts off rudely as the first scene begins, and is replaced by another cue. We hear several mentions of anti-war demonstrations but see only a fragment of a scene with a large crowd, indicating the deletion of a montage. The fierce storms and crazy weather that mark the approach of the Comet are accomplished with acceptable miniature effects, but are severely truncated as well. Two scenes use the signature flutter cutting seen in other classic Abel Gance silents, and the montages that haven't been altered are excellent. But the continuity in the scene of the elevator crash has been severely damaged. We never see Genevieve enter the elevator car, yet lines of dialogue hint that she is inside when it falls. Somebody apparently decided that they didn't like that scene, and mangled it with a re-cut.

The players aren't at all bad. Victor Francen fares particularly well in a difficult role. The problem is a naïve, emotional script that rushes from one sensational or miraculous scene to the next. The male characters are divided into noble heroes that follow the lead of the prophet

Jean, and dastardly villains like Schomburg, a war profiteer and rapist. Gance's daring passion play scene fumbles his intended point, that the church audience couldn't care less about religion. The play inspires lust, not spirituality – Schomburg wants to date the sexy actress playing Mary Magdalene.

The female characters are even more inconsistent. Jean's mother is an idealized stereotype while the raven-haired Isabelle and her friend "the princess" are mindless playgirls. Gance's women change character on a whim, as when Isabelle warns Martial in fit of jealousy. Perhaps poor continuity is at fault, but Genevieve is a laughable contradiction. She swears to serve Martial and shows no sign of doubting him. She then rushes back at the worst possible moment to rejoin the rapist Schomburg.

La fin du monde is hysterical pacifist propaganda that extends the comparatively reasonable thesis of Gance's earlier *J'Accuse!*, a horror movie in which the dead of WW1 refuse to stay dead because Europe has not taken the proper steps to insure a lasting peace. Gance would appear to be responding to the resurgence of Christian revivalism on the radio, and financial chaos and scandals in the French government. Jean speaks in humanist terms and never mentions Christianity, but his message is clear. Accompanied by doves, he is of course a literal Jesus figure preaching the spiritual salvation of mankind in The End of Days.

Frankly, I'd think that many 1931 audiences would find Gance's dress-up masquerade as Jesus to be in perfectly lousy taste. A scene of African natives speaking with accelerated 'Mickey Mouse' squeaked voices mars a montage of religious services around the world. Perhaps the producers added that detail. The producers did not excise a shot showing that Jean Novalic is inspired by the teachings of Kropotkin, a theorist who proposed Communist Anarchism as the perfect framework for society.

Others have seen Fascist tendencies in the film, reminding us that Gance's masterpiece *Napoleon* champions the emperor as a great Frenchman, not an enemy of liberty. The 'enlightened' Martial is definitely an autocrat; just as Schomburg accuses, he seizes leadership of the country with mass propaganda and by silencing the opposition. Martial murders his most important enemy in broad daylight. He galvanizes his supporters at a giant meeting that resembles a Nazi rally. *La fin du monde* endorses the idea that the masses should throw their support behind a strong leader with a righteous cause.

The film's most famous scene is an enormous orgy. Kevin Brownlow reported that a great many costumed extras were hired, the music and champagne were laid on and the crowd was told to 'have at it' while the camera crane moved overhead. [2] Even when trimmed for the release version, the spectacle outdoes the Biblical romps in De Mille epics. One brief shot appears to show dozens of lovers paired off on a mat on the floor. Of course, just as things are getting interesting, hooded monks enter and everyone starts praying instead.

La fin du monde sees the threatening comet as the salvation of mankind, just as weary diplomats and pundits periodically wish that one issue – or enemy – would appear to unite all peoples. To proclaim a Universal Government in the middle of a state of pandemonium is crazy, but even sillier is the notion that such a pact would be honored when the sun rises again the next day. Gance instead chooses to end on a banal pastoral scene.

Abel Gance undertook his first sound film standing at the forefront of French cinema, and came out almost ruined. The film ended his career as a freewheeling genius and turned him back to 'safe' projects. It's considered his worst movie. When film critic Jean-Luc Godard wished to belittle Gance in an interview, he simply title-dropped *La fin du monde*.

La fin du monde clearly influenced Wylie and Balmer's novels *When Worlds Collide* and *After Worlds Collide*, which imagine a Roosevelt-like project to build a Noah's Arc spaceship to escape a similar cosmic cataclysm. Instead of a spiritual revival, the American books suggest that a technological elite will earn the right to survive because they worship science. The rest of the world, including what Wylie and Balmer consider inferior races, is unworthy and must perish. In the American model too, religious fundamentalism eventually endorses Fascist solutions. 20th-century sci-fi is fundamentally political in nature – and the statements it makes cover the entire political spectrum. [3]

1. The 1934 English version *The End of the World* is only 54 minutes long, and some of that is a lengthy prologue lecture about our planetary system. Even a cursory look reveals that it consists mostly of scenes excised from the French version. A few minutes of duplicated dialogue exchanges frame long montages of grand speeches, world panic and destruction – and telling bits of action missing from the French cut! I frankly don't understand why nobody has endeavored to combine the two cuts into a more complete version.

2. As it turns out, *La fin du monde* was the film debut for an electronic musical instrument called the Ondes Martenot. It is featured in the foreground of the first big dinner scene.

3. An 18-minute 1930 film by Eugène Deslaw called *Autour de La Fin du Monde (Around the End of the World)* has seen screenings at film festivals lately. It collects screen tests and outtakes from *La fin du monde* and may have been some kind of promotional effort. Sadly, it contains no more orgy footage.

Guy Maddin's six-minute 2000 short *The Heart of the World* is a stylistic celebration of silent Soviet agit-prop cinema, but its theme and story are borrowed from *La fin du monde*. Two brothers, one a surrogate Christ figure, love an *Aelita*- like woman whose inverted telescope reports that the 'heart of the world' (a literal beating heart in the center of the Earth) is dying. She takes its place and becomes a humanistic Madonna, glowing with love that makes the world rejoice. The raw energy that fuels the Heart of the World is KINO ... cinema.

KOSMICHESKIY REYS: FANTASTICHESKAYA NOVELLA

Not available on DVD
Reviewed: October 19, 2006
1935 / B&W / 1:37 flat / 70 min. / *The Space Ship, Cosmic Voyage*
Cinematography Aleksandr Galperin. Art Direction Yuri Shvets, M. Tiunov, Alexsei Utkin. Special Effects Fodor Krasne. Technical Advisor Konstantin Tsiolkovsky. Written by Aleksandr Filimonov from the novel *Outside the Earth* by Konstantin Tsiolkovsky. Produced by Mosfilm. Directed by Vasili Zhuravlyov

In 2006 a touring series of Russian science fiction films organized by Robert Skotak included a 35mm print of 1935's **Kosmitcheskiy reys**. Most science fiction fans have never heard of this rare space voyage movie from Stalin's Soviet Union, a major missing link between Fritz Lang's *Woman in the Moon* and George Pal's *Destination Moon*. It's much more technically advanced than Lang's film, especially when the Cosmonauts reach the moon. Two colossal two-stage space ships are prepared for launch on a gigantic inclined ramp, an enormous miniature set reminiscent of the next year's *Things to Come*. One rocket is named "Joseph Stalin" and the other "Marshal Kliment Voroshilov" – a Soviet general who would figure heavily in purges to come. To buffer the acceleration of takeoff and the impact of the hard moon landing, the Cosmonauts enter chambers filled with liquid, a weird precursor to the tube-transformations in *This Island Earth* and *Forbidden Planet*. They explore the moon and rescue a housecat marooned in the wreck of a previous unmanned probe rocket. The old professor is trapped under a fallen boulder but signals for help with the boy's homemade pellet gun. With all of Earth's telescopes focusing on the moon, the Cosmonauts spread reflective patches that spell out the letters "CCCP." We don't get a good look at the flag that the old professor plants, but this Soviet expedition does *not* claim the moon for all mankind.

Although it premiered in 1936, *Kosmicheskiy reys: Fantasticheskaya novella* is a silent movie with inter-titles and a synchronized classical music score. The print is slightly cropped on the left and the top, indicating that it was originally filmed with a silent aperture and then reprinted with a music soundtrack covering the left extreme of the frame. The special effects by Fodor Krasne feature wide views of the Cosmodrome and long trucking shots around the giant rockets lying horizontally on their cradles. Some of these scenes appear to have been done with stop-motion animation, as both the camera and tiny animated vehicles do not always move smoothly. The full-sized sets are also vast, with the entrance to the rocket establishment looking like an enormous hotel lobby. The only plot involves a stuffy bureaucrat's attempt to prevent the old genius Pavel Ivanovich Sedikh (Sergei Petrovich Komarov) from taking the first moon flight. Pavel's wife is upset because he leaves a useless pair of boots behind. He ends up taking his secretary, Professor Marina (Ksenia Moskalenko), a beauty who displays a variety of healthy-looking collectivist smiles. Repeating a motif from the earlier Fritz Lang film, a kid stowaway named Andriocha Orlov (Vassili Gaponenko) proves to be a crackerjack Cosmonaut and saves the day.

The ship interior is roomier than the one in *Woman in the Moon* and resembles the fancy cabins in Toho spaceships from the late 1950s. Pavel's spacesuit radio and other small props appear to have been carved from wood.

The moon landing is accomplished in a crater scored with deep crevasses. Excellent stop-motion animation (with Harryhausen-like aerial bracing) shows the Cosmonauts leaping between giant rock formations and doing flips in the air, like the adventurers in H.G. Wells' novel *First Men In The Moon*. Their suits resemble deep-sea diving gear with flexible tubes coming from the helmets. Many accurate details are not fully explained to the audience – air locks, strap-holds on the ship interior, the low gravity on the moon. The *Joseph Stalin* has lost its oxygen supply, but Pavel finds frozen oxygen (it's -270° out there) left over from the moon's ancient atmosphere, so the Cosmonauts are saved after all.

Just as the MIIT (Moscow Institute for Interplanetary Travel) prepares to launch the second rocket on a rescue mission, the *Joseph Stalin* returns by parachute, landing right at the Academy's main entrance. Congratulations, speeches and general merry-making follow.

Kosmicheskiy reys is from a novel by the film's technical supervisor, the Russian space visionary Konstantin Tsiolkovsky (1857-1935). Tsiolkovsky, who died before the film was finished, is also credited with the "Space Elevator" concept featured in Arthur C. Clarke's book *The Fountains of Paradise*, and now being studied as a practical possibility. Tsiolkovsky also contributed to the earlier Russian political space film *Aelita*. He is considered the inspiration for the Russian space program that became a reality twenty years after his death.

As it is unclear what kind of distribution *Kosmicheskiy reys* had outside the Soviet Union, any influence it might have had on the genre is unknown. The only previous reference to it I have seen is in Phil Hardy's *Science Fiction Film Encyclopedia*, and the authors of that book may have sourced their information from a Soviet film catalogue.

THINGS TO COME

Reviewed July 25, 2007
1936 / B&W / 1:37 flat / **93** min.
Cinematography: Georges Périnal. Art
Direction: Vincent Korda. Special Effects:
Ned Mann, Lawrence Butler, Wally Veevers,
Edward Cohen, Peter Ellenshaw. Music:
Arthur Bliss. Written by H.G. Wells from his
novel *The Shape of Things to Come*. Produced by
Alexander Korda.
Directed by William Cameron Menzies.

One of the most impressive science fiction films
ever, H.G. Wells' *Things to Come* isn't given the
respect it deserves. A prestige production from
an England between the wars, it was originally
dismissed and largely ignored. Its much more
modest companion film *The Man Who Could
Work Miracles* was a big hit by comparison.

Quality prints of this Art Deco Utopian fantasy
have become rare. Viewers that can see beyond
the plastic-toga costumes worn by the swells of
2036 will find a film that predicts the Battle of
Britain four years ahead of time.

There are any number of ways to approach this
epic: as Wells' socialist riposte to Fritz Lang's
Metropolis; as a masterpiece whose reputation
might be reestablished if it could be properly
restored; and, more troublingly, as a curious expression of H.G. Wells' ideas about a eugenical-
ly-cleansed future for Mankind.

It was hoped that Network and Granada's
***Things to Come* 2-Disc Special Edition** would
be a restored 113 or even 117-minute version of
the film. That's not the case, but the release *does*
have a few new scenes. More below.

In 1936 peaceful Everytown (read: London)
braces for conflict, which comes in 1940 in the
form of massed air raids. A decades-long world
war ensues, bringing civilization to a halt. Thirty years later, the rubble-heap that was Everytown has survived a terrible plague called The
Walking Sickness. Its feudal ruler Rudolph,
The Boss (Ralph Richardson) wages un-mech-
anized war on neighboring fiefdoms to secure the raw materials for more sophisticated
weaponry. Into this Dark Age lands a futuristic airplane piloted by John Cabal (Raymond
Massey). Once a citizen of Everytown, Cabal is
now a member of a Basra-based technical guild
called *Wings over the World* that has developed
superior technology to defeat the warlords
and make a new start for mankind. The Boss
holds Cabal hostage but engineer Richard Gordon (Derrick De Marney), his wife Mary (Ann
Todd) and Doctor Harding (Maurice Braddell)
conspire to steal one of Everytown's antiquated biplanes to summon reinforcements. Giant
bombing planes from Basra drop the 'Gas of
Peace', conquering Everytown without bloodshed.

The New World Order begins. Decades of scientific advancements follow, re-engineering Earth into a peaceful technocracy of underground living. By 2036 society has built a giant Space Gun to shoot humans around the moon, but a group of dissident artists led by master sculptor Theotocopulos (Cedric Hardwicke) incites a mob to destroy it. The revolt fails. As the Moon capsule blazes to the stars, John's grandson Oswald Cabal pontificates on the destiny of Man.

Things to Come is a feast for the eyes and ears and the brain, too. Many of its special effects are still awe-inspiring, as is its sweeping symphonic music score. For detractors, the main objection is that its acting is disjointed and its dialogue is a constant flow of bald exposition and author's lectures. Ragged cuts made after release created continuity gaps that startle viewers. Author H. G. Wells mandated the lengthy speeches, to present his philosophical ideas about socialism and futurism.

Visually, *Things to Come* has few peers. William Cameron Menzies' designs are as massive as those in Fritz Lang's *Metropolis* and his cinematics benefit from more advanced editorial firepower. Sophisticated montages advance the story across years of war and turmoil. The opening musical montage of Christmas jitters and the later air raid on Everytown are successful examples of Eisensteinian montage, juxtaposing images of 'peace' and 'war.' The montage of the building of the futuristic city 'for Our Children's Children's Children' is a wonder of graphic industrial imagery. The score by Sir Arthur Bliss veers from martial tensions to airy reverence for a fantastic future.

Although some symbolic scenes some come off as stilted, others have undiminished power. The little girl who runs to John Cabal and a downed enemy pilot is a strange pre-echo of the tot seen in the 1964 war-themed campaign ad run by President Johnson to defeat Goldwater. The body on the barbed wire that dissolves to only a few remaining tatters, echoes a similar setup in Lewis Milestone's *All Quiet on the Western Front*. Ranting about 'sovereignty' in 1970, The Boss was immediately equated with Richard Nixon by the group of college peers to whom I showed *Things to Come* – in 1970! And the concluding image of the all-potent Oswald Cabal challenging the heavens has triple thematic echoes: back to the ending of Wells' book *The Food of the Gods*; and forward to both the conclusion of King Vidor's film of Ayn Rand's *The Fountainhead*, and to the Star Child of *2001: A Space Odyssey*.

Network and Granada TV's **Things to Come 2-Disc Special Edition** is a cleaner and more complete improvement on a previous Image disc. Several restored sequences bring the film back up to its original American release length. *Things to Come* seems to have been one of those unlucky pictures that was hacked by its own makers just prior to wide release and then cut further on subsequent runs. The discarded footage has not been located.

The BBFC measured *Things to Come* at 117 minutes when it gave its censor approval in 1936. Along the way version lengths of 113, 105 and 97 minutes have been recorded. The standard American cut clocks in at just under 93 minutes on the Image disc running at 24 fps. The Network cut comes to almost the exact same running time at 25 fps., which means that it is in reality about three minutes longer, and is probably the 97-minute cut.

Watching the film, I caught only three serious restorations. In the first sequence, Passworthy and Harding exit Cabal's house; the patriotic Passworthy talks about war as a merciless program of vermin extermination. This extra moment eliminates a ragged cut and smoothes the transition to the second 'war preparation' montage.

The second reinstated scene is the Boss Rudolph's drunken banquet, where we realize that he has other female favorites besides Margueretta Scott. The Boss makes a pig-headed speech about books being a nuisance and travel being unnecessary because good citizens belong at home. Unfortunately, this addition does nothing to mend the erratic continuity gaps in the scene that follows when Roxana goes down to talk with Cabal in his improvised cell.

The third reinstatement is a portion of dialogue during the grandfather / granddaughter's 2036 history lesson, including an unnecessary bit about sneezing. And that's it. The cut appears to be an export version prepared for America, and then trimmed a bit on arrival. All the major cuts must have happened earlier.

I watched *Things to Come* on an all-region DVD player, so the disc might look better on a PAL set. It was clean and smooth, but many scenes still displayed a bit of fluttering contrast – it's not a prime element in perfect condition. The best aspect of the transfer is that most of the flaws we're used to seeing in American copies are gone. Previously unstable splices and jarring timing changes have been eliminated. Dissolves and other transitions are much improved.

Strangely, the audio is just as difficult as ever to make out. The combination of a compressed track, boomy voices, clipped English enunciation and the 4% PAL speed-up make Network's disc still a hard listen – even with its many pops and flaws, the old Image track is easier to hear. No subtitles are provided to help out. On the other hand, Sir Arthur Bliss' bombastic score is better than ever, cutting through in places where it was once inaudible.

The extras feature the welcome involvement of fan-archivist Nick Cooper, who provides an authoritative feature commentary. He explains the twisted history of the film's many versions and restoration problems. The best extra is a *Virtual Extended Edition* that adds inter-title cards and text pages to show scenes and dialogue that were in the final script and were probably once a part of the film. These include an anti-Semitic scene with Roxana berating a merchant named Wadsky (Abraham Sofaer) for not giving her a first look at some new fabric. The extended cut stretches out to a whopping 134 minutes.

That bloated running time helps us understand why London Films went scissors-happy with the picture, as at least $2/3$ of the cut material consists of extended speeches between the characters. This isn't character dialogue; the actors simply 'orate' at each another. *Things to Come* already suffers from too many one-sided debates in which Wells' views always prevail. The situation invites a comparison to the film version of *The Fountainhead*. Author Ayn Rand also enjoyed dictatorial rights over the screenplay and her movie is also dominated by windy speeches. H.G. Wells' apparently had veto power over any attempt to trim his futuristic, socialist philosophizing. The wholesale cutting apparently occurred immediately after a brief premiere release. As shown in the *Virtual Extended Edition*, we lose Margaretta Scott's entire second role as Cabal's wife Rowena. Theotocopolous' dissident speech is reduced to a few lame fragments.

The other disc extras are interesting diversions. Sir Ralph Richardson makes an entertaining 40-minute appearance on an interview show, but says nothing about *Things to Come*. From 1971, sci-fi author Brian Aldiss stares at the camera in front of H.G. Wells' last London address and gives forth with an amusing discourse on the author's life and times. An original 1935 audio recording *The Wandering*

Sickness is a description of the fictional malady perhaps intended as an audition for a possible narrator. An image and artwork gallery comes direct from Nick Cooper's archive. An American reissue trailer is a ragged English original with a new distributor card slapped on the end.

Network and Granada's ***Things to Come 2-Disc Special Edition*** is still an incomplete copy of a film that one would think would have been preserved better than this ... but tragedies do happen. Any longer copy of *Things to Come* would be welcome. In the meantime, American viewers would love a Region 1 version of this release.

The screen's FIRST story of man's conquest of space!

ROCKETSHIP X-M

Image Reviewed: June 5, 2000
1950 / B&W / 1:37 flat full frame / 78 min.
Cinematography: Karl Struss. Special Effects: Jack Rabin. Music: Ferde Grofe. Written by Kurt Neumann and Dalton Trumbo (uncredited, unconfirmed). Produced by Murray Lerner, Kurt Neumann.
Directed by Kurt Neumann

As pointed out by notables such as Joe Dante, the first wave of 50s science fiction films included big-studio "A" pictures investigating the potential of the newfound genre. The early classics sought to exploit the vein struck by a pair of independent 1950 productions about space travel that premiered within weeks of one another. The Technicolor *Destination Moon* got all the press and won the blessing of the scientific establishment for its technical accuracy. The B&W upstart *Rocketship X-M* was filmed with a fraction of George Pal's budget ($94,000 to *Moon's* $600,000) and its science is incoherent. Yet *X-M* is *Moon's* equal in entertainment value: dramatically superior and just as interesting when discussing the beginnings of the science fiction boom.

Destination Moon struck a definite Cold War posture. An uncredited writer on *Rocketship X-M* may have been the blacklisted Dalton Trumbo, the populist author of sentimental and patriotic wartime hits like *Tender Comrade* and *A Guy Named Joe*. Trumbo's screenplays consistently extolled the virtues of Democratic principles, and he wrote some of the 50s most interesting scripts without credit while living in exile in Mexico.

Dr. Karl Eckstrom (John Emory) holds a press conference shortly before the launch of their Moon mission spaceship, the *X-M* (for eXpedition Moon). We meet his flight crew: lovely mathematician Lisa Van Horn (Osa Massen), Colonel Floyd Graham (Lloyd Bridges), nervous navigator Harry Chamberlin (Hugh O'Brien) and flight engineer Bill Corrigan (Noah Beery, Jr.), a drawling Texan. Narrowly missing some passing meteorites and 'stalled' in space while Eckstrom and Van Horn recalculate the fuel mixture, the ship accidentally goes into a sudden acceleration. The crew passes out. They awaken to find themselves hundreds of millions of miles off course, gaping through their rocket's portholes at the planet Mars.

Seizing the opportunity, the astronauts don oxygen masks and carry guns to explore the desert planet, and discover the ruins of an irradiated city. An advanced civilization has annihilated itself in a nuclear conflagration. The explorers have time to glimpse only a couple of artifacts before retreating in the face of climbing radiation levels. While they rest in a gully, humanoid shapes emerge from the canyon walls ...

Rocketship X-M is the 50s' first pacifist sci-fi film. Its dialogue mirrors *Destination Moon's* mention of moon-based rockets being an essential goal of any power seeking to dominate the Earth militarily. The script promotes sentimental stereotypes (softhearted Texan, unemotional scientist, etc. Lloyd Bridges' smugly insists that Osa Massen drop her slide rule and get serious about nesting.

This may be the first postwar feature film to offer a demonstration of the hazards of nuclear war. It needs to be remembered that almost all of 1950 popular culture supported the Atomic Energy Commission's pro-nuke public relations program. The 1949 *film noir D.O.A.* disguises its radiation-poisoning theme, but *Rocketship X-M* shows a Geiger counter hitting the red zone. Mars cannot be explored because the high roentgen count makes loitering too dangerous. In the year that conscience-stricken nuclear scientist Robert Oppenheimer was censored for saying negative things about the Bomb, this movie enlightened millions of American children with 'anti-American' speeches about nuclear folly. Dalton Trumbo had been a cheerleader for patriotism during WW2. If he indeed contributed to this screenplay, a case can be made that the blacklist turned him into a cheerful subversive critic, not of America but of its creeping militaristic blindness.

Rocketship X-M's astronaut martyrs deliver the message that nuclear war could destroy our civilization, just as the noble characters in Trumbo's wartime movies talked about a better world after the armistice. For the idealist Trumbo, personal problems are never as important as humanitarian values. The best America has to offer are being massacred by stone-age cavemen. We care about these heroes, and their deaths carry a sting of futility.

(Spoiler) The kids awed by *Rocketship X-M* on television in the late 50s were awed by its presentation of an altruistic doom similar to *Wake Island* or *The Alamo*, only with spaceships. Not only does everybody die, Mike Nelson from TV's *Sea Hunt* dies smiling, hugging the woman he loves in an explosive substitute sexual climax. Massen and Bridges' final pledge of love as X-M plummets into the Earth's atmosphere is almost traumatic. For kids who would never sit through *Wuthering Heights*, this all seemed incredibly important.

Rocketship X-M was released before David Lean's *Breaking the Sound Barrier*, a film that equated Progress with a suicidal eagerness to die testing new aircraft. Doctor Ralph Fleming (Morris Ankrum) learns of the loss of his Moon mission and immediately announces the beginning of the X-M 2 project. We 50s kids were indoctrinated with the idea that space exploration is a Holy Quest that must proceed no matter what the cost: NASA budget cuts and cold feet after the space shuttle disasters are unthinkable to the fans that grew up on the message of *Rocketship X-M* and *Things to Come*: Man's destiny is in the stars.

If *Rocketship X-M* employed a science advisor, someone left him bound and gagged in the corner. Every known rule of space travel is broken. Meteors whistle loudly by in the vacuum of space. One slip of the accelerator and the ship misses the Moon, arriving in Mars orbit only a few hours later. En route, the scientists work out the petty details of fuel mixtures, which should have been ascertained before a rocket was built. The strategy for the Mars landing is decided almost as an afterthought. Although unsurprised that their limited fuel takes them all the way to Mars, the survivors are shocked when their tanks run dry just as they return home.

Rocketship X-M's boffo box office was proof that science fiction success did not depend on scientific accuracy. Inane Z pictures like *Cat-Women*

of the Moon would proliferate for the remainder of the decade. With only a few exceptions, kids would have to wait until the 60s to see the subject attempted with both seriousness and high production values, in *Robinson Crusoe on Mars* and *First Men in the Moon*. *Rocketship X-M* was produced by one of the cheapest outfits in Hollywood, Lippert films, yet most of its production values are good. The red-toned Mars exteriors were shot on location in Death Valley and at Red Rock Canyon, a site familiar from the Westerns *The Big Country* and *Man of the West*. Perhaps the biggest production coup was signing composer Ferde Grofe, known for his famous *Grand Canyon Suite*. Grofe's romantic themes are just adequate but his Theremin-enhanced Mars music is weirdly impressive.

Unfussy journeyman director Kurt Neumann turned out a steady stream of low budget product in the 50s. His science fiction work was all filmed by Karl Struss and included the delirious *Kronos* and the gory *The Fly*, completed just before his death.

In the 1970s distributor Wade Williams hired some young special effects experts to shoot replacements for a few of the film's less-than-convincing special effects shots, including Dennis Muren, who went on to join the effects crew of *Star Wars*. The version of *Rocketship X-M* on disc is the original.

Image Entertainment's DVD of **Rocketship X-M** is made from great elements. The audio is almost perfect. The picture has a scratch here and there but otherwise is mint. The orange-toned Mars sequence is fine, with the matte paintings of the domed ruins in the background particularly so. Few 50s sci-fi efforts succeed as romantic melodramas, and *Rocketship X-M* consistently wins the approval of 'civilians'.

DESTINATION MOON

Image Reviewed February 26, 2000
1950 / Color / 1:37 flat / 92 min.
Cinematographer: Lionel Lindon. Production
design: Ernst Fegté. Technical advisor: Chesley
Bonestell. Music: Leith Stevens. Written
by Alford 'Rip' Van Ronkel and Robert A.
Heinlein. Produced by George Pal.
Directed by Irving Pichel.

In 1949 Hollywood just wasn't yet hip enough
to see the movie potential in outer space. Hi-tech
awareness had yet to grip the culture. *Things to
Come* and *Metropolis* were forgotten box office
flops and the only successful precedents were
Flash Gordon and *Buck Rogers*. Written sci-fi was
for undiscriminating boys and the flying saucer
fringe cult wasn't considered anything to base
a movie on. That's when some Hollywood independents made **Destination Moon**, the very

first film of the 50's science fiction craze and
America's late entry into serious science fiction
filmmaking.

Moon has a lofty pedigree. The script is co-
written by Robert Heinlein, the author of
Starship Troopers. Famed *Puppetoon* producer
George Pal, fresh from a lackluster first feature
about a mischievous squirrel, got the project
green-lit at Eagle-Lion. With the artwork of
Chesley Bonestell featured prominently in national magazines, *Destination Moon* enjoyed a
solid media push. It was forced to compete in
a filmic equivalent of the Space Race: Lippert's
Rocketship X-M was rushed into production
and actually came out a month before Pal's
color extravaganza.

When their latest V-2 rocket test fails and
government funding collapses, scientist Dr.
Charles Cargraves (Warner Anderson) and
space enthusiast General Thayer (Tom Powers)
enlist the aid of millionaire aircraft magnate
Jim Barnes (John Archer). Backed by a group
of patriotic industrialists, they build a private
ship at a desert base. A public uproar over
radiation safety threatens the rocket, but the
three idealists circumvent a court injunction by
launching ahead of schedule with a substitute
radio operator, Joe Sweeney (Dick Wesson). In
space, they almost lose a crewman when they
go outside the ship to free a frozen radio antenna. Barnes's landing expends too much fuel,
and after exploring the lunar surface they discover that they must drastically lighten ship.
No matter how much equipment they throw
overboard, it looks as though someone must
stay behind to allow the other three to return
to the Earth.

The thrilling novelty *Destination Moon* revived
the concept of space travel as a practical possibility, when lobbyists for such ideas attracted
the level of respect afforded common loonies.
George Pal wisely educates his audience with
a Woody Woodpecker cartoon sequence that

spells out the basics of space travel in a way any yahoo can understand. Comic Dick Wesson becomes an audience surrogate to whom the facts of weightlessness and the vacuum of space can be patiently and condescendingly explained. The movie is best appreciated as an early docu-drama, a dramatic educational film.

But *Destination Moon* is also groundbreaking hardcore science fiction. There's hardly anything fanciful about it – even *2001: A Space Odyssey* is less pure, with its aliens and mystical hoo-haw. Fritz Lang may have invented the countdown for *Woman in the Moon* but his rocket resembled an ugly cannon shell. *Destination Moon's* dazzling *Luna* set the new style for space vehicles. Featureless, dart-shaped chromium rockets would dominate the screen until the arrival of authentic space hardware. [1]

The 1969 Apollo moon landing bears eerie parallels to *Destination Moon*. Just as in the movie, Neil Armstrong's descent to the moon's surface required a last-second sideways maneuver to find an appropriate landing spot. The voyagers claim the moon in a formal speech not unlike Armstrong's, dedicating Earth's lifeless satellite to all the people of the Earth. Soon after the space program got rolling, Lyndon Johnson moved NASA headquarters to his home state of Texas. In *Destination Moon* one of the moneybags who bankrolls the moon shot is a drawling Texan who jokes that they'll have to build the rocket in the Lone Star State because it's the only place big enough.

Destination Moon is key evidence that the 50's space race was a military program promoted for the public as a noble scientific quest. The reactionary politics on view are startling.

When his test rocket blows up, Dr Cargraves claims that Red sabotage is responsible, and we are meant to agree. The moon project is a

no-go until its promoters play the "Red Card" and sermonize that whoever reaches the moon first will militarily control the Earth. Only then does the private sector fall obediently into line and do "what the government can't do" – i.e., fund politically sensitive military-space projects. The implication is that subversives in Washington have handcuffed America's defense ... at a time when Military expenditures were actually growing exponentially every year. When the Howard Hughes-like Barnes reads headlines warning that his atomic rocket poses a radiation hazard, he proclaims the news to be paid Communist propaganda orchestrated for the express purpose of hurting America. The publicity spurs Barnes to lie to the public, become ultra-secretive and break the law. *Destination Moon* isn't shown that much any more, but when it is these moments elicit audible gasps from the audience. The first American moon shot is made by zealots who thumb their noses at a court ordered delay, just because they might poison the Earth with a reactor-load of plutonium.

These were the years of secret government experiments exposing soldiers and civilians unknowingly to radioactive elements. 1949's noir thriller *D.O.A.* is about radiation poisoning, yet euphemistically buries the entire issue by renaming the malady that kills Edmond O'Brien as "luminous poisoning." Other pictures similarly downplay the effects of radiation. Radiation in science fiction would soon become a fantastic force that makes ants grow and people shrink. Not until 1959's *On The Beach* did a major film confront nuclear tampering as a bad thing that could destroy the world.

Image Entertainment's DVD of **Destination Moon** is a reasonably good copy of this Technicolor show that reveals the underpinnings of the Oscar-winning special effects. Wires are now visible holding up floating astronauts and spaceships, but we also see the beautiful detail in Chesley Bonestell's paintings. The only extra is an arresting trailer that pushes fun copy text like, "JOIN A WEIRD TRIP OF LUNAR EXPLORATION!" The cover artwork has a foldout with attractive color art and a brief but informative essay by well-known genre interviewer Tom Weaver.

1. The "ten, nine, eight ... " countdown was thrilling for us fifties kids ... a do-or-die, teeth-gritting ritual of anticipation that paid off with a deafening, blazing "Blast off!" Who said we didn't have sex in the 50's? The countdown idea became so ingrained in the world consciousness that when Toho made its *Uchu Daisenso (Battle in Outer Space)* in 1959, its Japanese soundtrack used a countdown – in English!

THE MAN FROM PLANET X

MGM Reviewed April 3, 2001
1951 / B&W / 1:37 flat / 71 min.
Cinematography: John L. Russell. Written and Produced by Aubrey Wisberg and Jack Pollexfen.
Directed by Edgar G. Ulmer

Much is made of the fact that *The Man From Planet X* features the first invasion from space, when the likely truth is that *The Thing from Another World* and *The Day the Earth Stood Still* were in production before this low-budget independent was conceived. A tiny movie of considerable merit, *Planet X* was once a joke when seen in spliced-up television prints. DVD restores the moody atmosphere of the legendary director Edgar G. Ulmer for all to see.

A strange invader in a metallic space capsule alights on a Scottish moor, much to the consternation of local scientists Professor Elliot (Raymond Bond) and Dr. Mears (William Schallert). American newsman John Lawrence (Robert Clarke) falls in love with Elliot's daughter Enid (Margaret Field, the mother of Sally Field) during the investigation. The visitor is from a rogue planetoid that will soon pass near the Earth. Our heroes capture the alien and attempt to communicate with him. The ambitious Mears tries to force the alien to give up more secrets; the spaceman responds by fortifying his landing site and taking Enid and others as hostages. John realizes that the alien is the first representative of a massive invasion. He must convince the local constable and outside authorities to use military force, before Planet X draws near and an attack can commence!

One of United Artists' first releases after its reorganization under Arthur Krim, *The Man From Planet X* is first and foremost an Edgar Ulmer film. The production values are minimal but a fog machine and some leftover pieces of a castle set make the 71 minutes of misty intrigue a stylist's delight. Half the film plays in front of painted backdrops or is dominated by foggy miniatures; the story stays in motion by sheer directorial skill.

Using a dreamlike flashback structure and portentous voiceovers, Ulmer assembles his cast in record time – pleasant hero, sweet heroine, unpleasant villain. The villain in this case is not the initially benign alien but the perfidious professor played by William Schallert, an actor who can surely list more bits in 50s science fiction movies than anyone.

Our alien is a mysterious fellow despite the threadbare production. His spaceship looks like a Christmas tree ornament and his spacesuit is a collection of plumbing accessories topped by a goldfish bowl. The alien's face is an unimpressive stiff mask. But when he leans unexpectedly

into the porthole to frighten Ms. Field we jump back as well. Z-movie favorite Robert Clarke makes an acceptable hero, if perhaps a bit too thoughtful and gentle for the he-man 1950s.

The treatment of the alien in *The Man From Planet X* is rather confused. A peaceful and cooperative guest, he falls victim to human cruelty and greed. Yet he uses a strange ray to turn earthmen into his slaves, and is the vanguard of a planned invasion (When? In the fifteen seconds it takes for the animated Planet X to zoom past the Earth?). Even with these powers, the alien is easily vanquished. It's best to enjoy the atmospheric thrills and not to challenge the film's less logical aspects.

MGM's DVD of ***The Man From Planet X*** is clean and smooth, with a pleasing gradation from dark skies through hazy grays to the shiny surface of the alien spaceship. The exciting trailer will grab and hold any kid's attention.

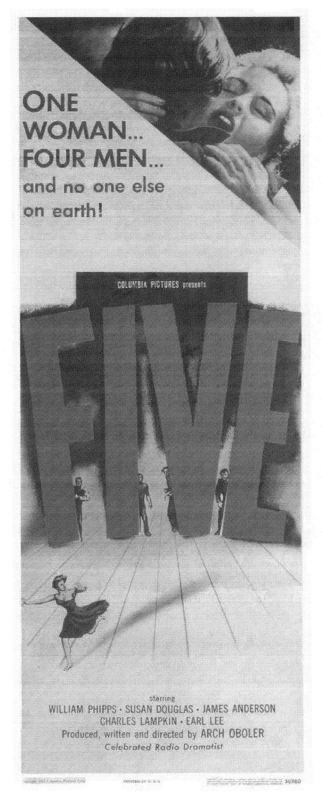

ONE WOMAN...
FOUR MEN...
and no one else
on earth!

COLUMBIA PICTURES presents

FIVE

starring
WILLIAM PHIPPS · SUSAN DOUGLAS · JAMES ANDERSON
CHARLES LAMPKIN · EARL LEE
Produced, written and directed by ARCH OBOLER
Celebrated Radio Dramatist

FIVE

Sony (DVD title: *5ive*)
Reviewed February 5, 2009
1951 / B&W / 1:37 flat / 93 min.
Cinematography Sid Lubow, Louis Clyde Stoumen; Original Music Henry Russell, Written by Arch Oboler, James Weldon Johnson.
Produced and Directed by Arch Oboler

Arch Oboler's *Five* is a significant oddity, an American art film that's also the first science fiction examination of the aftermath of a nuclear conflict. A minor success in 1951, it enjoyed a second life as a late-night movie, and many viewers have distinct memories of being touched by its realism and grim outlook. Is it really possible that the entire population of the planet could be wiped out by a nuclear war? Are the civil defense pamphlets not telling the whole truth?

A handful of people are marooned in the aftermath of an atomic exchange, and converge on an isolated house in a lonely landscape. Calm Michael (William Phipps) attends to the practical matters of hunting for food and growing a crop. Roseann (Susan Douglas) awaits the birth of her baby and clings to the hope that her husband may be alive back in the city. Timid bank clerk Mr. Barnstaple (Earl Lee) has snapped under the psychic pressure. Helping him is Charles, a black ex-G.I. (Charles Lampkin).

The last to show up is Eric (James Anderson), an arrogant mountain climber with no intention of pitching in for the common good. While the others work he forages for treasures in the cities below. Michael and Eric are both interested in Roseann, but she's too shaken to respond to their overtures. To keep the lone female for himself, Eric exploits Roseann's optimism, and offers to sneak her away to look for her husband.

The relentlessly downbeat *Five* has a raw look not seen in many mainstream American releases of the early 1950s, not even exploitation pictures. The gritty tone offers no assurance of a happy ending, and the birth of Roseann's baby only underlines the survivors' insecurity. The movie's visible pregnancy and breast-feeding scene were highly unusual for a movie with a Production Code seal. The racial theme is also handled with an uncommon directness. Eric tells Charles to his face that his presence offends him and insists that he leave. Charles' only response is to sigh: *"So. Now it's finally out."*

Five was filmed at Arch Oboler's distinctive Santa Monica Mountains Cliff House designed by the famed architect Frank Lloyd Wright. The film's style has similarities with experimental filmmaking of the time. Lap dissolves link huge close-ups with images of empty beaches and cloudy skies. The stark lighting and unforced blocking strive for emotional honesty. As little in Oboler's filmography suggests this kind of visual finesse, we may be tempted to credit some of the film's artistry to its "cinematographic consultant", accomplished photographer Louis Clyde Stoumen.

In the film's most suspenseful sequence Eric and Roseann return to downtown Los Angeles. Only a couple of streets are dressed with the expected ruined vehicles and skeletal corpses. Director Oboler evokes an appropriately bleak mood with up-angled shots of buildings passing by. A constant wail of civil defense sirens is heard on the soundtrack. The sirens are *psychological*, not literal – they cease only when Roseann finds what she's looking for.

The movie is more of a poetic allegory than a scientific documentary. The sudden gathering suggests more survivors, but Eric reportedly sailed from India to California without seeing a single living soul. Four of the five escaped the atom blasts because they were in unusual places when the bombs hit, but those circumstances wouldn't have made them any less susceptible to airborne radioactivity. Two group members come down with radiation poisoning, and it's possible that all may succumb in time.

Five reportedly cost only $75,000 to produce. It set the template for the post-atomic melodramas that followed: *The Day the World Ended*; *The World, the Flesh and the Devil*; *On the Beach, Last Woman on Earth*. We have the themes of Old Testament retribution and a new Adam and Eve, the isolated cabin setting and the exploration of a dead city. Dramatic conflicts form around racial prejudice and an amorous competition for the last surviving female. A lonely beach becomes a symbolic setting for the End of the World. *Five* distinguishes itself from other apocalyptic tales by its utter lack of sentimentality. One of the final scenes involves a tragedy rarely depicted in such explicit terms.

The fragile-looking Susan Douglas conveys terror and disorientation well. William Phipps (a character actor with small parts in quite a few 50s science fiction films) is a natural philosopher, although he makes a somewhat subdued leading man. James Anderson affects a French accent; the script explicitly labels his selfish arrogance as a sickness that should have died with the "old world". Earl Lee's feeble clerk represents the millions unequipped to cope with a world turned upside down. Charles Lampkin intones some moody Biblical verses, helping to integrate the Bible quotes that producer Oboler uses to bookend his unusual movie.

Sony's *Martini Movies* DVD of *Five* looks far better than any video copy previously available. The gray cinematography is properly represented. Cheap optical work mars some of the dissolves, leaving patterns of black specks on the screen. Sony's restoration work is particularly commendable when one knows the condition of the film elements. Many scenes in the original negative, worn out by over-printing were long ago replaced with dupe sections.

The audio quality is excellent. Although we're informed *Five* utilized an early magnetic film system to record direct sound on the set, its dialogue appears to have been expertly looped, especially the exteriors. The disc comes with an original trailer in near-perfect condition; it even uses the text phrase *"The Last Woman On Earth!"*

THE THING FROM ANOTHER WORLD

Warners Reviewed: August 7, 2003
1951 / B&W / 1:37 flat / **86**, 81 min.
Cinematography Russell Harlan. Original Music Dimitri Tiomkin. Written by Charles Lederer from a short story by John W. Campbell Jr. . Produced by Howard Hawks. Directed by Christian Nyby

Savant was too young to catch the first wave of classic 50s sci-fi, but fans about ten years older tell me that *The Thing from Another World* was the big scare picture of its day, the one that convinced kids that The Thing was hiding in their closets. Thirty soldiers and scientists at the North Pole duke it out with an entirely new kind of threat, a murderous life form from Outer Space. In one stroke, producers discovered that a successful sci-fi movie could dispense with visionary ideas and expensive special effects. The mysteries of space and technology could be a quick excuse for scary rubber monsters. *The Thing from Another World* has plenty of interesting ideas, but its high-tension thrills are what filled the theaters.

Captain Patrick Hendry (Kenneth Tobey) and his aircrew are sent to the Arctic research station of Doctor Arthur Carrington (Robert Cornthwaite). A nearby magnetic disturbance leads them to the crash site of what appears to be a genuine, honest-to-Dixie flying saucer. The craft is accidentally destroyed but the men recover the corpse of its occupant – an eight-foot, bald 'Thing' that quickly turns the ice station into a panic zone.

Almost everyone loves *The Thing from Another World*. In 1951 it raised the tempers of critics that had hoped the success of *Destination Moon* and *The Day the Earth Stood Still* would usher in a new genre dedicated to the progressive ideas of literary sci-fi. Howard Hawks' thriller took a scary short story with an interesting and cerebral concept – an alien that can duplicate other life forms – and reduced it to a militant face-off at the North Pole. Gun-toting heroes fight tooth and nail with a Frankenstein-like boogey man, and the Air Force comes out on top.

The mostly liberal sci-fi critics also resented the fact that the show stacks the deck in its opposition of soldiers against scientists. Kenneth Tobey's airmen are sentimental, funny and concerned by the problems of survival, whereas the egghead scientists' intellectual values run counter to the best interests of humanity. The soldiers aren't war lovers – they decry the invention of the atom bomb – but the blame for that is implicitly placed on the calculating, emotionless scientists. Robert Cornthwaite's suave researcher is enthused about the obviously dangerous monster, and considers it superior to Man. To him, knowledge is more important than human lives.

The Thing from Another World 's original script was even more unforgiving of the 'traitorous' scientists, a view that the final film takes pains to soften. Doctor Carrington's misjudgment is blamed on overwork. Carrington's own associates do not share his fanaticism. The soldiers respect Carrington's willingness to fight for his beliefs, especially when he proves his sincerity with a conspicuous act of bravery. But they remain convinced that he "doesn't think the way we do". Carrington's commitment to science is considered a menace, plain and simple.

The clever group staging of *The Thing* presents Howard Hawks' much-discussed 'male professional unit' in its most interesting form. No charismatic leader like Cary Grant or John Wayne emerges to tell us who's right. In his first crack at a leading role, the likeable Kenneth Tobey lacks the assumed authority of a Star Hero. In this case, it's a good thing. Because Tobey is not a star, we have no assurance that he will avoid becoming a victim of the bloodsucking carrot.

The rest of the ensemble is inspired. Scotty (Douglas Spencer of *This Island Earth*) is a daring front-line war correspondent. The fliers are a pleasant bunch without a dominant alpha male among them. Robert Nichols (he reads the magazine reference to flying saucers) is a familiar Hawks face also seen in *This Island Earth*. William Self, the fellow who didn't know the blanket was electric, became a network television executive. We all know Dewey Martin from his starring turn in *The Big Sky*.

These airmen have bonded through war experience and function as a natural unit. The scientists are, by contrast, individuals. When Carrington gathers them together it's a meeting, not a natural gathering of like-minded peers. The scientists present facts while the soldiers dispense decisions. When Carrington gives illogical or unwise instructions, his associates meekly obey instead of snapping back with an objection, as would one of Captain Hendry's men. The one scientist with a wife in tow (John Dierkes of "X," *the Man with the X-Ray Eyes*) is the first to defect to the soldiers' camp.

The arctic lab is a confined community in a death struggle. When monsters are banging on the door there isn't time to argue finer points of morality or philosophy. This makes *The Thing* an early manifestation of the Cold War edict that demands that all citizens are either 'with us or against us' against a perceived threat. 'United We Stand' yells the bumper sticker, but the real message is that there's an unspoken 'We' out there with the authority to decide policy, and the job for the rest of us is to follow. There's no room for dissenting Carringtons, no matter how sincere. This is War. [1]

Top-billed Margaret Sheridan is our heroine Nikki, a typical gutsy-but-sexy Hawks dame. NIkki doesn't lead any sing-a-longs (are we sure this is a Hawks movie?) but she uses her coffee pot as an excuse to butt in on the male discussion with little quips, like suggesting a possible defenses against a murderous vegetable. One kinky scene seems an outgrowth of Hawk's screwball comedies about emasculated men, *I Was a Male War Bride* and *Monkey Business.* Hendry is tied to a chair while Nikki feeds him drinks.

The confined warren of the arctic lab really looks assembled from prefab sections hauled in by plane, and the frequent icy breath of the actors reminds us that the cold up there is real. The rooms appear to have full ceilings. Some curious sets have big heat-losing windows (the General's windows have quaint curtains) and a couple of unlikely thin doorways open directly to the frozen outdoors: "Shut the door, it's 30 below outside". Other than that, we can easily believe we are where Hawks says we are.

The action scenes are terrific for 1951, especially a one-take fire scene with gallons of kerosene

splashed around. Note the mass of flames that erupts on and around the mattress in the corner, the one Nikki is under. I'm assuming that the featured players were replaced by stuntmen for this action. [2]

Appearances by The Thing (James Arness) are kept short and abrupt, with the result that he remains a frightening menace despite a somewhat ordinary design. The best shock moment is a quick view through a doorway. It's enhanced by an optical that slightly diffuses just that area of the picture in which Arness appears. It gives the shot an extra kick of weirdness, a "Did you see that?" quality.

A muted controversy exists over who directed *The Thing from Another World.* It's obviously Hawks, or the whole thing was planned and rehearsed by him. Editor Nyby needed a credit to join the Director's Guild and Hawks helped him out. Hawks probably wanted to disassociate himself from *The Thing* – I'm guessing that he didn't value a monster picture at the same level as the rest of his work. It had no stars, wasn't going to win any awards, etc. Hawks was right. As soon as sci-fi pictures became stereotyped as cheapies with no-name casts, a flashy poster and a rubber monster, mainstream directors avoided them.

Warners' DVD of **The Thing from Another World** is an okay but not stunning disc. An earlier Laserdisc reinstated a number of scenes trimmed for a reissue from a much-degraded 16mm source, but much of the movie looks slightly soft and washed-out. Also, three or four unaccountable breaks occur where frames are missing.

The reinstated scenes add up to almost five minutes. Important exchanges, briefings and the above-mentioned bondage scene fill in the characters and smooth out the story. Without these asides *The Thing* jumps from the point where the block of ice is stored away directly to the moment when the electric blanket is thrown over it.

Dimitri Tiomkin's jolting, aggressive music with its sharp notes and Theremin accents comes across in all its violent glory. It must have scared kids in '51 before the story even got going. The great score stays out of the way of the drama, blasting in whenever the audience needs shaking up.

The package box artwork adds a close-up of James Arness as the Thing to the old don't-show-the-monster ad art. A badly worn trailer consists almost completely of alternate takes, including several unused angles from the fire scene.

1. When Hendry assumes command from Carrington, Dewey Martin enforces the order by brandishing his rifle in Carrington's face, calmly hinting that he's willing to use it. When I was a kid I thought this was really cool. Now, it's caveman aggression.

2. Two odd details stick out during the Thing's final attack. The defenders barricade a hallway door with 4x4 timbers and strong braces. But when Arness enters, the door proves to open *the other way*, a gag right out of *Abbott and Costello meet Frankenstein*! A major continuity point follows immediately: Arness stomps in, each foot landing with a blast of Tiomkin's Mickey-Mouse'd music. The barricade is now a loose pile of lumber on the floor before him. We cut to the nervous defenders. When we cut back to Arness, a new 4x4 beam is lying just under his right arm, ready to pick up! There, now I've ruined the scene for everyone!

WHEN WORLDS COLLIDE

Paramount Reviewed October 5, 2001
1951 / Color / 1:37 flat / 83 min.
Cinematography: W. Howard Greene, John F. Seitz. Art Direction: Albert Nozaki, Hal Pereira. Original Music: Leith Stevens. Written by Sydney Boehm from the novel by Edwin Balmer & Philip Wylie. Produced by George Pal. Directed by Rudolph Maté

George Pal 's Technicolor *When Worlds Collide* is a naïve epic made fast on the heels of the producer's *Destination Moon*. A 1930s concoction from a novel surely influenced by Abel Gance's *La fin du monde*, this production skirts the racism of its literary source but expands on its religious framework. The show is bathed in the kind of sanctimony that typifies the movies of Cecil B. De Mille, for whom a script had been commissioned twenty years before.

Freelance pilot David Randall (Richard Derr) delivers telescope photographs from South Africa to the New York lab of scientist Cole Hendron (Larry Keating). The astronomical bottom line is that two rogue interstellar planets named Bellus and Zyra are going to destroy the Earth in only eight months' time. While Hendron scrambles to build a Space Ark to ferry a small group of humans out of harm's way, Randall finds himself attracted to Hendron's daughter Joyce (Barbara Rush). He works hard on the spaceship project, all the while knowing there's no reason to take a bush pilot along to help start a new world. Before the final impact, one of the planetoids will pass close enough to Earth to cause cataclysmic earthquakes and flooding. If the disasters prevent the Space Ark from being completed in time, it's possible that nobody will survive.

George Pal's *When Worlds Collide* won an Oscar for best special effects and was also nominated for best cinematography. The depression-era novel on which it was based now seems a radical reaction to the social instability of The Depression mixed with revivalist sentiment. The book and its sequel *After Worlds Collide* are filled with racist hatred for anything Asian, yet were standard fare in school libraries of the 1960s.

Devout producer Pal retains the book's Christ metaphor: the stellar cataclysm is a thinly disguised Second Coming. Two heavenly bodies, the planet Bronson Alpha (or Bellus in the film) and its smaller satellite Bronson Beta (Zyra) will intersect Earth's orbit in only eight months. Representing the Old Testament Jehovah, Bellus will smash the Earth to pulp, killing every living soul. But Earth has a chance for redemption. A few weeks before the arrival of Bellus, its moon Zyra will pass close enough to cause massive earthquakes, tidal waves and other assorted havoc. Like Jesus Christ, Zyra is both a warning and a potential savior. Only a Chosen Few will be saved: technocrats daring enough to build Space Arks to fly to Zyra.

Seen today, Pal's epic is a charming hoot. It begins and ends with the ponderous opening and closing of a Bible. Bellus, schmellus, we know who's really wiping out the Earth! The inside of the Space Ark is arrayed like a church with the faithful in the pews and the pilots (deacons?) up in the pulpit. The chosen passengers are a technological Elect. Their peers left behind immediately riot to steal seats on the only ride off the planet. *When Worlds Collide* is a delirious End Of Days story.

The scientific details of George Pal's Space Ark are rather sketchy, especially after the fastidiously accurate *Destination Moon*. Eight months isn't long enough to perfect a pencil sharpener but the Arkian engineers are able to research, design, build and test an advanced rocket ship as civilization crumbles around them. The admittedly breathtaking Space Ark is launched from a ramp that goes down into a valley before zooming up the next mountainside. The super rocket's fuel gauge is a simple indicator marked 'full', 'half' and 'empty'. [1]

The manifest for this joy ride is also amusing. Domestic farm animals are brought on board two by two, Noah-style, as if a single pair of animals could restore a species. The same logic applies to the paired-off sixteen or so couples who win the lottery to take the trip. Their key function is presumably to make babies for the future of mankind. Nowadays, it would seem obvious that if a Space Ark could only hold forty people, the best hope for mankind would be to choose brilliant female scientists, doctors and engineers as passengers, all young and all fit to bear children. The male component of the passenger list would be test tubes of sperm for later artificial insemination. Why waste cargo weight on a bunch of redundant drones, when breeder females are needed? Is *When Worlds Collide* interested in saving mankind, or does a sexual fantasy lurk behind the Bible talk? This no-boys-allowed rational approach would surely upset the Strangeloves and Turgidsons of our present political system.

The dramatic and moral logic of *When Worlds Collide* is equally thoughtless. Essential project personnel risk their lives taking supplies to flood survivors who are doomed anyway. In the lottery for the forty seats on the Ark, not one of the young engineers objects when project leader Cole Hendron arbitrarily reserves space for his daughter, her boyfriend, a kid rescued from a rooftop and a stray dog. Hendron also bends the rules to allow yet another lottery loser to take cuts in the line for the Ark, to stay with her boyfriend. No wonder the losers are rioting!

Multimillionaire investor Stanton (John Hoyt) is refused his agreed-upon ticket to ride because he's a cynical malcontent. How his riches financed the Ark is a mystery, when a big point is made that money no longer has value after the end of the world is announced. A cripple restricted to a wheelchair, Stanton prefigures *Doctor Strangelove* when the coming of doomsday unaccountably restores his ability to walk. Since the genial, gentle George Pal was serious about his Sunday school Bible theme, this is clearly meant to be an apocalyptic miracle. You've got ten minutes to live, Mr. Moneybags, so have yourself a stroll.

The only preparation for arrival on Zyra is a crash landing, which is accomplished on a handy mountaintop snowfield. Aerial glimpses of the terrain show only ice and dense clouds for hundreds of miles. Yet when the hatch is opened, the view awaiting Earth's exiles is that of a verdant paradise complete with an inspirational sunset and unexplained (unless one takes into account the book *After Worlds Collide*) pyramid-like structures on the horizon. The cocksure pilot throws open the airlock without first testing the atmosphere because, "It's the only place we can go!"

The special effects wowed 'em in 1951 and can still spark imagination and wonder. A beauti-

ful silver colossus, the Space Ark stands silhouetted against the dramatic painted skies. The onrushing Bellus looming in the night sky is appropriately frightful. Except for some poorly scaled fire and smoke, most of the effects shots are breathtaking.

The disasters of the first passing of the rogue planets aren't as impressive as they once were. A fairly successful matte shot of water pouring into Manhattan is followed by a just-passable painting of ocean liners capsized next to the Chrysler building. The rest of the footage is culled from every Technicolor volcano, flood, and earthquake stock shot that George Pal could get his hands on, including outtakes from *For Whom the Bell Tolls* and *Crash Dive*.

Paramount's DVD of **When Worlds Collide** is visually disappointing. The deluxe laser disc of a few years back (with its isolated music track!) is still the better show. The DVD image is on the harsh side, with annoying fringing appearing against lines of strong contrast. Frequent shots of newspaper headlines have annoying contrast colors outlining what should be plain black letters on white. An expert I saw the disc with suspected an overuse of edge enhancement. These will be less of a bother on smaller monitors, but on a big set it looks as if one's television rabbit ears need tweaking.

1. Arthur C. Clarke once criticized the launch ramp in *When Worlds Collide*, claiming that the roller-coaster ride down one mountain and up the next would waste the rocket's forward impetus by transferring it to the ground as it took the curve. The rocket might as well just start from the bottom of the ravine. But Clarke missed a key detail: The fuel and power being used to accelerate the ship down the ramp come from the sled it rests on, not the ship itself. The rocket's engines aren't ignited until the second, "Up" half of the roller coaster ramp. The spaceship is already speeding at 100 mph or so when its on-board engines come into use.

THE MAN IN THE WHITE SUIT

Anchor Bay Reviewed: October 22, 2002
1951 / B&W / 1:37 flat / 85 min.
Cinematography Douglas Slocombe. Original
Music Benjamin Frankel. Written by John
Dighton, Alexander Mackendrick and Roger
MacDougall. Produced by Michael Balcon,
Sidney Cole.
Directed by Alexander Mackendrick

The Man in the White Suit is a nearly perfect
satire, one of the best of the celebrated Ealing
comedies. It carries some genuinely profound
themes about progress versus economic realities. Science fiction claims the movie because it
centers on a world altering, potentially menacing invention. The noble ambitions of its hero
prove to be against the general good of society.
As in many films of the early 1950s, science is
made the scapegoat for all of man's woes.

Research chemist Sidney Stratton (Guinness)
steals equipment and laboratory space to perfect
his fantastic 'long molecule' synthetic fiber. He's
fired from the textile mill of Michael Corland
(Michael Gough) but sets up shop in the nearby
facilities of Alan Birnley (Cecil Parker), where
he manages a breakthrough. Caught in the act,
Sidney is nevertheless given a lab of his own
and *carte blanche* to make good on his theories,
thanks to the intervention of Birnley's daughter,
Daphne (Joan Greenwood), who sees Sidney as
an idealistic crusader. Sidney succeeds in creating a cloth that doesn't wear out and never gets
dirty, but what should be embraced as a miracle
turns into a nightmare.

Sidney Stratton's indestructible cloth most likely
would upset the economic balance of the world.
Textiles are a labor-intensive industry and perish-
able clothing needs to be cleaned, repaired and
replaced. The labor spokesmen whine about retaining their hard-won concessions but are correct
when they complain that Stanley's cloth will put
them all out of work. *The Man in the White Suit* is
the rare picture that acknowledges that man relates to the basics of his life (food, employment,
etc.) not directly but through social and economic
conventions. Even when the conventions are obsolete, they are still needed. This recognition of
political complexity is especially sophisticated
when compared to emotionally based movie
treatments of the labor-management-technology
triangle, starting way back with *Metropolis*.

Guinness's Stratton is Ibsen's *Enemy of the People*
and a White Knight of truth. The film is a great
lesson-teacher for kids, or anyone complacent
enough to believe that all social problems are sol-
uble in terms of right and wrong. Although on a
crusade to save the world, Sydney is both human
and fallible, and has an ego that seeks recognition,
wealth and love. He's a little like the character K
from Kafka's *The Trial*, who sees himself as a victim yet elevates his personal ego over the general
welfare of society at large. Sidney's scientific urge
makes him a dangerous, if loveable, imp.

One might not perceive these depths in *The Man in the White Suit,* as the film maintains a constant flow of verbal and slapstick humor. Farcical misunderstandings lead to chases worthy of Chaplin and Keaton, as with Sidney's hilarious attempt to gain entrance to the Birnley manse. Sidney's takeover of Birnley's lab is a wonderful pre-*Brazil* view of power interpreted as office space. The lab manager Hoskins (Henry Mollinson) is shoved into a jammed closet, and must wear a blitz helmet against Sidney's explosive experiments. The funny semi-musical noises made by Sidney's synthetic fiber apparatus were adapted into a novelty song that became popular on the British radio.

Starry-eyed and dreamy, Guinness makes Sidney into a loveable Quixote character. Joan Greenwood's voice is a sexy, velvety croak when she's inspired by his impossible dream. Stuffy Cecil Parker and the crassly thick Michael Gough are the imbecilic captains of industry, and fifteen years after *The Bride of Frankenstein* Ernest Thesiger is grandly anemic as the Machiavellian textile kingpin. The movie has great fun making their line of limousines appear like a funeral cortege.

There's a bit of the class clash of *A Place in the Sun* working here too. Sidney first captures the eye of Bertha, the union-obsessed working girl (Vida Hope) but her adoration can't compete with the moneyed charms of textile princess Daphne. This added bit of tension is not all that flattering to the Sidney Stratton character. When he wanders off, contemplating the 'fix' for his failed invention and blinded to its questionable social effects, he could easily be some scientist enraptured by an idea for a new kind of super-weapon.

Anchor Bay's ***The Man in the White Suit*** is blessed with a near-perfect transfer. The soundtrack is equally strong. No subtitle tracks are included, but the clipped English dialogue is easy to understand. The disc comes with an original trailer and a lengthy text essay on Guinness' career by the capable Avie Hern.

FROM OUT OF SPACE....
A WARNING AND AN ULTIMATUM!

THE DAY THE EARTH STOOD STILL

MICHAEL RENNIE · PATRICIA NEAL · HUGH MARLOWE

THE DAY THE EARTH STOOD STILL

Fox Blu-ray Reviewed December 6, 2008
1951 / B&W / 1:37 flat / 92 min.
Cinematography Leo Tover. Art Direction Addison Hehr, Lyle Wheeler. Original Music Bernard Herrmann. Written by Edmund H. North from the story *Farewell to the Master* by Harry Bates. Produced by Julian Blaustein. Directed by Robert Wise

Possibly the most beloved science Fiction movie of the 50s, ***The Day the Earth Stood Still*** was produced when Hollywood could still perceive a movie about a man from space as an 'A' production. After a flurry of top-end product, space and monster operas were consigned to the independent ghetto, with only occasional exceptions like *20,000 Leagues Under the Sea* or *Forbidden Planet* displaying the genre's grand possibilities.

Simultaneously pacifist and fascist in its concept, this audience pleaser is so appealing that liberal thinkers don't look past the "Socialists from Space" angle to see the kind of conceptual rhubarb writer Edmund H. North is selling. *The Day the Earth Stood Still* pulls us into its post-modern thrills by pushing the right Cold War buttons. We can save the world, but only if we can remember those three magic words.

A silvery flying saucer lands on the Mall in Washington D.C. and throws the entire country into a panic. From it emerges Klaatu (Michael Rennie), an ascetic, humorless messenger who asks to speak to all the people of Earth, all at once. Foiling the Army's attempt lock him up, Klaatu masquerades as an Earthling and meets the residents of Mrs. Barley's boarding house, especially war widow Helen Benson (Patricia Neal) and her curious son Bobby (Billy Gray). Bobby is the first to realize that Klaatu is Not of This Earth, but as a police dragnet closes in, Helen's jealous fiancé Tom Stevens (Hugh Marlowe) is the Judas that betrays the stranger from Space. The big problem is Klaatu's robot policeman companion Gort (Lock Martin). Should the trigger-happy authorities kill the spaceman, Gort is programmed to destroy the world.

The Day the Earth Stood Still was one of *Cinefantastique* magazine's first classic profile articles; researcher Steven Jay Rubin collected the entire back story of its making. The movie was conceived before *Destination Moon* and Claude Rains was the first choice to play Klaatu. Rubin also nailed the movie's three dominant themes – two of them hot-button topics that at the time could be approached only through the smokescreen of genre filmmaking. Deservedly or not, this is the cornerstone of Deep-Think sci-fi of the Liberal Kind.

The first theme is of course the Flying Saucer craze. *The Man From Planet X's* confused and potentially benign alien actually touched down first. Fans of Steven Spielberg's *Close Encoun-* *ters of the Third Kind* think that all previous sci-fi movies featured hostile invaders, forgetting that initial efforts like *It Came from Outer Space* also soft-pedaled the menace angle. Then *The War of the Worlds* hit and visitors from the stars became synonymous with ray guns and destruction.

Flying Saucer hysteria, based on several hard-to-discount sightings in the late 40s, has since been pegged as a religious phenomenon. [1] Scholars that study belief systems from Christianity to phrenology think that people invest their faith in the craze because Flying Saucers have an immediacy missing from organized churches. Why not believe that an advanced civilization of interstellar people will soon arrive to solve our problems? *The Day the Earth Stood Still's* miraculous space ship landing definitely evokes the Biblical Rapture – an irrational idea fully exploited in *Close Encounters*.

Then there's the straight-on Church theme. In 1950 America was experiencing a revivalist comeback spurred by TV preachers like Billy Graham. The revivalists hit the theme of the Second Coming for all it was worth, and a sizeable segment of the country began living their secular lives – and casting their votes – exactly as dictated from the pulpits.

Unfortunately, the revivalist messages were mostly isolationist, know-nothing and backward; based on a Love that was 9/10ths paternalistic authoritarianism and fear. Foreigners, non-whites, non-fundamentalists were all considered suspicious. Fundamentalists and the Anti-Communists had much in common – the scholars list some forms of Anti-Communism as a belief system of its own. An enemy to loathe seemed to be all the faith many Americans needed. A cadre of devils had betrayed us to the Russians and the Red Chinese, and they must be rooted out.

The America that greets Klaatu is at perpetual war and flailing at ideological enemies. Massive arms, aviation and space research programs were under way to counter perceived Soviet super-weapons. Media pundits gained popularity by hyping the invisible menace. People on the streets were just plain scared. A joke of the day was that if Jesus came back, we'd nuke him.

The Day the Earth Stood Still is a sci-fi parable on that exact theme. The original short story *Farewell to the Master* is an okay pulp piece with a twist – Harry Bates' robot Gnut turns out to be the dominant alien, and Klaatu merely his organic PR spokesman, a sidekick along for the ride. The screen version instead gives us a full-on allegory.

The film's Christ parallel is well known. One of the first dialogue lines is, "Holy Christmas!" Klaatu takes the name Carpenter. He frets over the perfect non-violent Miracle to convince mankind of his limitless power. Murdered by the Army, Klaatu returns from the dead with final words of hope for our backward race, a message of paternal authority from all-powerful super beings. Not often cited is the detail, during a nighttime visit to his spaceship, of the Army's barbed wire falling across Klaatu's face – a modern crown of thorns.

Klaatu's smug attitude is evident from the beginning; attempts to keep him under lock and key merely amuse him. The fugitive space man falls into an immediate mutual attraction with war widow Helen Benson and her son. Patricia Neal plays the widow with dignity and skepticism and becomes our surrogate in the story. When Helen finally buys into Klaatu's mission and defies the military (which seems to be in charge of everything), she follows a higher truth than official fear. [2]

The religious angle may have been what shielded *The Day the Earth Stood Still* from the red-baiting media in and outside of Hollywood. Fundamentalists would surely recognize the Christ parallel and approve the movie's championing of a faith-based morality. Hollywood was certainly in step

with that aspect – the Production Code's only objection to the script was to demand that Klaatu's apparent resurrection be clarified as only temporary – the power to give life "is reserved by The Almighty Spirit".

The supposed Utopia represented by Klaatu's Federation of Planets is more than a little disturbing. Jesus preached Love and offered a reprieve from the blood and thunder of the Old Testament Jehovah, who had already destroyed the world once in anger. Klaatu doesn't come on a mission of enlightenment and his race has little interest in Earth culture. Klaatu speaks perfect Oxford English but is ignorant about how we live – trains, flashlights and locked doors are novelties to him. More importantly, he is unaware of the nature of our wars.

Nope, Klaatu is not here to save the heathen, but to smite the wicked. He isn't interested in our petty squabbles and doesn't leave any monoliths behind to help us along. We're to get our act together or suffer annihilation. Klaatu's farewell speech, a kind of rebuttal to Oswald Cabal's ode to conquerors of the universe in *Things to Come,* is a final warning, a direct threat, an ultimatum.

Pacifists of 1951 were surely impressed to see America criticized as an aggressor nation. But did anybody consider the 'superior' society Klaatu describes? It's a Robotocracy of implacable mechanical policemen that watch over everything and respond to 'aggression' with ruthless force. The Gortian race doesn't hand out tickets or slap hands – instant disintegration is the only response in its bag of tricks. Klaatu's race has ceded total control to the robots and is said to be free of wars and dissent. Of course, if the Federation of Planets ever decides that it doesn't need robotic executioners on every street corner, they'll be out of luck – Gort doesn't have an off switch. *The Day the Earth Stood Still* is a good think piece for those who promote Law And Order as a universal solution. Whose law? Whose order? What Klaatu is really selling is a dictatorship far worse than anything Stalin or Mao could dream up. [3]

The Day the Earth Stood Still works best as a parable about the petty differences between Earthly nations. If we can get along with an alien like Klaatu, why can't we settle our differences with our brother humans? Poor Mr. Harley's protest that politics prevent him from fulfilling Klaatu's demands earns the spaceman's ire, and our scorn. But Klaatu isn't much different from the colonists that 'discovered' America or India, couldn't make the uncooperative natives see things the right way and started shooting. Behind Klaatu at all times stands Gort, the enforcer. Weapons have the loudest voice even when they're just sitting quietly. It always comes down to brute force.

As an emotional experience, few sci-fi films can beat Robert Wise's show. The documentary surface ups the tension and Bernard Herrman's sublime score tells the story in operatic movements. We have rational, likeable Helen Benson and the Albert Einstein substitute Professor Barnhardt to root for. The villain informs on Klaatu (Jesus) with selfish excuses: "I don't care about the rest of the world." "Somebody's got to get rid of him!" [4]

Darryl Zanuck's production is sublime. The cleanly designed saucer, the robot Gort and Klaatu's garb do indeed seem the products of alien technology. The Fox studio's location expertise meshes perfectly with Robert Wise's Val Lewton-esque touches of personal unease. Bobby's night walk to the Mall is as tense as anything in *Cat People*; when stalked by the menacing robot, Helen's panic is sheer unthinking terror.

The picture manages warm touches and a lively sense of humor. Billy Gray is terrific as the normal kid-cum-diamond thief. Klaatu's power outage demo has its amusing aspects and Professor Barnhardt happily gloats when his secretary admits to being frightened.

The sparingly used optical magic of saucer landings and death rays is superb, greatly aided by sound effects and Herrmann's quavering Theremin. Gort's visor slides open to reveal a pulsing light of death that shoots like a bullet, a reverse ricochet sound, actually. Gort is an inverse Knight of the Round table, one that responds to cold programming instead of a chivalric code.

The Day the Earth Stood Still pulls its audience so firmly into its spell that its inconsistencies only become obvious after repeated viewings. Klaatu's initial wounding by a nervous soldier gets big gasps and 'boos' from audiences, when in actuality the spaceman kind of asks for it. If the L.A.P.D. has already drawn its guns, try reaching into your clothing for an unfamiliar object and see what happens. Our trigger-happy attitude is no excuse, but ignorance is a two-way street. Had they cared enough, Klaatu's race could have studied ours for a minute or two.

Although it encases Gort in plastic, the Army posts only two soldiers to guard what anyone can see is a weapon of limitless mass destruction. Access to the site isn't even restricted. At the very least they'd evacuate the city and ring the saucer with more firepower. A real flying saucer and alien robot are sitting on a baseball diamond in the park and nobody seems to care, not even the press. If this really happened, the Mall would more likely than not become the destination of a mass exodus. Every pilgrim en route to Mecca or the Vatican would buy a ticket to Washington instead.

Klaatu's language is extremely efficient. "Gort, Klaatu barada nikto" is the message (and a wrong one – Helen doesn't repeat Klaatu's exact words). If the first two words are names, than barada nikto translates roughly as, "Stash the lady in the ship and call headquarters for instructions." Either that, or it also tells Gort to recover Klaatu's body and warm it up in the microwave.

Gort, a ten-foot metal Golem, scorches his way out of a solid block of plastic, marches across a major city, burns down the wall of a jail and carries kaput Klaatu back to the Mall – and nobody sees him! That's pretty good when one considers that Klaatu couldn't shake the Army's dragnet just an hour before. [5] Also puzzling is the fact that Klaatu's limitless technology can neutralize all electric power selectively, all over the Earth, yet Klaatu cannot fulfill his mission by simply communicating to the whole Earth, all at once. The benevolent alien Overlords of Arthur C. Clarke's *Childhood's End* solved that problem, no sweat.

Relax, Savant, it's just a movie. All of these objections are hooey in a film that keeps us at the edge of our seats, eager to hear every detail and catch every nuance. The international group of scientists that receives Klaatu's imperious ultimatum has no power to implement any of his demands. Who listens to scientists? Our days to becoming a burnt-out cinder are numbered indeed.

We're more concerned with the walking-dead version of Klaatu, who apparently is running on borrowed batteries. Does his smile to Helen have a tinge of bittersweet interstellar romance? Does he perhaps have a twin brother who'll come back to spirit Helen away to a galactic Casbah? Or is Gort a trigger-happy chaperone, willing to roast playboy Klaatu should he go soft for an Earth dame?

The Day the Earth Stood Still is a highly successful message movie. Its Christian theme is ultimately a muddle, but it does communicate some things loud and clear. War is an atrocity to be avoided at all cost. Interstellar peace begins with treating our friends, relatives and everyone we meet with kindness and respect. True Christians don't allow suspicion and fear to guide their actions or mask weakness with blind aggression. This is one science fiction classic that will never fade away.

Fox's *The Day the Earth Stood Still* is the first 50's sci-fi classic to be presented in Blu-ray. The restored, remastered B&W film looks and sounds immaculate. The movie's clean lines and simple compositions only improve with the added detail. We can see tiny human figures running away from Klaatu's space ship as it lands on the D.C. Mall, and the imperfections in both the ship and the rubber Gort costume are now much more in evidence. Watch Gort's arms and legs carefully and you'll see that more than one shot reveals large laces on the side meant to face away from the camera.

Most of the film's later scenes take place at night, under eerie lighting that complements Bernard Herrmann's sensational music score. The remixed soundtrack is sharper and more defined than I've ever heard it before; in the lossless Blu-ray audio format Gort's ray blasts are a marvel of audio construction, with sound effects nested *inside* sound effects. In addition to Spanish and French tracks, an isolated score track is included. Much of the film unspools with a documentary-like directness; Herrmann's cues are used almost exclusively in scenes involving alien activity.

Some worthy extras from the previous *Studio Classics* DVD are not present. Older copies are worth saving for interviews with Robert Wise and contributions by the likes of Bob Burns, Robert Skotak and Joe Dante. The older commentary by Robert Wise and writer-director Nicholas Meyer has been retained, accompanied by a music-centric new commentary with Nick Redman and three music historians. Several new featurettes are included. *The Making of ...* is an acceptable overview piece;. *Decoding "Klaatu Barada Nikto": Science Fiction as Metaphor* interprets the film's famous quote. Fat galleries of stills and artwork are included along with an interactive press book.

The Astounding Harry Bates and *Edmund North, the Man Who Made the Earth Stand Still* are respectful tributes to the film's authors. Jamieson

K. Price recites Bates' original short story *Fare-well to the Master*. The best new extra is *A Brief History of Flying Saucers*, an excellent analysis of the flying saucer craze as examined by cultists, debunkers and the commercial opportunists of Roswell, New Mexico. The piece offers several famous bits of saucer footage, most of which look terribly phony.

The fun continues with three items based on the use of the electronic Theremin in the film's soundtrack. A montage of newsreel clips from the early '50s shows the media's contempt for our Communist foes. Contrasting that is Edmund North's 1982 film *Race to Oblivion*, made for an anti-nuke coalition. It features doctors and scientists proclaiming the unsurvivabilty of a nuclear war. Activist actor Burt Lancaster interviews a scarred Los Angeles nurse who was a victim of the Hiroshima bombing. Back in the early 1950s, political advocacy films of this sort were considered traitorous propaganda.

1. Dr. Christopher Cook, ed. *Pears Encyclopedia* 1988-89, Pelham Books, London. Reprinted in *Information Please Almanac*, Houghton Mifflin 1990.

2. Patricia Neal's character is both sensitive and mature. She's woman enough to say goodbye to the super-man from space without as much as a whimper of personal feeling. It's all in the eyes – Helen's love is the kind that can save the world and ask nothing in return.

3. This became a cautionary message in 1969's *Colossus: The Forbin Project*. America and Russia hand over their strategic defense to computers. The machines immediately take over the world, enslaving us to save us from ourselves.

4. As witness *Them!* and *Invaders from Mars*, tow-headed American boys are the darlings and first boosters of our U.S. Army. Tom Stevens is a known rat right from the beginning. The real Judas of *The Day the Earth Stood Still* is that jerk kid outside the boarding house that cheerfully tells the M.P.'s that Klaatu Went Thataway.

5. Gort's record for stealth was broken only by Dean Parkin in Bert Gordon's 1958 *War of the Colossal Beast*: A 60-foot giant breaks loose from a hangar at Los Angeles International Airport and disappears into the city. He later turns up 22 miles away in Griffith Park!

RED PLANET MARS

Not on DVD Reviewed June 24, 2009
1952 / B&W / 1:37 flat / 87 min.
Cinematography Joseph F. Biroc. Music Mahlon Merrick. Written by John L. Balderson, Anthony Veiller from a play by Balderson and John Hoare. Produced by Donald Hyde, Anthony Veiller. Directed by Harry Horner.

The relatively obscure **Red Planet Mars** is a pro-Christian anti-Communist sci-fi melodrama, a politically radical film that advocates the conversion of the United States to a Christian theocracy. Released by United Artists, the independent production was made by industry professionals with impressive credits. Despite its title (and poster graphics depicting a futuristic Martian city) the film takes place entirely in a few earthbound settings. It dramatizes the popular desire for God to appear from outer space to solve all earthly problems.

There's certainly no rule against filmmaking advocating a religious point of view. Producers during the studio heyday traditionally did well with Bible themes, whether sincere or not. The influence of Catholic censors in the enforcement of the Production Code frequently resulted in Christian-friendly changes to films of all kinds, as we've seen with *The Day the Earth Stood Still*. But films that combine religious conversion with radical politics are usually remembered only as eccentric curiosities. *Gabriel Over the White House* (1933) is about a corrupt President, miraculously revived from an auto accident, who saves the United States by assuming "benign" dictatorial powers. One of the more controversial MGM pictures of 1950 was William Wellman's *The Next Voice You Hear,* a strange parable in which the voice of God (unheard) speaks to all mankind on the radio.

The political fantasy of *Red Planet Mars* exploits a number of anxieties of the early postwar years. Total victory brought not peace but a hostile confrontation with Communist regimes noted for suppressing religious freedom. Although America's power and influence was at an all-time high, the public felt threatened from abroad and betrayed from within. Americans wishing that the complexities of postwar politics would just *go away,* turned for relief to the politically conservative sermons broadcast over their new television sets.

(Full Synopsis): The near future. Radio researchers and good Christians Chris and Linda Cronyn (Peter Graves & Andrea King) desire a better world for their two boys. Using a special hydrogen valve confiscated from the Nazis, they've been sending radio messages to Mars. An astronomer shows them photographic proof that Martians are using canals to irrigate their crops with water from Mars's polar ice cap. Monitored by Navy signals expert Admiral Carey (Walter Sande), the Cronyns transmit a mathematical code to Mars. A few minutes later, a response proves that they've contacted intelligent life. Soon they're receiving and decoding amazing messages, which are broadcast around the world. The Martian lifespan is 300 years. Martian agriculture is advanced far beyond ours. They've tapped "Cosmic energy" as a source of unlimited power.

The effect of these revelations is almost instantaneous. Life insurance policies are cancelled, farm prices crash and steel mills and mines close. Democratic economies are threatened with collapse. To avert disaster, the President (Willis Bouchey) declares all Mars communications top secret. Washington takes over the decoding of messages, which are no longer made public.

As it turns out, the "messages from Mars" are actually being sent from a remote lab in the Andes. Franz Calder, the Nazi scientist who invented the hydrogen valve, is purposely fabricating fake messages to disrupt the enemies of the Soviet Union. Russian spymaster Arjenian (Marvin Miller) is delighted with Calder's scheme. But subsequent messages change in tone, when Chris and Linda ask how the Martians maintain peace. Responses decoded by the military reveal that Mars is ruled by a "supreme authority" that visited the Earth and preached peace "seven lifetimes ago" – when Jesus walked. Declaring that *"Now we're following the star of Bethlehem"*, the President releases the Christian-themed messages. Millions flock to churches. The news is also broadcast on Voice of America behind the Iron Curtain. Russian peasants retrieve long-hidden Eastern Orthodox artifacts and rise up in demonstrations.

An avalanche wipes out Calder's lab, and the messages from Mars cease. The popular uprising overturns the Soviet government, and a priest takes charge in the Kremlin. Churches reopen. All world conflict comes to an end as Russia's armies stand down.

The Cronyn family is celebrating the birth of "The Blessed Generation" when Calder shows up at their guarded radio observatory to reveal what he has done. The Nazi has proof that Washington faked the religious messages for obvious propaganda reasons. Calder now intends to reveal the hoax, so that the world will once again fall into secular chaos. Chris and Linda realize that the only way to stop this modern anti-Christ is to ignite the unstable hydrogen valve and become martyrs for the new age of Christian peace. Yet, at the last moment, a *genuine* message comes through from Mars …

At a first viewing the outlandish *Red Planet Mars* takes one's breath away: God is alive and well and living on Mars. The anti-Communist propaganda message is that the solution to the world's problems is universal Christian fundamentalism.

The movie assumes that its audience believes Communists to be vile, godless villains. The Soviet Premier is a bloodthirsty despot eager to shoot dissidents and execute underlings who bring bad news. Linda Cronyn's exaggerated position speeches advocate more radical opinions. She argues that science is evil and will advance mankind to oblivion. After all, "Mars means war".

Headline montages and TV reports (on a wall-mounted flat screen monitor!) show the world in turmoil. The public initially blames the Cronyns for the economic plunge into chaos, and then flock to worship when the Mars messages turn religious. The film's one bit of comedy relief depicts a heavy drinker impressed by the sermons from Mars. He throws away his booze and drags his wife to church, "just for insurance".

The abrupt plot reversals at the climax are a bit rushed, causing many viewers to come away with the impression that all the Mars messages are fakes. 1952 viewers also noted the resemblance between actor Willis Bouchey and Presidential candidate Dwight Eisenhower, and took *Red Planet Mars* as an endorsement of the Republican ticket for the November election. In the filmmakers' view the U.S. should be a Christian nation with no separation between church and state – and the military as well, considering that the government appears to be led by literal Christian Soldiers. *Red Planet Mars* can't be dismissed as a relic of its time, because a sizeable minority today advocates just this viewpoint.

The film concludes like a barnstorming morality play. The anti-Christ is vanquished and the enlightened Cronyns go to their heavenly reward. In Washington, the President addresses the Union as if preaching to a national congregation, declaring the Cronyns' orphans to be both blessed and fortunate. The last fragment of authentic Mars message (which verifies the truth of the others) is, *"Ye have done well, my good -"* The President knows his Bible, and completes God's message: *"… my good and faithful servants."* Let the religious conversion begin.

1957's *The 27th Day* is a similar, if basically secular, Cold War parable. Aliens intent on conquering our planet give representative earthlings capsules capable of wiping out life on an entire continent. The aliens claim that they are morally incapable of killing, yet hypocritically lend us the means to kill ourselves. In the appallingly crude twist ending, a capsule is altered to kill "only the enemies of human freedom". Naturally, all those terrible communists magically disappear; the finish is an undisguised *reverse Rapture*. Such a perverted fairy tale makes *Red Planet Mars* seem rational by comparison.

A cross-section of Americans congregates in a Manhattan bar – newscaster Vince Potter (Gerald Mohr); beautiful Carla Sanford (Peggie Castle); industrialist George Sylvester (Robert Bice); Arizona rancher Ed Mulfory (Erik Blythe) and blustering congressman Arthur Harroway (Wade Crosby). All are entranced by yet another patron, the confident, mysterious Mr. Ohman (Dan O'Herlihy). War breaks out in the form of a massive Russian invasion using Atomic bombs. Alaska and Washington State are overrun. Sylvester and Mulfory catch one of the last flights to the coast, but meet horrible fates at the hands of ruthless invaders. New York City is nuked, and skyscrapers collapse as enemy troops blast their way in. Vince tries to shield his new girlfriend Carla but to no avail. All wish they had been a trifle more committed to their country's defense ...

Cheap, clever, outrageous, *Invasion, USA* is the most militant Cold War 'scare' picture. Unlike Arch Oboler's pacifist weepie *Five*, this show depicts a Soviet Union so aggressive, Senator Joe McCarthy wouldn't recognize it. [1]

The tricky plot centers on a half-dozen stereotypes interpreted by actors best suited to chewing scenery. Oily lothario Gerald Mohr began by playing gigolos in pictures like *Gilda*. Mohr's cool TV newsman moves in on curvaceous Peggie Castle like a Tex Avery wolf, practically diving down her dress. Castle comes off as less an actress than a tough girl who won a wrestling match on a casting couch.

The other bar patrons react stoically to a screenplay that requires them to be shot down like dogs. The congressman is felled before a statue of George Washington. Luckless rancher Ed is drowned like a rat when the Commies strike Boulder Dam with an A-bomb. The film's touch of genius is Dan O'Herlihy, that little-used actor who can be seen as an IRA killer in Carol Reed's *Odd Man Out*, and as *Robinson Crusoe* in Luis Buñuel's screen classic. He's also 'The Old Man'

INVASION, USA

Synapse Reviewed: April 2, 2002
1952 / B&W / 1:37 flat / 74 min.
Cinematography John L. Russell. Music Albert Glasser. Written by Robert Smith and Franz Spencer. Produced by Joseph Justman, Robert Smith & Albert Zugsmith.
Directed by Alfred E. Green

This key picture of the 1950s played constantly on television before disappearing in the early 1970s. *Invasion, USA* is a bizarre call to arms against an all-out Communist onslaught. Characterizations and dialogue reach new heights of camp hilarity, beginning with a Criswell-like 'forecaster' who mesmerizes a group of bar patrons. Synapse Films' DVD is strongly recommended for jaw-dropping sociology and group viewing fun.

in the first two *RoboCop* movies. O'Herlihy's Ohman claims to know the future. He offers his barroom congregation a look at the George Bailey – like possibilities of Things to Come, should America not get down to the business of girding the loins of its defense machine.

The impression given is that America is sitting on its hands waiting for a Pearl Harbor-style sneak attack because defense spending is hogtied. In reality, our military in 1952 was growing by leaps and bounds. The U.S.A.'s armed forces were everywhere, intimidating our enemies with more sophisticated weaponry than any nation in history.

Invasion, USA's unprovoked nuclear war is visualized via a barrage of stock film footage, augmented by a few grainy shots of Soviet MIGS. After a while we don't know what we're looking at – 'Russian' planes are often American jets with USAF markings, and the enemy bombers are our own B29s and B36s. Our war surplus must have gotten wa-ay out of hand.

Nervous news bulletins tell us that, "The enemy is wearing our uniforms to create confusion," a gambit that allows the Soviet invaders to be represented by stock footage of U.S. troops. When broadcasting mass attacks 'live from the scene' using 'remote control units', the live television feed is somehow beautifully edited. *Invasion, USA's* battle scenes play like an extended version of the montage that opens *The Road Warrior*. The crude imagery works even though many shots are flopped, with writing on airplanes written backwards, etc.

Augmented by Albert Glasser's relentless score, the stock footage battles build a mounting feeling of hysteria – a panicky approximation of what an invasion might be like. News anchors list familiar cities and landmarks as overrun, with deaths reaching into the thousands, a la Howard Koch's famous *War of the Worlds* radio broadcast.

The script takes great pains not to verbally identify the invaders as Russian. A roomful of Russki generals wear quasi-Nazi uniforms and speak with accents that sound Russian, German, and Spanish – sometimes in the same sentence! The top general is addressed as, 'Excellency'. The most frequent Russian dialogue line is a spirited, "Bombs a-Vey!"

The invasion is credible if you can for a moment believe that the Russians had the capability to move millions of men by air. The Reds make a clean sweep of the West Coast, knocking out airfields along the way with Atomic weapons. Even when it pretends that the U.S. has no warning system for just such an attack, *Invasion, USA* makes a lot more sense than the later *Red Dawn*, a similar but inferior retro take on the same subject. Being sillier than this film is not easy. [2]

The brief, under-produced dramatic scenes raise hokum to a new level. Just as the Soviet troops bash down his door, the industrialist's meek window washer proudly reveals that he's a deep-cover Commie agent. The barflies at Tim's get soused as they make wisecracks at the doom reports on the tube. Lowly airline counterperson Noel Neill must tell a female customer that no flights are scheduled to Montana ... because it's been nuked. As the other airline customers soberly watch the lady stagger away, we almost expect to hear Neill chirp, "Next!"

The East coast invasion is wonderfully silly. An enemy soldier in GI garb is unmasked when he doesn't know that the Chicago Cubs are not, 'leetle bears'. His comrades blast their way into rear-projected Senate building interiors and machine-gun the congressmen ... rather similarly to *Mars Attacks!* Like Joel McCrea in *Foreign Correspondent*, Gerald Mohr stoically broadcasts as New York falls. He can't save Peggie Castle's Carla from the fat Russian slob that crashes into her apartment. The goon rips her dress across the shoulder in the censor-approved manner afforded all dream girls in science fiction movies. Poor Carla meets a fate identical to the 'Broadway Baby' of *Gold Diggers of 1935*, only this time there's no kitty cat left behind to mourn her.

Jack Rabin's special effects in *Invasion, USA* are outrageously ambitious. Nuclear strikes are depicted by superimposing a nighttime bomb blast over various targets, in quick cuts that exploit the iconic impact of the mushroom cloud. When NYC is nuked our lovers are buried alive under a cascade of bricks and masonry, but of course are unharmed. One solitary break-apart model skyscraper collapses in flames. It may be the only model constructed for the film, for in the disc extras we see Castle and Neill posing beside it for a publicity still – in bathing suits! The hyped-up context makes firecrackers and cigarette smoke superimposed over cityscapes more effective than they should be. The silly flood that overruns the family fleeing Boulder Dam is a fall-down hoot – with a mountain of out-of-scale water visible through the rear window, the rancher pleads with the cabbie to drive faster!

Synapse's 'Atomic Special Edition' of **Invasion, USA** looks very good, with almost no print damage. The extras begin with a trio of amateurish interviews with Dan O'Herlihy, William Schallert and Noel Neill. Two official defense department audio recordings are included, *The Complacent Americans* and *If the Bomb Falls*. The best extra is a 30-minute cut-down of the hour-long public information short subject *Red Nightmare*. Warners made it in 1962 for the Defense Department. Jack Kelly, Jack Webb and Andrew Duggan star, and Robert Conrad and Peter Breck show up in bits.

Jack Webb serves as an omniscient *Our Town*-like host. Family man Jack Kelly has an *It's a Wonderful Life* – like nightmare in an alternate reality in which his wife and teenagers have become collectivist zombies and prattle incessant

commie-speak. Attending Sunday school and making a personal phone call are now treasonous activities. The show trial on view, however, would seem to be an accurate portrayal of practices in modern dictatorships ... even though it equally resembles a McCarthy witch hunt. Jack Webb returns at the end, still in *Our Town* mode, to deliver a conservative ode to 'Freedom'. A depressing montage equates Liberty with consumer goods and ugly tract homes. A brief clip from *The Pajama Game* can be seen in the Americana sequence, if one looks fast.

1. *Daily Variety's* review of December 4, 1952 sees *Invasion, USA* as a perfect 'scare' movie conducive to boffo box office. *Variety* reviews are fascinating because they so rigorously divorce a movie's content from its commercial appeal.

2. To be fair, history-buff screenwriter John Milius wanted 1984's *Red Dawn* to be much more of a fantasy, and cites MGM interference for turning his show into a throwback killer-Commie movie.

INVADERS FROM MARS

Image An extended essay from 1999, "The Ultimate Invaders from Mars"
1953 / Color / 1:37 flat / 78 min.
Cinematography John F. Seitz. Music Raoul Kraushaar. Written by Richard Blake, story by John Tucker Battle. Produced by Edward L. Alperson.
Designed and Directed by William Cameron Menzies

1953's **Invaders from Mars** has been a personal fascination since childhood. It hasn't been analyzed in a way that really captures its genius; of all 50s sci-fi I think it is the most visually inspired and a work worthy of the term 'great art.' My argument to support this contention is based on the movie we all can see. This synopsis of *Invaders from Mars* gives little indication of its visual riches:

Young David MacLean (Jimmy Hunt) witnesses the landing of a flying saucer. Burrowing into a sand pit, the Martians trap David's kindly father George (Leif Erickson) and plant a radio control device in his neck. Now the invaders' zombie-agent, George MacLean lures others into the pit: David's mother Mary (Hillary Brooke), army General Mayberry. The Martians soon control the local police as well. Traumatized to find his family transformed into inhuman automatons, David confides in his friend, local astronomer Dr. Stuart Kelston (Arthur Franz). With the help of attractive public health nurse Dr. Pat Blake (Helena Carter) they determine that the Martian invaders plan to sabotage Coral Bluffs, a local atomic rocket base. The Army surrounds the sand pit. Captured by the Martians, David and Pat are ushered into the buried Martian saucer and confront a disembodied, tentacled head in a glass globe. This "Martian Intelligence" commands a crew of bug-eyed Mutant slaves and uses radio-telepathy to control its human agents. Colonel Fielding (Morris Ankrum) launches a rescue mission into the maze of Martian tunnels, freeing Pat before she can be implanted with a control device. David mans an alien infrared ray gun to burn an exit tunnel to the surface, and the soldiers and scientists escape. When the Army's explosives finally detonate, David wakes up. His entire adventure was nothing but a dream. But was it? Once again, David is awakened by the sound of an approaching spacecraft.

PART ONE: Background.

William Cameron Menzies. *Invaders from Mars* was made relatively early in the 50s sci-fi cycle, when the field was still dominated by "A" quality efforts. A script by John Tucker Battle eventually landed with producer Edward L. Alperson, who entrusted the entire project to the legendary film designer and director William Cameron Menzies. Menzies invented the concept of production design on silent epics like 1922's *The Thief of Baghdad*. His unique graphic sense often graced the films of Sam Wood (*Our Town*, *For Whom the Bell Tolls*, *King's Row*), and he made Hollywood history for David O. Selznick on *Gone With the Wind* by unifying the contributions of a half-dozen directors.

Menzies directed several earlier films, most notably *Things to Come*. Another fantastic Menzies effort was *The Whip Hand*, a thriller in which a journalist discovers a nest of postwar Nazis seeking to launch a fourth Reich in America. After the film was completely finished by producer Stanley Rubin, Howard Hughes decreed that it be reworked to turn the Nazis into Communists experimenting with biological warfare weapons. No other Hollywood film demonstrates as well the interchangeablilty of Nazis and "Commies" in those politically charged years.

The Production. *Invaders from Mars* was filmed in color, a luxury that gave it an edge in 1953 Hollywood. Original prints have an otherworldly color texture, with slimy greens and blues and vivid reds. *Invaders from Mars* was not shot in 3D, even though Menzies' depth-enhancing design conveys more depth than many real 3D pictures.

Most of the movie was filmed on inexpensive but carefully designed sets. One oft-repeated bit of trivia is that the bubbles lining the walls of the Martian tunnels were inflated condoms. Some sets were cleverly recycled. Assassination target Dr. Wilson's lab is the same set as the forbidding Police station, redressed. Special effects man Jack Cosgrove executed a number of effective matte paintings. David's house and the telescopic view of the atomic rocket are both mattes. Some of the saucer interiors are augmented with clever glass paintings, such as the dynamic angle down the glass tube above the Martian operating table.

The Infamous Zippered Aliens. Casual sci-fi bashers have plenty of ammunition to hurl at *Invaders from Mars*. Most often derided are the plush velour jumpsuits worn by the green Martian slaves. Writers Robert Skotak and Scot Holton report that a friend of the producer whipped up these suits on her Singer sewing machine practically overnight; this accounts for the legendary zippers running up their spines. The bug-eyed Martian face is a simple plastic eye-nose-mouth combo mask worn like sunglasses. In stills, the Martian slaves are reminiscent of the moth-eaten Cat Suits seen in *The Bad and the Beautiful*, the ones the wardrobe man tries to push on producer Kirk Douglas. Not the most convincing Aliens concocted for the screen.... point granted.

The Sand Pit Hill Set. Menzies appears to have put the bulk of his construction budget into one large, remarkable set, the hill leading to the Sand Pit behind David's house. A slightly curved path marked by a broad plank fence winds up the hill between some leafless black tree trunks. Atop the hill, the blackened fence dips out of sight into the largely unseen Sand Pit beyond.

On first glance the hill appears to be a flat-perspective, diorama-like design reminiscent of the footbridge in the 1919 *Cabinet of Caligari*. The hill resembles a painted backdrop, but when an actor walks up the path all sense of perspective goes haywire. The hill resembles a two-dimensional painting, but when three-dimensional people walk 'into' it, they defy visual logic and diminish in size: it's a "reverse forced-perspective" optical illusion. George MacLean seems to get smaller than he should when he reaches the top of the hill, and he takes a lot of steps to get there. The trees at the rear of the set give conflicting perspective clues, so it almost looks as if George MacLean is shrinking as he walks. The subtle effect is more easily appreciated on a large screen.

Stock Footage. *Invaders from Mars* is shamelessly padded with stock footage. Large sections of a WW2 training film represent the regiments

Colonel Fielding summons to surround the Sand Pit. It's clear that no money was available to film the National Guard, as *The War of the Worlds* and *The Day the Earth Stood Still* did to such good effect. Ditto all of the footage of tanks pulling into position amid the greenery around the Sand Pit: it's all stock footage. More padding is evident when Doctor Kelston realigns his telescope. Long, uninterrupted takes of the Observatory's rotating cupola bring the movie to a dead stop.

The Strange Repetition of shots. The biggest invitation for nitpickers in *Invaders from Mars* is the constant and obvious repetition of shots. When those aforementioned tanks open fire, a handful of angles are reused over and over. One specific image of a shell blast is repeated at least a dozen times.

Not just stock footage is repeated. In the Martians' underground lair, shots of shuffling Martian slaves and running soldiers look suspiciously recycled. There seem to have been at most three actual camera angles in the Martian tunnel set. The same six velour Martians shambling past, repeated three times, become eighteen alien slaves. These angles have also been flopped left-to-right, and the flopped versions repeated too! The same three-bubble pattern on the back wall of a tunnel can be seen repeated in over 50% of the shots, often edited back to back. Likewise, when David's parents flee the army in a two-angle no-budget car chase, both shots are flopped horizontally, and shown again.

During the underground fighting, two and three-shot sequences are repeated in their entirety. Inside the saucer Sgt. Rinaldi (Max Wagner) drags David from the operation room and down to the next level. When David breaks free and runs back upstairs, the same exact shots are reused to show the Sergeant carrying David down a second time. When a group of soldiers shoots a Martian slave ("Blast him!"), the fallen alien gets back up again, seemingly

unharmed. The soldiers doggedly try it again. The sequence of them shooting and the Martian slave toppling, is repeated exactly as shown just seconds before.

Crazy Suspense Editing. *Invaders from Mars* uses a 'deadline' tension device to depict the struggle to escape from the saucer before the army's demolition charges blow it up. A huge close-up of the bomb's time delay readout is inter-cut with views of the fleeing soldiers and the surface of the Sand Pit. Editors normally 'cheat' the timing of sequences of this kind, stretching the material in the service of suspense: clock the bomb countdown in *Goldfinger* sometime. Here in *Invaders* the bomb's second-hand defies all logic, repeatedly passing the same numbers on its dial. Also stretched beyond reason is the saucer's initial emergence from the Sand Pit. Surely nobody expected anyone over the age of six to accept this sequence at face value.

If a filmmaker shoots twenty minutes of film stock and makes a ten-minute movie out of it, the show is said to have a 2-to-1 shooting ratio. The joke to *Invaders* is that there are so many repeated shots, its shooting ratio is 1-to-2 !

A Bizarre Montage like No Other. This is the point where *Invaders from Mars* becomes an editorial tour-de-force. The parallel actions of ticking bomb, rising saucer and fleeing troops overlap to a point where time stops progressing altogether. David never reaches the bottom of the hill; the saucer never breaks free of the Sand Pit. David runs for his life in an unending close-up. Then, a prolonged optical montage begins. Striking images and violent action from earlier scenes are superimposed over David's running face and inter-cut with that same repeated shell blast.

After working itself into a martial frenzy, the music downshifts into a previously unheard ethereal theme not unlike the conclusion of Gustav Holst's *The Planets*. David's running, already reduced to a non-progressing state, now goes in *reverse*, as another series of superimposed images begins, now playing *backwards*. These superimpositions are non-violent but eerily disturbing. David leaps from the embrace of his mother. The zombie police chief (Bert Freed) puts his hat on. The odd visions then dissolve into a star-scape of planets receding, retreating away from us. Concurrent with a clap of thunder, a final explosion breaks the montage and restores David to his bedroom. The 'dream' part of *Invaders from Mars* is over. Savant hasn't yet read anything about *Invaders* that satisfactorily resolves the meaning behind Menzies' and editor Arthur Roberts' crazy quilt editing of this last reel.

A Victim of Version Manipulation. The American cut of *Invaders from Mars* is about 78 minutes long. A few months after it was completed, Arthur Franz, Helena Carter and young Jimmy Hunt were rehired for retakes to address the demands of foreign distributors. England nixed the dream structure of *Invaders* outright, for reasons that are unclear. It's the same structure used in *The Wizard of Oz*, after all, not to mention the British horror classic *Dead of Night*. An inexpressive angle was filmed of the three actors reaching the bottom of the hill and ducking behind an Army vehicle. The animated landing scene was reversed to make the saucer look as if it were taking off, with an added flash to show it being destroyed by the Army's bomb. A prop tree tips over, lamely. Pat glibly announces that, with the control source destroyed, David's parents are now safe. Then comes a dissolve to David sleeping. Like replacement parents, Drs. Kelston and Blake look on approvingly from David's bedroom doorway: 'He'll be safe now". End of show.

The muddled English ending skips the weird montage altogether, trimming several minutes of running time. To compensate, a *second* new scene was filmed with the same three actors. This new footage appears in the observatory when the trio discusses the likelihood of living beings on Mars. Jimmy Hunt's neck is suddenly two inches longer and his haircut has changed. Dr. Kelston takes his two visitors to a previously unseen corner to view an album of news clippings of flying saucer sightings. He opens a cabinet and produces models of three 'typical' saucer shapes. David seems already familiar with these exhibits. After several minutes of dull discussion, an impressed Pat accompanies the two UFO experts back to the desk, where they resume their seating positions so the film can pick up where it left off.

PART TWO: Cinematic Dreamscape.

Jimmy Hunt, the talented child actor of *Invaders from Mars*, appears at an even younger age in *Pitfall*, a moody 1948 film noir. Jimmy plays the five or six year-old son of disenchanted husband Dick Powell, who can't understand why his loving wife and good job don't satisfy him. A telling scene in *Pitfall* occurs when little Jimmy wakes from a nightmare. Something was threatening him *at his window*. Jimmy's mother (Jane Wyatt, later of *Father Knows Best*) is at a loss to guess what could disturb a boy in such a peaceful suburban environment. Dad picks up a stack of – what else – 'trashy' comics: "Now it's comic books. Where does he get this stuff?" Scapegoats are already being sought for the lack of direction in American life, an absence of values that evokes an un-nameable fear in both little Jimmy and his father. Something is uneasy about the times themselves, and no one seems able to identify the cause.

In *Invaders from Mars* David MacLean has a BIG nightmare, and once again his parents blame it on trashy comic books. Think of *Invaders* as a 50s, post-modern version of *The Wizard of Oz*. in Dorothy's circa-1900 world of dull rural sameness a dream is a chance to escape into a magical realm. Dorothy's strange journey reveals the truth behind the surface of her real world. Authority figures are without substance, and conflicts rage between powers of Good and Bad that ordinary people do not understand. If Dorothy is brave and virtuous she may find her way home, and perhaps discover truths about herself.

Dorothy's idealized Kansas has one quality David MacLean's does not: a sense of security. David's dream is a result of the pressures in his daily life, not an escape from them. It's not a magical place Over the Rainbow that one can enter like a Tex Avery cartoon character: "Technicolor Begins Here"; David's alternate reality is indistinguishable from his real world. As in Dorothy's Oz, familiar faces populate David's dream, but they don't affect dress-up disguises. They're instead sinister doppelgängers of their 'real' selves.

Director William Cameron Menzies doesn't explicitly identify David MacLean's adventure as a subjective nightmare. Adults are dismissive of tales that turn out to be dreams. A four-year-old needs to be reassured that Dorothy really didn't go to a place called Oz, but adults aren't going to be fooled. David MacLean's nightmare isn't revealed until the end, after 75 minutes of illogical characters and plotting. Illogical to an adult mindset, that is.

Invaders from Mars has a reputation for scaring the hell out of children because it's that rare film engineered around adolescent fears. The nightmare is not only shown from little David's point of view, it is restricted to his limited frame of reference. In *Pitfall*, Dick Powell's disenchantment is having an unnoticed psychological effect on his son, who perhaps worries that his father doesn't love him. If the pressures of 1953 are making adults paranoid, what effect are they having on the children?

We know that the 'real' David MacLean has loving parents and is a precocious astronomy buff. His father might be an engineer working on a secret project. David *probably* has a neighbor friend named Kathy Wilson (Janine Perreau) [1] whose father *might* work at the same project. That's about all we are told regarding David's 'reality'. Everything in David's nightmare is a distorted projection of his waking world and not to be trusted. There are no reassuring 'winks' to the audience, no loveable Scarecrow who resembles a farmhand back home. David wishes he had an astronomer for a friend; he seemingly also has a good idea of the woman he wants in his life as well – sexy Pat Blake (Helena Carter).

Fantasies present us with crazy-mirror visions of our own real world, visions that comment on our everyday realities. [2] David MacLean feels insecure, therefore his dream parents 'aren't really his parents'. Authority figures are remote and inclined to disbelieve him. "Those trashy comic books" have populated David's imagination with flying saucers and aliens. Beyond those observations, most reviewers can't fathom the rest of the film, let alone the continuity anomalies detailed earlier in this article.

The brilliance of *Invaders from Mars* is that all the 'weirdness' does make sense. It isn't convincing to an adult sensibility because a 10-year-old, David himself, is 'writing the script' and 'painting the scenery'. *Invaders from Mars* is a surreal parade of non-sequitur dialogue, plot illogic and crazy character behavior. To an impressionable ten-year old of 1953, comic book flying saucers and aliens have a credibility equal to headlines about atom bombs, brainwashing and foreign conspiracies. Taken literally, *Invaders from Mars* is incoherent. Taken like, say, Lewis Carrol's *Alice through the Looking Glass*, it's a mother lode of engrossing ideas.

Breaking Down the Pulp.

Titles: The martial marching music behind the titles blends with an eerie suspense theme as planets and moons drift by ... in 1953, Outer space is Big Science, and Big Science is Military Science. The music's real theme is a Brave New Future of aggression, expanding into outer space.

Norman Rockwell Opening: In a few brief scenes Menzies and writer Richard Blake sketch a happy family just as succinctly as would the famous Saturday Evening Post illustrator. David and his father's 3 A.M. telescope fun is as wholesome as a fishing trip. The only odd notes are the weird green-bluish colors and Menzies' precise use of gigantic close-ups. Parents Mary and George MacLean are nurturing and sweethearted even when awakened in the middle of the night. They're too perfect to be true.

Saucer Landing: Our first darkened view of The Hill looks like a flat storybook illustration. When the Saucer lands at 4:41 A.M., David doesn't shrink in terror, he wonders out loud: "Gee whiz!" He's the first of the *Cinefantastique* sense-of-wonder boys, Spielberg's inspiration for *Close Encounters of the Third Kind.*

Dream-Logic Visuals: At sunrise we see Menzies' minimalist art direction at its most uncanny. Rooms are simple one or two-wall sets. The view out David's back door shows only a naked tree and an almost empty horizon. Shots alternate between wide, flattish domestic masters and intense choker close-ups, usually accompanied by blasts of music. There is no action montage per se; only tableaux and obsessive details. The policeman's huge shoulder looms above little David, who strains to see something on the back of his neck.

Discontinuity of Angles: In the earlier part of the story The Hill is always seen from a single wide-angle view. It's an oneiric repeated dream image, the kind that never changes. When George or Mary step into The Hill set, they enter a different dimension. The action on The Hill remains limited to a handful of obsessive angles: A close-up of a character in danger, a funnel of sinking sand forming in the Pit, and back to the ultra-wide unchanging Hill, as if it were alive and responsible.

Bizarre Music: Credited composer Raoul Kraushaar, or whoever really created the jolting, schizophrenic score for *Invaders*, invests The Hill and its grasping Sand Pit with an eerie, stomach-twisting vocal effect that seems an inversion of a stock 'heavenly chorus.' This creepy collection of slippery tones will grab the attention of any child. It's more disturbing than a Theremin, if only because of that instrument's overuse. The chorus seems to be part of the musical score until Sgt. Rinaldi disappears into the Sand Pit. David blurts out, "That noise!" as if hearing it for the first time. Do the Martians sing as they operate their sand trap, or is David hearing the soundtrack of his own dream? Later, both David and Pat hear the 'music' just before they are captured. And the entire cast reacts similarly to a choral burst as the saucer prepares to lift off. David's dream fully enlists the soundtrack in its surrealism.

Overplayed Villainy: Because David is orchestrating the Dream Logic, his parents behave like the baddies in his comic books: if this were a realistic photoplay, father's sullen demeanor and explosive anger would have Mary MacLean running to the neighbors for help. George MacLean's menacing invitation to show his wife something in the Sand Pit plays like a come-on line for Bluto in a *Popeye* cartoon. And after Mary too is possessed, they huddle and exchange sinister stage-whisper conspiratorial asides. Even Forrest Gump would be dialing the F.B.I..

When quisling Mary hugs her son at the Police Station she raises an eyebrow and addresses the camera directly, as if saying, "Yes, I'm possessed". Pokerfaced Police Chief Barrows (Bert Freed) confronts the camera with a look that says, "Yeah, I'm one of 'em too. Got a problem with that?" Menzies makes the weirdness all the more apparent by shooting the Chief's signature close-up in *reverse*. [3] The faces of these zombified humans mirror the emotionless-but-intense expression of the as-yet unseen Martian Intelligence controlling them.

A Kafka Collection of Characters: David MacLean is fully cognizant of his own powerlessness and lack of credibility. Protected, sheltered and ignorant of anything beyond their Davy Crockett coonskin caps, many 1950s kids weren't the streetwise, economy-driving consumers we know today. Nobody takes David seriously, not Mrs. Wilson nor the gas-station attendant Jim, who instantly betrays his confidence. Even the benign Desk Sergeant Finley (Walter Sande) isn't going to understand David's predicament. David is in a psychological Hell where his pleas fall on deaf ears, a dark corner darker than that of the most luckless noir protagonist: Your parents have become unfeeling monsters, part of a vast conspiracy to conquer the Earth. Only you know about it, but nobody will even listen to you. You're just a kid.

A Sex Life for David MacLean: Richard Staehling, in a hilarious article about Teen films of the 50s, [4] wrote that teenagers didn't exist as a cultural concept before James Dean. *Invaders from Mars* shows what a 1953 ten year-old really is thinking. David probably isn't getting any peeks at the first issue of *Playboy* but he knows what makes Virginia Mayo different from Aunt Virginia. David's Mom comes from the glamour-girl mold herself. Incidentally, Hillary Brooke already carried a mild taint of villainy, as she played the foil to Gale Storm in television's *My Little Margie*.

David's playmate Kathy Wilson is seen only in her 'zombie' state. The creepy look of triumph in her giant close-ups has a hint of the boyhood sexual distrust of girls that society still doesn't know how to acknowledge. Little girls (when I grew up in the 50s) were smarter and better behaved. They tended to be trusted more than little boys. Some had actually been told facts about sex, when most of us boys didn't have a clue. When hanky-panky got started, it quite often was girl-initiated. 50s culture tightly pigeonholed proper little girl behavior, making Kathy's 'knowing' smile seem sexually precocious, dangerous. Next stop, Patty McCormick in *The Bad Seed*.

But the big burner in David's love life is Dr. Pat Blake, the nurse who wears two-tone high heels and (we imagine) an intoxicating perfume. A crimson handkerchief sticks fashionably, daringly out of her designer nurse's uniform. She's as tender as David's mother but accepts him as an adult in all matters. Pat Blake doesn't leave David's side from the moment she finds him. Forget stuffy Astronomer Kelston: it's David and Pat all the way. When manhandled by the Martian slaves, Pat's tailored uniform is torn at the shoulder *just so*, the way every heroine in action movies from Joanne Dru (*Red River*) to Virginia Mayo to Maureen O'Hara seem to have their dresses torn at the shoulder. *Invaders from Mars* reveals this cliché as a little boy sex-thing. Naked woman aren't yet a fixture of David's psyche, but he's getting there. The arresting close-up of Pat resting peacefully on the Martians' glass operating table, one shoulder bared with a diamond-like needle pulsing slowly toward the back of her neck, is a penetration image charged with concepts of sex and rape, innocence and violation. Perhaps the 'real' David MacLean has a crush on his school nurse, who is sweet to him. A lot of adolescent confusion, angst and guilt comes when a boy realizes that the older women to whom he's attracted are going to be 'gotten' by males other than himself. The threat of the Martians taking away David's 'girl' overrides even his anxiety about his parents' fate.

That Wacky Dr. Kelston: Anyone doubting that the 'text' of *Invaders* comes directly from the mind of 10-year-old David MacLean should view this scene first. David's imagined best friend Dr. Stuart Kelston (Arthur Franz) smokes a pipe and works in an observatory with backlit murals on the walls. Kelston pulls the darndest, most ridiculous notions out of thin air, just to lay a foundation of explanations for the Martians that will soon be making their first appearance. He advances a series of illogical, baseless non-sequiturs: the Martians are visiting the Earth in Motherships, they live underground on Mars and have bred a race of synthetic human slaves called Mutants! David chimes in with cheery support. Pat's polite objection is met with the "I'm a scientist" retort made hilarious years later in *Ghostbusters*. A scientist's work, apparently, is to invent ridiculous theories and believe them until they're disproved. Pat has the gall to ask a couple of mild questions, both of which are dismissed with meaningless allusions to public skepticism of the airplane.

We've already heard the bizarre dialog where George tells Mary all about the 'secret' work at the Coral Bluffs plant. When she asks what it is, her husband chuckles and replies, "Honey, you know I can't talk about that". If George MacLean has a loose concept of national security, Kelston is a madman. He spills the beans to David and Pat about the secret rocket project, which, naturally, is military in nature. The scientific / military collusion seems complete when Dr. Kelston talks to his Coral Bluffs Army contact, Colonel Fielding. There's no hint of ideological conflict between scientist and soldier here, not even the token rebellion given Dr. Carrington in *The Thing*. David's adolescent view is clearly right wing ... Oppenheimers need not apply.

"A real General wouldn't say that": The soldiers show up led by the Gung-Ho Colonel Fielding, who behaves as if his life has been spent waiting on full alert for a cue to start fighting Martians. His phone calls set in motion the stock footage padding detailed earlier. More evidence of the dream-logic of events: Fielding and company climb up on David's roof to observe the Sand Pit. That they look so ridiculous perched up there among the gables can only be because the visual is David's dream notion of what being on the roof would be like – because he's never been allowed up there.

U.S. Troops, the Ultimate Heroes: When films of the early 50s are written up, there's little mention of the fact that the majority of the young adult men on view were not long before part of a civilian army with an entirely different attitude to combat than today's glamorized gladiators. Vet James Whitmore in *Them!* is the prime example of the sane & humane ideal of the American warrior circa 1954: decency personified, there to protect and serve.

This idea emerges in unexpected genres. The horde of police that raids the oil refinery at the end of the gangster film *White Heat* evokes a vision of criminals at war with an America that <u>is</u> an army. David MacLean seems to hold this same attitude. The soldiers in his dream are perfectly disciplined. They follow ridiculous orders and ignore the presence of dishy dame Pat Blake. Army engineer Captain Roth (Milburn Stone) is as scientifically clairvoyant as civilian Dr. Kelston. He somehow knows all about infrared ray guns that can melt tunnels in the earth, and instantly diagnoses the control device retrieved from the late Kathy Wilson's skull. A couple of minutes later, he's got it re-wired as a divining rod to locate the Martian tunnels. Roth has perhaps *Invaders'* most absurd dialogue line: "Don't worry son. They aren't going to use a complicated device like this just to kill people." He gives David a reassuring pat on the head. Most 50's sci-fi films idolize the Army the same way David idolizes brave Sgt. Rinaldi, who charges single-handedly up The Hill like John Wayne in *The Sands of Iwo Jima*.

Dream tension. The furious action that concludes *Invaders from Mars* becomes even more dreamlike with the repetitions of shots and scenes. Dialogue lines are also repeated, especially young David's "Colonel Fielding! Colonel Fielding!" that becomes an unending echo. These repetition patterns make the ending more dreamlike in two ways. First, a high level of anxiety is maintained while the actual story progression slows to a crawl. A classic nightmare situation is 'running in place but not getting anywhere', exactly the sensation imparted to *Invaders*. Second, the repetition forces us to fixate on images that keep returning with the obsessive quality of dream logic. In our dreams, shocking moments seem to hang forever in the consciousness, or illogically "come back again, but for the first time", over and over.

The dream logic of *Invaders* reverses cause & effect, observation & explanation. The 'surprises' found in the underground Martian nest are not surprises at all, having been fully described earlier by Dr. Kelston and Captain Roth. "Mutants!" shouts David at his first sight of the huge green Martian slaves. [5] Zombie Sgt. Rinaldi's verbal intro for the "Martian Intelligence" is completely redundant. David pummels the fishbowl as if having always known that the sphinx inside is fully in charge. The most illogical event in the tunnels is David's ability to recognize and operate the clarinet-like infrared tunneling ray gun. Neither David nor anybody else has seen it function, yet David takes charge and leaps into action, an instant ray gun expert. David MacLean's dream may be a mirror for his anxieties, but there's plenty of room within to cast himself as the know-it-all hero.

David MacLean's dream-confusion between wish fulfillment and dread becomes complete as the climax draws near. The ending montage has several dynamic up-tempo changes, as when the tanks fire to begin the assault on the underground tunnels. But, at the height of the tension, when David is running in place during the escape, time-progression comes to a standstill. The rising arc of tension breaks, with a music change (a harp arpeggio) and the addition of the superimposed bits of visuals mentioned before. As the music score becomes more ethereal, the dream seems to fold in upon itself, laying itself to rest even as David continues running, still unreleased from his nightmare. The oddly reversed scenes that conclude the montage are like fading mirage memories, those striking mental images that disappear when one tries to remember them.

If this were a normal dream, in the morning David would have a burst of memory, a sudden consciousness of an entire scenario populated with details and events. But it would be fleeting, because only some dreams fully resolve in the light of day. Most evaporate in the act of recall, leaving behind only random images of uncertain significance. The strongest of these surface every once in a while into normal consciousness, as disconnected mysteries.

William Cameron Menzies' direction and unforgettable images are what make *Invaders* perhaps the most accurate nightmare film of its day. The topography of its dreamscape is surely more familiar than the 'art film' dreams of Fellini and Bergman. That the nightmare of *Invaders from Mars* sums up the shared anxieties underlying the sheltered, secure 50s childhoods of David MacLean, myself, and millions of American boys like us possibly limits its relevance to its era – which is not exactly the same as, "dated". Does the dream world of *Invaders from Mars* 'speak' to modern audiences? Or is it an artifact solely for the appreciation of sci-fi fans? Savant would like to know.

1. Savant met Janine Perreau in 1997; her actress sister Gigi was directing a play at my daughter's school. A popular child performer, Janine remembers Mr. Menzies being nice, and having to pick flowers and drop through a trap door on the hill where a stagehand caught her! She's proud of her 'zombie' close-ups, and was happy to be told that yes, she is probably

the first "possessed" child on the American screen, years before *The Innocents, Village of the Damned*, and *The Exorcist*.

2. Savant remembers the 'Ahhs' of approval from the audience during a screening of *The NeverEnding Story* when the terrifying 'Nothing' is explained: what seems a shallow fairy tale suddenly becomes multi-dimensional, and meaningful.

3. Shooting this CU in reverse was probably a practical aid to allow the actor to start on his mark, perfectly framed and in focus, before stepping back away from the camera. But it still comes off as bizarrely pre-Lynchian.

4. Staehling, Richard, *From Rock Around the Clock to The Trip: The Truth about Teen Movies* Kings of the Bs, A. Dutton 1975 NYC, Edited by Todd McCarthy and Charles Flynn.

5. The mutants always remind Savant of the Winkie Guards from *The Wizard of Oz* ... something about the noses, and their slavish stupidity.

IT CAME FROM OUTER SPACE

Universal Reviewed May 16, 2002
1953 / B&W / 1:37 flat / 81 min.
Cinematography Clifford Stine. Art Direction Robert Boyle. Makeup & Special effects Jack Kevan, Bud Westmore, David S. Horsley. Written by Harry Essex from a story by Ray Bradbury. Produced by William Alland. Directed by Jack Arnold

Universal's first '50s science fiction offering is a tale of alien visitation from an original script by Ray Bradbury, whose florid and poetic dialogue still survives in some sequences. Bradbury's starry-eyed hero offers plenty of optimistic speculation about the first meeting of two interstellar civilizations. Originally shown in 3D, *It Came From Outer Space* has dated somewhat but still impresses with its message of inter-species tolerance. It's also the first sci-fi film by '50s cult director Jack Arnold.

Author and amateur astronomer John Putnam (Richard Carlson) is showing the stars to his fiancée Ellen Fields (Barbara Rush of *When Worlds Collide*) when they witness the landing of a meteor-like vessel from Outer Space. Only John sees the ship before a landslide buries it at the bottom of a deep crater. He has no luck convincing anyone that aliens have arrived on Earth, even after a spate of strange kidnappings. Sheriff Matt Warren (Charles Drake) is persuaded that something's wrong out at the crater only when Ellen disappears as well – replaced, it seems, by some kind of eerie copy.

The smoothly directed *It Came From Outer Space* overcomes its standard studio production values with some adept visual design and the sincerity of its actors, particularly Richard Carlson. The B&W photography can't hide the fake studio sets and the overall style reminds us more of early television than a big screen movie. But Jack Arnold manages some impressive sights: the initial view of the globular, honeycombed ship under the crumbling rocks; the loneliness of the open desert, which already resembles the surface of an alien planet; the feeling of a space-age fairy tale as John Putnam follows a trail of glittering stardust across his living room floor.

The aliens in *It Came From Outer Space* are shape shifting star travelers detoured to Earth for repairs. They are normally huge, hulking eye-creatures but can impersonate humans to move freely among us. The duplicates look correct but lack normal human mannerisms and speak with hollow, haunted voices. This concept quickly became filmed sci-fi's most overworked cliché, making *It Came From Outer Space* no longer seem as fresh as it should.

Underrated stylist Jack Arnold manages some strange and affecting Cocteau-like moments.

Putnam pleads with two silent telephone linemen he finds hiding in a storeroom: "Who are you? Why have you come here?" In one magical image, an alien posing as Ellen stands on a rough desert hill, wearing an incongruous evening gown and flowing scarf.

Early '50s sci-fi frequently describes space civilizations as having high moral standards, only to show them reflecting more of our own species' blind aggression. When Putnam finally meets an alien Xenomorph face-to-face, it happens to be the one that has copied his appearance: he tries to understand the aliens' predicament as he talks to his own doppelgänger. Although the aliens may be correct in assuming that Arizonans would shoot first and get sociable later, they offer no explanation for aiming a death ray at the obviously friendly Putnam. They claim that Earthlings are hostile yet persist in kidnapping innocent people and threatening our planet with destruction. As the space ship blasts into the night sky Putnam is still spouting happy-talk about the wonderful visit from space. In actuality, the entire episode is a miserable failure of interstellar diplomacy.

An over-familiarity with the film's themes has taken its toll. Luckily, its poetic qualities haven't diminished.

Savant saw a full Polaroid 3D presentation of *It Came From Outer Space* back in 1972. The illusion was stunning, with the rockslide sequence indeed making us bob our heads reflexively. In 3D many scenes have the look of a paper diorama. But the mist and smoke look great, as do some of the elaborate special effects. Only the fake soundstage deserts are less convincing in 3-D. Also, the shots of the comet-like space ship blazing over the desert use a cartoon matte around the trailing sparks that never blends well with the sky.

Other 3D details: original stereoscopic prints have only one intermission to change reels, not two as described in the disc's commentary and docu. The 3D version uses different title cards and a special intermission card, with a twinkling star background. The trailer and the cast run at the end of the movie pay rather ungallant attention to buxom Kathleen Hughes, encouraging the expectation that the 3D effect would, heh heh, make all kinds of interesting things project from the screen.

Universal's DVD of *It Came From Outer Space* is a rush job. The cover art is indifferent and the menus are unusually difficult to read. The extras compensate somewhat. A thorough commentary track by author and genre interviewer Tom Weaver claims that although writer Harry Essex wrote the film's final draft, the story concepts and situations are all Ray Bradbury's. Weaver refers several times to "this widescreen presentation" of the movie, but the transfer on view is flat full-frame. The two-channel stereo track is an original mix from 1953, when 3D depth extended to the audio as well.

The David J. Skal docu, *The Universe According to Universal* lacks behind-the-scenes photos and direct witnesses: I guess Barbara Rush wasn't game to talk about her beginnings in science fiction. Universal marketing would seem to be the culprit, as the piece references video titles with little relevance to the outer space theme.

THE BEAST FROM 20,000 FATHOMS

Warners Reviewed: October 20, 2003
1953 / B&W / 1:37 flat / 80 min.
Cinematography Jack Russell. Production Designer Eugène Lourié. Special Animation Effects Ray Harryhausen. Written by Fred Freiberger, Eugène Lourié, Louis Morheim, Robert Smith from the Saturday Evening Post short story *The Fog Horn* by Ray Bradbury. Produced by Bernard W. Burton, Hal E. Chester, Jack Dietz
Directed by Eugène Lourié

This endearingly juvenile but visually impressive thriller is the first 50s science fiction picture to feature a giant, city-attacking monster. An independent production brought in-house at Warner Bros., it launched Ray Harryhausen as a major solo special effects talent. Unable to afford the complex miniatures and glass paintings used on the Willis O'Brien film *Mighty Joe Young*, Ray invented his own method of combining animated models with realistic settings, a system he used throughout his career. The result is the Rhedosaurus, a charismatic dinosaur that invites us along for a madcap Manhattan weekend.

> Tom Nesbitt (Paul Christian *aka* Paul Hubschmid) is collecting data from an arctic atom blast when he's almost killed by what he insists is a prehistoric monster. Recovering in New York, Tom befriends paleontologist Professor Thurgood Elson (Cecil Kellaway) and his research assistant Lee Hunter (Paula Raymond). They begin to believe Tom's tale when a chain of strange events and sightings appears to be moving from Baffin Bay toward New York City. Deducing that Nesbitt's monster is returning to its ancestral spawning grounds off Long Island, Elson undertakes to trawl the sound in a diving bell in hopes of catching a glimpse of a 'paleolithic survival'.

In the disc's generous interview extras, Ray Harryhausen explains the felicitous coincidences that led to his fashioning the animation effects for a story written by his childhood pal Ray Bradbury. Perhaps reacting to the socko 1952 reissue of *King Kong*, the writers of this programmer updated their prehistoric monster with an unlikely atomic motivation. The script dawdles until the beastie's third act appearance, introducing a score of what would become giant monster clichés. There's a hero with a story nobody will believe, the kindly scientist with the shapely assistant for the hero to fall in love with, terrified witnesses, initial monster sightings in isolated locales and finally, an all-out attack on a major city. That template for monster mayhem was repeated almost without variation in scores of 50s productions – Toho's *Gojira* is an obvious inspirational offspring. When Harryhausen began his Dynamation career two years later with Charles Schneer, their first picture *It Came from Beneath the Sea* was a typical programmer in the subgenre initiated by his own *The Beast*. Columbia's 1998 *Godzilla* is really an elaborate remake of this film, right down to the details: The monster sinks a

fishing boat and the Army shoots at it from the Manhattan rooftops.

Everybody loves Ray Harryhausen's Rhedosaurus, a massive monster that elicited raves from *Variety*: "... makes King Kong look like a chimpanzee ... the sight of it stalking the canyons of New York is awesome..." Using character animation skills he perfected for *Mighty Joe Young*, Ray gives his dinosaur an appealing reptilian personality. It looks like a scaly, pissed-off puppy, disoriented by the changes in its New York hometown that happened in the 30 million years it's been asleep. David Buttolph's magisterial score and hundreds of terrified New Yawkers greet the Rhedosaurus when he alights just south of the Brooklyn Bridge; the vaguely fantastic setting of a Coney Island roller coaster is chosen for a climactic showdown.

Harryhausen's effects are superb. His composites of miniatures and miniature rear-projection are nearly perfect and his lighting of the Beast is carefully matched. An especially effective sight is the upward view of the monster's head as it strides up Wall Street, with the skyscrapers towering over him. In the nighttime scenes, the monster squints in the glare of the searchlights; Harryhausen's mannequin appears giant and imposing even in down-angles that should by rights diminish its menace. Almost every scene has memorable bits of business – the monster gently paws a wrecked car before charging into an intersection like a prehistoric Ratzo Rizzo: "I'm walkin' here!"

The dinosaur has a frightening encounter with a New York beat patrolman. The cop calmly unloads his pistol at the beast and while reloading is snapped up like an after-dinner mint. This first 50s giant monster movie defines a new, anonymous kind of terror: death is no longer Gothic or romantic as in a 30s horror film, but an undignified and meaningless obliteration. In the new scale of things, individual lives mean nothing.

The aftermath of the monster's first appearance is marked by a 'voice of doom' broadcast montage that says a couple of hundred people lost their lives in the 'worst disaster in New York history'. Recent history is a terrible realization of the chaos of 50s monster films that created thrills by reveling in fantasized calamities. This kind of existential, almost surreal terror puts *The Beast From 20,000 Fathoms* soundly in the sci-fi territory of brave new worlds.

Mention needs to be made of Eugène Lourié, the art director of classic French movies who later became a director and special effects expert (*Crack in the World*). The Beast must have put Lourié in a rut, because he ended up remaking it twice, more or less. *The Giant Behemoth* is a cheap derivative with less imaginative effects by Willis O'Brien, but Lourié's 1961 *Gorgo* is a lavish Technicolor production. Lourié's designs in *The Beast* are simple but effective, with a memorable museum interior and a claustrophobic diving bell. His impressive military planning room would be repeated on a bigger scale for *Gorgo*. Ray Harryhausen's personal artistry may have been augmented by the Frenchman's concepts for key effects scenes, such as the superb attack on the Nova Scotia lighthouse, rendered in dramatic silhouette.

The human actors are secondary to the monster. As 'Paul Christian', Paul Hubschmid of Fritz Lang's *The Tiger of Eschnapur* is a stalwart hero. Paula Raymond is merely okay but Cecil Kellaway wins our hearts with his adorable scientist routine. It's sad to see Kenneth Tobey playing a second-string Army officer after doing so well in *The Thing from Another World*; when actors discovered that sci-fi movies were not a path to better roles, the field was cleared for the likes of Richard Carlson, Peter Graves and Richard Denning. From the Warners stock company comes Donald Woods, and every kid immediately recognizes Lee Van Cleef as the army sharpshooter who picks his teeth with a grenade rifle.

The Beast From 20,000 Fathoms was a huge success. Even though Jack Warner hated monster movies, it probably initiated the production of the next year's *Them!* As was typical back then, 'movie magic' didn't make stars of its artisans or even guarantee them work; Harryhausen's phone didn't ring any more regularly than did his mentor Willis O'Brien's. Fortunately, Harryhausen soon linked up with a young producer willing to commit to his effects-based fantasy ideas, and won himself an active and rewarding career.

Warners' DVD of *The Beast From 20,000 Fathoms* is in even better shape than the 1993 laser disc. The extras include the original trailer, with its great copy: "The Beast! The Beast! THE BEAST!"

This disc has two fine interview featurettes: One on the making of the picture and another taped at a reception for old friends Harryhausen and Ray Bradbury. Bradbury is in a wheelchair and on the frail side but his enthusiasm for dinosaurs and his old pal is undiminished.

THE WAR OF THE WORLDS

Paramount Reviewed: October 20, 2005
1953 / Color / 1:37 flat / 85 min.
Cinematography George Barnes. Art
Direction Al Nozaki, Hal Pereira. Music
Leith Stevens. Special Visual Effects
Gordon Jennings. Written by Barre Lyndon
from the novel by H.G. Wells. Produced
by George Pal.
Directed by Byron Haskin

The War of the Worlds is an ambitious, intelligent and exciting adventure that combines H.G. Wells' original tale with 1950s invasion panic: what would happen if our enemies possessed unstoppable weapons of super-destruction? George Pal's movie was advertised as a class offering – the posters showed only the title and an abstract claw clutching at the Earth from the depths of outer space.

Paramount's Special Collector's Edition replaces a 1999 release of indifferent quality. The 2005 Steven Spielberg remake clearly inspired this reissue; I only wish the industry would also do lavish remakes of great movies that didn't turn out to be classics, like John Wyndham's *The Day of the Triffids*.

Vacationing Pacific Tech scientist Dr. Clayton Forrester (Gene Barry) investigates when a meteor lands intact in a California forest. He meets attractive librarian Sylvia Van Buren (Ann Robinson) at the impact site and waits for the oddly shaped meteor to cool off to permit further examination. But the meteor is really one of many alien invasion landing craft, from which emerge gigantic hovering fighting machines armed with heat rays and disintegrator beams, and protected from attack by invisible force fields. They begin an assault on Earth, destroying everything man-made. Clayton and Sylvia return to Pacific Tech to formulate a scientific defense, but the alien onslaught is too intense. The world quickly loses ground to the invaders.

Savant saw *The War of the Worlds* in 1964 as a surprise second feature on a kiddie double-bill, with an audience clearly shaken by the sheer power of George Pal's exciting blitzkrieg from outer space. We weren't accustomed to such effective filmmaking in our monster movies: I remember audible expressions of nervousness when the unseen aliens prepare to launch their attack, and screams with the first blast of their heat ray. When the alien creeps into the crushed farmhouse, kids were ready to cry. The sound track is a barrage of weird noises and threatening explosions. It was a real thrill ride with emotional highs and lows and special effects that at the time simply looked real: buildings burn and telephone lines melt as the war machines glided down city streets. The Japanese *The Mysterians* is an imaginative fantasy, but it's scary only once or twice. *The War of the Worlds* kept me at the edge of my seat for its entire running time, mouth agape.

The motivating factor behind the show is war fear, something that producer George Pal knew well, having been chased from Europe by the Germans in the 1930s. Capitals of great and beautiful cities fell one after another in a matter of weeks, a trauma that Americans haven't experienced since our Civil War. H.G. Wells' 1898 book could be interpreted as a fearful look forward at a century that promised Brave New Wars employing ever more lethal applications of technology. Pal's movie version updates the story to the Cold War years and removes Wells' mostly first-person POV, which had centered on an everyman hero desperate to reunite with his wife. But the basic tale is retained. The unstoppable alien invasion is "a rout of civilization, a massacre of mankind."

The alien menace is brilliantly updated. Albert Nozaki's sinister fighting machines have an extra-terrestrial appeal combining the animal forms of a manta ray and a cobra snake. They seem to fly, even though it is established that their means of support is an invisible electronic tripod correlating to Wells' original mechanical legs. Charles Gemora's makeshift Martian is a hideous crab-like biped with a three-hued color television camera for an eye. Wells' investigatory tentacle becomes a spy camera resembling the gladiator helmet of the God of War.

Swift pacing and jarring set pieces keep us on edge by alternating relatively serene passages with intensely violent or suspenseful highlights. A nervous newsreel (shades of the other Welles' *Citizen Kane*) is followed by a real estate tour of potential planets for invasion, with Wells' poetic preamble spoken by Sir Cedric Hardwicke. Pal and Haskin bridge transitions with loud noises and abrupt cuts, like the unscrewed lid sliding from atop the alien landing craft. The prelude to battle builds unbearable tension as Lewis Martin's gentle preacher greets the alien vanguard with a pacifist plea ... a thematic repeat of Dr. Carrington's altruistic gesture in *The Thing from Another World*. The most cinematic moment is when the aliens open fire. A yellow heat ray blast cuts to a red-tinted close-up of Ann Robinson screaming. Colonel Heffner (Vernon Rich) shouts "Let 'em have it!" and the barrage begins. It's a stunning sequence.

The War of the Worlds was nominated for best editing and sound effects. Ordinary battle scenarios stress the glory of American firepower but here we watch while guns and cannons blast away to no effect whatsoever. The aliens sit behind their protective blisters for a few moments, as if relieved to be met with such puny resistance. When they counterattack, two kinds of rays (and their associated weird sound effects) blast away in a cyclone of white-hot sparks and green 'meson flux.' It's like using a blowtorch on an ant's nest.

The authorities don't take long to reach the conclusion that's already on the mind of every eight year-old kid in the audience ... let's nuke these bastards, and fast. A delegation of military brass and media descend on the La Puente hills fully expecting to liquidate their foe. [1] They're more than a little distressed when the A-bomb just puts a nice shine on the alien fighting craft. That's where the film's camp dialogue cuts in, with hard-bitten Major General Les Tremayne's tantrum: "Guns, tanks, bombs – they're like toys against them!" So much for the arms race.

From this point forward the fate of the world is in God's hands. George Pal was a sincerely devout fellow and this picture's miraculous conclusion might as well be divine intervention by way of natural selection. The aliens are susceptible to ordinary bacteria and fall fast when they approach our (presumably filthy) population centers. Humanity is saved by God's microscopic creations.

The emotional finish is melodramatic in the extreme. But it is both tasteful and appropriate to the dire circumstances – Sylvia and Clayton are reunited among refugees in a church, cowering helpless as war machines close in for the kill. *The War of the Worlds* endures with only a few unintentional laughs, and its uplifting finale is still impressive.

Paramount has given its Special Edition of *The War of the Worlds* everything that fans might have hoped for. Besides an original mono track, the much more lively stereophonic track heard on the 1995 laserdisc makes its reappearance and is a big plus. It may be a Chace reprocessing job – in his commentary Joe Dante tells us that the real stereo audio was lost long ago.

The picture looks far sharper than the earlier disc in both film mastering and digital formatting. This means that the forest of fine wires supporting the fighting machines is now more visible than ever, so we can't have everything. There was no CG wire removal in 1953 and erasing them now would be blatant revisionism – so I'm surprised that it hasn't been done yet.

Paramount has added a number of good extras. The original trailer is here along with the entire 1939 Orson Welles radio show. A making-of reappraisal featurette interviews the film's assistant director with some videotaped remarks by designer Al Nozaki and input from stars Gene Barry and Ann Robinson. Both actors contribute to an audio commentary and discuss their careers at length. Barry seems to finally realize that this picture is the one he'll be remembered for.

Another Sparkhill short subject provides a good overview of H.G. Wells as a science fiction writer, skipping his other careers as an erratic pundit, free-sex advocate and espouser of socialist and futurist causes. A second commentary track is an informative and often funny teaming of a great trio: superfan and artifact custodian Bob Burns, science fiction film authority Bill Warren and congenial director Joe Dante. Dante has often served as a classy host at Cinematheque screenings and on DVD extras. Bill Warren regales us with little-known facts about the original 1924 Paramount script prepared for Cecil B. DeMille and offers numerous interesting observations. Leave out the Hardwicke narration and a wild guess by actor Paul Birch, for instance, and there is no direct reference in the movie that the invaders come from Mars. Dante brings up the influential *Classics Illustrated* comic book design for the alien tripods, to which Spielberg reverted for his interesting remake.

The chrome monsters from the comic were ingrained in Savant's childhood as well; they sent me right to Wells' book, which became the first novel I can remember reading.

The trio also point out the film's prodigious host of name bit players, including many that are almost unrecognizable ... Paul Frees, William Phipps, Henry Brandon, Jack Kruschen, Edgar Barrier, Russ Bender, Russ Conway, Ralph Dumke, Ned Glass, Carolyn Jones, Alvy Moore and Walter Sande. Elsewhere we're directed to admire an image of Woody Woodpecker in a treetop as a cylinder descends over the National Forest.

1. La Puente is pictured as practically a wilderness, a last-ditch stopgap at the gates to Los Angeles. In a visual that suggests a weird inversion of The Sermon on the Mount, a crowd of extras witnesses the invaders withstand a heavenly atomic inferno. Today this part of Southern California is solid suburbs as far as the eye can see.

CREATURE FROM THE BLACK LAGOON
REVENGE OF THE CREATURE
THE CREATURE WALKS AMONG US

Universal Reviewed: November 10, 2004
1954-56 / B&W / 1:37 flat / 79, 82, 78 min.
Cinematography: William E. Snyder; Charles
S. Welbourne; Maury Gertsman. Written by
Maurice Zimm, Arthur A. Ross, Harry Essex;
William Alland, Martin Berkeley; Arthur A.
Ross. Produced by William Alland.
Directed by Jack Arnold; Jack Arnold; John
Sherwood

The best and practically the only original 1950s
movie monster is everyone's favorite denizen
of the Amazon, The Creature, a.k.a. The Gill
Man. Drummed up by Universal when studios were still putting resources and effort into
far-out fantasy, the Creature is a beautifully
designed and executed fish-monster, perhaps
the best rubber-suited thing Hollywood ever
turned out. He appeals to kids who like their
monsters big, slimy and savage, and his three
starring vehicles barely tap his potential. Universal's *Legacy Collection* gathers the original
feature and its two sequels together for the first
time. The Gill Man would certainly give a bull-
froggian roar of approval.

Creature from the Black Lagoon: Idealistic scientist David Reed (Richard Carlson), adventur-
er-investor Mark Williams (Richard Denning)
and curvaceous Kay (Julia Adams) penetrate
the Black Lagoon to search for a full fossil to
match the skeletal claw discovered by professor Carl Maia (Antonio Moreno). They are
greeted by an aquatic man-fish that takes an instant shine to the way Kay fills out a contoured
swimsuit. The Gill Man decimates the supporting cast while the leads debate the best way to
capture it; after blocking the exit from the Lagoon the wily Devonian goes a step further and
claims Kay as a romantic spoil of war. But you
know what they say about fish and visitors after three days.

Revenge of the Creature picks up immediately
with a new group that snares the Gill Man and
carts him off to a Florida seaquarium, there to be
chained to the bottom of an exotic fish tank like
a sideshow freak. Scientists Clete Ferguson and
Helen Dobson (John Agar & Lori Nelson) carry on
a spirited romance within sight of the jealous Gill
Man, prompting a timely escape and predictable
panic. The amphibious Don Juan claws Helen's
dog into puppy chow and attempts to tow her to
South America, but is undone by the necessity of
leaving her on the beach while he takes periodic
breathing breaks in the surf. Clete tricks his romantic rival into releasing Helen by using lessons
taught during negative-reinforcement sessions: to
be exact, yelling "stop" into a megaphone.

The Creature Walks Among Us finds a third
gaggle of scientists bagging the Creature in his

Florida bayou hideout, accidentally giving him serious burns in the process. The Gill Man's fish scales are removed, revealing a fleshy proto-man underneath. Dr. Thomas Morgan (Rex Reason) opens up the monster's unused lungs, permanently transforming him into a land-based creature. Morgan preaches kindness but the moneybags behind the research William Barton (Jeff Morrow) treats the Creature as he does everyone else in his life – as his property to do with as he wishes. Wife Marcia Barton (Leigh Snowden) has already wrapped boat skipper Jed Grant (Gregg Palmer) around her finger and reveals that she really wants handsome Dr. Morgan. Disturbed by the human duplicity, the Creature rebels against being penned in with the sheep and goes on a well-deserved rampage.

They may be neither classy nor classics but the Creature movies remain an entertaining trilogy well above the standards of most 50s monster movies, even Universal's. The three pictures contain a wealth of lore and anecdotal incident, most of it covered in the set's docu and three commentary tracks. But a few points stand out.

Derived neither from a book nor a recorded legend, the Creature is a Hollywood original, a newly minted fish story. The presence of the scientists lends a progressive veneer to a concept that has little to do with the 50s sci-fi craze; as Tom Weaver prodded producer Alland to admit, the concept is a retread of *King Kong*, which had enjoyed an enormously popular theatrical revival in 1952. The first two movies combined retrace the same story: the monster strives to possess the leading lady.

The first movie was made by eager talent itching to pull off a scare-show in 3D. Unpretentious director Jack Arnold was less interesting than the fantastic subjects he ended up helming for the studio system; he'd later transcend the sci-fi ghetto with his wonderful *The Incredible Shrinking Man*. With the exception of a few atmospheric moments, the Creature is a threat

only because the situation is in his favor – he attacks underwater and in dark, confined spaces. Cast members remain relaxed even when aware that a menace could be sneaking up on them; blasts of trumpet music accompany the monster's every un-sensational appearance. The Creature does a lot of reaching blindly onto footpaths and through portholes with a trembling claw that's supposed to terrify us. Instead, we admire the artful sculpting of his webby-scaled paw.

The first two movies were in 3D and looked great in a process that thrived on artificial thrills: hands poking into the camera, the Creature leaping up a ten-foot aquarium wall into a giant groggy close-up. In the original Polaroid projection system, audiences saw underwater scenes in 3D for the first time, an extra gimmick that added to the novelty. I was too young to be there in person, but I'll bet that the Creature was kind of a tongue-in-cheek nostalgic holdover from the old 30s monsters, the ones most 50s kids would have to wait until the 1956 *Shock Theater* package to see on TV. The Gill Man is funny but also cool – we watch to see how human he is. He turns out to be everyone's favorite kind of monster, a basic nice guy who makes mincemeat of the humans because they won't leave him alone, or because he's attracted to a girl from the wrong side of the evolutionary tree. He's at least as convincing as the human cast, and we sympathize with his problems.

I always thought that the true sequel to *Creature from the Black Lagoon* should be a courtroom drama. Let's see, eight scientists go into the jungle and only four come back. Several mutilated corpses and an alibi about a fish-man being responsible? No photos, no evidence, no nothing. I see some long prison terms in the future.

The Revenge of the Creature and *The Creature Walks Among Us* are okay follow-ups but neither builds on the Creature's character. The predictable *Revenge* reduces the Gill Man to a goldfish in a bowl getting poked by an electric prod, which incidentally would almost certainly shock everything else in the water too. The film has about eight minutes of classy rampage action: a car overturned, a baby menaced, the Gill Man snatching his late night date from the dance floor of a restaurant bar. The rest is scientific doubletalk, travelogue filler and abortive suspense scenes. The Creature turns Peeping Tom to spy on Lori Nelson in her bathroom, something that even giant *Tarantulas* tend to do in Universal City. Some scenes, like the one where the Creature swims 'with' Lori and tickles her heel, cover the same ground as the original. The posse that tracks him down at the end isn't very interesting but the nighttime photography is. Also, the cast of the first film smoothed out the dialogue scenes, but *Revenge* doesn't even pretend that its script is worth listening to. Lori Nelson's offhand explanation of ichthyology shows that she can barely pronounce the word.

By the time of *The Creature Walks Among Us* Universal's monsters had been relegated to the lowest tier of production. Ambitious fantasies like *The Mole People* ended up resembling PRC groaners of ten years before. Writer Arthur Ross (reportedly the true auteur of the first film) tailored a cost-cutting sequel with a clever ruse: instead of another difficult shoot with those tricky rubber full-body suits, *Walks* recycles outtakes from the first two films. The creature is soon transformed into a more easily managed monster with just a head mask, new hands and new feet. A gunnysack Zoot suit covers the rest of him. Voila! Except for a few new shots for the capture scene, the full crew of latex wranglers can be replaced by one or two guys touching up a couple of masks. Any big actor can don the gear, and he doesn't have to wear an unbearable rubber suit for eight hours straight.

Our former Gill-Man is reduced to a shuffling lummox in a sheep pen, dealing with vague new feelings that aren't fully articulated by the script or the direction. The Creature kills an in-

surgent mountain lion as if deciding he's now the protector of wooly rights. Some fish, as they say.

Yet *The Creature Walks Among Us* has the germ of a solid monster idea lacking in most formulaic efforts. Obnoxious big boss Jeff Morrow creates a hostile atmosphere that drives his wife to lure other males into compromising situations. She's played as a brazen tramp by *Kiss Me Deadly's* "No" girl, Leigh Snowden. Halo-pure Rex Reason remains chaste, yet steps in at the finale to claim Snowden's dance card. In a pre-echo of the violent rebellion of *The Birds*, the Creature observes all the human treachery, and when he can't stand any more rips free of his cage to smite the offenders. So he's also become a moral judge as well. Doubtless this was all made possible simply because the studio didn't care about the picture. You can bet that few top execs actually attended screenings.

Director John Sherwood arranges the best action in the trilogy when the Creature invades the mansion house to punish the abusive Jeff Morrow. Excellent blocking shows the monster pursuing his prey through a series of rooms. He spots Morrow out of the corner of his eye and barrels through a window to cut off his escape. The violence is laid out for maximum involvement.

The ending *almost* works. The escaped monster stands overlooking the sea. He can no longer breathe underwater, so he's a goner for sure. But does the Creature know that? Does he think he's going home, or is he committing suicide? If the final shot of the monster lumbering toward the surf weren't so artlessly filmed, this ending could have been truly enigmatic and thought-provoking.

Universal's two-disc **Creature from the Black Lagoon The Legacy Collection** comes in a fancy display box. The quality is excellent, although all three movies should be enhanced for widescreen. The studio's preferred ratio can be seen in the text blocks used for the title and credit sequences. If one masks off the top and bottom on a widescreen TV, all the lettering fits perfectly. Heads are never cut off and all essential action is still there, even on the first film.

In his excellent commentary, Tom Weaver identifies as a blooper a telephone pole that can be seen as the explorers first enter the forbidden Black Lagoon. It's not a blooper at all. When cropped to a more-correct 1:78, the pole isn't visible.

Weaver's commentary continues on the new-to-DVD sequels, joined by Bob Burns and Lori Nelson for some lively banter. The only docu is David J. Skal's elaborate piece that came with the original *Creature* disc, which covers all three films and just about every other Gill-Man related piece of Hollywood lore, even the monster's mention in Billy Wilder's *The Seven-Year Itch*. Since the Creature inspired Marilyn Monroe's emotional outburst on her way to that famous subway grating, I always thought it appropriate that the famous photo of her skirt flying over her head should have an added scaly claw reaching up from below.

Last thoughts: In the first film, is the Creature's roommate the *Phantom of the Opera*? What are those organ pipe-like columns doing in his sub-aquatic lair? Also: The Gill Man comes from the headwaters of a tributary of the Amazon, which should make him a fresh-water kind of guy. Why doesn't he turn belly-up and croak when they dump him into a salt-water ocean-arium tank? Hm?

GOG

Not on DVD Reviewed: September 5, 2007
1954 / Color (3D) / 1:37 flat / 85 min.
Lothrop B. Worth. Production Design William Ferrari. Written by Ivan Tors, Tom Taggart, Richard G. Taylor. Produced by Ivan Tors. Directed by Herbert L. Strock

Producer Ivan Tors continued the science-oriented spirit of George Pal's *Destination Moon* with an informal trilogy of thrillers about the fictional OSI, the Office of Scientific Investigation. In 1953's *The Magnetic Monster* a 'lone wolf' researcher synthesizes a dangerous element, which then must be neutralized in a giant reactor. An elaborate effects sequence from the 1934 German film *Gold* was lifted to provide the expensive-looking finale. *Riders to the Stars* (1954) followed daring rocket pilots into space to capture meteorites so that scientists can discover what protects them from cosmic rays. *GOG* is an even more elaborate espionage thriller about high-tech mayhem in a top-secret government research lab.

Special OSI agent David Sheppard (Richard Egan) arrives at a secret desert installation to investigate the murders of several scientists. Lab director Dr. Van Ness (Herbert Marshall, repeating from *Riders to the Stars*) shows Taggart various experiments underway at the underground lab, which is overseen by a computer called Novac, or The Brain. David also meets up with Joanna Merritt (Constance Dowling), Van Ness's assistant. Only slowly does it become clear that Novac and its robot helpers GOG and MAGOG are being influenced by outside saboteurs.

GOG is perhaps the first 50s sci-fi thriller to glamorize the technical marvels of America's Military-Industrial Complex. Far removed from ordinary life, scientists and government agents live and work in a futuristic secret base buried in the desert. The super-computer Novac runs everything, from individual experiments to the base defense system: solar mirrors hidden in the sagebrush. Novac can automatically activate any dial, lever and door latch in the building, not to mention dispatch a pair of tank-like robots to service the atomic reactor. The five-level underground plant is nearly identical to the Wildfire Station in Michael Crichton's later *The Andromeda Strain.* Its walls are a Pentagon-approved beige and blue, with glass bricks from a garden store providing design accents. And of course, no futuristic environment can do without one critical detail: automatic sliding doors.

The Office of Scientific Investigation is a secret intelligence agency overseeing the nation's military research. Executive Van Ness explains that the base is building a solar powered space station that will also serve as an orbital platform for a heat ray weapon to be trained on the earth below. The murders have placed the base on high alert, but Miss Merritt assures us that as soon as the space station is launched we'll have nothing to fear. Once the death ray is in orbit, America will dominate the world. Once again, sci-fi entertainment celebrates military aggression.

The film alternates between endless technical exposition and a series of bizarre murders. Beautiful female assistants aid the middle-aged researchers; a married doctor played by Philip Van Zandt loiters during a centrifuge experiment to ogle a shapely test subject. Like exhibits at a Junior High Science Fair, victims are dispatched by high frequency audio, freezing, etc. Investigator Sheppard must have flunked physics in High School because he spends critical investigation time listening as various experts explain rudimentary scientific concepts. A casual demonstration of the focusing-mirror heat ray involves incinerating a detailed table-top miniature; we wonder if the lab maintains its own model shop, just to keep up with the need for dramatic demos.

Audiences not intimidated by scientific doubletalk easily solve the film's mystery, making agent Sheppard look completely incompetent. The experts babble on constantly about the concept of remote control, but are shocked to learn that sinister foreign interests might control Novac with radio waves beamed from a rocket plane high in the stratosphere. When components for the computer were assembled in "a neutral European country", enemy spies added their own secret transmitter. The climax has David and Joanna battling the assassin robots GOG and MAGOG for control of the reactor room.

The patriotic and upbeat *GOG* reassures its viewers that nuclear problems are nothing to be worried about. Our lovers are accidentally irradiated but are last seen happy and smiling in the lab hospital: "The doctors say we'll be okay, we just got a little too much radiation!"

Savant saw *GOG* at a 3D festival in 2003 with director Herbert Strock and actor William Schallert in attendance. Strock said that although most of his production effort went into the depth process, as far as he knew, *GOG* was publicly screened in 3D only once. The film is much less exciting when seen flat. Schallert checked his employment notebook for 1954 and found that he worked on the film for three days: his lab assistant character is strangled by MAGOG.

GOG remains an ideological souvenir from a time when the H-Bomb lifted the arms race to a new level of tension. The prescription is always the same: more secrecy, better bombs and space research to dominate the globe with 'peace-keeping' weapons. The happy ending of *GOG* reinforces the climate of Cold War terror. [1]

1. The spy thriller *The Satan Bug* (1965) is about an almost identical desert lab making doomsday viruses; a secret agent goes into action when biological weapons disappear from the inventory. As it turns out, the deadly vials are being used to blackmail the government into closing down the research station. The highly questionable finale refuses to make a moral statement about germ warfare – the emergency is quietly resolved and the biological experiments can continue. The world is 'safe' once more.

THEM!

Warners Reviewed: August 11, 2002
1954 / B&W / 1:37 flat / 94 min.
Cinematography Sid Hickox. Art Direction Stanley Fleischer. Editor Thomas Reilly. Music Bronislau Kaper. Written by Ted Sherdeman from a story by George Worthing Yates.
Produced by David Weisbart.
Directed by Gordon Douglas

The key science fiction film *Them!* transcends its reputation as "that movie about giant ants". The nicely budgeted thriller was made at a time when each studio still had a house style: *Them!* enjoys the crisp photography of Sid Hickox (*White Heat*), great montages, a brassy and aggressive Warners music score and a trim, action-packed script. It has been described as a film noir, which is only partially true: the world has been transformed into a bold new battleground for a struggle against a totalitarian enemy that cannot be bargained with.

> New Mexico State Policeman Sgt. Ben Peterson (James Whitmore) finds the tiny daughter of an FBI agent (Sandy Descher) wandering in the desert. Both of her vacationing parents and the owner of a general store have been killed under baffling circumstances. An odd footprint sent to Washington summons FBI agent Robert Graham (James Arness) and entomologists Dr. Harold Medford (Edmund Gwenn) and his daughter Pat (Joan Weldon). Together they discover that a nest of enormous mutated ants has broken out. The world may be overrun by hordes of killer monster insects.

In 1954, cheaper independent product was already starting to infiltrate science fiction filmmaking. No-budget shows like *Target: Earth!* no longer required big stars and spectacle to attract audiences. Why spend hundreds of thousands of dollars to earn what Herman Cohen or Lippert were getting by spending fifty or sixty?

Warners resisted the new fantastic genre until 1953's *The Beast from 20,000 Fathoms*. According to film historian Steve Rubin, *Them!* was planned as an expensive 'A' picture in color and 3D. [1] The studio had already pared down an original story that involved battles in the NYC subways on a scale more grandiose than *The War of the Worlds*. Instead of contacting then still-unknown effects man Ray Harryhausen, the job of creating an ant army fell to studio craftsmen eager for the challenge.

The whole point of doing the ants live-action was because *Them!* was to be filmed in 3D, making mattes and other effects difficult if not impossible. Several functioning ant models were built: articulated whole insects that moved on the front of fork lifts, hydraulic and electric models with working heads, antennae and mandibles; and simple balanced 'wobbly' heads that waved their antennae when agitated by wind machines. The cleverness extended to the eyes, plastic bubbles filled with multicolored soapy oils and glitter. Animated by washing-machine agitators, the sparkly liquid slooshed around and made the inexpressive ant faces seem alive. [2]

Jack Warner hit the brakes twice during preproduction. The 3D was abandoned first, and then just two days before filming Warner decreed that the show would not be in color either. Warner hated monster movies, an opinion that didn't change even when *Them!* became the studio's biggest moneymaker of the year. No *Son of Them!* ever had a chance.

Although director Gordon Douglas was incensed to see his solid-A picture reduced to uppity B status, it didn't dampen his enthusiasm: *Them!* may be his best-directed action feature. [3] The story creates sympathetic characters and builds logically on its investigation in the desert. Nowhere is the show treated as if it were a down-market monster movie, a fault tainting some similar productions over at Universal. A believable noir world is sketched as cops and soldiers go about their mundane jobs. Victims have caring families and the survival of individuals is always kept at the highest level of importance. An advisor who suggests that two young boys be sacrificed to guarantee a 'sanitary' means of disposing of the ants is usually booed in theaters. *Them!* is one of the few monster movies with a big emotional appeal.

Douglas's New Mexico desert is no place for a casual stroll, as in *Tarantula*. The little lost girl opens the picture with a different kind of poetry – the absolute innocent alone in a hostile and alien world. Forget the singing cowboys ... there's radioactivity out there.

The midnight visit to Gramps' store is truly frightening. Sgt. Peterson and his buddy Ed Blackburn (Chris Drake) move through the windblown wreck with guns drawn. A radio is playing and the men listen to a vaguely threatening news report. The ex-soldiers are in a new kind of war against a new kind of foe that invades from within.

The emotional center of the film is James Whitmore's Sgt. Peterson. Whitmore had started over at MGM, where he had personified a rather condescending average American Joe in producer Dore Schary's *The Next Voice You Hear*. Whitmore made his strongest impression as soldiers and cops. His Sgt. Peterson is a humanistic everyman, the WW2 veteran dedicated to keeping the peace and saving small children. He's how we baby boomers like to remember our fathers, gentle men who had once been to war and now wanted something different.

James Arness at this time was a bona fide protégé of John Wayne doing his darndest to elbow his way into a career. Arness' delivery, mannerisms etc. are almost laughably patterned on Wayne's style. The terrifying finale of *Them!* abandons the handsome FBI man Arness in the dark, with clicking monsters closing in from all sides. Prescription? Open up with your Tommy gun in all directions at once, and hope for the best.

Edmund Gwenn tempers his dotty *House on 34th Street* persona with grim, oracle-like predictions of a world poised on the brink of a strange new age. Unlike the philosophical split of *The Thing from Another World*, the warriors and eggheads of *Them!* have achieved consensus. The Washingtonians take some convincing, but once they're on board America becomes an efficient self-healing machine – the military-industrial-political complex Eisenhower warned about. Unlike the real Oppenheimers of 50s America, Gwenn's Dr. Medford isn't sidelined or considered a dissident: the generals don't make a move without his okay. It takes a pro like Gwenn to make the character both serious and comic, as almost every scene ends with him fielding a doomsday zinger: "Man, as the dominant life form on Earth, may soon be extinct."

Joan Weldon's stock scientist's daughter Pat Medford predicts another unsettling post-nuke change taking place, a Cold War version of women's liberation. We'd think that Pat's scientific expertise would enhance her social mobility. It instead frees her to don a uniform and join the he-men to help fight America's enemies. Pat is plenty eager for the job. She's the least emotional and easily the most bloodthirsty of the bunch, as evinced by her callous order: "Burn everything in here! Burn it all!"

Them!'s visuals suggest that to survive in the new Atomic Age of Terror, man will have to become more like savage ants. By show's end all the major characters have been converted into soldiers. The heroes wear bug-like goggles and creep through tunnels to locate and destroy the enemy. The utter kill-worthiness of the giant ants is never questioned, as it is indeed 'Them' or 'Us.' [4]

Two latter day sci-fi films with giant insects are obviously influenced by *Them!* Sigourney Weaver's character in James Cameron's *Aliens* combines the ruthless take-charge aggression of Pat Medford with the humanism of Sgt. Peterson. Both films stress sensitive sequences involving children traumatized by the insect monsters. Paul Verhoeven's *Starship Troopers* pits futuristic soldiers against militant space-bugs but ironically demands that we understand that the war being waged is totally hypocritical. [5]

The bit player list is a who's who of interesting folk like William Schallert, Leonard Nimoy, Richard Deacon, Dub Taylor and Olin Howland. The capable Mary Alan Hokanson deserved a better career for her role as the distraught mother. Fess Parker jumped from unknown player to media hero when Walt Disney caught his animated performance here and signed him to play Davy Crockett.

The exciting score by Bronislau Kaper was recorded a few years back as one of the first entries in the *Monstrous Movie Music CD* series. It included the uncut ending, which builds to a powerful finale. As with many Warners films of the time, tight editing hurries the last shot, so as to rush to the 'The End' card and get those house lights up. A comparison with the CD shows how the music editors radically up-cut the original ending fanfare.

Warner's DVD of *Them!* is a pleasant surprise. Judging by the shape of the title blocks the correct aspect ratio is probably 1:66. Cropping off the flat full-frame transfer in a 16:9 television looks best, even though it's a bit too tight on the bottom. The comic-book menus are colorful and cute but also difficult to navigate. One of the text extras is a cursory history of big bug movies. The terrific trailer communicates the desired 'gotta see' quality and ends with a boffo graphic gag where the four letters of the title spell out words like Terror! and Horror!

The best extra is a selection of raw outtakes that offer a clear look at the giant ant props. Critics can complain that they're too slow and creep too mechanically, but stop-motion animation would have had a feel totally different to the in-your-face chompers seen here. The outtakes prove that superior editing makes the ants look good: individual shots are kept brief, with extra motion imparted via camera pans and tilts. A couple of wide unused takes on a static ant show how bad it could have been. As soon as the ants are motionless they look ridiculous, like the gorilla robot in the 1976 *King Kong*. Carefully edited and augmented with sound effects, windblown sand, explosions, flames and falling timbers, they're a knockout.

The box art is a faithful collage from the original posters that featured cartoonish cat-eyed bug monsters. A 'scrambling citizen' motif is repeated from *The Beast from 20,000 Fathoms'* key art. Screams a blonde: "Kill one and two take

its place!" The DVD liner copy hits the nail on the head when it suggests that *Them!* gets better with age – this is the 1950s radioactive monster movie, and it's just as exciting now as it was back then.

1. The key research source for this film is a 1974 *Cinefantastique* article on *Them!* by Steve Rubin (Volume 3, Number 4). Rubin's *Cinefantastique's* essays were some of the first decently researched and authoritative critical writing on science fiction.

2. Effects men were utterly invisible in the industry before Douglas Trumbull and *2001: A Space Odyssey*. Only technicians and a few insiders were aware of someone like Willis O'Brien. *The Beast* should have led to a studio contract for Harryhausen but the industry just didn't work that way. Technicians were like carpenters – anybody below the level of Director of Photography was treated like day labor. It took magazines like *Famous Monsters* to raise awareness of effects wizards, and not until *Star Wars* was there an explosion in effects superstardom. A few of the acolytes of Ray Harryhausen that had been scraping around making a living in television commercials then became the hottest tickets in Hollywood.

3. I've heard the story that director Douglas had the main title card of several original prints brightly colored at his own expense, so as to thumb his nose at Jack Warner for canceling the color for the movie, a story that is probably apocryphal. The DVD of *Them!* displays the title in bright red and blue. Bill Shaffer tells me that he's seen a collectors' original 35mm print with the color title, indicating that whole runs of prints had it, and not just the few.

4. According to William Johnson in *Focus on the Science Fiction Film* (Prentice-Hall, 1972) "*Twentieth Century* magazine denounced *Them!* as a vicious allegory calling for the extermination not of giant ants but of Communists." The analogy still holds. The giant ants are considered so dangerous that the campaign against them is hidden from the public. An FBI agent orders the covert arrest of a citizen in the interest of national security. The investigation overrides local jurisdictions and declares martial law in L.A. – essentially the military taking over an entire city for its own protection. The hysterical view of Communists is that their ideology makes them implacable, ungodly aliens: flamethrowers are too good for 'em.

5. Of course, *Aliens* inverts *Them!'s* politics. By the 1980s America is so militaristically aggressive that the Army and Big Business promote the terror of the insect monsters, which are desired as a weapon.

GOJIRA & GODZILLA, KING OF THE MONSTERS!

Classic Media Reviewed: August 27, 2006
B&W / 1:37 flat full frame

The giant Japanese monster **Godzilla** has occupied the public imagination for over fifty years, weathering innumerable sequels as well as Sony's ill-fated 1998 remake. Because his films quickly became badly dubbed kiddie TV fodder, the fire-breathing aquatic dragon has at times been more of an adolescent joke than a serious film subject.

Most American viewers were deprived of the ability to see Japanese fantasy films in their original versions. Heard in the correct language, they play like real movies and yield unexpected treasures such as added scenes and terrific original music tracks, sometimes in stereophonic sound. Latter-day *Godzilla* movies increased

interest in the 'classics', and after years of disappointing gray-market offerings we started seeing licensed DVDs of great Japanese fantasy.

The 1954 Japanese cut of *Gojira* received its first official American theatrical release in 2004. An enthusiastic audience was surprised to encounter a thoughtful and sobering meditation on nuclear war by the only country to suffer an atomic attack – and filmed only nine years after the fact. *Gojira* is paired on a double-disc special edition with its American variant version (the one we've been watching for the last half-century) *Godzilla, King of the Monsters!*

GOJIRA

1954 / 98 min. / **Japanese with English subtitles**
Cinematography Masao Tamai. Special Visual Effects Eiji Tsuburaya. Music Akira Ifukube. Written by Ishiro Honda, Shigeru Kayama, Takeo Murata. Produced by Tomoyuki Tanaka. Directed by Ishirô Honda

An unknown radioactive force is sinking Japanese ships. Searching for the cause, scientist Dr. Yamane (Takashi Shimura) travels to a tiny fishing island and is confronted by a colossal water dragon, which soon lays waste to a large area of Tokyo. Conventional armaments prove useless, which puts the eccentric Dr. Serizawa (Akihiko Hirata) in a bind. He's invented a new weapon he calls an "Oxygen Destroyer" but refuses to use it on moral grounds. Serizawa's fiancée Emiko Yamane (Momoko Kochi) begs the scientist to reconsider.

By now most fantasy film fans are aware that the original *Gojira* is a serious picture. *Gojira* revisits the still-fresh horror of much of urban Japan being burned or blasted by long-range bombers. Faced by a radioactive monster from the ocean, Takashi Shimura's somber scientist behaves as if Japan were repaying a terrible karmic debt through yet another ordeal by fire. Subway passengers lament the idea of going back into those smelly shelters again. And a war widow clutches her children as buildings crumble around them, crying, "We will be with daddy soon." It all plays like national masochism of the highest order.

Military efforts are useless but heroism is expressed in the operatic self-sacrifice of the lonely and mysterious Dr. Serizawa, an odd character pictured as an unnatural freak. Like Rotwang of *Metropolis*, Serizawa has a physical infirmity (the eye patch) that suggests an intense but limited vision. The technical décor of his 'mad lab' is reminiscent of Rotwang's electro-alchemy experiments. Serizawa's science obsession has left him with little social sense or sex drive. He watches as the handsome Ogata (Akira Takarada) charms his fiancée Emiko right out from under his test tube.

Serizawa's scientist carries the same dubious moral burden that was heaped onto American scientists after the development of the bomb. Politicians are gregarious and military men are heroes, but scientists are shifty 'unknown quantities' that don't think as do you or I. Their inventions bring bad news and cause unwelcome changes. Serizawa doesn't want to repeat the error of the Manhattan Project by allowing the awful potential of his discovery to be exploited for war. He keeps faith with his scientific ethics by carrying out a death pact.

The film implies that the developers of the American bomb were traitors to mankind. That faulty judgment is based on the misapprehension that scientists in any country exercise control over their work or what its eventual application might be. Participants in the Manhattan Project displayed the wide range of political beliefs that might be found in any group of intellectuals. Considered difficult to control, they were asked to sign loyalty oaths and heavily investigated.

Few scientists would identify with Doctor Serizawa, who produces his miracle weapon alone in a brick basement lab, like a gothic Frankenstein figure. Serizawa's 'moral choice' is to take

his secret with him to the grave, withholding his Oxygen Destroyer from the hands of evil men. Baloney. After the demo in Tokyo Bay, every nation with a University system would instantly assign a crack team to retrace Serizawa's research.

Gojira's outlandish contribution to 20th century mythology is to envision an abstract concept – atomic anxiety – as a Golem-like force of nature. *Gojira* is an implacable atomic enemy, a mobile natural disaster, a typhoon in the form of a firestorm. Plot-wise, the film is a bald rip-off of *The Beast From 20,000 Fathoms*, in which the monster's nuclear origin is little more than a convenient gimmick. No explanation is given for Gojira's genesis, or why he wants to trample Tokyo into the mud. He just *is*. The film is aimed at the mass denial of the Japanese public, to face an intimate horror that had been swept under the rug for nine years.

We're told that *Gojira* came at a time of expansion at the Toho studio and was not a cheap picture. Eiji Tsuburaya's effects are all very good for the time, and some are excellent. Ishiro Honda's masterful direction creates a nightmarish spectacle, a destructive juggernaut that crushes in slow strides. Akira Ifukube's grim music intensifies the dread with deep, slow themes for the monster and a somber march to represent Japan's futile defense. It's important to point out that *Gojira* victimizes the whole city and not just a select group of individuals; the entire first wave of Japanese *kaiju* and science fiction films would threaten society as a whole. The highest social virtue is always identified as selfless teamwork in the defense of the nation.

Later Toho monsters concentrated more on spectacular thrills than anti-war statements. *Rodan* is a romantic "double suicide" tale of flying gods doomed to perish in volcanic fire. *The Mysterians* is a rallying call to repel conquering foreign influences. *Mothra* pits the forces of storybook magic against predatory material commercialism. Quite a few 'lowly' Japanese monster movies of the 50s and 60s display thematic riches that put the average science fiction extravaganza to shame.

GODZILLA, KING OF THE MONSTERS!
1956 / 80 min. / English dub version
Additional actors: Raymond Burr, Frank Iwanaga Additional Cinematography Guy Roe. Editor Terry O. Morse. Written by Al C. Ward. Produced by Edward B. Barison, Richard Kay, Joseph E. Levine, Harry Rybnick. English Version Directed by Terry O. Morse

In 1954 only a handful of Japanese films had been exhibited in the United States outside Japanese-American neighborhoods. Japanese art was something to be found in museums and jokes about cheap Japanese toys reflected American ignorance of the country's post-war economic boom. Everyone "knew" that anything Made in Japan was inferior. Anti-Japanese sentiment was still easy to find: why spend a dime that might find its way back to the people who gave us Pearl Harbor?

This was an obvious problem for the exploitation promoters that eyed big $$ potential in *Gojira*'s special effects scenes. To make *Gojira* look like any other Yankee film shot in an 'exotic' Eastern land, American version director Terry Morse back-grounded the original storyline and inserted an American actor as the star. Character actor Raymond Burr got the job as Steve Martin, intrepid foreign news correspondent. Morse pulled off one of the more clever cinematic retrofit jobs in film history by making Steve a fly-on-the-wall witness to the events of the original film.

Terry Morse analyzed the original film to see where Raymond Burr could be sandwiched in. He filmed the actor against a few judiciously-chosen wild walls and surrounded him with just enough bystanders from Los Angeles' Little Tokyo to fool the casual viewer. The entire original narrative becomes Steve Martin's feverish memory after barely surviving a direct Godzilla attack. Aided by shrewd English scripting, the new scenes inter-cut well; Raymond Burr indeed appears to be in the middle of the chaos.

We all know the rest of the story, as the American *Godzilla* became a smash international success only two years after its Japanese debut. Fledgling mogul Joseph Levine thought up a dozen advertising tag lines and ended up using them all in an unending litany of hectoring hyperbole:

"Incredible, Unstoppable Titan of Terror!" "Is Godzilla fantasy or a prophecy of doom?" "Fantastic beyond comprehension, beyond compare! Astounding beyond belief!" "Terror staggers the mind as the gargantuan creature of the sea surges up on a tidal wave of destruction to wreak vengeance on the Earth!" "Civilization crumbles as its death rays blast a city of six million from the face of the Earth!" "Mightiest Monster! Mightiest Melodrama of them All!"

Godzilla hit American screens in 1956 and attracted a sizeable audience that surely included a surfeit of hyperactive kids. Godzilla's legend grew slowly but steadily through sequels, toys and playground mythmaking: *Yeah, yeah, King Kong is cool but Godzilla would just step on him, dork."* Although Godzilla eventually morphed into a clownish gang leader, rallying Mothra and Rodan to defeat outer-space freaks like King "Look Ma, no arms!" Ghidorah, he kept his original bad-dude reputation. The original film never fell out of favor.

The *Godzilla – Gojira Deluxe Collector's Edition – The Official U.S. & Japanese film Versions* elevates the general stature of the Godzilla franchise. The handsome packaging for the reasonably priced disc says 'quality special edition' all the way.

Although it still looks well worn, this transfer is a great improvement. The scratching is minimized and the film retains its gray-grayer-black texture. *Godzilla* always looked darker and had tight framing that chopped off the top of the picture. It too is greatly improved, to the point that we can appreciate how close Guy Roe's new photography comes to matching the original. This version includes the echo-y footfalls heard over black (no Transworld logo), until the "King of the Monsters!" main title zooms up on Godzilla's metallic roar. Also included is a set of "Jewell Enterprises" end titles (matted to 1:75!) showing all the American credits over an oddly patterned background.

Godzilla authorities Steve Ryfle and Ed Godziszewsky double up on commentaries for both features to cover All Things Godzilla in an efficient and entertaining matter. They separate publicity myth from practical reality – producer Tomoyuki Tanaka may claim otherwise but the previous year's Ray Harryhausen movie is referenced as his inspiration. Gojira was even originally scripted to destroy a lighthouse.

Steve and Ed consider the "what Godzilla means" controversy from several interesting angles without insisting on a particular interpretation. They downplay the notion (instigated by a Japanese dialogue reference) that the Dr. Serizawa character collaborated with Nazi scientists during WW2. The experts include sound bites from one of the original importers and the screenwriter who came up with the surprisingly good American dialogue and narration. Two docu featurettes cover the original film's story development and the construction of the rubber monster suit. We see plenty of images of the men who made the monsters and fascinating behind-the-scenes shots of the rubber-suited characters taking breaks between stomp Tokyo duties.

Colorful menus featuring original poster artwork take us to the original trailer. The set comes in a sturdy 'Little Golden Book'- style case with the two discs in plastic holders. A slick twelve-page insert booklet has more stills, acknowledgements and a lengthy text essay by Steve Ryfle called *Godzilla's Footprint*.

20,000 LEAGUES UNDER THE SEA
Disney Reviewed: May 12, 2003
1954 / Color / 2:55 widescreen / 127 min. Cinematography Franz Planer. Production Designer Harper Goff (uncredited). Art Direction John Meehan. Editor Elmo Williams. Music Paul Smith. Written by Earl Felton from the novel *Vingt Mille Lieues sous les mers* by Jules Verne. Produced by Walt Disney.
Directed by Richard Fleischer

One the best projects Walt Disney ever undertook, *20,000 Leagues Under the Sea* is an exciting and faithful adaptation of Jules Verne's most popular 'Voyage Extraordinaire'. Received as a breathtaking wonder upon its Christmas release in 1954, it retained its glow through many reissues. For his first big screen live-action effort, Disney picked a property with countless unknown production hazards. It would be filmed in the new CinemaScope screen process, for which few lenses were available. It required special effects nobody had seen before. Disney needed the best technical resources in Hollywood, when he was known primarily as an animation producer.

1870. 'Alarming rumors' of a monster have emptied the sea lanes. The United States dispatches a warship to track it down, and invites French scientist Professor Arronax (Paul Lukas) and his faithful aide Conseil (Peter Lorre). When the monster destroys the ship, the Frenchmen and harpoonist Ned Land (Kirk Douglas) swim to its floating hulk, which turns out to be a submersible watercraft. It's the Nautilus, the invention of mad avenger Captain Nemo (James Mason), who exercises his grudge against colonial powers by sinking their war fleets and munitions shipments. At first charmed by Nemo's personal undersea empire, the three captives soon conspire to find a way to put an end to Nemo's engine of destruction.

20,000 Leagues Under the Sea opens with a screen bathed in light from a rippling underwater source, signaling the mystery and spectacle to come. It is not long before we're completely immersed in Captain Nemo's fantastic underwater world, cruising in a submarine so well designed that we accept its reality without question. An iris window allows magical views of the deep, and the craft's comfortable interiors are invitingly believable.

Today, the most startling aspect of *Leagues* is its political tone. Disney provides a song, a trained seal and comedy between Kirk Douglas' blustery seaman and Peter Lorre's dour valet, but the film's overall impression is dark and moody. His Captain Nemo is an escaped slave, once an Eastern prince, who somehow became a scientific genius, developing futuristic technologies solely for revenge.

By today's standards Nemo is now easily recognized as a Terrorist, a political zealot who uses violence to strike back at those that tortured and murdered his family. In the original book Nemo is motivated by spite for what he refers to as "that hated nation". If Jules Verne had added a religious motive, Nemo would be a clear cipher for Osama Bin Laden, and his futuristic submarine a weapon of mass destruction.

James Mason's Captain Nemo glowers and fumes with an intensity that overshadows the whole enterprise. His singular vendetta is echoed in grand shots of the Nautilus prowling slowly in the blue depths to the determined chords of Paul Smith's music score. Nemo is the original unconscious manifestation of (literal) sub-versive hatred, a pacifist who declares war on the rest of the world.

The movie endorses the humanistic reason of the dull Professor Arronax, who pegs Nemo as a misguided idealist. Yet Nemo is a magnificent antihero. When set next to the jocular Kirk Douglas, who pulls faces and acts all hale and hearty, James Mason's gloom wins every time; he's obsession personified. Seven years later Vincent Price got a shot at a similar Verne character in the under-produced *Master of the World*, but couldn't match Mason's intensity.

The adventures of the Nautilus are magnificently realized. The sub cruises beneath the waves and navigates submerged tunnels like a beautiful but dangerous sea creature. Its attack churns a terrifying wake as its glowing eyes scream across the water's surface. A knifelike bow spur rips through the hulls of warships. Kiddie matinee audiences cheered at the film's trailer, which opened with the high-pitched Tasmanian Devil whine of the Nautilus zooming toward us, its wake splashing over its yellow "eyes".

The end of the Nautilus is a bleak götterdämmerung that includes a suicide pact between

Nemo and his dedicated crew. The loyal first officer is played by Robert J. Wilke, an actor associated exclusively with degenerate outlaw villains. The book had the damaged sub disappear in a Norwegian maelstrom, but writer Earl Fenton incorporates ideas from *Mysterious Island* and other Verne stories. Nemo returns to his secret island base only to discover it overrun by colonial troops. We get a quick impression of his super lab (complete with a radar dish – in 1870? – before Nemo throws a patented *Bride of Frankenstein* lever to blow it all to kingdom come.

Not only does Nemo prevent 'that hated nation' from stealing his scientific secrets, he gets a revenge of sorts by nuking a small army and navy of assorted national interests. Nobody ever points out that Disney's family fantasy ends with the murder of hundreds of First World colonials, in a visual that replays the Bikini H-blast right down to the inclusion of a circle of moored warships. There isn't a similar scene in films until the overtly radical *Giù la testa (Duck, You Sucker!)* in which James Coburn gleefully "rids the world of a few uniforms" by dynamiting an entire army. Nemo may be a warped madman, but every audience I ever saw the picture with wanted him to survive and sink every warship afloat.

Disney's DVD of **20,000 Leagues Under the Sea** looks fine in enhanced widescreen that doesn't quite display the full original 2:55 aspect ratio. Disney composes the opening titles for standard 1:33 screens, knowing that his film would eventually be shown on television. The disc's new docu is a much better piece than the 1954 television show that served as a primetime ad for the movie. Walt must have laughed all the way to the bank, as the networks paid him big $$ to advertise his own product. Along with input from director Richard Fleischer, critic Rudy Behlmer and an enthusiastic Kirk Douglas, we see several reels' worth of fascinating behind-the-scenes footage.

The unsung genius Harper Goff gets the nod as the film's most important creative contributor. His submarine design has never been beaten. Goff found an excellent workaround for the scarcity of CinemaScope lenses. "Squeezed" models of the *Nautilus* were built and photographed with ordinary flat optics. When anamorphically stretched in projection, they produced superior 'Scope images!

A docu on the combined genius of Verne and Disney focuses mostly on Disney. A 'Disney Studio Album' for 1954 is a montage of the studio's insane roster of fiscally risky activities in that pivotal year. The short subject *The Humboldt Squid* raises our awareness of the power and danger of real squids. They actually do swim both ways, forwards and backwards, as pictured in the film.

The extras also include 16mm footage of the first abortive attempt at the Squid scene, showing the rubber monster in flat lighting before a sunset backdrop. One of Disney's best qualities was his willingness to Bet the Farm on his instincts. When Squid One proved a dud he redoubled his effort, and the final scene is a remarkable improvement.

REVENGE OF THE CREATURE
(see page 70)

CONQUEST OF SPACE

Paramount October 30, 2004
1955 / Color / 1:78 widescreen / 81 min.
Cinematography Lionel Lindon. Music by
Van Cleave. Written by Philip Yordan. Barré
Lyndon, George Worthing Yates, James
O'Hanlon from books by Chesley Bonestell,
Willy Ley and Wernher von Braun. Produced
by George Pal.
Directed by Byron Haskin

One of the biggest disappointments of the first
wave of 1950s science fiction, *Conquest of Space*
seriously hindered the career of its producer
George Pal. Originally planned and rejected
as a follow-up to Pal's original blockbuster
Destination Moon, the film is burdened with an
unsatisfactory script about a commander that
goes crazy and tries to sabotage a Mars mission.

Worse, the ambitious special effects are some of
the first to garner jeers for their lack of realism.

The box office failure of *Conquest of Space*
popped the balloon of the science fiction craze,
at least as far as expensive productions were
concerned. Previously, name actors had little to
gain from starring in a sci-fi thriller, but from
here on it was more often than not a career kiss
of death.

> The 1980s. Spacemen assemble a moon rocket
> in Earth orbit, wondering why its landing craft
> needs wings. A handpicked crew lives on a diet
> of pills while other space station personnel get
> steak and turkey. Dr. Fenton (William Hopper)
> arrives with the news that the mission target is
> Mars, not the Moon. One astronaut has already
> washed out due to space sickness. The willful
> commander General Merritt (Walter Brooke)
> denies that he also suffers from nervous fatigue
> and bulls ahead to command the mission, ac-
> companied by his reluctant son Captain Barney
> Merritt (Eric Fleming). The flight proceeds as
> planned with only one hitch: General Merritt
> goes off his rocker with religious delusions, con-
> vinced that the blasphemous trip to Mars is tres-
> passing on God's domain.

George Pal was a sweet-natured and devout
man. Bible themes marked all of his previous
work, even his moralizing Puppetoons. It looks
as though Pal was steamrolled by studio pressure on *Conquest of Space*, mainly through the
plot hook of the commander's religious melt-
down en route to Mars. The final script is a hash
of bad writing and screwball ideas.

Outer space in *Conquest of Space* is colorful but
not very consistent. Hand-painted mattes on
the space wheel yield fluttering edges on of
parts of the station. The Paramount brass may
have kept a tight budgetary rein on Pal's effects
team, forcing them to accept composites that
needed one or two extra tries to succeed. The

optical experts do away with mattes where possible, resulting in transparent spacemen flying between shuttles and the wheel. The models appear to be built on a smallish scale. When the space station wobbles under a meteorite bombardment, it looks like a toy.

Not all of the film's science is good. A moon mission becomes a Mars mission as easily as pulling out a new set of maps, and some technological details are highly oversimplified. How does one cross a hundred yards of space with no tether and no means of propulsion? Just have someone give you a good push. How many astronauts would they lose that way? "Oops, sorry Fred!"

This is the first space movie I can think of that has no scenes on Earth, although I'm sure someone can point out a *Flash Gordon* serial that came before. A one-world international political body rules the planet. That's a far cry from the jingoistic militarism of the average sci-fi film, in which, as Pauline Kael once put it, spacemen race to the heavens with itchy trigger fingers on their ray guns.

The spacemen are a mix of altruistic scientists and guys you'd expect to find in a filling station, with a very *Destination Moon-* like Brooklyn bozo along for cheap laughs. Phil Foster is more lovable than his predecessor, but he's an awfully dumb type to take on a Mars mission.

The real joy killer is the movie's central conflict. Walter Brooke's mad space captain is a maverick unsuited for normal command, let alone this kind of hazardous undertaking. Merritt has bullied his son into becoming a space cadet; his only friend is a fanatical sergeant straight from a bad WW2 movie (Mickey Shaughnessy). Even before the launch Brooke is spouting freaky Bible babble, telling his crew that the abominable mission needs to be aborted. Nobody does anything about it. Here's one space odyssey that needs a HAL computer along to terminate

some life functions, for the greater good.

The lack of rational thought is best exhibited in a speech by a dedicated Japanese botanist (Benson Fong of *Our Man Flint*). The botanist offers an unsolicited, hair-brained apology for WW2: Pearl Harbor might not have been necessary if Japanese nutrition had been better and they'd been able to grow bigger and taller like occidentals. This speech never fails to make audiences gasp. Was the final author of *Conquest of Space* a precocious 6th grader? Amiable producer Pal never had much of a grip on complex issues, to the detriment of several otherwise honorable efforts: *When Worlds Collide, Atlantis, the Lost Continent, The Power*.

The space flight is standard stuff with some nice touches. The astronauts must evade a giant rolling asteroid similar to the lethal planetoid from *Gorath*. They jet out of the way in a dynamic maneuver copied by the later *Starship Troopers*. A meteorite zaps through poor Ross Martin like a sniper bullet, and his faceplate mists blood red. He's given a brief but eerie burial in space. At least the talented Martin makes it more than halfway through this picture; in *Colossus of New York* a truck crushes him in the very first scene!

The ship is obviously rolling through outer space on uneven rails, accompanied by spacey Van Cleave music trills. For some reason, Mars is incredibly dull. There's no sense of wonder or mystery about the landscape. Except for Benson Fong's efforts to get a seed to sprout, nothing much happens. I won't give away the plot, but a fight between the commander and his son is resolved with the sergeant bringing ridiculously unsubstantiated charges against Merritt junior. Events perk up for a last-minute Mars-quake and re-launch, but overall this is a slow 81 minutes. I can see 1955 space enthusiasts feeling oddly disappointed.

Interestingly, the only time the movie jumps to life is at a pre-launch dinner party that treats the spacemen to entertainment and personal messages from home. Phil Foster gets a testimonial from his steady girl (played by Joan Shawlee of *Some Like it Hot* and *The Apartment*) who is clearly two-timing him. Ross Martin's scientist hears from his mother in Germany. To entertain the boys, Rosemary Clooney performs a Harem musical number lifted from 1954's *Here Come the Girls*.

Actor Eric Fleming made *Queen of Outer Space* and retreated to TV's *Rawhide*, only to be overshadowed by his co-star Clint Eastwood. Walter Brooke stayed with character parts, to become famous twelve years later by saying the immortal word "Plastics!" to Dustin Hoffman in *The Graduate*.

Paramount's DVD of **Conquest of Space** is an excellent DVD presentation. It is properly formatted in an enhanced transfer that crops away a lot of dead space above and below, in the process eliminating some of the worst of the mattes. On television, I remember seeing whole parts of the space station blooped away on individual frames. The picture is a bit soft and grainy, but that may be a function of the effects work. No extras are included.

THIS ISLAND EARTH

Universal Reviewed: August 25, 2006
1955 / Color / 1:37 flat / 87 min.
Cinematography Clifford Stine. Art Direction Alexander Golitzen, Richard H. Riedel. Written by Franklin Coen, Edward G. O'Callaghan from a story by Raymond F. Jones. Produced by William Alland.
Directed by Joseph Newman

A core classic 1950s science fiction film with the decade's most poetic title, **This Island Earth** is the first interstellar space opera in color. Its story comes straight from the pulp magazines, and features a two-fisted scientist playboy hero who matches wits with extraterrestrials and sexy Faith Domergue. As with *Star Wars* twenty-two years later, we're lifted from the mundane cares of a complacent world into the middle of an interplanetary war.

The Technicolor production was a huge expense for Universal, which committed a sizeable budget to a story requiring elaborate props, costumes and wall-to-wall optical effects. It was the high point of William Alland's monster cycle and the cost may have soured the studio's commitment to science fiction: after *This Island Earth* fantastic subject matter at Universal began to taper off.

An inferior disc appeared in the first months of DVD and has become a collector's item. The feature had already suffered a humiliating roasting in the theatrical *Mystery Science Theater 3000* movie. Perhaps this disc will help restore *This Island Earth* to its deserved place near the top ranks of 50s sci-fi.

> Scientist, playboy and jet pilot Dr. Cal Meacham (Rex Reason) returns from the Pentagon to the Ryberg Lab in California to find an impressive invitation waiting for him, in a weird form: a catalog for advanced electronic hardware no one has ever heard of. Cal and his trusty sidekick Joe Wilson (Robert Nichols) order a kit for a strange piece of machinery. It proves to be a communication device called an Interociter. On its triangular screen appears Exeter (Jeff Morrow), a confident white haired executive with an unnaturally high forehead. Exeter reveals that Cal's assembly of the Interociter is a sort of an entry exam, and Cal is tempted by the promise of even more sophisticated technology – knowledge too advanced to have originated on Earth. A pilot-less DC-3 airplane arrives to spirit Cal to a secret research center. On the way Cal meets up with fellow invitee Dr. Ruth Adams (Faith Domergue), with whom he had a 'summer fling' a few seasons back. Only Ruth now denies that it ever happened.

By 1955 fantastic space movies were tapering off into more economical monster thrillers. The print ads for *This Island Earth* promised the heavens to sci-fi fans. Poster art displayed hordes of bug-brained mutated extraterrestrials, plus the added pulp thrill of warring space armadas clashing in the skies.

The dramatics are barely above the naïve level of 'space cadet' television fare. Cal Meachum is the kind of nuclear physicist that David MacLean of *Invaders from Mars* might idolize, a guy who knows his way around an alien do-it-yourself electronics project. Cal flies his own Air Force jet, hobnobs with 'the big boys' at the Pentagon (no Oppenheimer he) and goes in for quickie romances at summer seminars in Vermont. The wholly independent Cal determines his own agenda, even if it means ducking his official responsibilities to volunteer to be 'kidnapped' by the benevolently brainy Exeter. One of the film's genuinely warm touches is its sympathetic farewell to Cal's assistant Joe Wilson (Robert Nichols). Poor Joe watches his boss disappear, and has to walk away alone in the fog. Exciting space adventures with sexy partners are the exclusive domain of handsome heroes.

Once installed in Exeter's secret lab (in the state of Georgia!), Cal finds himself among a group of international scientists synthesizing new sources of atomic power. Incredibly trusting, Cal, Ruth and Steve Carlson go along with the mysterious mission until they decide that (duh) there's a lot about Exeter and his odd associates that they don't understand: Exeter and his creepy assistant Brack (Lance Fuller) both have similar "subtle" indentations in their foreheads ... [1]

Politically, the film is a silly mess, with America's top scientists foolishly lending their talents to what looks like a blatant foreign conspiracy to steal our top tech secrets – a "brain drain". The poetry kicks in when the scientists decide to escape. The space-age trappings catch up to the kiddie plot and Cal & Ruth are "hurtled into an adventure beyond the stars" to "challenge the unearthly furies of an outlaw planet gone mad". Exeter is revealed as a recruiting agent for his home world of Metaluna, which is desperate for outside technical assistance. Exeter's superiors are fighting a losing war with the planet Zahgon, whose dart-shaped siege spaceships are blasting Metaluna to bits. With Metaluna's 'ionization shield' about to give out, Exeter transports Cal and Ruth across the galaxy, to help formulate a last-ditch defense.

One effect in the space ship is particularly expressive. In the same way that the space soldiers in *Forbidden Planet* must be dematerialized while their ship slips into Hyperdrive, the passengers on Exeter's palatial spaceship must have their molecules reconfigured to exist in Metaluna's altered conditions. Entering narrow tubes, Cal and Ruth are electronically disintegrated and reconstructed before our eyes, almost like Claude Rains in *The Invisible Man*. The simple matte effect is a startling expression of science fiction's 'fear of the unknown": To exist in the unnatural future, we'll have to be transformed by our own technology.

The characters aren't very well defined, except perhaps for Jeff Morrow's Exeter, the Alien Without A Country who retains his ethics amid all the interplanetary double-crossing. Exeter is interesting because, unlike the faultless, clueless leads, his integrity is heavily compromised: Transporting Atomic Scientists across State Lines to Build Weapons of Mass Destruction? The split between high pulp art and artless dime store scripting hobbles *This Island Earth*, but its juvenile surface hides a fascinating interior.

Our Earth couple has barely arrived on Metaluna when the Zahgon missiles break through. We get the idea that Metaluna didn't properly prioritize planetary defense, and is now suffering annihilation at the hands of a barbaric enemy. We see no ordinary citizens in the ruins. "That was an educational complex," wails Exeter, letting all of us Earthly pacifists know that our right to higher thinking has been secured only through military vigilance. The sympathetic Exeter has no stomach for expedient brutality, and rebels when the sinister Monitor (Douglas Spencer) orders that Cal and Ruth be brainwashed.

The film is a visual knockout, using special effects that are state-of-the-art for 1955. The robot plane that serves as a modern version of a "ghost coach" and a cat that detects Neutrino Rays mix well with outrageous ideas such as an entire green hill revealed to be a hidden flying saucer, or an airplane captured in the belly of a gigantic spaceship. The planet Metaluna is encased in a crumbling outer shell dotted with 'Swiss cheese' craters. Zahgonian bombs have scarred this outside barrier. The planet's defensive force field is giving way to the constant bombardment.

This Island Earth has the distinction of being the first 50s sci-fi picture to be given a thorough genre analysis, courtesy of Raymond Durgnat in his 1967 book *Films and Feelings*. Alongside brilliant chapters on *Johnny Guitar* and *Psycho*, Durgnat breaks the space movie into its component themes, such as "Brains." Cal Meacham is smart, and is therefore an attractive, Brainy guy. The Metalunans have a 'Brain shortage' and therefore must enlist and even kidnap Brains. They're so 'Brainy' that their heads have apparently expanded. But too much Brain is not a good thing. The Metaluna Mutant has the biggest Brain of all, yet is an unintelligent monster.

Durgnat also sees the movie as an analogy for the Cold War: Earth scientists Meacham and Adams are caught between competing civilizations. To save themselves from the implacable Zahgonians the 'good' Metalunans must resort to morally reprehensible methods – kidnapping, mind control. But we're not at all certain that Metaluna represents "the good guys". The Monitor behaves like Hitler in his bunker, fighting a losing battle. For all we know, the Zahgonians may actually be avenging greater Metalunan war crimes. The implication is that

Earthlings need to shake free of isolationist complacency. We are just one island amid many others in space.

If the film's visuals are poetry, the dialogue is pulp junk. Cal's craziest line of stalwart Hero-speak reads as if it were inserted to assure church groups that Faith still rules the moral fabric of futurism: "Our true size is the size of our God." We really expect the entire cast – Exeter, The Monitor, and even the Mutant – to stare at each other in search of an explanation for Cal's bizarre remark. At the finale, Exeter under-reacts to the obliteration of his home planet with the trite 'feel good' observation that the resulting atomic fire may provide sunshine for 'some other world.' That sounds similar to the Fascist sentiment that the best use for 'unfortunate races' is to become the fertilizer for a more deserving society.

This Island Earth's benchmark for quality space opera stood for only one year, until the debut of MGM's *Forbidden Planet*. Universal's special effects have a gaudy Technicolor sheen yet lack depth and detail. The flying saucer model actually looks smaller than it is, while too much of Metaluna is created through matte paintings with faulty perspectives. Just the same, the general look of Metaluna comes closer to the pulp-novel ethos than any other 50s sci-fi film. NASA's real rockets would soon make this romantic view of outer space obsolete.

The movie was almost too big a project for Universal-International, which had just finished spending a small fortune on rubber suits for its *Creature* monster and wasn't interested in repeating the experience. Both the Metaluna Mutant and the upcoming *Mole People* wear substantial clothing to simplify their design. The studio had no intention to make expensive effects pictures an ongoing habit. [2]

Some sources state that the film was shot in 3-Strip Technicolor, which author/researcher Robert Skotak confirms is partly true. Live action without effects was done 3-Strip but material needing optical effects was not. Behind-the-scenes stills show ordinary Mitchell cameras being used on the special effects stage. Technicolor printing made possible some jarringly gaudy effects, as when Neutrino ray explosions are rendered in contrasting primary colors.

Universal's DVD of *This Island Earth* is a welcome release for fans of 50s science fiction. Until *Star Wars* came along, this space fantasy and *Forbidden Planet* had no rivals. For those of us who remember 35mm Technicolor prints no video transfer is going to compare, but this rather grainy and flat encoding is not the wonderful restoration we hoped for. The flat transfer makes the Metalunan interiors look unnecessarily empty.

The only extra is the hysteria-driven trailer that shouts "2 & 1/2 YEARS IN THE MAKING!" That's a shame, because *This Island Earth's* imaginative ad campaign boasted several exciting and colorful poster concepts.

1. *This Island Earth* is the key example of a production with insufficient coordination between the director/writing team and the effects/design team. The script and dialogue mention 'subtle' differences in the head shape of the Metalunan characters. Yet their foreheads are almost laughably exaggerated, like the Coneheads from *Saturday Night Live*. With Exeter and Brack obvious aliens from the get-go, Cal, Ruth and Steve look foolish discussing their vague suspicions.

2. The go-to authority on all things *This Island Earth* is author and effects man Robert Skotak, a heavy contributor to a highly collectible 1989 *Universal Filmscripts* Series publication on the film. Robert's research into classic 50s science fiction movies is unequalled. Skotak reports that a more credible brownish appearance for the Mutant was scuttled in favor of a candy-colored blue-and-red. No wonder that the Metaluna Mutant looks twice as impressive in B&W stills; one would think a kindergarten class was in charge of his final colors. Not fully integrated into the script (Skotak says that the writers resisted its inclusion), the Mutant remains the film's most memorable visual.

WALT DISNEY IN SPACE AND BEYOND

Walt Disney Treasures: Tomorrowland
Disney Reviewed: May 13, 2004

1955 / B&W & Color / 1:37 flat full frame / 4 hours

This collection of Tomorrowland- themed television programs contains **Man in Space**, **Man and the Moon** and **Mars and Beyond,** Walt Disney's trilogy of edu-tainment shows that charted a course for the following decade's space program. The 1955 and 1959 broadcasts of the trilogy were as important to the development of filmed science fiction as any feature release. Although the initial broadcast was in B&W, Disney filmed them in expensive color – demonstrating the showman's faith in his work.

Disc host Leonard Maltin provides necessary context and exposition to enable viewers to appreciate the effort and genius that went into these shows, produced when Disney was more than a little preoccupied with the debut of his Disneyland theme park. Writer and animation director Ward Kimball directs and hosts the programs, which feature a mix of interviews, graphics, animation, photography and even a live-action space sequence. The special effects on view are better than similar work in George Pal's *Conquest of Space* made the same year.

NASA did not yet exist in 1955. Chesley Bonestell's space art coffee table books were popular but I credit this landmark TV trilogy with convincing America that space travel was really going to happen. The only obvious objection was money – the show proposes hardware and rockets that would easily cost more than what the country was worth. Yet, when John F. Kennedy launched his Moon program five years later America was primed for the adventure. Disney's seal of approval had a lot to do with it.

Director Kimball uses the "infotainment" formula that worked so well in his *Victory Through Air Power*. Each show opens with a light comedic segment providing background information. Breezy animated gags explain man's ancient curiosity for the stars and our popular romantic notions regarding the moon. The last show has fun with our fascination with pulp fantasy visions of Mars and space. A hilarious riff on "the typical space monster story" satirizes the sci-fi genre with the wit and accuracy of a *Mad* magazine layout.

Animation fans will be intrigued by the variety of styles employed. The look of the artwork changes with every new subject. The writing, visual invention and communication skill are at the highest level of sophistication.

After the comedy section, *Man in Space* teaches the space travel basics required to get a man into orbit. The concepts of escape velocity, multi- staged rockets and orbits are presented using animated lecture boards and beautiful conceptual drawings. Just as in *The Right Stuff*, America's space race brain trust is all German. It's amusing to see and hear Deutschland's best, Werner von Braun, Willy Ley etc., explaining theories for us just as they must have done for the Nazi command fifteen years earlier. [1]

The U.S. Army didn't transplant them to New Mexico for nothing – these guys know their stuff. Their accents and origin go unmentioned even when a clip from Fritz Lang's 1929 *Woman in the Moon* demonstrates that they have been popularizing their space dreams for decades.

Disney's space launch is depicted with beautiful conceptual animation. The daring design of the giant-finned rockets (immortalized in styrene model kits, 1955's new hobby rage) and the details of the orbiting mission are a good match for what we saw later with the Apollo program. The engineering of a space station differs from how we're doing it now, but the visuals of worker-bee space suits buzzing around assembling the orbiting wheel are fascinating. Placing nuclear reactors in orbit is taken as a routine idea. We haven't been told much about that in real life because there's an associated risk of poisoning the entire planet. Tsk, tsk, details.

After a whimsical look at mankind's love affair with the moon, with examples from Baron Munchausen to kid's nursery rhymes, *Man and the Moon* settles in for the main course, the construction in orbit of a lunar spacecraft. Here the show switches to live-action sets, actors and special effects. The crew is young, white and appropriately bland. The commander (Frank Gerstle) looks like Sergeant Rock, reinforcing the Cold War notion that any bold quest needs a military man in command.

The spaceship set and spacesuits are exceptionally good, and the color visual effects are much better than those in the George Pal movie. Exterior shots use automated animation similar to the motion control of twenty years later. Unlike *Conquest of Space* there are no traveling mattes. [2]

Passing over the dark side of the moon, the astronauts fire flares to see the landscape below. A final flash reveals a hidden alien base as postulated in the later fantasy *The Mysterians*. This odd dash of fantastic provocation goes unexplained, teasing the audience with the idea that the ultimate goal of this obsession with hardware is the search for life in space.

The final episode *Mars and Beyond* moves from the fantastic dreams of the past to wild speculations of life elsewhere in our solar system. A date isn't specified but we now have atomic spaceships that look like colossal parasols. A string of six of them heads off to Mars, cueing the deep-think boys to come up with wonderful visualizations of abstract scientific concepts.

The episode begins with a star field backed by a "heavenly" score reminiscent of the opening of *Invaders from Mars*. We're offered possible ways living things could have adapted to the hostile conditions on other planets. Every animation trick in the book is employed, until Mars is overgrown with monstrous vegetation more frightening than anything in the sci-fi pulps. When the text postulates crystal creatures based on silicon instead of carbon, we see visuals identical to those in *The Andromeda Strain*, made sixteen years later.

The show also examines the possibility that man might reach his mental and physical limits in the disorienting void of space. How does one cope with conceptual vertigo when every direction is "down" into a black nothingness that goes on into infinity?

Disney's filmmakers undersand what the science fiction craze is all about. The show nails the sense of wonder, pulp monster fun and the youthful fascination with technology. Then it transcends itself with visions of man's place in the universe. *Mars and Beyond* takes us into a cold scientific future that promises the eventual unlocking of all the mysteries of the cosmos – without one mention of God or religion. That's pretty risky stuff for the middle 1950s.

Disney In Space has yet to be discussed in critical examinations of the science fiction film genre, yet it appears to be one of its most important milestones. When space travel became the property of nonfiction news shows and newspaper headlines the majority of sci-fi movies retreated to juvenile fantasy.

Disc Two of the **Tomorrowland** Tin shows Disney's 'vision' adapting to corporate needs. Also made for TV, *Eyes in Outer Space* and *Our Friend the Atom* reveal a new condescending attitude to the public. There's nothing malign about touting the promise of the atom in 1955. That it didn't deliver an endless supply of clean energy or usher the world into a new era of peace and security is not Disney's fault. However, the Genie out of the Bottle imagery swiped from *The Thief of Bagdad* makes it seem as though Disney has decided to lecture us with the same methods designed to reach kindergartners.

Between then and roughly 1966, when we see Walt demonstrating his Epcot plans, something went wrong with Disney's Tomorrowland ideas. The proposed Utopia of Epcot seems as unlivable as the porcelain towers in the 1936 *Things to Come*. People movers and monorails are fine (if you're not handicapped), but the regimentation of our lives into an orderly ant-hill of proscribed motions is no more attractive than the model's antiseptic-looking residential areas. The basic living structure is a single-family mansion and there aren't very many of them. Will we be a wealthy, educated and birth-controlled happy hive of obedient citizens? Or is Disney proposing that those structures closer

to the center of town (away from the green-belt gardens) are the living quarters for a working underclass?

One look at the Epcot plans and my father re-iterated the old saw that Kubla Khan made the perfect city but forgot to create the perfect people to live in them. Nobody's yet conceived of a societal structure that didn't rely on poor labor forced to work for its survival. Our cities are an organized chaos of petty disputes and nagging inequities, but at least they're a living adventure. We don't wake up in the morning to be moved about like Hostess Twinkies on a *Koyaanisqatsi* conveyor belt.

The guest interview section bears this out. Author Ray Bradbury praises Walt but has lost his optimism for endless futures of improvement. It's a far cry from his speech to my High School in 1968 when he said that world peace would prevail when consumer realities conquer Red China and Chairman Mao can't find a parking space. Chief Imagineer Marty Sklar has fascinating insights into the social engineering ideas that began with the designs for Disneyland. But what sneaks into the stew is the domination of a little thing called "corporate sponsorship". Disney designed key installations for corporate sponsors at the 1964 World's Fair, some of which were later relocated to the Anaheim park. The vapid "It's a Small World" ride still draws crowds.

In the Space shows and other earlier docu-essays, Disney's storytelling had always used cartoons and humor to secure audience attention for the serious content. The empty "It's a Small World" has no serious content and no message beyond Hallmark card drivel. The world is a bloody slaughterhouse of political, racial and religious terror? Give them dancing dolls of peace singing a dippy song.

The old docus occasionally simplified concepts but the "Carousel of Progress" exhibit briefly shown in Sklar's interview scrupulously avoided explaining anything, as if doing so were a waste of time. The exhibit insinuated that our future is the exclusive domain of benevolent corporations. The Carousel explained the world thusly: 1) The household appliances in grandma's house were cute and funny. They must have laughed all the time! Look at the funny dog! 2) Yes, our present power utilities are far too vast and complicated for us, your corporate masters, to explain to you right now. Just keep paying your bills and stop asking questions. 3) The future is all rosy and you'll be warm and snug in your beds. Just don't put any restraint on our schemes to control the world and every facet of your insignificant lives. We'll make sure that you get plenty of sports, fast food and wholesome Disney entertainment.

I learned nothing from the insultingly patronizing Carousel except that a paternalistic corporation wanted me to be passive and leave technology to "those who knew better." [3]

That's the real drama played out in the second half of the Tomorrowland Tin – the dreams of a fantastic future soaring into corporate feudalism. Medical cures, public safety and who eats and who starves are now determined by the national interest, as defined by and for big corporations. Disney's pioneering vision was watered down to satisfy the aims and public images of its corporate sponsors. All we're left with is nostalgia for the days of bold space exploration in silvery rocket ships.

Disney's **Walt Disney Treaures: Tomorrowland – Disney in Space and Beyond** set is a thing of beauty. The contents are in tip-top shape. Only the title and credit sequences of the three space shows are in B&W; the rest of the material is in perfectly preserved color. The disc includes a limited selection of behind-the-scenes stills, art conceptualizations, storyboards, etc. The set doesn't end on the strongest of notes – Disc one

is fabulous and Disc 2 not as dazzling – but *Disney in Space* is essential viewing.

1. Gary Teetzel pointed out that Willy Ley's voice seems to have been completely dubbed by Paul Frees with a convincing German accent.

2. The "adventures" in flight are almost identical to those encountered in *Destination Moon*. The repair of the meteorite impact with a convenient plug is pretty amusing; the routine fix makes a great comparison with the do-or-die crisis management and techno-panic of *Apollo 13*.

3. I think the perceived malice in my attitude toward *It's a Small World* and *The Carousel of Progress* stemmed from the fact that my graduating class faced being drafted and sent to Vietnam. We still wanted to believe in Uncle Walt but his park responded to the crazy world with silly singing dolls and patronizing messages from big companies. After the inspired satire of *The President's Analyst*, the Disney way of communication with a smile now seemed an insult, a tool to encourage conformity.

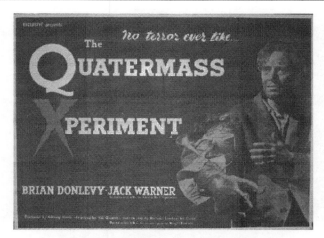

THE QUATERMASS XPERIMENT

MGM Reviewed: 2007
1955 / B&W / 1:37 flat / 82 min.
Cinematography Walter Harvey. Music James Bernard. Makeup Phil Leakey. Written by Richard Landau, Val Guest from a teleplay by Nigel Kneale. Produced by Anthony Hinds. Directed by Val Guest

The Quatermass Xperiment holds a high roost in filmed sci-fi; as England's first 50s success in the genre it enabled its maker Hammer Films to get a leg up in the industry. Adapted from Nigel Kneale's sensationally popular 1953 television serial, the space thriller unfolds as a deceptively ordinary police mystery. Writer Nigel Kneale's very different kind of invasion from beyond involves not an alien armada but a biological contamination. If a ship from the tropics can transport a deadly virus back to Europe, why can't a rocket mission unknowingly carry some unimaginable contagion back from outer space?

Hammer helped their thriller become a smash hit in England by incorporating the adults-only 'Certificate X' rating into its title. As the popular Quatermass character meant nothing to American audiences, United Artists imported the film under the unsavory title *The Creeping Unknown*. Under either title, its story concept is probably the most imitated in filmed science fiction.

Professor Bernard Quatermass (Brian Donlevy) rushes to the crash site of his first manned rocket. When the cockpit is opened only astronaut Victor Carroon (Richard Wordsworth) stumbles out; the others are missing even though they could not possibly have left the ship. Victor is in a sickly trance and is unable to speak. Carroon's tissues are undergoing disturbing changes. Convinced that the rude Quatermass is holding her husband for his own interests, Judith Carroon (Margia Dean) bribes a private detective to help the now deranged astronaut escape into the streets. Briscoe and Quatermass make a chilling discovery: an unknown living entity entered the spaceship in flight, consumed the other two astronauts and took up residence in Carroon's body. Victor is now absorbing other organisms (a cactus plant, zoo animals, unlucky humans) for raw materials. By the time Quatermass corners Carroon in Westminster Abbey, the astronaut has become a jellyfish-like mass of protoplasm.

The Quatermass Xperiment is superior to comparable inexpensive monster thrillers of its day because its creature is much more than a man in a scary costume. The film personifies primal fears of personal decay and disease in the pitiful astronaut played by the gaunt, suffering Richard Wordsworth. As sympathetic as Frankenstein's monster, Victor Carroon has a Karloff-like encounter with a small girl played by Jane Asher, a future Paul McCartney girlfriend and accomplished actress (*Alfie*). The alien creature grows inside the pathetic Carroon and rearranges his internal structure. Compelled to jam his hand into a cactus plant, Carroon is soon walking around with an arm and fist bloated into a twisted, thorned growth. By the time he's killing zoo animals, we see only his eye, and hear him dragging his bulk along the ground.

Writer-director Val Guest distills Kneale's multipart teleplay into eighty suspenseful minutes. Kneale objected to his kindly Quatermass character being given to the American actor Brian Donlevy, who plays the scientist as bull-headed and belligerent. Quatermass is continually shouting people down as he blurts out new bits of exposition. Project assistant Marsh (Maurice Kaufmann) recovers an automatic camera from the spaceship cockpit, allowing the investigators to see glimpses of what happened out in space. But when Carroon escapes Quatermass has no choice but to help Scotland Yard's Inspecor Lomax (Jack Warner) track him down.

Carroon's transformation into a mollusk-like creature presents a sticky extermination problem while introducing new ideas to the science fiction film. The first men into space have given an undesirable alien entity an opportunity to explore *us.* What would previously be explained as demonic possession is now parasitic possession. *The Quatermass Xperiment* dispenses completely with the notion that the unknown is God's domain, and that scientists are trespassers. Carroon and his crew are aware that their lives are at risk, and the failure of Quatermass's first space rocket only makes him more determined to try it again. The Professor wastes no time mourning; the next rocket is waiting to launch.

Val Guest gives his film a documentary flavor; the low budget shows when a nighttime dragnet scene incorporates stock shots from an earlier film. A country fire brigade arrives to cool the crash-landed rocket, which sticks out of the ground like a dart. In London, Carroon makes contact with various working-folk, including Thora Hird's alcoholic street lady. A laboratory sample of the space creature is an amoeba-like thing that attempts to consume some test mice. But until the climax, all we see of Carroon's final form are snail-like slime trails on cobblestone streets.

Hammer Films acquired all three BBC Quatermass serials and followed up quickly with the best film adaptation, *Quatermass 2.* The third installment was delayed by seven years while the studio pursued gothic horror subjects. Packed with imaginative ideas, Nigel Kneale's Quatermass trilogy is now considered a high point of British science fiction filmmaking.

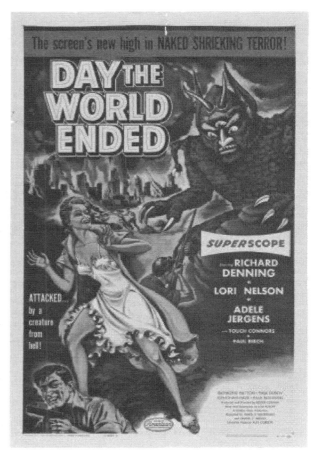

DAY THE WORLD ENDED

Lionsgate Reviewed May 2, 2006
1955 / B&W / 2:1 flat letterbox / 79 min.
Cinematography Jock Feindel. Mutant Costume Paul Blaisdell. Original Music Ronald Stein. Written by Lou Rusoff. Produced by Roger Corman, Alex Gordon.
Directed by Roger Corman.

This Roger Corman and Alex Gordon production was made when the American-International Company was still called American Releasing Corp. After teaching himself to direct in four quickie westerns, Roger doubled back to the science fiction subject matter of the micro-budgeted Lippert release *Monster from the Ocean Floor,* his first success. By 1955 the only substantial post-apocalyptic film was still Columbia's grim and prophetic *Five.* Lou Rusoff's rushed script for

Day the World Ended reads like *Key Largo* with nuclear fallout, sprinkled with a dash of quasi-Biblical fantasy. The science in this quickie is bogus and the dramatics are crude, but its storyline is unbreakable.

It is Total Destruction Day plus one. Survivalist Jim Maddison (Paul Birch) and his virginal daughter Louise (Lori Nelson of *Revenge of the Creature*) are safe because his house is in a canyon surrounded by lead ore, where the "winds will keep the radioactive fallout away." Jim has provisions for three but Louise's fiancé has apparently perished with the rest of the world. Jim grudgingly admits several more survivors: handsome young geologist Rick (Richard Denning), gangster Tony Lamont and his stripper girlfriend Ruby (Mike "Touch" Connors & Adele Jergens), prospector Pete and his donkey Diablo (Raymond Hatton and a donkey) and the mentally unbalanced Radek (Paul Dubov). All are healthy except for Radek, who mumbles about eating red meat and dismisses his severe radiation burns as no bother. Tough-guy Tony makes a play for Louise while Jim and Rick concern themselves with the problem of nuclear mutations – Radek's skin seems to be getting scaly. With the food running out and tempers running short, everyone is in danger. Louise keeps hearing high frequency noises that nobody else hears ... sounds that seem to be coming from the deadly wasteland outside the protected canyon.

Day the World Ended is a natural for penny-pinching Roger Corman. A home in the Hollywood Hills serves as Jim's survivalist hideaway and a large pond at the Sportsman's Lodge in Studio City is used for the swimming scenes. The rest of the movie is filmed in the good old Bronson Caverns quarry, a Griffith Park location that must have been busy every day of the week in the 1950s. Watch carefully and you'll see the hikers pass a crooked tree branch over a path that sees similar duty in Don Siegel's *Invasion of the Body Snatchers*. Add one interior set and you've got an instant Corman quickie.

The script is a paranoid stew of faulty science. Radioactive fallout will disperse anywhere a breeze blows, invalidating the nonsense about a protected canyon. Rusoff's visually effective smoke clouds outside the canyon aren't scientific either. The script implies that atom scientists are withholding the information that atomic test animals suffered grotesque mutations, forgetting that a mutation by definition happens to the *offspring* of an irradiated creature.

But Rusoff and Corman's atomic nonsense makes good poetic sense. Irradiated bodies grow scales to fend off more radiation, neatly motivating the monster transformations. The mutants also turn cannibalistic and savage, giving us the idea that WW3 will split humanity into separate Jekyll & Hyde species along the Darwinian lines introduced by H.G. Wells in *The Time Machine*. Corman's mutant also resembles a horned devil, conjuring a vision of a Hell on Earth to match the film's Biblical references. [1]

The players are stock but also professional. Richard Denning seems ready to take on any role that gives him star billing. Lori Nelson is cute and concerned and Touch Connors can snarl on cue. All must have gotten their roles by proving to Corman that he'd never suffer a ruined take due to a blown line. Beautiful Adele Jergens, a statuesque Virginia Mayo type, has the most fun as a gun moll with a heart. She's amusing even when faking her exotic dance routines. Corman wisely resisted the temptation to make Ruby beg for a drink, like Claire Trevor in *Key Largo*: bottles and drinks would mean more props and more continuity worries. Although much of the film plays on a strictly cornball level – no actorly introspection or nuances – everyone is singing in the same key.

The mutant monster is the first of Paul Blaisdell's full body suit creations and although it has earned a nostalgic place in our hearts, it's pretty tacky both in design and execution.

The face is crude and the horns are as rubbery as the crumbly-foam skin; Blaisdell's skinny shoulders are obviously enhanced by football pads to lend the creature an imposing build. A second set of vestigial clawed arms sprout from its shoulders, like epaulets. "Marty" the mutant must carry Lori Nelson in some shots, a task that must have been a real strain on Blaisdell.

(spoiler) The story resolves on Biblical terms when a purifying rainfall washes away the Atomic Sin. It's pointless to insist that the rain would simply bring the irradiated dust in the air to the ground. This rain kills the mutants and cleans the Earth of all atomic residues, allowing the survivors to go forth like a new Adam and Eve. Corman inserts perhaps his first instance of directorial inspiration by fixating on a tell-tale snapshot of Louise with her lost fiancée. She takes one last look at the photo before leaving, and Corman dissolves to the dead mutant. Coupled with Louise's unexplained telepathy, the dissolve tells us beyond a doubt that the mutant was Louise's fiancée.

Day the World Ended shows Corman becoming a more relaxed director. He may be unwilling to slow down long enough to finesse his visuals, but he at least sets his angles up with an eye for relationships. The modest success of this programmer led Corman to churn out a number of cheap but intriguing sci-fi thrillers in fast succession.

Lionsgate's *Samuel Z. Arkoff Collection Cult Classics* presentation of **Day the World Ended** is a sticky evaluation subject. *Day* is a SuperScope release and the transfer provided is the flat-letterboxed version shown on AMC in 1998 or so. Lionsgate may not be the company to blame, at least not directly. I've been told that the Arkoff Collection was peddled to more than one home video distributor and rejected for transfer quality. It appears that the present copyright holders have little interest in the legacy represented

by the films and prefer to cash in with the minimum necessary investment.

1. The idea of creatures becoming immune to radiation, like fakirs "acclimating" themselves to poisons, crops up again in Joseph Losey's thoughtful Ban-the-Bomb apocalyptic fantasy *These Are the Damned (The Damned)*.

TARANTULA

Universal Reviewed September 22, 2006
1955. / 1:33 flat / 80 min.
Cinematography George Robinson. Special
effects David S. Horsley. Written by Jack
Arnold, Robert M. Fresco, Martin Berkeley.
Produced by William Alland.
Directed by Jack Arnold.

Universal entered the Big Bug business when William Alland lifted the premise of Warners' giant hit *Them!* and placed it in a budget version of the desert town from *It Came from Outer Space*. Thus was launched a hundred film-school treatises extolling the Arnoldian Desert Motif. Yet *Tarantula* works up its own broth of monster thrills and strange poetic effects. While the human characters exchange small talk a colossal black arachnid stalks the wide-open desert spaces. As big as a mountain, it nevertheless escapes detection while snacking on various peripheral characters in approved monster-on-the-loose fashion.

> Professor Gerald Deemer (Leo G. Carroll) and his two associates have been toying with a radioactive growth-inducing serum because in twenty years (= 1975) overpopulation will bring about epidemics of starvation. Through a regrettable sequence of events, all three researchers receive injections, resulting in disfigurement and eventual death. Deemer's new assistant Stephanie 'Steve' Clayton (Mara Corday) arrives to find Deemer's lab in disarray. She and the town doctor Matt Hastings (John Agar) discover that a test spider has escaped from the lab and grown to gargantuan proportions. It's roaming the countryside devouring horses, truckloads of beef and the truck drivers as well.

Tarantula subscribes to the can't-miss formula for 50s monster entertainment: make sure your monster is bigger than last year's. Led by optical whiz David S. Horsley, the Universal effects department puts a lot of effort into forty or so angles showing the giant spider striding down highways, knocking over power lines and sneaking up on unlucky motorists. As with the previous year's giant ants, the outsized crawling bug is accompanied by a loud signature noise that sounds like sizzling bacon. Unlike the ants, the only practical full-scale part of the spider we see is one hairy fang that smashes through a roof.

Gigantism in movies is hard to pull off. The design geniuses behind *Metropolis* and *King Kong* knew how to cheat the scale of our perceptions to make things LOOK REALLY BIG, a skill unknown to the makers of *Beginning of the End* and *The Giant Gila Monster*. Here the Universal optical department succeeds most of the time. The monster shots were done by shooting various spiders high-speed (to get the slow motion) and in deep-focus. White plaster miniature landscapes were shaped to conform to the contours of the real desert in the live-action footage. When carefully matted into the picture the spider seems to 'fit' the hills and rocks, and even throws a shadow. The sight of the spider stepping over an outcropping two or three miles away is undeniably impressive. With one telltale leg silently peeking over the horizon, he makes a wonderfully subtle entrance creeping up behind a pair of friendly prospectors.

Perspective issues remain, as the hairy arachnid has a tendency to appear a mile across in the far background, only to shrink to a hundred feet or so when he reaches the foreground. Since the performing spiders could only be guided with jets of air, Horsley's camera team must have burned up a lot of film to get useable footage, and been grateful whenever an angle matched up at all. It looks as though they weren't allowed to finesse the shots, as several show the spider's legs disappearing into mattes that cut across the sky. In a few others, parts of the spider are transparent.

But the effect can be stunning. One pre-dawn moment places Universal's ubiquitous Southern mansion on the right side of the screen, with a real desert landscape dominating the left. Off in the distance we can see the tarantula advancing this-a-way, an "Arizona Highways" calendar gone surreal. It seems to be crawling into our reality from another dimension. He's a horrifying menace, but still so far away that it's much too soon to panic. I have nightmares like this.

In its best entrance, the spider suddenly reveals itself to the cast as they stand by their cars on stretch of desert road. It charges up over the crest of a hill and then freezes, as if holding still to evaluate its new dining opportunity. Then it resumes its machine-like crawl, accompanied by Henry Mancini's menace music, recycled from *This Island Earth.* [1]

Lovely Mara Corday has the task of looking concerned while pretending to be a top research assistant in designer clothes. It's neither her nor John Agar's fault that the script keeps them way behind the story curve, always asking questions when the audience already knows the answers. Agar's scripted reveries about the desert may be based on Richard Carlson's speeches from *It Came from Outer Space*, but he hasn't the chops to deliver them. Leo G. Carroll does well with his sad tale of mix-ups in the lab, although we never understand exactly why these scientists would consider taking a drug that makes bunnies and hamsters into 'sizeable beasts'. Haven't they seen *King Size Canary*, the Tex Avery cartoon? Speaking of which, Carroll's elaborate, Quasimodo-eyed makeup makes him into a dead ringer for Avery's Droopy Dog character.

Tarantula collapses into hilarity at least once, when the giant spider (partially in its poorly-matched puppet version, the one seen on the poster) imitates King Kong by peeking through a convenient giant-size window into Mara Corday's dressing room. She strolls to and fro (and even looks in a mirror) but never notices a fif-

teen-foot monster eyeball ogling her only a few feet away. When the spider subsequently climbs on top of the house and proceeds to batter it to pieces, it really appears to be, uh, aroused. The filmmakers had to be aware of this association; it must have been screamingly funny in 1955 drive-ins.

Clint Eastwood (or at least his voice and eyes) is the pilot guiding the Napalm strike that turns the spider into a big fireball. *Tarantula* has always been a guilty favorite of giant monster fans, and fits in there right behind the top ten or so sci-fi offerings of the 1950s.

Tarantula's flat transfer crops perfectly on a 16:9 television, removing large areas of compositionally dead space above and below the action. I wish Universal had seen fit to go to the extra trouble of enhanced widescreen. The only extra is a beat-up trailer.

1. The 'charge in and freeze' entrance seems to have inspired the third *Lord of the Rings* movie when the spider monster Shelob suddenly appears from a mountainside cave. Cartoonist Gahan Wilson captured *Tarantula's* surreal gigantism effect in a Playboy cartoon around 1967. Two guys at a tiny highway burger shack stare at the dark hills far away. One of the hills is really a toad-like monster with two gigantic eyes, and it looks like it's crawling their way. Realizing that the shack's neon sign reads "EAT", one customer says, "Good God – do you think it can READ?"

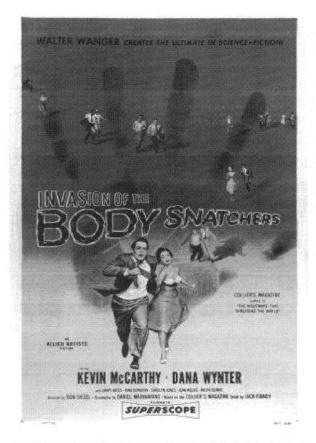

indistinguishable from normal people. The identity-theft idea from John W. Campbell Jr.'s *Who Goes There?* at last finds its full expression.

> Several patients of Dr. Miles Bennell (Kevin McCarthy) report that their relatives are impostors, or 'not themselves'. In each case the delusion passes quickly, but the deeper suspicions of Miles and his friend Becky Driscoll (Dana Wynter) are confirmed when writer Jack Belicec (King Donovan) discovers a 'blank' body slowly taking on Jack's physical characteristics. A fantastic biological conspiracy has seized the town: seedpods from outer space are replacing human beings with passive duplicates, simulacra devoid of emotion. Local farmers are growing more pods to spread the menace to other communities. Realizing that the local authorities have been taken over, the couple has no choice but to flee for their lives.

While fifties science fiction visualized Cold War anxieties as giant monsters and mechanized invasions from space, *films noir* made do with a more insidious post-nuclear disquiet. The alienation becomes complete in *Kiss Me Deadly* when thieves and detectives foolishly treat a powerful atomic device as they would any contraband for barter. But the most paranoid fifties film is *Invasion of the Body Snatchers*. In place of a corrupt noir underworld *Invasion* fashions a political allegory about infiltration and possession: exposure to dangerous ideas will transform a person into the agent of a conformist alien ideology. The conspiracy spreads through the sleepy town of Santa Mira until the Pod contagion is disseminated at open street rallies. Duplicated lawmen forcibly arrest citizens in broad daylight so they can be replicated and replaced by the sinister pods. The normal population is slowly displaced by unfeeling pod people, new additions to a vast conspiracy intent on eradicating humanity.

Behind the political threat is the traumatic personal fear of losing one's identity, one's human

INVASION OF THE BODY SNATCHERS

Republic Reviewed: July 26, 2007
1956 / B&W / 2:1 flat letterboxed / 83 min.
Cinematography Ellsworth Fredericks. Written by Daniel Mainwaring, Richard Collins (uncredited) based on a 1954 serial in *Collier's* magazine by Jack Finney. Produced by Walter Wanger
Directed by Son Siegel.

The inspired *Invasion of the Body Snatchers* reinvents the alien invasion plot as a paranoid fantasy, lifting filmed science fiction to a new level of sophistication. Because he's just a kid, David MacLean of *Invaders from Mars* has difficulty spreading the word about Martians. Jack Finney's chilling concept supposes that an alien invasion is underway, all around us, but it can't be stopped because the human victims – actually duplicated substitutes – are nearly essence. Miles and Becky become a hunted minority in a new order of conformity to a collective will. The 'traditional value' Miles fights to retain is his essential individuality. Trapped with a pod that will duplicate him if he falls asleep, Miles must listen while a pod version of his psychiatrist friend Dr. Danny Kaufmann (Larry Gates) tells him that love is a painful illusion, and that mankind will be better off without emotions.

Miles and Becky already know emotional displacement and disillusion from their own divorces. Replacement by a pod is the ultimate horror. Emotional bonds and family ties vanish; a pod's only loyalty is to its own kind. Miles observes an unnaturally tranquil family placing a fresh pod next to a baby's crib: after the duplication, there'll be 'no more tears'. Miles and Becky's fugitive struggle against the ideological/biological invasion forces them to bond much like the lovers of *Gun Crazy* or *They Live By Night*. But love is powerless against the totalitarian onslaught of the pods.

The political message behind *Invasion of the Body Snatchers'* alien conspiracy is teasingly ambiguous. Conservatives interpret the pods as placeholders for Communism, and the film stays consistent with the notion that Communism is an ideological disease. A healthy citizen inculcated with sick Marxist ideas, becomes a less-than-human Communist. Liberals can easily interpret *Invasion* as an allegory for what they perceive as the mindless conformity of the Eisenhower years. The conformist establishment cannot abide intellectual writers and non-conformist dissidents. The pods reduce humans to complacent ciphers that calmly abide by the will of the majority.

A brilliant piece of sustained suspense, *Invasion of the Body Snatchers* is perhaps the best job of direction by the talented Don Siegel. Siegel emphasizes a claustrophobic removal of options as the pods close in, until our lovers must hide in a broom closet and pray they won't be detected.

Key personnel have discounted the idea that dialogue director Sam Peckinpah rewrote the script by *noir* screenwriter Daniel Mainwaring (*Out of the Past*, *The Phenix City Story*). Mainwaring references the small-town ambience of Hitchcock's *Shadow of a Doubt* as a model for Santa Mira and establishes many 'givens' associated with subsequent conspiracy fantasies. Terrible secrets hide behind a veneer of normality. As officials and law officers are the first to be duplicated, our trust in authority is undermined. Even a telephone operator is an enemy pod person, blandly telling Miles that *all* of the phone lines are out of service. Trust and hope crumble as Miles and Becky find that their friends and loved ones are now enemy conspirators. It may already be too late to summon help from out of town.

Ellsworth Frederick's photographic style alternates between ordinary daylight and hallucinatory night scenes, as with the unnerving deep focus view of the fresh pod on Jack Belicec's pool table. King Donovan and a young Carolyn Jones provide excellent support as the Belicecs. The two couples discover the full horror of the pod duplication process while enjoying an old-fashioned backyard barbecue. Just a few feet away, obscene lumps of vegetable tissue are rapidly taking on their likenesses.

Don Siegel's first cut told the story straight and ended with a close-up of Miles Bennell shouting, "You're next!" followed by an abrupt cut to black. Allied Artists insisted that the ending be lightened, which delayed *Invasion* for several months. Producer Walter Wanger engaged Orson Welles to appear in bookend 'storytelling' segments but when filming time came couldn't locate the actor. To protect as much of his creation as possible, Don Siegel directed the added flashback bookends showing the frantic Miles Bennell being examined by doubting doctors. The new voiceovers actually enhance the mood of the film, but Siegel makes sure that the ending isn't too hopeful or reassuring. The pods still seem well on their way to victory.

Republic's DVD of *Invasion of the Body Snatchers* was one of the earliest DVD releases and is sorely in need of restoration and remastering. The non-enhanced letterboxed transfer is adequate for small monitors but falls apart on larger displays. The film was formatted in SuperScope, which used ordinary cameras and lenses, tightly cropping the top and bottom of the image to make a widescreen theatrical presentation. The flat transfer on the flip side pan-scans the existing widescreen rectangle, resulting in an effective image smaller than 16mm. It is quite possible that the film was hard-matted in the camera, leaving no extra image area above and below the SuperScope rectangle.

An attractive extra is a 1985 television interview with actor Kevin McCarthy conducted by TV personality Tom Hatten.

FORBIDDEN PLANET

Warners Blu-ray Reviewed: November 12, 2006
1956 / Color / 2:35 widescreen / 98 min.
Cinematography George J. Folsey. Production Design Irving Block. Art Direction Cedric Gibbons, Arthur Lonergan. Film Editor Ferris Webster. Electronic Tonalities Louis and Bebe Barron. Written by Cyril Hume, Irving Block, Allen Adler. Produced by Nicholas Nayfack. Directed by Fred McLeod Wilcox

Many 50s films set off with the germ of a good speculative idea, but 1956's *Forbidden Planet* may be the lone effort that embraces the genre's potential, backed by the *committed* production resources of a major studio. The futuristic science on view is more than an excuse for a monster; entire sequences are dedicated to the exploration of abstract, wondrous concepts. It is also perhaps the first "out of this world" film that really shows what special effects can accomplish when a sizeable budget is allocated. Other sci-fi tales limited their depictions of spaceships and strange environments to a few scenes, or even a few shots. *Forbidden Planet* is the first film to take place entirely within a fantastic futuristic world, all of which had to be conceived and constructed from the stage floor up.

Star cruiser C-57D returns to the planet Altair-4 to check up on the complement of the spaceship Bellerophon, an expedition that disappeared there ten years before. They find only Edward Morbius (Walter Pidgeon) and his daughter Altaira (Anne Francis), living alone with an amazing robot named Robby. Displeased by his host's insistence that they leave, Commander John Adams (Leslie Nielsen) presses for more information on the fate of the other Bellerophon colonists, and an explanation for Morbius' possession of scientific knowledge far in advance of Earth's. Morbius' secrecy and an awareness of a strange ghostlike presence on Altair-4 convince Adams that further investigation is required ... even when Morbius alludes to dire consequences.

Forbidden Planet was a gift to fans hungry for a *real* space opera, with all the trimmings: an engaging script, romance and a congenial robot butler named Robby to amuse space-crazy kids. The film's middling box office performance can only be chalked up to a miscalculation of the public's interest in the genre. By 1956 audiences had been burned by plenty of cheap pictures hiding behind attractive ad campaigns. Space pictures were out of the mainstream, something for teenagers. This epic did good business but not enough to justify its enormous cost: *Earth vs. the Flying Saucers* earned almost as much, but was made for relative peanuts.

All that means nothing in the long run, for *Forbidden Planet* has persisted as the wonder film of its time. Kids hungry for a glimpse of a

rocket or a neat special effect sat astonished at the film's surfeit of futuristic hardware. The previous year's *This Island Earth* seemed cheap by comparison, with its cartoonish Mutant and a spaceship interior that used glass bricks from the garden store. There's no waiting until Act 2 to see something unusual. A beautiful space cruiser glides through the frame in the very first shot, followed by one amazing visual after another: a planet turning in space, a glowing eclipse, a saucer landing in an eerie desert under a green sky. The characters are professional spacemen and not gawking civilians. And that's only the beginning of the wonders to be found on Altair-4.

Forbidden Planet's vision is like the Monsanto Kitchen of the Future, with a little sex. Anne Francis' virginal Altaira communes telepathically with a deer and a tiger, providing a thematic harmony with the mythological. Altaira's miniskirt and coquettish ignorance of 'space wolves' only makes her more attractive to the space troopers, who might as well be Yankee sailors in an unfamiliar port.

Allen Adler and Irving Block's story appealed to MGM's Dore Schary because it transcends space opera hardware. The back-story for the "Fatal Planet" still energizes the imagination. In the middle of the movie, the narrative stops dead still for what is essentially a fifteen-minute archeological rumination, an investigation of an extinct civilization. The ancient Krel are long gone but their technology lives on in the form of an amazing twenty-square mile power plant and machine complex that still functions under the surface of the planet. Morbius says that he's tapped a tiny portion of its knowledge, doubled his own brainpower and used it to 'cobble together' wonders like Robby.

(spoiler) The mystery of the *Forbidden Planet* is based on Freudian principles spelled out in the script as clearly as are Isaac Asimov's Laws of Robotics, the ethical 'prime directives' that govern Robby the Robot. Morbius reveals that the giant Krel machines were built to convert desires into physical realities *by thought alone*, without "instrumentalities." Each Krel citizen was set free of the physical limitations of their bodies, essentially becoming Demigods. The very human-seeming Krel didn't realize that they would be giving this power not only to their ethical conscious selves, but also to their unknown secret subconscious selves. Soon after the Krel activated their massive machine, they perished in an orgy of destruction and murder. Morbius has yet to realize that the secret of the Krel applies to him as well. When his fellow colonists disagreed with his 'enlightened' decisions, his subconscious manifested an Id Monster to destroy them.

That's deep-dish stuff for a 'fifties space opera partially aimed at kiddies, and it opens many channels of thought. First, the Krel machines resemble a modern computer on a vast scale. They link the entire planet and its inhabitants in a World Wide Web that goes beyond communication to *perform physical actions*. It's as if a 'flame' E-mail had the power to punch the recipient in the nose. If the Web suddenly projected our unexpressed malign thoughts into violent actions, the result would certainly resemble the Freudian holocaust described in *Forbidden Planet*.

Morbius is a dark character. His conscious mind has invented the benign Robby and built a beautiful oasis in the Altairian desert, but his elevated intelligence is mirrored by an unconscious sense of superiority and a lust for power. The Id is his Mr. Hyde, so to speak. The public Morbius honestly hopes that his visitors will leave before his paradise is disturbed. He's also a father engaged in a vague competition with his daughter's suitors. The expression "Nobody is good enough for my daughter" is easily interpreted as incestuous. In this case Morbius' subconscious wishes to keep defending its kin, even when that function is no longer wanted.

To take this one step further, *Forbidden Planet*

displays a refined version of the argument introduced in *The Thing from Another World*. Howard Hawks' film asserts that scientists live by cold rules of logic disconnected from faith and sentiment. Science itself is therefore anti-humanistic and not to be trusted. Pure science, *The Thing* teaches, is an ideology unto itself, an unholy cult. Hawks' film came out strongly in favor of the patriotic, aggressive soldiers and against Dr. Carrington, the pacifist & defeatist scientist.

Forbidden Planet's Morbius is a more refined Dr. Carrington, a liberal monster as defined by conservatives. He's an elitist convinced of the superiority of his viewpoint; other men are midgets by comparison. But Morbius is overblown with hubris. He's supremely intelligent, yet must have the lowdown about the Id and the 'primitive savage' explained to him by the relatively unintelligent (but socially conformist) Captain Adams. Only Adams brings up the subject of God and spirituality. Morbius is damned because his new intellect has him knocking on the door of God-hood, a religious taboo even when done for the most benign of reasons. Being Super-Smart feeds the Ego, which makes one disloyal to one's fellows (Adams even uses the word comrades) and thus untrustworthy. Dr. Morbius might be a reaction to Ayn Rand, an anti- Howard Roark. The common good requires the elimination of the occasional visionary egghead, as they tend to be wholly irresponsible.

The conclusion reaffirms the necessity of moral suppression. Inner demons must be held in check by laws and limits. The super-science of the Krel was BAD, and God-fearing humans have no use for it. Nobody cries when Altair-4 is eradicated by an atomic blast. The Production Code gets its pro-religious message out as well. In space, God can hear you pray.

Pauline Kael's *Forbidden Planet* review noted its clever adaptation of Shakespeare's *The Tempest* and also expressed her disappointment in the film's conception of a militaristic space-age future. Our brave spacemen tote ray guns; force is a first option. Outer space is an extension of the Wild West, where one anticipates violence and aggression in every encounter. Although *Forbidden Planet's* ideas run deep, its surface is firmly anchored in the middle of the Cold War.

Warners' Blu-ray of **Forbidden Planet** is spectacular. Color values are stable, as is the picture as a whole, and the greatly increased sharpness allows us a much better look at props, settings, and special effects. A couple of the shots of the C-57D circling Altair look better than their counterparts in the first *Star Wars* film... the magic of MGM's low-tech effects really jumps off the screen. The added resolution also allows us to scrutinize the faces of the crewmembers, even in the film's medium-wide shots. Now we can more easily pick out James Drury from *The Virginian* and Morgan Jones from Roger Corman's *Not of this Earth*.

We do wish some extra resources had been available to spot-clean a few scenes. We certainly wouldn't want an automatic program to soften the image as we've noticed in some Universal discs. But some manual anti-dot work would have helped the impressive scenes using mattes and opticals. Somebody did finally think to slightly enlarge the shots of Morbius' steel shutters closing, which have always betrayed flickering splice marks with every jump-cut panel banging into place.

The extras port over everything from the 2006 *Ultimate Collector's Edition*. They appear to be sourced in standard definition and of course encoded in HD on the single Blu-ray disc. A set of work print excerpts from the early Criterion disc originally came from a 16mm print sent to aid Louis and Bebe Barron in concocting their revolutionary synthetic soundscapes and 'electronic tonalities' score. A set of 'lost' scenes is just some effects outtakes, unaccountably transferred pan-scan -- or perhaps shot flat? "Lost Footage' doesn't seem an accurate description, but who's complaining?

The extras include material old and new. Walter Pidgeon interacts with Robby while plugging the film on an MGM TV show. A new interview docu rounds up a number of critics and interested parties such as Dennis Muren, Phil Tippet and the welcome Bill Warren to express why *Forbidden Planet* was the effects 'n' fantasy touchstone for their later ambitions. Anne Francis is there as well. The relatively lavish TCM docu *Watch the Skies!* presents similar sentiments from top 'student filmmaker' -era directors -- Steven Spielberg, George Lucas, John Carpenter, Ridley Scott and James Cameron -- and extends the field of investigation to the whole decade of 50s sci-fi. Another new featurette examines the design and construction of Robby the Robot, still the most popular and recognizable movie robot and far more practical than those *Star Wars* pretenders. Actually, none of them are capable of using an ordinary flight of stairs, that I can see.

Robby also makes an appearance in an entire episode of TV's *Thin Man*. A full second feature is the 1957 **The Invisible Boy**, in B&W and widescreen. Deserving of its own review, the film will strike viewers as a retreat to the level of typical 50s sci-fi, albeit with some fanciful touches. A scientist's mischievous son uses a super computer to make himself invisible and befriends a robot (Robby) that falls under evil influences, like the research robot tanks in Ivan Tors' GOG. Besides the expected robot rampage and army retaliation, the film shows the kid using his invisibility for some rather disturbingly naughty purposes ... like peeping into his parents' bedroom!

All that is missing from the fancy 2006 DVD set is that edition's colorful tin "lunchbox" case and the little Robby the Robot toy. But sci-fi fans that have never seen the impressive *Forbidden Planet* on a large screen should be impressed by its spectacular thrills.

WORLD WITHOUT END

Warners Reviewed: July 31, 2008
1956 / Color / 2:35 widescreen / 81 min.
Cinematography Ellsworth Fredericks,
Original Music Leith Stevens, Produced by
Richard V. Heermance.
Written and Directed by Edward Bernds.

World Without End is a real oddity. It was written and directed by Edward Bernds, who as the B-picture industry imploded fanned out into westerns, sci-fi teen exploitation and Three Stooges features. His movie begins as a space adventure but spends most of its time within skimpy Allied Artists sets and on location at Stony Point in the northwest San Fernando Valley. The 'exotic future society' on view isn't much different from lost kingdoms in adventure tales from the

Arabian Knights to Tarzan movies. The main theme is that we coddled Americans need to get tough and fight for our place in the sun. As an added thrill, Bernds' movie exploits the "space babe" formula of groaners like *Cat Women of the Moon*. His futuristic pin-ups look great in abbreviated outfits designed by none other than girlie art maestro Alberto Vargas.

Mars explorers John Borden, Eldon Galbraithe, Herbert Ellis and Hank Jaffe (Hugh Marlowe, Nelson Leigh, Rod Taylor & Christopher Dark) undergo a freakish acceleration on their trip home, and are catapulted through a dimensional portal. They awaken on a snowy peak and hike down to discover that centuries have passed; it is 550 years into the future. Deformed "Mutates" rule the earth's surface while a dwindling civilization of cowardly men and oversexed women subsists in a cozy underground city. Elaine (Shawn Smith of *The Land Unknown* and *It! The Terror from Beyond Space*), Deena (Lisa Montell) and the highborn Garnet (Nancy Gates) take an instant shine to the manly astronauts from the past. Jealous official Mories (Booth Colman) connives against the newcomers, convincing the council that their plan to re-conquer the surface world is a return to man's ancient violence and irresponsibility. Mories frames the newcomers for a murder in a bid to see them banished to certain death above.

In his core study *Keep Watching the Skies*, fifties' sci-fi authority Bill Warren pegs *World Without End*'s status as an inverted adaptation of the classic novel *The Time Machine*. This version's monstrous Morlocks enjoy the sunshine while the effete Eloi hide in caves. H.G. Wells' tale has an anti-war, humanistic message, whereas Bernds' screenplay alters the formula to celebrate the macho territorial imperative. Our gutsy astronauts teach the pacifist pansies of the 25th century how to get out there and kick ass, Yankee style.

The film's exiting posters and promo artwork promise the delirious adventures featured on the covers of sci-fi pulp fiction, but the movie dispenses with its outer space content in only eight minutes. Weak spaceship scenes (recycled, along with some rubber spiders, for AA's later *Queen of Outer Space*) give way to indifferent locations familiar from series westerns. The architecture of the underground city favors triangular arches made of plywood. Colors are bright but Ellsworth Fredericks' lighting is flat and inexpressive.

Amusing boy-girl flirtations offset the weak intrigues at court. Hugh Marlowe immediately hits it off with comely Nancy Gates (*Comanche Station*, *Some Came Running*), who parades a stunning pair of legs in Vargas' cutesy-pie outfits. Shawn Smith beams happily at the sight of Rod Taylor's bare chest. Dark-haired Lisa Montell, playing a former slave girl of the Mutates, falls hopelessly in love with Taylor as well. The rugged Taylor would soon play The Time Traveler in George Pal's version of H.G. Wells' original; we wonder if his bright attitude here helped win him roles in *Giant* and *Raintree County*. The professor (Nelson Leigh, a "star" of now-campy civil defense shorts treating atomic war as an inconvenience) stays out of the running for female companionship, while the fourth astronaut remains gloomy over the loss of his wife and children, left 500 years in the past.

To reclaim the quality real estate topside, the four spacemen fabricate a bazooka and go Mutate hunting. The action is limited to rock hopping and tame wrestling amid very ordinary surroundings. A number of bizarre and disturbing Mutate make-ups, with bulging eyes and rearranged facial features, are seen almost exclusively in wide shots. The MPAA may have warned Allied Artists away from horror close-ups, but it's equally likely that Bernd's standoffish style (and the limitations of his Cinema-Scope lens) kept the camera further back.

Speaking of CinemaScope, *World Without End* has been shown pan-scanned for over fifty years; this is its first disc release. The wide compositions no longer crop characters off screen but the 'Scope frame doesn't reveal anything particularly distinctive about the visuals. Edward Bernds' direction is mostly flat and static. The film's tagline reads *CinemaScope's First Science-Fiction Thriller Hurls You into the Year 2508!* but MGM's *Forbidden Planet* seems to have beaten it into theaters by a couple of weeks. They also aren't counting Disney's *20,000 Leagues Under the Sea*, released more than a year earlier.

Presented in an enhanced transfer with good color, the guilty favorite *World Without End* has an effective score by Leith Stevens. No extras are included.

THE CREATURE WALKS AMONG US
(see page 70)

GODZILLA, KING OF THE MONSTERS
(see page 81)

EARTH VS. THE FLYING SAUCERS

Sony Blu-ray Reviewed: September 26, 2002
1956 / B&W / 1:78 widescreen / 83 min.
Cinematography Fred Jackman Jr. Special
Effects Ray Harryhausen. Written by
Donald E. Keyhoe, Curt Siodmak, George
Worthing Yates, Raymond T. Marcus.
Produced by Sam Katzman, Charles H.
Schneer.
Directed by Fred F. Sears

Ray Harryhausen's ambitious second outing
with producer Charles H. Schneer took a break
from rampaging monsters to create an armada
of invading interplanetary spaceships. Naïve
and rather stiffly directed, this all-out invasion
film was one of the most popular science fiction
attractions of the 1950s.

Unknown forces are knocking Project Skyhook's
satellites out of orbit, frustrating Dr. Russell
Marvin (Hugh Marlowe). Flying saucers land
at Marvin's rocket base, disgorging aliens with
powerful energy rays that blow the installation
to bits. Marvin and his new bride Carol (Joan
Taylor) are the only survivors. It soon becomes
apparent that the saucer men intend to conquer
the world. In a secret lab, Mr. and Mrs. Marvin
perfect radio weapons capable of interrupting
the saucers' levitation beam. They had better get
them working quickly, as a fleet of the spinning
discs is heading toward Washington, D.C.!

As serious about its interplanetary menace as *It
Came from Beneath the Sea* is about a mighty mol-
lusk from the deep, ***Earth vs. the Flying Saucers***
was a matinee gold mine whose title tells all. It
didn't take long for word of mouth to let the kids
know that this one was a keeper. Nervously spinning saucers make good on their threats with
jazzy disintegration rays and sawblade sound effects in scenes of aerial combat and mass destruction. The thrill factor of this budget programmer
equaled the much more lavish *The War of the
Worlds*.

Ray Harryhausen was still establishing his cre-
dentials with producing partner Charles H.
Schneer, here under the guidance of Columbia
cheapskate Sam Katzman. Harryhausen's greater ambitions were in larger-scale fantasy films
with mythological beasts, but as outer space and
atomic monsters were the rage in 1956, he directed his technical skills to the challenge of giving life and personality to alien flying machines.
His dynamic saucers scream as they accelerate.
A part of their outer rim spins madly, a trouble-
some animation chore that lends nervousness
to their mechanical menace and imparts a gyro-
scopic, Frisbee logic to their levitation.

A judicious use of stock footage allows Harryhausen to create some impressive illusions. Test
rockets explode harmlessly into the saucers and
real airplanes (drones?) disintegrate when hit by

animated saucer rays. Identifiable landmarks were as necessary for movie monsters as they were for Alfred Hitchcock, and several highly detailed models of Washington, D.C. buildings and monuments are used for the eye-popping finale. Kids accustomed to getting one or two 'neato' effects per matinee were served a veritable smorgasbord of destruction, as marble columns and hallowed domes crumble onto helpless citizens.

The key compliment to Harryhausen's visualization is that it is his saucers, not *The Day the Earth Stood Still's* glowing pie plate or *The Mysterians'* nifty flying eyes that have persisted as the iconic Unidentified Flying Objects of the 1950s. Tim Burton copied this design for his invasion comedy *Mars Attacks!* He even parodied Harryhausen's great set pieces, like the spectacle of the Washington Monument crashing down on terrorized victims.

Kids and adults catching up with *Earth vs. the Flying Saucers* at this late date may not react as favorably. Digital effects achieve the kinds of tricks seen here so much better that what was once awe-inspiring may now just seem silly. Harryhausen fans don't need lectures, but others become more appreciative when informed that Ray worked practically alone with found materials. His miraculous illusions probably cost little more than the utter garbage seen in a turkey like *The Giant Claw*.

Earth vs. the Flying Saucers earns an "A" for action and a "D" for story detail. The authorities stand with their hands in their pockets and wait for "Do-oc-k-t-e-r-r Ma-ahr-r-r-v-i-i-n", as spoken by Paul Frees' warbling alien voice, to save the day. Marvin comes up with anti-saucer weapons faster than a magician can pull rabbits out of a hat. Chief of Staff Thomas Browne Henry notes that only 9 days remain to save the world, while circling the number '9' on a cheap printed stationary pad that reads, 'From the Desk of ... Chief of Staff!' The action is rushed, with lines and situations lifted practically verbatim from *This Island Earth*: "What a beautiful planet." / "Thank God it's still here."

Hugh Marlowe is an odd choice of hero considering his earlier role as the hiss-able villain of *The Day the Earth Stood Still*. He has a flat delivery and a perpetual grump act going, and is the least imaginative, most military-minded sci-fi scientist of the 50s. Joan Taylor (soon to come back for more punishment in *20 Million Miles to Earth*) lends the show a fair amount of tension, and good old Morris Ankrum has a nice bit as the general given a Plexiglas skull by the nefarious saucer men. The picture breaks down in the dullsville direction of Fred F. Sears, who manages to rob the scenes with the helmeted saucermen of their potential thrills. In still poses the bulbous, silver saucer dudes look great. They have ray guns in place of hands and go about their business in sinister little groups.

There's a heap of stock footage in this show. From *The Day the Earth Stood Still* come textless title shots of planets and stars in space, outtakes of people running from the baseball field, and even a shot of the collected scientists from the famous conclusion. *The War of the Worlds* is represented by shots of pileups on freeways and the iconic angle of L.A. City Hall being blown to bits. Sam Katzman was an equal opportunity stock library pillager.

The second unit work at the end is a real letdown. Limited location angles are padded with shots of rather pitiful 'interference ray' trucks driving through a Hollywood residential back lot. The editor in Savant still wants to cut the sequence down to its thrilling essentials. But the saucer thrills knocked 'em dead in 1956, and are still a heap of fun now.

Columbia Tristar's DVD of **Earth vs. the Flying Saucers** encodes a 16:9 widescreen version that approximates what was shown on 1956 screens. Some fans accustomed to seeing the film un-matted may be alarmed that the extreme tops and bottoms of shots are cropped away.

The best extra is a nifty Ray Harryhausen interview conducted by amiable director Joe Dante.

They handle a saucer animation model – it's pretty darn small! – and discuss the finer points of UFO movies. The flying saucer sound effect was found when producer Schneer heard the effluent (polite word) being pumped through the giant pipes in the sewage treatment plant that serves as the movie's rocket base set.

SOMEWHERE IN THIS WORLD STALKS A THING THAT-IS...

NOT OF THIS EARTH

PAUL BIRCH · BEVERLY GARLAND · MORGAN JONES

A Roger Corman Production · Screenplay by CHARLES B. GRIFFITH and MARK HANNA · Produced and Directed by ROGER CORMAN
AN ALLIED ARTISTS PICTURE

NOT OF THIS EARTH & ATTACK OF THE CRAB MONSTERS

Shout! Factory Reviewed December 28, 2010
1957 / B&W / 1:78 widescreen / 67 & 62 min.
Cinematography John J. Mescall, Floyd Crosby.
Music Ronald Stein.
Written by Charles B. Griffith, Mark Hanna.
Produced and
Directed by Roger Corman

Producer-director Roger Corman seems to have regarded his low-budget sci-fi films for A.I.P. and Allied Artists as practical exercises in creating releasable attractions for as little cash outlay as possible. Yet each show has a strong central idea as well as a monster for the box office. Back in 1972, Corman told interviewer William Johnson that he chose material looking for a sense of excitement within the story, plus a theme of some importance. He also admitted that he was never really satisfied with his work in the field. Just the same, Corman's early efforts hold up extremely well.

The Allied Artists poster for 1957's *Not of This Earth* depicts the Earth engulfed by a tentacled monster, which in the movie turns out to be a minor sidebar critter. With little more than a couple of barely-adequate props, *Not of This Earth* conjures an interesting story of an invasion by vampires from a distant planet.

A secret agent from Davanna, Paul Johnson (Paul Birch) looks like a human but has no normal internal organs. His alien eyes can hypnotize and kill; he hides them behind dark glasses (a motif repeated in "X" and *Tomb of Ligeia*). Paul teleports blood samples back to Davanna through a matter-transmitting device that predates *The Fly*. He murders a teenaged girl and uses his chauffeur Jeremy (Jonathan Haze) to ensnare other victims. Johnson hypnotizes a doctor (William Roerick) into studying Earth-Davanna blood compatibility issues, and hires live-in nurse Nadine Storey (Beverly Garland) to give him daily transfusions. Taking an interest in Nadine, a motor patrolman (Morgan Jones) grows suspicious of her oddball employer, who never removes his sunglasses.

Not of This Earth extracts a maximum of interest from the frightening pupil-less white contact lenses worn by actor Paul Birch. Paul Johnson converses telepathically -- in Chinese when required -- yet is a stranger to human ways. Like Jean-Luc Godard's Lemmy Caution, he is only one of a series of invading alien agents. We learn in voiceover that Davanna's blood supply is all but exhausted, and that Paul's mission is a desperate attempt to locate a fresh source. At one point Paul encounters another Davannan, a beautiful female vampire (Anna Lee Carroll) who has teleported to Earth to avoid starvation. Paul tries to feed her blood stolen from a doctor's lab, but makes a fatal mistake.

Paul Johnson has alien weaknesses that prove to be his undoing. Chased barefoot through Griffith Park, Beverly Garland's spunky nurse saves herself by the same means that will neutralize William Castle's *The Tingler* two years later. The abbreviated feature may appear insubstantial, but Charles B. Griffith and Mark Hanna's neatly constructed screenplay never drags its feet.

Not of This Earth can boast a brief but beloved appearance by the favorite Corman actor Dick Miller, as a luckless vacuum cleaner salesman who lives to regret the words, "No flip-flop". When his leading player Paul Birch reportedly walked off the film, Corman replaced him in a number of scenes with a so-so double. Few viewers even noticed!

Attack of the Crab Monsters was filmed next, to fill out an Allied Artists "Terrorama!" double bill for early 1957. Charles B. Griffith's screenplay keeps the monster thriller hopping for just over an hour, as a core of scientists and adventurers battle telepathic mutated monsters.

A team of Navy researchers lands on an atomic test island, where a previous expedition has disappeared without a trace. Despite the freak decapitation of a sailor, the scientists calmly observe that the island is being undermined bit by bit by unknown forces. Scientist Martha Hunter (Pamela Duncan of *The Undead*) is awakened in the night by the voice of one of the members of the first doomed expedition. As they are slowly picked off by unseen foes, the survivors learn the island's horrific secret: a pair of mutated super-crabs has evolved a completely different atomic structure. Not only are the crabs telepathic, they absorb the consciousness of anyone they devour. Martha and scientists Dale Drewer and Hank Chapman (Richard Garland & Russell Johnson) watch helplessly as the crabs reduce the island to a single outcropping of rock, leaving no avenue of escape.

Jokes abound about *Attack of the Crab Monsters*, from the story about tennis shoes being visible under the klunky Fiberglas crab mock-up to its campy title, the ultimate '50s monster movie moniker. Corman avoids any direct depiction of the destruction of the island, yet his film is strangely convincing. We *hear* hundreds of acres collapsing into the ocean, and people *report* that they just saw a beach or a mountain disappear. Corman's haste shows in a mismatch between dialogue and visuals. A character remarks about the unearthly quiet, and we're told that all animal life has departed from the island. Then the film cuts to various crabs and a noisy flight of seagulls taking off.

Corman can't film spectacular effects but he can afford ideas, and Charles Griffith comes up with a winner. When a "missing" scientist calls to Martha in the night, his personality is now possessed and controlled by one of the monsters. The crabs can tap the mental patterns of every person they consume. We expect monsters to eat people, but the idea of being "incorporated" into a monster's psyche is an atomic age equivalent of the living death of vampire movies. The crabs use their victim's personalities to lure more victims. *Crabs* reaches beyond the concept of the Remote Control of Human Beings to envision human identity as a non-spiritual pattern that can be ingested and put to use for another species.

Corman's film does have its ragged edges. The crabs are never particularly convincing. A scientist loses his hand simply because a small rock falls on it, a development that now seems absurd after the harrowing drama *127 Hours*. The crabs carefully sabotage the team's radio, neatly slicing each vacuum tube in half. We have difficulty visualizing the giant claw prop doing anything more delicate than bashing in a door. For his underwater scenes Corman films at the Marineland of the Pacific amusement park. All looks well until we become aware of the far side of the park's water tank.

Allied Artists may have suggested actor Richard Garland, who played a small but impressive part opposite Gary Cooper in the previous year's *Friendly Persuasion*. Russell Johnson later found immortality as The Professor in *Gilligan's Island*, a show that should have filmed an episode called *Gilligan Versus the Crab Monsters*: "A Three-Hour Cruise... to Terror!"

Shout Factory's discs of **Not of This Earth** and **Attack of the Crab Monsters** are good transfers enhanced for widescreen. Both titles carry audio commentaries by Tom Weaver and John & Mike Brunas. Weaver refers to original scripts and shooting schedules and offers reliable information on the rumored falling-out between director Corman and actor Paul Birch.

X THE UNKNOWN

Anchor Bay Reviewed: September 16, 2000
1956 / B&W / 1:37 flat / 91 min.
Cinematography Gerald Gibbs. Film Editor James Needs. Original Music James Bernard. Writing credits Jimmy Sangster. Produced by Michael Carreras, Anthony Hinds.
Directed by Leslie Norman

Hammer's *The Quatermass Xperiment* concluded with its astronaut hero devolving into a disgusting shapeless monster. In the next three years, similar protoplasm monsters would ooze from the popular cinema of America (*The Blob*), Japan (*The H-Man*) and Italy (*Caltiki, il mostro immortale*). But the boys at Bray beat them all with what American showmen would call a quickie follow-up:

X the Unknown. A fast script was commissioned from Hammer production manager and first time screenwriter Jimmy Sangster. The title was chosen to again capitalize on the English Certificate X, Adults only rating. Hammer contracted an American character actor to guarantee an overseas sale.

Dr. Adam Royston (Dean Jagger) conducts radio experiments in search of a method to neutralize radioactivity. A muddy Y-shaped gash erupts on a nearby Scottish military test range and a soldier is burned to death by an unseen radiation source. Inspector McGill (Leo McKern) joins Royston in the search for a mystery killer that soon adds a young boy and a philandering hospital intern to its list of victims. Royston hits upon a fantastic but dead-on accurate theory: a primordial life form within the Earth that feeds on radiation has been lured to the surface by man's nuclear energy activities. After assaulting Royston's research plant and consuming the fuel rods from its reactor, "X" flows back to the crack on the test range. Since weapons are ineffective against a wave of deadly radioactive mud, only Royston's radio theories have a chance of stopping the shapeless monster.

X the Unknown shapes up as an efficient if somewhat subdued monster thriller. Jimmy Sangster's formulaic script follows the American blueprint: a rural setting and a selection of victims that include an adorable child and a pair of illicit lovers. Sangster's characters are calm and unflappable, even the usually brash Leo McKern, so good in Val Guest's *The Day the Earth Caught Fire*. This helps maintain a hysteria-free mood, but some of the supporting players come off as colorless. The bald, unglamorous Dean Jagger holds screen center. Confronted with conflicting clues, Gene Barry or Richard Carlson would rattle off crackpot techno-babble. Jagger's Dr. Royston simply admits that he doesn't know what's going on, and that's that.

Jagger's appearance in Leo McCarey's witch-hunt anthem *My Son John* must have been no accident, for the Oscar winner (for *Twelve O'Clock High*) refused to work with initial director Joseph Losey, one of the most talented of the refugees from the American blacklist. Director Leslie Norman later moved on to success in television. But Hammer must have been impressed by Losey, for he came back several years later to helm the CinemaScope culmination of Hammer's early science fiction films, the ambitious *These are The Damned*.

Radioactivity was the buzzword most often evoked to animate otherwise unmotivated '50s monsters. *X the Unknown* is unusual in that it is about radiation and little else. Unlike American movies that soft-pedaled the downside of the nuclear industry, Sangster actually exaggerates the dangers of radiation burns. The victims of *X* swell like sponges and melt like popsicles in a blast furnace. When the living slime is finally seen, it gallops across a field and convincingly bulldozes a stone wall. It's all the more menacing for being so banal: just a mass of deadly ook.

There are almost no women in Sangster's slim story, an oversight that gives credence to Peter Hutchings' curious cinematic analysis. [1] The critic scores points with his observations about weak English heroes dominated by female monsters, but his comparison of *The Quatermass Xperiment* and *X the Unknown* would seem meant only for symbol-happy semiologists. To Hutchings, *Xperiment's* phallic rocket sticking up in a farmyard, is complimented by *X's* vaginal gash in the Earth, a Terran womb that unleashes the ultimate 'Earth Mother' monster. Such a reading conjures memories of the gleefully obscene outer space creatures jerry-rigged to spice up Francis Coppola's patchwork space movie *Battle Beyond the Sun*.

At one point, soldiers attempt to suppress the Unknown X by sealing the fissure with explosives and paving it over. The Hutchings thought process would imply that the stodgy military is operating in sexual denial, and trying to fit Mother Nature with a concrete chastity belt.

Anchor Bay's DVD of *X the Unknown* includes an excellent transfer, handsome animated menus and a trailer. The shots of melting victims are more complete than was evident on earlier TV prints. Editorially, only the unusually long Warner logo over James Bernard's typical nervous-strings title music seems a bit odd.

1. Hutchings, Peter, **Hammer and Beyond, The British Horror Film** Manchester University Press, 1993

THE INCREDIBLE SHRINKING MAN

Universal Reviewed September 19, 2006
1957 / 1:78 widescreen / 81 min.
Cinematography by Ellis W. Carter, Clifford Stine. Art Direction Robert Clatworthy, Alexander Golitzen. Special Effects Charles Baker, Everett H. Broussard, Roswell A. Hoffmann, Fred Knoth, Tom McCrory. Written by Richard Matheson from his novel *The Shrinking Man*. Produced by Albert Zugsmith.
Directed by Jack Arnold

The Incredible Shrinking Man is the happy exception to formulaic and predictable studio genre work. Producer Albert Zugsmith had enjoyed a solid hit with Douglas Sirk's star-studded *Written on the Wind* and was making more Universal pictures with bigger names like Jeff Chandler. Zugsmith decided that Richard Matheson's novel *The Shrinking Man* would be perfect for an offbeat science fiction tale. Either somebody had imagination or the project was green-lit during vacation time, because *The Incredible Shrinking Man* outdoes all of William Alland's sci-fi efforts. Kids loved the miniaturization effects, a trick relegated mostly to comedy fantasies since the failure of Paramount's *Dr. Cyclops* back in 1940. Matheson's adult, thoughtful script crystallizes Cold War phobias much as had the previous year's *Invasion of the Body Snatchers*. Seeing a chance to 'make a good one', Jack Arnold contributed his best job of direction. What might have been a shaggy-dog story with an unsatisfying twist ending becomes a wondrous delight. *The Incredible Shrinking Man* is science fiction poetry and the most profound sci-fi film of the fifties.

Ad writer Robert Scott Carey (Grant Williams) notices that he's gradually losing both height and weight. He consults Drs. Bramson and Silver (William Schallert & Raymond Bailey), who are at first baffled. Like a reverse cancer, the tissues and organs of Carey's entire body are shrinking a fraction of an inch each day. The specialists soon formulate a theory of what happened, and work tirelessly to halt Scott's malady. Scott loses his job, retires from the world and hides like a freak. He sells his story to the press. Eventually so small that he can live in a doll's house, Scott is irritable and tyrannical with his long-suffering wife Louise (Randy Stuart). He's still shrinking with no end in sight – when the cat, long banished from the house, sneaks back inside....

The Gothic tradition conceives of horror in terms of suffering and death, and the loss of one's soul to bestiality or the Devil. The Cold War fears of the 1950s unleashed a new existential crisis on the public psyche. Don Siegel's *Invasion of the Body Snatchers* is about depersonalization and the loss of identity. It encourages the suspicion that appearances lie, that the world we think we know may be a vast political conspiracy.

The Incredible Shrinking Man exploits a new post-atomic fear of a world in which common values, presumed facts and assumed conventions might be completely transformed. An implacable fate threatens to end Scott Carey's life, and even worse, render it meaningless.

There is a classic kind of character that discovers his true nature by losing or casting off artificial and material things; many philosophies including the Christian faith tell us that this is a path to spiritual grace. Carey goes through a similar process except that his spiritual growth is an involuntary ordeal. As he shrinks bit by bit toward that inescapable zero of personal oblivion, Carey loses everything by which he defines himself. First his clothes don't fit. Then his wedding ring falls off. The doctors concentrate on Scott's biological problem but nobody knows how to deal with his mental state. Scott's wife must mother him like a child. Man becomes toy, husband a helpless baby.

Matheson's original novel emphasized Carey's sexual trauma as he realizes that he's no longer going to be intimate with his wife, and that she undoubtedly will have to find someone else. His resentment grows with his forced isolation. He knows that his personality is changing along with his situation. He can't help it.

A normal 1957 movie would have to dodge this sex angle but *Shrinking Man* takes pains to keep it at the forefront. Tiny Scott shouts at his wife, demanding that she come straight home from the store. Nothing she does is good enough. He tries to maintain his dominant attitude, the one that could 'order' Louise to bring him a beer as part of a conventionally equitable relationship. In his jeans and tennis shoes, sitting on a chair with his feet barely reaching the end of the cushion, Scott at first looks like a little kid. Having a sex drive with such a small body must seem like a horrible joke, a castration nightmare out of Jim Thompson's *The Nothing Man*.

At one point Carey wanders out to the carnival. He meets a young midget (April Kent) and begs for her company, seeking the security any kind of 'normalcy' can give him. Carey becomes both abusive and unfaithful, but he has no psychological choice – he's desperate to keep himself intact, to remain a man. Even the companionship of midgets does not last when he continues to shrink smaller than they. Carey doesn't know it yet, but his only certainty is eternal change, and utter isolation in the knowledge that his fate must ultimately be faced alone. Already withdrawn from his normal suburban existence, Scott is drifting into neurosis when events plunge him into a miniature Robinson Crusoe world.

The horrors in Scott Carey's cellar express a chaotic condition beyond simple disproportion; only in a paranoid fantasy could one's own mundane basement turn this hostile. *Shrinking Man's* surreal re-ordering of existing reality resembles *Alice Through the Looking Glass*. Alice's dream terrors came from nursery rhymes; Carey's emerge from the pages of pulp fantasy in the form of a nastily tangible spider. Scott rallies his courage by flexing an ancient human instinct, the Territorial Imperative. The big unknowns can be staved off if one busies one's self with the immediate problem of survival. How else has the human race survived so long?

Victory over the spider once again forces Scott to consider his bleak future, but now he realizes that he's no longer afraid. That's when *The Incredible Shrinking Man* pulls out its ace, an ethereal conclusion that reportedly was not written by Matheson and was added against his wishes. Some philosophies seek truth by engaging in the search for one's true self. Others teach that one can find truth only by casting off the ego and joining a larger natural order apart from material values. Only a fraction of an inch tall, Scott is able to walk through a barrier that previously blocked him. Nothing in his world will ever be the same, but he looks up at the sky and experiences a revelation: The distant stars haven't changed at all.

"And I felt myself melting..." I've been at screenings in which one can feel an "ahh" rise from the audience when the camera pulls back on Carey's words. Many people, especially kids that might never have considered the possibility of transcendence, can feel the pull on some part of their minds. As Scott continues with his final speech, *Shrinking Man* achieves the most profound "Sense of Wonder" in the genre. Scott's concluding revelation, sometimes interpreted as an ethereal surrender to fate or even an expression of the death experience, is a triumph over complacent existence. With the simple defiant words "I Still Exist", Robert Scott Carey becomes a hero of the Atomic Age. [1]

When I first wrote about *The Incredible Shrinking Man* in 1981 it seemed that Scott Carey's battle with the spider was one of the best special effects sequences ever made. It's still good but modern fans will have no trouble picking apart the perspective tricks, split screens and traveling mattes. One wishes all the original optical elements existed so the shots could be re-composited more

perfectly – shadows for the tiny Scott, etc. But the imagination in Matheson's script makes perfect effects unnecessary. *Shrinking Man* works because of its sharp observations, like Scott's wedding ring falling off just as he and Louise affirm their unbreakable union. It hits exactly the right note.

It is hard to believe that the film's downbeat ending ever made it through the script stage. In practically every other show of this kind (even today), the doctors find the antidote and the story fades out with the situation solved. Think of *Outbreak*, in which a single injection halts a deadly virus and magically repairs organ and tissue damage! Once Scott falls into the cellar and becomes part of the alternate miniature underworld, he is never heard from again. His wife will always think that she is a widow. Just as Scott's adventure is beginning, she drives away and never comes back. *The Incredible Shrinking Man* deals with the infinite and finality. [2]

The source of Scott's trouble is at first a mystery, and then a theory. It eventually becomes irrelevant. The film's first potent image is a man alone facing an approaching 'mystery cloud'. There's no escaping the cloud; all Carey can do is watch it overtake him. The fantastic story is unharmed by the utter absurdity of the film's supposed science – for Scott to shrink so perfectly his cells would have to shrink proportionately, not just diminish. And how can hard bones become smaller – once formed, they're largely inert. Scott's plight is better off left as a philosophical enigma.

Universal presents its DVD of **The Incredible Shrinking Man** in a beautiful enhanced widescreen 1:78. Savant hasn't seen it this way since 1973 at the Los Angeles County Museum with Richard Matheson in attendance. The restored screen shape reveals visual harmonies lacking in older flat transfers. Although filmed with flat spherical lenses, *Shrinking Man* was hard-matted in the camera (and/or the optical printer) to eliminate the need to do effects for areas of the frame not intended to be projected. The earlier transfers took a 1:33 piece out of the middle of the already-matted frame (just as had *Invasion of the Body Snatchers* when formatted for television), resulting in a fuzzy, severely cropped image. [3]

The compositional improvement is evident all through the picture. Scott and Louise no longer talk to each other from extremes of the frame. The perspective angle down the cellar shelf to the spider's web now looks like quite a hike. By now effects cameraman Clifford Stine had gained plenty of experience with spiders, and with Arnold's guidance pulls off a terrific series of effects angles and moving shots.

Clear sound augments the sharp picture; Ray Anthony's trumpet calls over the main titles while the little Scott Carey figure shrinks, and shrinks.... We hear a smattering of *Written on the Wind*-ish soap opera music on Scott's radio, making his shut-in home life seem even drabber. As an extra, we're offered the Saul Bass-like teaser trailer with Orson Welles. It doesn't even use scenes from the movie. With Welles reading the narration, we'll believe anything can happen.

1. Another movie from 1957 deals with a woman of modest means, set in her ways, not too bright but with a good heart. Cheated and robbed, she loses her house, her possessions and her money, until at the end she's walking along with nothing, a total vagrant. In the last shot she turns at the camera and smiles. She's still there. She retains some human essence that cannot be taken away. She looks through the fourth wall, right into us. The movie is Federico Fellini's best, *The Nights of Cabiria*, and it practically parallels *The Incredible Shrinking Man*.

2. Many psychedelic song lyrics sound faintly ridiculous now. The Moody Blues' space-themed album *To Our Children's Children's Children* riffs on *2001* to revisit older sci-fi ideas. The lyric "You've Got to Take the Journey Out and In" seems connected to *Shrinking Man's* idea of infinity, where the impossibly big and the impossibly small meet "like the closing of a gigantic circle". In other words, it's all in your heads, pilgrims. If you want go to the stars, you have to come to terms with the secrets of the atom. If you want to embrace the universe, you must also look deep inside yourself. Pass it this way, please.

3. At that old Museum screening Matheson practically apologized for the movie, telling the audience he hated its altered ending. Much later, he saw it again and changed his mind.

KRONOS

Image Reviewed: April 27, 2000
1957 / B&W / 2:35 flat letterbox / 78 min. Cinematography Karl Struss. Production Designer Theobold Holsopple. Music Paul Sawtell and Bert Shefter. Writing credits Irving Block, Lawrence J. Goldman and Jack Rabin, from a story by Irving Block. Produced by Irving Block, Louis DeWitt, Kurt Neumann and Jack Rabin. Directed by Kurt Neumann

Kurt Neumann's *Kronos* is an over-achieving near classic in a year noted for cheap exploitation monster movies. It has always earned positive notices; contemporary reviewers impressed by its special effects thought it equal to many a higher budgeted effort.

Irving Block and Jack Rabin ran an all-purpose

optical house serving the needs of independent productions, and their work can be seen in everything from *Monster from Green Hell* to *Night of the Hunter*. With effects man Louis DeWitt, the ambitious duo also dabbled in writing and production, making the extremely low-budget *Unknown World* in 1951. A screen treatment by Block became MGM's ambitious, intelligent *Forbidden Planet*. *Kronos* benefits from a similar 'big concept' sci-fi premise. Its star is a titanic cubic Tinkertoy, an alien robot sent to drain every erg and kilowatt of energy from the Earth for the benefit of its unseen controllers.

An electrical life form from outer space penetrates the desert research facility Labcentral by possessing a truck driver. The alien energy transfers itself to the lab's director, Dr. Hubbell Eliot (John Emery). Obeying orders from space, Eliot covertly directs the landing in Mexico of a mystery UFO. LabCentral's top scientists Dr. Leslie Gaskell, Vera Hunter and Arnold Culver (Jeff Morrow, Barbara Lawrence, George O'Hanlon) go to Mexico to investigate, and discover Kronos, a giant robot. A metallic dome tops the robot's two upright cubes; it stands on piston legs. Guided from afar by Dr. Eliot, the robot marches across the countryside in search of power plants. Now called Kronos, it vacuums up power with plasma storms, electric bolts and ray blasts, growing in size as it converts energy into matter. A B47 bomber is recalled when our heroes determine that a nuclear blast would counterproductively feed the titan more energy. Kronos employs a pre-*Star Trek* tractor beam to pull the bomber to its target – and emerges from the mushroom cloud exponentially larger, seemingly a mile or more tall. Now an unstoppable colossus, Kronos marches on a panic-stricken Los Angeles.

The Kronos accumulator is a wonderfully compact science fiction concept. It can be interpreted as a comment on gluttonous consumerism but more easily represents an impersonal mechanism by which a technological culture feeds off one less advanced. Like Brazilian Indians watching their rain forest cleared away acre by acre, humans fret helplessly as Kronos steals the Earth's resources.

The design of the titan is brilliant: Earth is invaded by Abstract Art from outer space. A simple collection of shapes with neither style nor personality, Kronos defies analysis. Stanley Kubrick surely learned a lesson here; like Arthur Clarke's Monolith, this alien apparition doesn't date. The robot stands on the horizon with its head in the clouds, an unexplainable manifestation of an unknowable Future. [1]

In its second half *Kronos* becomes a series of unique special effects sequences accomplished through simple opticals and superior design. Cel animation is used for a few shots, which at the time were criticized by scoffers who didn't want animated cartoons in their sci-fi films. Today, that's almost all there is to special effects.

The vast glowing shape glimpsed on the Pacific horizon is yet another architectural dome menace from 1957 (the others are *The Mysterians* and *Quatermass 2*). Giant piston-feet appear to level a path as the robot glides forward in a few animated long shots. The camera pans across matte paintings that depict Kronos plowing giant grooves into Mexican valleys.

At the Navarez Electro Plant a riot of rays and smoke is superimposed over Lionel-gauge train model switch towers and signal arches. In the final assault on L.A., simple dots superimposed on a photo of the Los Feliz hills represent lights going out as Kronos drains the city's power, grid by grid. Equally important to these destructive spectacles is the film's creative sound design. Whistles, klaxons and crackling electricity accompany explosions and ray gun noises, and fuse with Paul Sawtell and Bert Shefter's thunderous music score into a sci-fi Wall Of Sound. The main musical theme, by the way, reappeared in both the 1958 *It! The Terror* from Beyond Space and 1959's Gigantis The Fire Monster.

Some visuals are disturbingly organic. Crackling liquid metal represents the alien life form exiting the dead body of Dr. Eliot, and eerie waves of energy ebb and flow from Kronos as it vacuums up power. Some of these waves appear to be cleverly superimposed shots of foamy surf at the seashore. In an interview, Block said one angle of the giant Kronos standing alone in the desert was achieved by putting the model on a white sheet, which was then airbrushed to approximate hills and rocks.

The dramatics in Kronos follow the glib formula of the "typical space monster story" lampooned in Walt Disney's Mars and Beyond TV show. Research scientist Dr. Leslie Gaskell (Jeff Morrow) is also a helicopter pilot. His egghead sidekick Dr. Arnold Culver (George O'Hanlon) doesn't claim to understand the caprices of his own SUSIE, a computer given a female nickname and credited with a femme personality. Gaskell is a workaholic emasculated by the demands of his job. His ever-patient girlfriend/lab assistant Vera (Barbara Lawrence of Thieves' Highway) doesn't rate twenty seconds of his attention, let alone a night out at the movies. Since LabCentral is shown to be in a remote corner of the California desert, it must be quite a drive to the drive-in. Kronos has one of the 50s best howler romantic dialogue lines, delivered by Morrow during a soggy clinch on a Mexican beach:

"Do you think you'll be able to respect a husband who probably pulled the biggest scientific boner of all time?"

LabCentral recycles set constructions for the Fox films Desk Set and The Day the Earth Stood Still. Another clue that Kronos was produced on the Fox lot is the use of the pop song Something's Gotta Give as soundtrack source music. Kronos' trek through Mexico reveals numerous cutaways to CinemaScope stock footage filmed in Hawaii. One angle shows Kronos threatening a sugar-cane field as hundreds of Hawaiians flee in panic. If Savant is not mistaken, the depression in the hills behind Kronos is Kolekole Pass, the infamous route taken by the torpedo planes that bombed Pearl Harbor!

Kronos' most sublime moment involves the H-bomb. When the alien tractor beam draws the B47 inexorably into an H-blast, the angles and cutting enforce a sense of impending doom, until the screen whites out at the point of impact. The effect prefigures the climactic bombing scene in Dr. Strangelove and works almost as well.

Other details show a lack of production coordination. Gaskell and Culver follow the UFO's descent on a mysterious telescope scanner that displays its image like a television, with automatic cuts. Newscasters hold up sketches for the studio cameras, one of which shows a full-sized colossus on a rampage, the monster that Kronos has not yet become. It may be the same illustration used for the film's key ad art.

When the possessed Dr. Eliot tells his associates how to defeat Kronos they start the tape recorder rolling a sentence or two after he begins talking. When the tape is replayed, Eliot's entire speech is recorded.

Dr. Eliot electrocutes his psychiatrist (Morris Ankrum) at an indoor transformer power station of the kind that serves a large building. This hospital's transformer substation is located in the office of the head of Psychiatric Treatment, a few steps from his consulting desk. Is the good doctor conducting shock treatment trials on elephants?

That scene may not be an intentional joke, but the conclusion surely is. Our scientist heroes look on in relief as their dime store physics succeed in making the robot invader melt and crumble like the Krel door in Forbidden Planet.

Then Kronos suddenly erupts in a nuclear explosion, a giant stock shot blasteroonie. This is happening right in the middle of Los Angeles, not out in the desert somewhere – Kronos appears to be standing in Atwater, just behind Dodger Stadium. A few seconds after the devastating blast, sidekick Arnie cheerfully tells Gaskell and Vera that they still might make it to a late show! Wearing what, radiation suits?

Image's DVD of *Kronos* is a clean flat letterboxed transfer from good elements. Scratches and damage are limited mostly to the copious stock footage on view. The aural detail in the cacophonous destruction scenes is striking – one can hear the transformers blowing as Kronos drains L.A.'s power in a rolling blackout (which happens every time we have a heat wave). An effective trailer is the only extra.

Kronos has remained a compelling cosmic Golem thanks to an intriguing concept and superior design. Savant rates the show an A-, right up there under the top classics of the genre.

1. In the 1970s, the NBC Broadcast Studios in Burbank displayed a logo sculpture that looked a lot like Kronos, at least the two-cubes part. Anyone coming to see a Johnny Carson *Tonight Show* taping would wait in line by it. At the time, David Allen's animation studio was just a few doors away; he once entertained the idea of sneaking over there at night and crowning the sculpture with a homemade antenna dome.

OUT-OF-SPACE CREATURE INVADES THE EARTH!

20 MILLION MILES TO EARTH

WILLIAM HOPPER · JOAN TAYLOR

20 MILLION MILES TO EARTH

Sony Blu-ray Reviewed: July 22, 2007
1957 / B&W / 1:78 widescreen / 82 min.
Cinematography Irving Lippman, Carlo Ventimiglia. Visual Effects Ray Harryhausen. Written by Christopher Knopf, Bob Williams, story by Charlott Knight. Produced by Charles H. Schneer.
Directed by Nathan Juran

Ray Harryhausen's last B&W movie shows the animator at the height of his technical prowess, single-handedly creating fantastic movie magic from an unpromising space monster tale. Called an Ymir everywhere but in the movie itself, his Venusian visitor is a fascinating creature, a stranger in a strange world that battles an elephant amid familiar Roman landmarks.

Spaceman Colonel Bob Calder (William Hopper) is the only survivor of a secret voyage to Venus that crashes into the sea upon its return. A young Italian boy (Bart Bradley) finds a silicone-like object washed ashore and brings it to traveling zoologist Dr. Leonardo (Frank Puglia). Leonardo is amazed when the translucent glob hatches a small humanoid lizard beast with a bifurcated tail and an otherworldly howl. He's even more amazed when the unknown animal grows much larger in only a few hours. Calder identifies it as a specimen from his spaceship and says that the creatures were relatively harmless back on Venus. When attacked by a dog and a farmer's pitchfork, the still-growing Ymir goes on a rampage.

20 Million Miles to Earth delivers far better goods than most monster thrillers of the late '50s. Kids love the imaginative illusions of the Ymir smashing through ancient pillars, crushing cars and wrestling a bull elephant to the ground. No fumbled super-imposures or lame cutaways here – when the Ymir picks up a screaming victim, we see them both in the same shot.

After working so hard to wreck San Francisco and Washington D.C. in epics about giant octopi and flying saucers, Harryhausen indulged his personal wish to see Europe by filming *20 Million Miles to Earth*'s second-unit scenes in Rome. The functional script invents a token romance for nurse "almost a doctor" Joan Taylor (back for more after *Earth versus the Flying Saucers*), and some depressingly phony rural Italians. William Hopper does as good as can be expected in his spaceman role but is easily upstaged by bit player Tito Vuolo, who plays a stock Italian police chief.

Harryhausen's acknowledged classics are the larger-scaled fantasies made after he successfully integrated color into his Dynamation process, but *20 Million* has a balance lacking in some of the later films. Because of his successful association with producer Charles Schneer, Harryhausen became the first special effects artisan-star, creating the whole film practically on his own. A modern digital picture can credit four or five hundred effects people but at this point in his career, Harryhausen didn't even use an assistant.

The Ymir is a humanoid alien with a dinosaur-like head reminiscent of a Jupiterian monster from Ray's home movie experiments. The goat-legs make the Ymir more bird-like than simian but Harryhausen imparts a few 'Mighty Joe Young' body motions to the creature. We like the weird Ymir; we respect his right to live because he's an embodiment of his creator-animator's personality.

The moodily lit and expertly blocked scenes of the Ymir trapped in the barn are some of Harryhausen's best B&W work. The illusion of Hopper poking the monster with a pole is so nicely judged, we forget we're watching a trick shot. With a monster this charming, it seems churlish to take *20 Million Miles to Earth* to task for its lack of character development. The Ymir has some sympathetic moments when it tries to relate to a lamb but it remains a dumb animal, never making a connection with the humans. *Mighty Joe Young* had us all in tears and we were really saddened to see the monstrous *Beast* shot down in flames. The Ymir seems a missed opportunity.

But the spectacle we get is top quality. Harryhausen's Dynamation 'reality sandwich' effect creates convincing views of the monster loose in the streets of Rome. Art director-turned film director Nathan Juran must have impressed his producers because they re-teamed with him twice more.

Sensing that the 'monster wrecks city' theme had been played out, after *20 Million Miles to Earth* Ray and Charles upgraded their ambitions to color costume fantasies, for which Columbia was willing to invest more money. Their next show *The 7th Voyage of Sinbad* hit the jackpot. The bold music of Bernard Herrmann blended perfectly with Harryhausen's animated magic, carrying his work to the next level of wonder.

Sony's fancy **50th Anniversary Edition** flatters Ray Harryhausen's semi-classic. The transfer is the same as the earlier 2002 DVD release. A second colorized version is a good tinting job of the kind seen in B&W photos turned into color lobby cards. The Ymir is almost exactly the same dull green no matter what the lighting circumstances. Dressed up in uniform, paint-by-number colors, Harryhausen's clever effects look more than ever like little toy dioramas. I'm glad that Columbia has only three B&W Harryhausens to screw around with in this way. Hollywood has yet to find a way to reap a profit by destroying a film outright. If an extra nickel could be made that way, I think movies would already be disappearing.

Ray Harryhausen plays a big role in the copious extras. The featurette *The Colorization Process* plays like an infomercial. The best extra is the Harryhausen commentary with effects artists Dennis Muren & Phil Tippett. There's no let-up in Muren and Tippett's technical questions. When Ray dodges a query with, "A magician needs to keep his secrets", or, "You shouldn't be concentrating on details like that", Tippett and Muren just keep the questions coming. Tim Burton also interviews Ray, and looks genuinely charmed to be talking with one of his heroes. Other extras include an interview with star Joan Taylor and music expert David Schecter's profile of composer Mischa Bakaleinikoff.

QUATERMASS 2

Anchor Bay Reviewed: May 20, 2000
1957 / B&W / 1:37 flat / *Enemy from Space*
Cinematography Gerald Gibbs. Art Director Bernard Robinson. Editor James Needs. Music James Bernard. Writers Val Guest and Nigel Kneale, from a BBC teleplay by Nigel Kneale. Produced by Michael Carreras and Anthony Hinds.
Directed by Val Guest

The reputation of *Quatermass 2*, the first sequel to *The Quatermass Xperiment* has skyrocketed in recent years. United Artists released this masterpiece in the U.S. in 1957 as *Enemy From Space*. It disappeared from television in the 60s and fell into undeserved obscurity. Along with Fritz Lang's *The 1,000 Eyes of Dr. Mabuse*, *Quatermass 2* is the missing link in the progression of pop pulp sci-fi from the serial thrillers of the 40s to the James Bond films of the 60s.

The Rocket Research Group headed by Dr. Bernard Quatermass (Brian Donlevy) is being disbanded and its funds reallocated. With his atomic rocket standing idle on its launch pad, the arrogant and bullying Profesor Q turns his attention to a new phenomenon – strange objects falling from the skies that can mysteriously infect people. He discovers that the Winnerden Flats township has been razed to make way for a secret scientific establishment, the very one that has siphoned off the Rocket Group's funding. Even stranger, the secret plant bears a close resemblance to Quatermass's own proposed Moon base.

Q's assistant Marsh (Bryan Forbes) is infected by one of the projectile-like meteorites, which renders him unconscious and leaves a wicked scar. Sinister guards then appear from the Winnerden plant and spirit Marsh away at gunpoint. In London, Quatermass finds that everyone with knowledge of the mystery refuses to talk about it. Inspector Lomax, his old Scotland Yard pal (John Longden) puts him in contact with Vincent Broadhead, a dissident Parliament Minister (Tom Chatto). Broadhead wangles himself and Quatermass passes for an inspection tour of the Winnerden facility, which is rumored to be making synthetic food. But as they enter the security gate and are politely herded past the zombie-like guards toward a giant domed structure, Quatermass is formulating his own theory ... invasion from outer space.

The original 1955 Quatermass 2 television serial spread its story over five episodes and its action over a larger number of characters. It ended with a trip into space to confront the interplanetary threat, a conclusion identical to that of 1996's Independence Day. Author Nigel Kneale hated American actor Brian Donlevy's blunt and unsentimental interpretation of the Quatermass character, but director Guest's condensation of the serial's action into 80 minutes of intense plotting is superb. The film version slowly reveals the mechanics of alien possession elaborated in the teleplay, reducing what would now be obvious repetition to the sinister image of the alien 'mark' as it turns up in increasingly higher levels of government ... in Scotland Yard and the Houses of Parliament.

Although Americans must have (erroneously) thought the film derivative of Don Siegel's Invasion of the Body Snatchers, Quatermass 2 approaches its invasion-by-possession theme from a more political angle. The socialist-leaning postwar England, already satirized in George Orwell's 1984, is envisioned as a bureaucratic system of secrets and therefore the perfect environment for invasion. With just a few key people under alien influence, all of England is ripe for the taking.

Once Quatermass makes contact with the tumor-like Winnerden plant, Quatermass 2 hits high gear and never lets up. Key themes from future conspiracy movies emerge fully developed. Stonewalled for information, Quatermass rails that invoking "Top Secret" classification is an excuse to ignore the law. Equally chilling (and aided by James Bernard's nervous music) are details as subtle as our Professor observing truckloads of building materials bearing the Winnerden symbol moving unnoticed through the streets of London. The invasion is everywhere, yet undetected. This may be the birth of paranoid cinema.

The zombie guards wear bullet-shaped helmets and aim machine pistols through goggled gas masks. They're an immediate visual link to the gas-masked ant fighters of Them! The alien threat in Quatermass is a composite being, whose individual parts arrive meteorite-by-meteorite. The creatures have strength only as a combined mass. This alien intelligence considers individual humans as it does its own basic units – as disposable functionaries. The invasion is as much political as biological, a brilliant twist that makes this Hammer film as relevant today as the more celebrated Don Siegel classic.

When the Winnerden workers initiate bloody revolt the havoc is indistinguishable from a labor insurrection. Only the abstraction of fantasy saved *Q2* from the British censor.

Also on display is Hammer's willingness to play rough. *Q2* features some grotesque killings that are shockingly graphic for 1957: *"Those pipes are blocked with human pulp!"* Made at the same time as the gory *The Curse of Frankenstein*, *Q2* uses many familiar Hammer personnel, including composer Bernard, editor James Needs and makeup artist Phil Leakey. The mark of infection is treated like a mark of the Devil, giving the political-biological threat a supernatural taint. [1] One look at Public Relations Officer John Van Eyssen (Jonathan Harker from *Horror of Dracula*) and we know something is up.

Kneale and Guest's *Quatermass 2* also distills the basis of the generic James Bond movie. Uniquely equipped to root out a subversive conspiracy, Quatermass locates a mysterious technological complex guarded by a ruthless army. At first single-handedly, and then with the help of small force of fighters, he penetrates the awesome establishment, puts paid to its ringleaders and blows it all to bits. This basic formula was repeated ad infinitum in *Dr. No,* two *Flint* movies, four *Matt Helm* movies, dozens of *Man from Uncle* episodes, etc. The theme of a sinister secret government project may be what attracted Hammer to what became Joseph Losey's *These Are The Damned* several years later. [2]

Quatermass 2 also marks the end of the British 'we won the war' genre that Peter Hutchings claims was an effort by a geo-politically impotent nation to bask in its recent war glory. The unsung hero of *Q2* is the professor's second-in-command, the unglamorous, bookish Dr. Tom Brand (William Franklyn). In a parallel to the end of *The Bridge on the River Kwai*, Brand valiantly sacrifices himself by diving at a launch trigger rigged like the dynamite detonator Alec Guinness falls on in the David Lean film. Brand is no semi-quisling like *Kwai's* Colonel Nicholson; he walks through a machine gun blast to save the day, as gallant as the hero of any 'Queen and Country' epic. [3]

Quatermass 2 draws its images from interesting sources. The machine gun battle in the chemical plant is practically a replay of the end of *White Heat*. The vision of tiny figures approaching an immense dome on the horizon is echoed in the same year's *Chikyu Boeigun (The Mysterians)*; both films evoke a post-modern feeling of humanity walking with trepidation toward a looming, science fiction Future.

After all the mystery, in its last moments *Quatermass 2* transforms into an almost Godzilla-like monster movie. The Professor peers into the mystery dome and sees nothing less than a colossal heap of alien protoplasm. The sight of the usually unflappable Quatermass recoiling in shock is priceless – how can anybody defeat that? The oozing blob is a challenge to man's claim for a spiritual status above the rest of nature. If communication were possible Quatermass might say, *"You think you're so all-powerful, and you're just a disgusting assemblage of individual cells."* The blob might well respond, *"Just what do you think you are?"*

Quatermass 2 reveals its most disturbing surprises when we're least prepared. Wandering in the weird landscape of the Winnerden synthetic food plant, the Professor hears a scream. From the top of a globular holding tank descends a lone figure, choking, covered head to toe in a black, smoldering, caustic mystery substance. He begs Quatermass not to touch him, and collapses on the ground: *"Quatermass! This is the food! And it burns!"*

Anchor Bay's transfer of **Quatermass 2** was reportedly taken from an English archive print. The dark opening scene has been digitally brightened, resulting in a grainy pincushion effect. Beyond that only a few more shots are affected. The rest of the picture is sharp and bright.

A trailer is included for the American version, *Enemy from Space*. Val Guest and Nigel Kneale are welcome guests on a feature-length commentary. Kneale doesn't take Guest to task for simplifying the television plays and Guest doesn't try to make a case about his film versions being better. It's fortuitous that the commentary of these elderly gentlemen was recorded while it could be. Jolly good.

There are classic science fiction movies and essential ones, and *Quatermass 2* sits firmly in both categories. In the pantheon of British science fiction it is paramount, with *These are the Damned* and *Day the Earth Caught Fire* only one notch below. Anchor Bay's long-awaited DVD is a very welcome release indeed.

1. In *Future Tense* author John Brosnan noted that the alien mark is V-shaped, and thus evokes the 'V for Victory' sign immortalized by Churchill in WW2. The socialist government so easily penetrated in *Q2* is a direct result of that war, and now its own symbol is being turned against England. Those scurvy socialists are relocating the working populace to soulless temporary housing in communities cut off from society. The work town's buses are abandoned. Does nobody go anywhere anymore?

2. This trend is of course the subject of Jean-Luc Godard's *Alphaville*, where citizens are reduced to zombie-like ants when deprived of the support of their all-controlling computer Alpha-60.

3. Hutchings, Peter *Hammer and Beyond, The British Horror Film*.

BEGINNING OF THE END

Image Reviewed: March 8, 2003
1957 / B&W / 1:78 widescreen / 76 min.
Cinematography Jack A. Marta. Art Direction Walter E. Keller. Editor Aaron Stell. Music Albert Glasser. Written by Fred Freiberger and Lester Gorn.
Produced, Directed and Special Effects by Bert I. Gordon

Released by the short-lived AB-PT Pictures Corp. (ABC Broadcasting and Paramount Theaters), *Beginning of the End* is one of filmmaker Bert I. Gordon's best efforts. It's a smartly paced and ambitiously assembled plagiarism job on Gordon Douglas's *Them!*, from plot and dialogue all the way to the blatant rip-off of the first film's poster art. Awkward at best, this generic 50s Big Bug movie shows the American wing of the genre descending into lower quality productions.

When the Illinois town of Ludlow is leveled overnight, hotshot New York news hen Audrey Ames (Peggie Castle) is on the case, nosing around the Army-imposed information blackout. Given special privileges by Colonel Sturgeon (Thomas Browne Henry), Audrey visits the agricultural lab of Dr. Ed Wainright (Peter Graves) whose sloppy work with isotopes has bred a race of humungous, voracious locusts. Army scoffing turns to grim determination when hordes of king-size bugs overrun the National Guard; the regular army moves in but can't stop the onslaught from mowing down city after city on its way to Chicago. Only entomologist Ed has a chance of finding the insects' weakness before General Hanson (Morris Ankrum) gives the order to nuke the Windy City.

With a directing career pretty much based on H.G. Wells' *The Food of the Gods*, and being a handy man with do-it-yourself special effects, Bert I. Gordon generally struck out big-time whenever he tried something original. He did his best work when creating, ah, *tributes* to other people's hit monster movies. This film's resemblance to *Them!* is explicit. *Beginning of the End* starts with two cops investigating a disappearance, tasks the Army and government entomologists with figuring out the mystery and then moves its climax to a major city imperiled by the insect foe. The title is a dialogue line that mimics Edmund Gwenn's grim warnings of apocalypse in the previous Big Bug picture. Warners had *Them!'s* original script rewritten to eliminate expensive scenes indicating massive monster battles. Gordon's version retains all of those grandiose story ideas, and solves the budget problem by using laughably poor effects work.

Gordon worked out an effects matting system that successfully composited images with an in-camera bi-pack method rather than costly optical printing. The clever technique yields arresting images that get the job done in a messy Z-picture sort of way. *Beginning of the End* uses this traveling matte process to place macro-photographed locusts into dozens of live-action backgrounds. The bugs look like cutouts pasted onto the screen. Elsewhere, a lot of rear-projection effects are utilized along with extremely ineffective footage of live locusts crawling on photo-blowups of streets and buildings. The 50s were notorious for energetic monster movies with pitiful effects. Although Gordon's technical finesse would never earn respect from the industry, it was good enough to satisfy the market. Anybody complaining would first have to admit they bought a ticket to a picture about giant grasshoppers.

The plot and its trimmings are unconvincing and implausible. Pretty Peggie Castle (*Invasion, U.S.A*) looks sexy in her tight skirts and silk blouses but never once behaves like a journalist. She turns into a heavy-breathing along-for-the-ride type soon after linking up with hunky Peter Graves. Graves' glorified gardener is surprised when his jumbo plant experimental station creates giant insects farther up the food chain. Reliable General Morris Ankrum tells us with a straight face that he plans to save Chicago by blowing it up with a nuclear bomb.

The science is unbelievably naïve, with concepts covered in the standard BIG-ordon method: a technical point is offered, and then immediately explained in words suited to a kindergartner. Graves uses isotopes, which are like a substitute sun (?) to make his plants grow 24 hours a day. Tomatoes thus mutate as big as beach balls, etc. Graves' helper (Than Wyenn) lost his voice and hearing because of a little 'radiation accident', tsk tsk. Wyenn can't hear anything but offers smiling reactions to things the other two are saying, even when their backs are turned and he can't read their lips. It is strange that Wyenn is so relaxed, because Castle and Graves ignore him almost completely, in scenes surreal enough to fit into a Buñuel movie.

Headlines, telegrams, and radio voices inform us that towns are wiped out and divisions of soldiers are devoured by the locust hordes, although we actually *see* next to nothing. With the majority of the relevant action happening off-screen, *Beginning of the End* makes do with a couple of tensely edited battle scenes that at least give the impression that some fierce fighting is going on, even if the miniature bugs never fit into the live-action stock shots. When thousands of locusts are supposed to be overrunning Chicago, making a beeline for Graves' high-frequency transmitter, we're shown a handful of bugs going in no particular direction. The mass drowning in Lake Michigan is covered in two or three brief cuts of insects bobbing around in what might be Gordon's kitchen sink.

The upshot of all this is that the goofy and inept *Beginning of the End* is irresistible.

Image's DVD of **Beginning of the End** is a pristine presentation that enables a close examination of the effects processes. For instance, a bug photographed crawling on a photo blowup of a building, results in an image of a 3-dimensional insect against an indistinct and flat-looking photo. Even us 50s kids could see through the effect.

Interestingly, the enhanced matting crops away what was once the film's main joke, a shot or two where the bugs crawl off the buildings, and keep crawling onto the sky background. Those mistakes must all have happened up near the top of the frame that the matting cuts off. After 40 years of open-matte TV viewing, we find out that Bert is innocent of that particular charge.

Director-producer and enthusiastic genre collector Bruce Kimmel hosts a friendly commentary with Gordon's ex-wife Flora and daughter Susan. Although Flora assisted Bert and is more

than qualified to speak authoritatively about the effects, she seems to have forgotten the picture almost entirely.

One detail in *Beginning of the End* threw Savant for a loop: when the first squad of soldiers retreats from the big bugs at the destroyed grain warehouse, television prints contained a truly awful effect shot. Near the end of the sequence, where the camera pans left with a fleeing Army truck, a locust enters from screen right and chases it. The bug's legs don't move, resulting in an ambitious shot that fails miserably. But that effect isn't in this print – the truck shot still is, but without the bug matted in.

SCIENCE-FICTION'S MOST ASTOUNDING STORY!

THE BRAIN from PLANET AROUS

JOHN AGAR · JOYCE MEADOWS · ROBERT FULLER

THE BRAIN FROM PLANET AROUS

Image Reviewed: March 5, 2001
1957 / B&W / 1:37 flat / 70 min.
Cinematography / Producer Jacques
Marquette. Makeup Jack Pierce. Written by
Ray Buffum.
Directed by Nathan Hertz

A silly film for the neck 'n' pet drive-in crowd, *The Brain From Planet Arous* is great entertainment. It may be played straight, but at heart it knows it's a comedy.

Scientist Steve March (John Agar) and his assistant Dan Murphy (Robert Fuller) investigate an unexpected radiation source at Mystery Mountain, and encounter a bulbous floating brain named Gor (voice: Dale Tate). Gloating that he's here to conquer the earth, Gor kills Dan with rays from his glowing eyes and takes possession of Steve. Delighted at having a human body to inhabit, Gor wastes no time aggressively groping ("Heh Heh") Steve's girlfriend Sally Fallon (Joyce Meadows) and making megalomaniacal speeches to Sally's father John (Thomas Browne Henry). Gor/Steve uses his mental powers to blow up an airplane. He aims to enslave humanity and build an armada of spaceships with which to conquer his home planet. Suspicious of Steve's odd behavior, Sally and John find Dan's burned body at Mystery Mountain and meet Vol, another Brain from the Planet Arous. Soft spoken and benign ("Nice dog, nice dog"), Vol announces that he's a policeman come to capture the criminal Gor. But Vol needs a little assistance, in the form of a volunteer living body to possess while on the case.

As can be gathered from the synopsis, this isn't *The Day the Earth Stood Still*; any sillier and *Arous* would be an episode of *Rocky & Bullwinkle*. Those looking for laughs will find no end of absurdities, what with a giant floating brain with headlight-like eyes chortling in anticipation of earthly sex. Teenagers necked in *Invasion of the Saucermen* but this film's possessed John Agar is so hot for poor Joyce Meadows that he tears her clothing. Many space aliens *talk* about mating with earth women but the libidinous Gor gets right down to business.

Arous billboards the singular talents of John Agar, then near the end of a string of ever-worsening science fiction roles. Uninteresting as just plain Steve, Agar is terrific when possessed by the malevolent party balloon from space. Agar puts snap into his comic-book threats. He ends almost every sentence chortling like Simon Legree. The effect is as if Agar himself is crazy – it's funny and weird at the same time. Agar must have hated donning the painful-looking silvery contact lenses, as we see them only once or twice. The cutaways to Agar's grinning face as he uses his super eye-power to zap planes or simulate atomic explosions, appear to be the same shot.

The production values are modest but polished. Director Nathan Juran hides behind his middle name as he did for *Attack of the 50 Foot Woman*. His expert and expressive direction is nothing to be ashamed of. Juran frequently arranges for Agar to face us with his back to other actors, flashing a knowing smirk whenever a puny earthling (Gor uses those exact words) says something that strikes him as funny. Juran films one of Gor's power-mad speeches through a water cooler bottle to distort John Agar's face. It's as effective as its antecedent in *The Wizard of Oz*, where Margaret Hamilton's face is distorted in a crystal ball.

The playing is always earnest. Meadows and Agar go at their noble profession even when swinging axes at Gor's "fissure of Rolando", as if the inflated brain were a birthday piñata. Meadows is particularly convincing at expressing distress when lustfully pawed by Steve, knowing he really isn't her boyfriend – a thought that surely was going through a lot of pony-tailed heads at the drive-in.

The Brain from Planet Arous was a reasonable hit, enabling its producer Howco to follow with a score of ever-worse features, like *Teenage Monster*. (We called them "How Come?" movies.) *Variety* gave it a positive review, as opposed to its total slam of the superior *Quatermass 2 (Enemy From Space)* just a few months before. By late 1957, a Hollywood overdosed by cheap sci-fi welcomed this show's sense of humor.

Image's DVD of **The Brain from Planet Arous** is one of Wade Williams' better releases. Savant only saw a few marks on the print source. A raggedly edited trailer does a good job of making the film look exciting.

THE ABOMINABLE SNOWMAN

Anchor Bay Reviewed: August 7, 2000
1957 / B&W / 2:35 widescreen / *The Abominable Snowman of the Himalayas*
Cinematography Arthur Grant. Production Designer Bernard Robinson. Editor Bill Lenny. Written by Nigel Kneale from his story *The Creature*. Produced by Aubrey Baring, Michael Carreras, Anthony Nelson-Keys.
Directed by Val Guest

Reviewers didn't have had much to say about the remarkable **The Abominable Snowman**. Monster fans weren't charmed by its reluctance to show the title characters. Hammer aficionados preferred the company's Technicolor horrors. But this Nigel Kneale teleplay adaptation, like his earlier Quatermass series, is a genre film of rare power.

Botanists John Rollason (Peter Cushing) and Peter Fox (Richard Wattis) are the guests of the kindly but mysterious Tibetan Lhama (Arnold Marle), who meddles in John's research and his relationship with his wife Helen (Maureen Connell). Blustering American explorer / promoter Tom Friend (Forrest Tucker) arrives, and proposes a daring winter climb to observe a real Yeti, the purported Abominable Snowman. Over Helen's objections and the subtle warnings of the Lhama, John joins the Friend expedition. But out in the deep snow, Friend proves to be a liar: he plans to capture a Yeti, and if that doesn't work, kill one. At first the expedition seems a failure. Friend has already huckstered a phony wolf-child in India, and he's prepared to pass off a snow monkey as an exhibit debunking the Yeti myth. The real snowmen abruptly appear. A trap set by the reckless Ed Shelley (Robert Brown) breaks the ankle of team member Mc-Nee (Michael Brill), who goes quietly insane watching a gigantic Yeti hand reach into his tent. John realizes too late that the Yeti are actually ultra-intelligent beings, that use telepathic powers to manipulate the minds of the surviving expedition members.

The Abominable Snowman reminds one of other B&W Hammerscope productions that didn't share in the popularity of the company's flat Technicolor shockers: *The Stranglers of Bombay, These Are the Damned. Snowman* integrates impressive interior sets with footage shot in the Pyrenees.

Nigel Kneale's script is a neat re-think of the setup of Frank Capra's *Lost Horizon*, proposing a human-alien relationship that would be further developed in his conceptual masterwork *Quatermass and the Pit*. Cushing plays a warm and likeable scientist who, much like Ronald Colman in the Capra film, is manipulated by a Tibetan Lhama. Instead of divulging spiritual secrets, this Lhama keeps Cushing's Rollason almost completely in the dark. Both

Lhamas sense that the end of humanity is near. In this science fiction update, the wise guru of the Himalayas knows of the existence of a 'better mankind', one that isn't strictly human. An evolutionary fork apart from men and apes, the Yeti have waited patiently for the apocalypse to allow them to inherit the earth from undeserving, violent Man.

Kneale makes most of the Lhama's ambiguous actions, and the story's resolution is intriguingly ambivalent. Does the Lhama guide Rollason into joining the Friend expedition? Does he protect the Yeti through sympathetic wisdom, or do the Yeti control him as he seems to control others? Are the Yeti really the next masters of the Earth, as in *The Planet of the Apes*, or are they an ultra-sophisticated invasion from outer space, using the Lhama as a puppet? There's no doubting the telepathic connection between the Lhama and the Yeti, between the Yeti and the expedition, and between the Lhama and Helen when she launches her 'intuitive' rescue mission. Does the Lhama save John Rollason because he recognizes a Ronald Colman-like kindred spirit, or is he callously using Rollason to quash curiosity about the Yeti?

The tease ending of *The Abominable Snowman* is priceless. A rescued John Rollason meekly endorses the Lhama's assertion that, "There is no Yeti". One angle gives the impression that John is lying voluntarily, morally converted to the Lhama's position, as was *Lost Horizon's* Ronald Colman. But in his final close-up, Cushing's pale, staring face conveys an impression of involuntary brainwashing. When Savant saw *The Abominable Snowman* as a child, this ending seemed merely abrupt: "What, no more monsters?" The film now plays as a mature ecological fable, as powerful as any cautionary documentary. It belongs on a double bill with John Huston's majestic *The Roots of Heaven*, one of few commercial films to take human species arrogance as its subject.

Kneale's characters are basically decent, even the opportunistic Tom Friend. Ed Shelly is a thoughtless adventurer-pirate, but he's also has good qualities. Kneale doesn't suggest that an appreciation of a 'correct' point of view is going to redeem either of them. On the other hand, Rollason's gentle partner is granted atypical respect. Richard Wattis often plays a silly-ass twit (his general in *Casino Royale*, for one), but this supporting role is given careful depth.

Viewers can easily assign the Tom Friend character's attitude to 'Ugly American' stereotyping, and maybe they have a point. Unfavorably compared with Dr. Rollason, Friend probably represents everything about Brian Donlevy's Quatermass that Kneale hated. Had Cushing played Professor Quatermass, perhaps history would have seen a series of Technicolor Hammer science fiction films!

Anchor Bay's DVD of **The Abominable Snowman** is for most of us the first opportunity to really see this movie. Also included is an American trailer that adds the extra words *of the Himalayas* to the title ... and presents the Lhama as a stock menace by implying that the fainted Helen is being delivered to him for illicit purposes! Finishing the extras is an engrossing full-length commentary by director Guest and author Kneale, similar to the one on *Quatermass 2*.

FROM BEHIND THE MOON THEY COME...

TO INVADE THE EARTH! ABDUCT ITS WOMEN LEVEL ITS CITIES

"THE MYSTERIANS"

In BIG SCREEN COLOR!

GREATEST SCIENCE-FICTION PICTURE EVER CONCEIVED BY THE MIND OF MAN

CHIKYU BOEIGUN

Media Blasters / Tokyo Shock Reviewed: March 28, 2005
1957 / Color / 2:35 widescreen / ~~88~~ 85 min. / *The Mysterians*
Cinematography Hajime Koizumi. Production Designer Teruaki Abe. Music Akira Ifukube. Written by Shigeru Kayama, Takeshi Kimura, Jojiro Okami. Produced by Tomoyuki Tanaka. Directed by Ishiro Honda

Savant is a booster of the first wave of fantastic Japanese spectaculars from roughly 1957 to 1964. *The Mysterians* was one of the company's first efforts in color and Tohoscope. It's patterned after *The War of the Worlds* by way of *Flash Gordon*, with a little added Japanese flavoring.

The American version of *The Mysterians* fell into the shadowy world of questionable rights only a few years after its 1959 debut. For decades the only viewing choice were gray market VHS tapes of old television prints. The 16mm optical tracks for these prints were printed with an annoying flutter that ruined Akira Ifukube's relentless martial music score. This uncut and authorized Japanese edition is mastered from Toho sources with excellent color and sound.

At a country festival, scientist Ryoichi Shirahashi (Akihiko Hirata) upsets his sister Etsuko (Yumi Shirakawa) and his date Hiroko Iwamoto (Momoko Kochi) with his sullen and withdrawn attitude. A strange forest fire interrupts the festival, and Ryochi disappears. The next day the entire hamlet is destroyed when the ground beneath it subsides. Ryoichi's colleague and friend Joji Atsumi (Kenji Sahara) investigates and finds that the ground nearby is radioactive – and hot! A giant robot called Moguera appears from a mountain fissure. The Japan Defense Force mobilizes to stop it, but shortly thereafter a giant whirling dome rises out of the earth near a lake at the foot of Mt. Fuji. A delegation of scientists, including Joji and his *sensai* Dr. Adachi (Takashi Shimura) are greeted by a group of helmeted, caped men from the planet Mysteroid. The aliens have established a temporary base on the far side of the moon because their own world has been destroyed by intergalactic war. Ryoichi appears on television in his new role as spokesman for the Mysterians, who demand a few hectares of land and the right to replenish their race by mating with earth women. The Japanese officials don't like the invaders' rampaging robots or their take-first, ask-later policy, and vow to resist.

RKO acquired *The Mysterians* just as the studio folded in 1958. The film migrated to MGM in a fire-sale deal that accounts for the American rights drifting almost immediately into limbo. Many surviving advertising materials still bear RKO's imprint. In contrast to the lavish original Japanese artwork, the U.S. ad campaign appears to have been designed by amateurs.

Finally reaching U.S. screens in 1959, *The Mysterians* was a kiddie matinee hit that helped Toho license more films to Columbia (*The H-Man, Battle in Outer Space, Mothra*), Universal (*King Kong vs. Godzilla*), Warners (*Gigantis the Fire Monster*) and American-International (*Matango, Atragon*).

Toho's first outer space epic displays a slightly juvenile house style of fanta-science that appeals to many adults as well. The film's personal stories quickly take a back seat to unending battle scenes. Jarring music crashes in as the Mysteroid battle dome repels wave after wave of attacks by Sherman tanks and Super Sabre jets. The sky fills with battling flying saucers and the noisy blasting of colorful death rays.

The Defense Force musters fleets of futuristic super-weapons against the invaders. Twin aerial battleships called Beta-One and Beta-Two float horizontally on jets of air. Their primary weapon is an untested American atomic cannon. The Markalite looks like a colossal radio telescope mounted on a tripod, with three army tanks for feet. Its dish antenna gathers the Mysteroid rays, amplifies them and then shoots them back again. Those clairvoyant Americans have been developing defensive weapons against unknown technologies!

All of this hardware makes *The Mysterians* a wall-to-wall toy bonanza. The tanks and the jets are the usual wire-rigged models, as are the Mysterians' little hot-rod flying saucers, still the coolest rides in the galaxy. Beta-One and Beta-Two must have been designed as marketable toys; the Japanese at the time were very big on gaudy electric gizmos with flashing lights that rolled on the floor. [1]

The buildup to the first appearance of the robot Moguera was a white-knuckle experience for little kids back in 1959 – its emergence from a mountainside is stunning. The American cut never explains that the robot's purpose is to dig subterranean tunnels. A brief added scene shows a second Moguera buzz-sawing its way underground. It undermines one of the Markalite weapons during the final battle.

The film has more than its share of core science fiction poetry. Fleeing Moguera over a railroad bridge, Joji and Etsuko notice a trio of flying saucers flitting across the sky. Joji has seen a forest fire that burns from the roots up and an entire valley that's been tossed about as if it were in a blender. The saucers finally make sense of it all. Professor Adachi and his colleagues walk toward the eerie dome that waits threateningly on the horizon. We puny Earthlings have been ushered into a frightening future of alien technology.

The invaders prove to have the same needs as earthly men when they demand mating rights with Japanese women. Joji and his countrymen aren't about to give up their most precious possessions without a fight. Of course, neither side thinks to ask the women if they might *want* to become the consorts of space pirates. The kidnapping of Etsuko and Hiroko is a ghostly time-out from the noise of battle. Two saucers dim their lights and park motionless above Etsuko's house. Helmeted Mysterians descend on cables, seize the swooning damsels and disappear with them into the saucer's underbelly. Kidnapped by sex-starved aliens!

The Mysterians themselves are pure *Flash Gordon* villains that enjoy issuing ultimatums and rub their hands in anticipation of villages being inundated by their artificial floods. When all is said and done, the pitiful intruders crawl back to their saucers and flee to their retreating space station. Better luck next time, losers. [2]

The Japanese title *Chikyu boeigun* means "Earth Defense Force," an imaginary military branch of the United Nations. American films like *The War of the Worlds* emphasize the futility of resisting the superior weaponry of the invaders from space. Whereas our films presume that civilian populations are one step away from panic or mob violence, these Japanese fantasies see things differently. At every cataclysmic disaster, invasion or Kaiju threat, civil defense monitors help the public flee from danger. The crowds run, but it's an orderly evacuation and not a rout like the chaotic mob scenes in the English *Gorgo*.

The Japanese military response is also a group effort. Every meeting and decision takes place in a room crammed with dozens of officials and experts working as a team. The humble Dr. Adachi repeatedly defers to the communal will. Individual attacks are usually suicide efforts, as with the tank commander who ends up popping out of his miniature tank like a Jack-in-the-Box. Responsibility to the needs of the group is of paramount importance. That's what makes it necessary for the turncoat Ryoichi to atone by forfeiting his life, even though a scientist like him is presumably worth more to society alive and productive. *The Mysterians* is a conservative fantasy.

This martial fantasy is also a product of an officially pacifist nation. In his *Science Fiction Encyclopedia* Phil Hardy contends that *The Mysterians* is pointedly anti-American. The alien invaders that want military bases on Japanese soil and mating rights with Japanese women are a transparent cipher for occupying U.S. forces. Note that the Americans played by George Furness and Harold Conway are meant to be United Nations officials. When the miraculous new weapons arrive from America (on U.S. cargo planes) Japanese personnel take them into battle.

Most everyone will recognize actor Takashi Shimura from *Seven Samurai*. Mysterian leader Yoshio Tsuchiya played Rikichi in the same film. One of the gangsters in *Mothra*, Tetsu Nakamura, has a small role as a scientist. Momoko Kochi, the actress with the cute Gene Tierney- like overbite, had a more demanding role in the original *Gojira*.

Daily Variety's assessment of *The Mysterians* as "a red-blooded phantasmagoria" still holds true. Spread out across a large monitor, Toho's thriller is a spectacular action circus of spaceships, death rays, explosions and wholesale destruction.

Media Blasters' Tokyo Shock DVD of **The Mysterians** is a fine video presentation. The enhanced picture is brightly colored, with good black levels. The multi-hued rays, color-coded Mysterian costumes and crimson flamethrower blasts all look correct.

The Mysterians marked Toho's entry into full-on optical printer work. It's easy to tell when a shot becomes an optical because the screen is suddenly inundated with white specks of dust, hair and other flotsam. It's possible that digital image processing has been applied, as the white dirt-storms are slightly subdued and the image a tiny bit softer.

The original Japanese sound is robust and the Akira Ifukube music plays at original levels. Newly recorded English and Spanish dub tracks appear as well. Media Blasters has also isolated Akira Ifukube's superb music score, a gallery of hypnotic martial rhythms that alternate between an insistent march to honor the defenders and jarring brassy notes representing the Mysterian threat. When the first Markalite weapon rockets onto the battlefield, the raucous swipes of the brass section sound like the slashes of a giant metallic sword.

Latter-day Toho special effects supervisors Koichi Kawakita and Shinji Higuchi speak on a feature-length commentary track, subtitled in English. They marvel at production values

that are routinely denied today's Japanese films: crowd scenes and the giant miniatures that special effects supervisor Eiji Tsuburaya used for his pre-CGI visuals. Fantastic action toys are a big part of the appeal of *The Mysterians*; the computer graphics employed in new pictures haven't the same quality. The commentators say that their desire to remake *Mysterians* finds no interest.

1. My pre-teen daughter thought those Mysteroid helmets with the vertical white patches covering the nose and the mouth make them look like parrots: "Look, it's Attack of the Parakeet People!"

2. Advertising executives in the satirical black comedy *Giants and Toys* released soon after *The Mysterians* play with new space toys and use them to hawk their candy products. Interestingly, *The Mysterians* includes several product placements for a major Japanese candy company.

VYNALEZ ZKAZY

Not on Region 1 DVD Reviewed: January 10, 2010
1958 / B&W / 1:33 flat / 85 min. / *The Fabulous World of Jules Verne*
Cinematography: Antonin Horak, Bohuslav Pikhart, Jiri Tarantik. Music Zdenek Liska. Written by Frantisek Hrubin, Milan Vacha, Jiri Brdecka, Karel Zeman from the novel *Face au drapeau* by Jules Verne. Produced by Zdenek Novak.
Production Design and Directed by Karel Zeman

Movie kids in the early 1960s kept their radar tuned for anything with Jules Verne attached, and producers knew it. We loved *20,000 Leagues Under the Sea* and *Journey to the Center of the Earth;* the less discriminating (or younger) among us also loved A.I.P.'s cut-rate *Master of the World.* Long before we had a clue that any-body in Czechoslovakia made movies, many of us ran to a Warner Bros. matinee picture called *The Fabulous World of Jules Verne.*

Our initial impression was disappointment, as *The Fabulous World of Jules Verne* was more like an animated movie than a live-action extravaganza. But too many outright charming things were happening not to be entertained, and it took only a few minutes for the film's magic spell to settle in. The story played almost like a silent movie, but every single shot was a new discovery, a "hey, look at that" moment.

It wasn't until 1970 that I encountered the movie in John Baxter's book *Science Fiction Film.* As with several other Soviet Bloc pictures we'd seen in edited form this picture makes quite a different impression in its original version. It is really **Vynález Zkázy** from 1958. The title translates as *A Deadly Invention.* Karel Zeman died in 1989. Considered something of a national treasure in Czechoslovakia, he's best known here for a color version of *Baron Munchausen* filmed with similar techniques, that at one time showed frequently on American television.

Zeman made a number of films with roughly the same method, a combination of theatrical and film techniques stylized to resemble vintage illustrations that used parallel line patterns to suggest shading and texture in a printing technology with a limited range of contrast. Zeman achieves his effects with flat scenery, special three-dimensional props (some of them mechanical), miniature mattes, texture superimpositions and stop-motion animation. The images are so sharp and consistent that we suspect that little if any optical work was done. Many scenes look patently artificial, reproducing old-fashioned ideas of altered perspective. Others are so good that we can't tell whether most of what we're looking at is a live set, an animated drawing, or a miniature diorama. Some of the flat cel animation (birds, etc.) betrays its origin but the stop-motion model work is often extremely smooth. Everything is textured with parallel lines, from costumes to the paneling of walls; it's as if we were in a steel-engraved world suspended somewhere between 2D and 3D.

The story combines a specific Verne tale with ideas from *20,00 Leagues* and *Mysterious Island*. After a brief overview of the marvelous world of new inventions (including Robur's flying helicopter boat, the *Albatross*) we settle into a charming, fantastic adventure. Pirates kidnap Professor Roch (Arnost Navratil), and also his new assistant, Simon Hart (Lubor Tokos). They're transferred to the amazing submarine of the nefarious Count Artigas (Miroslav Holub), which then sinks a ship by ramming it. We watch the ship settle to the bottom through the submarine's quaint picture windows. Beautiful Jana (Jana Zatloukalova) frees some birds as her ship goes down, a gesture linking *Vynález Zkázy* with the "End of an Age" nostalgia of Georges Franju's *Judex*. Characters behave in a subdued and civilized manner no matter how dire the circumstances, establishing a charmingly ironic distance from the material – women in sedate old engravings never scream or grin, you know. With Zeman's deliberate pacing inviting us to savor every picture-book image, the movie takes on a wonderfully droll quality.

Later on, the love-struck Hart climbs a castle wall to talk to Jana. She asks him to wait until she makes herself decent, which requires that the fellow cling precariously to the outside of her window for a few extra moments. The comment on proper decorum elicited applause from an adult audience keen to savor the film's finer subtleties.

The rest of the plot is designed to showcase Artigas' amazing Nemo-like world. Jana is rescued and hidden from the other prisoners. The submarine reaches the Count's secret island base through an underwater tunnel, as in the Disney version. Artigas tricks Professor Roch into refining his atomic energy invention into a new kind of explosive. While Roch works on heavy water issues and a giant reactor, Artigas builds a giant cannon. Hart succeeds in sending out a distress message but is prevented from contacting Roch or the mystery girl. He tries to escape while helping Artigas's divers repair a telegraph cable, just as an outside submarine arrives to investigate. Left unconscious at the bottom of the underwater tunnel, Hart is picked up by the bulbous mini-sub that paddles through the water like a turtle (more guaranteed applause from kids and adults alike). But it is sunk by Artigas's larger submarine. Presumed dead, Hart returns to the secret lab and escapes with Jana in an observation balloon. Artigas prepares to sink the enemy fleet with cannon shells loaded with Roch's new super-explosive. That's when Professor Roch realizes that he must take direct responsibility for his deadly invention.

Vynález Zkázy will be an unending delight for anybody with a visual imagination. The submarines cruise past stylized fish. Undersea divers ride little mechanical submarine bicycles. Pirates sharpen their swords in uniform motions, as if they were playing in a string section. Upon finding a treasure chest, two pirates begin a duel, at the bottom of the sea. Roch's lab is a forest of crazy steam-pistons in motion, all of which appear to be optical-illusion flat animated stage props. News from the outside world comes via a fanciful pre-cinema "movie" projector that uses giant picture wheels similar to a View-Master setup.

Left at the bottom of the underwater tunnel with his air running low, Hart hallucinates fish that fold into each other like a kaleidoscope, turning into butterflies. A giant squid blackens the screen with its ink, as Hart and the pirates defend themselves with axes. One-off jokes proliferate, as when Artigas arms himself with a spring-loaded wind-up repeating pistol to shoot down Hart's balloon. The explosive finale has an anti-nuke tone, but one contained by the context. There's not a hint of a propagandistic message.

Vynález Zkázy is highly cinematic – its whimsical "world" of Jules Verne couldn't be accomplished as either an old illustration or a live-action movie. The charm comes directly from Zeman's ingenious filming methods. We get the idea that if an 1865 daydreamer could imagine a magic-lantern movie of Verne's marvels, it might look a little like this. The visual magic here dwarfs most modern fantasies, where photo-real images are a routine, and the magic is frequently lost in creativity-by-committee.

Warners' re-edited version *The Fabulous World of Jules Verne* is reportedly a couple of minutes shorter, even with an introduction by Hugh Downs (then an announcer for Jack Paar). Zeman's processes were given the name "Mystimation", clearly inspired by Ray Harryhausen's Dynamation moniker. *Variety* caught the original film at the 1958 Brussels film festival and gave it a lukewarm review, as it often did with foreign productions regardless of quality. When reviewed as a Warners release three years later, the coverage is twice as long and more optimistic about the film's commercial possibilities.

I've since been able to see Karel Zeman's follow-ups *The Stolen Airship* (*Ukradena vzducholod*; 1967) and *On the Comet* (*Na komete*;1971) which have special qualities of their own but are not as exciting. I understand that these films are available on disc in other countries; *Vynález Zkázy* would make a marvelous, classy addition to the Criterion Collection.

THE FLY
RETURN OF THE FLY
CURSE OF THE FLY

Fox Reviewed September 6, 2007
2:35 widescreen
The Fly
1958 / Color / 94 min.
Return of the Fly
1959 / B&W / 80 min.
Curse of the Fly
1965 / B&W / 86 min.
Starring Vincent Price, Patricia Owens, Herbert Marshall, Al (David) Hedison, Brett Halsey, Brian Donlevy, George Baker, Carole Gray.
Directed by Kurt Neumann, Edward Bernds, Don Sharp

The three films in Fox's *The Fly Collection* originate with the 1957 short story by George Langelaan first published in *Playboy*. The idea of matter teleportation probably occurred to the writer the moment he heard an explanation of the workings of television. If images can be broadcast from one location to another, why not objects? Langelaan's brief exercise in horror was a natural for the movies at a time when cheap independents about mutated bugs were packing the drive-ins. The major studios stepped in looking for easy pickings. Paramount hired William Alland away from Universal for *The Space Children* and *Colossus of New York* and made a killing with a tiny independent acquisition, *The Blob*. Independent producer Robert L. Lippert couldn't sign his name to *The Fly* but apparently produced that film and several other Fox releases, such as *She Devil*, under the "Regalscope" banner. Presented in color and stereophonic sound, *The Fly* became one of the biggest hits of 1958. The genuinely icky concept definitely had legs: Fox followed it up with two cheap sequels. David Cronenberg's remake 28 years later is a minor masterpiece that in many ways improves on the original.

THE FLY

1958/ Color / 94 min. Cinematography Karl Struss. Music Paul Sawtell. Written by James Clavell, from a story by George Langelaan. Produced and Directed by Kurt Neumann

The Fly is a clever crossover concoction that places its disturbing concept within the romantic format of the 'woman's picture'. Set in a fashionable home in Montreal, the story is structured as a flashback murder confession. Audiences were surprised and shocked by the film's horror aspects. Like a technological cousin of the cockroach freak in Kafka's *Metamorphosis*, the lady of the house must deal with a husband with the head of an insect.

Inspector Charas (Herbert Marshall) finds brilliant researcher Andre Delambre's (Al "David" Hedison) head and arm crushed in a machine press, and his widow Helene (Patricia Owens) in a state of confused denial. Andre's businessman brother François (Vincent Price) senses that Helene is lying about what really happened, and tricks her into a full explanation: Andre had invented an amazing matter transmitter and was teleporting objects from one booth to another in his basement lab. He foolishly tried to teleport himself, unaware that a fly was in the booth with him...

Robert L. Lippert may have been drawn to *The Fly* because of similarities to the English *The Quatermass Xperiment*, on which he had served as an uncredited producer. Both films are about sympathetic men transformed against their will into horrible monsters. Andre Delambre emerges from the teleportation booth with the head and claw of a fly, while somewhere in the house buzzes a confused fly with Andre's head and hand. Sympathy for the understandably distraught Helene creates interest for a concept that by all rights should be plain silly, especially when the tiny fly, caught in a spider's web, squeals *"Help me!"* Yet the image of the nightmarish, agonized face in the web can't be forgotten.

Director Kurt Neumann's straightforward storytelling masks some of *The Fly*'s non-existent logic. The malfunctioning matter transmitter makes radically inconsistent errors with each use. After the dematerialized cat becomes lost en route to the second booth, Andre hears it meeyowing, like a ghost. We also wonder how the fly head got bigger and Andre's head smaller. It still appears to be Andre's brain in there, at least until he tells Helene that he's losing his will to that of the fly. At one point Andre confesses that he's not sure how parts of his own machine work, and hasn't a clue why some transmissions are successful and others are not. That doesn't sound very scientific. [1]

Instead of sending Andre back to engineering school the script opts for the easy out of proclaiming that the researcher meddled with things Man was not meant to know. François Delambre tells little Phillipe that his father was a lot like Columbus, an explorer into the unknown. Writer Richard Hodgens points out that, "what will be remembered is that Father was like a fly." [2]

Andre's teleportations are orchestrated with a dramatic fanfare of flashing lights and audio while the witnesses wear dark goggles, as if watching a nuclear blast. The reveal of the frightening fly's head is quite a shock, as is his compound eye's POV of Helene's reaction, a pattern of dozens of screaming faces. The head-crushing business with the machine press accounts for more horror trauma and the final scene at the spider's web is justly famous. Vincent Price, Patricia Owens and Herbert Marshall put across some very unlikely scenes by taking everything seriously.

The Fly has survived with its original stereo track intact. Fox played up the classy production values, only for the show to include a CinemaScope and color close-up of a dirty trash can, complete with flies buzzing in multi-channel sound.

The Fly is a good enhanced transfer with accurate color. Actor David Hedison appears on a commentary. His memories are quite vivid and host David Del Valle adds his personal recollections of Vincent Price. Hedison wishes that his transformation into the fly-monster could have been more gradual, enabling him to perform a Jekyll-Hyde scene.

RETURN OF THE FLY

1959 / B&W / 80 min. Cinematography Brydon Baker. Music Paul Sawtell, Bert Shefter. Producer Bernard Glasser. Written and Directed by Edward L. Bernds

The immediate follow-up **Return of the Fly** rushes to deliver same-but-different monster thrills, retaining CinemaScope but dropping the Color by Deluxe. This time the matter trans-

mitter has a problem with gigantism, resulting in a fly's head that resembles an insectoid beach ball. The film is an official sequel with Vincent Price returning as François Delambre. Fifteen years have passed and little Phillipe (Charles Herbert in the first film) is now grown up. François' hair is grayer but the rest of the world hasn't changed. Director Ed Bernds' rushed script takes a page from a Universal Frankenstein sequel – the son returns to repeat his father's tragic experiment.

Young Phillipe Delambre (Brett Halsey) attends his mother's funeral and reopens his father's matter transmitter lab. Phillipe corrects his Andre's engineering mistakes, but is victimized by his unscrupulous business partners. They hijack the invention and dispose of Phillipe by tossing him into the teleporter with a fly. Realizing that the monster wandering the countryside is his nephew, François thinks he can save him – but he first needs to do some essential fly catching.

The relatively cheap *Return of the Fly* was a moderate success despite an unimaginative script. The amazing teleporter is now merely a device to create instant monsters, as seen with an unlucky fellow who emerges from the process with the paws of a rat. Phillipe commits a couple of vengeance murders when trapped in the monster fly's head. Since he has an ironclad "it was the fly" defense, nobody mentions trouble with the law. Edward Bernds' direction is lively and Vincent Price has some good moments as the concerned Uncle. Audiences laughed when the tiny fly squeals *"Help, Cecile!"* but I remember hearing applause at the conclusion when Phillipe is restored intact.

After this film and its double bill partner *The Alligator People*, Fox released fewer small-scale B&W creature features. Only a handful would come out in the next five years or so, including the undernourished efforts *The Hand of Death* and *The Day Mars Invaded Earth*. [2]

Return of the Fly is a good enhanced transfer of a cheaply made picture with variable original photography. On some scenes the 'Scope lenses look a bit out of adjustment, and a few inserts are on the fuzzy side.

CURSE OF THE FLY

1965 / B&W / 80 min. Cinematography Basil Emmott. Music Paul Sawtell, Bert Shefter. Written by Harry Spalding. Producers Robert L. Lippert, Jack Parsons. Directed by Don Sharp

Robert Lippert was finally able to take a screen credit six years later on *Curse of the Fly*, probably because he had relocated to England. Even cheaper than the first sequel, *Curse* suffers from a rushed production and a haphazard script. Director Don Sharp adds a handful of effective stylistic touches and some of the acting is quite good; for fans of teleportation looking for something completely different, *Curse* certainly tries. For starters, no fly appears in the film.

Henri Delambre (Brian Donlevy) and his sons have continued the researches of Andre and Phillipe. Their machine can transmit people between teleportation chambers located in Montreal and London, but gruesome accidents have created a number of problems both scientific and legal. Henri is suspected in the disappearances of various test subjects that are now horrible mutations hidden in cells on the Delambre property. Some of the successful teleportees end up aging rapidly, or are left with radiation burns. The household attracts the interest of the law when Martin Delambre (George Baker of *On Her Majesty's Secret Service*) brings home a new wife, the unstable Patricia (Carole Gray). Henri's objection to the marriage seems reasonable after we find out that Martin periodically suffers from horrible skin lesions. Neither father nor son can prevent Patricia from discovering the teleportation equipment, or finding the zombie-like mutations locked in the stables.

Science is never easy in science fiction films. The Delambre family develops a wonderful invention but becomes mired in lawbreaking, murders and madness. Although we welcome a sequel where Andre's machine finally gets to teleport people across the globe, that aspect of *Curse of the Fly* is largely left unexplored. The bulk of the film repeats the structure of *The Alligator People*, following the beautiful Carole Gray as she learns the secret of the spooky Delambre mansion. A cop investigating the family visits the blind, infirm Inspector Charas, this time played by Charles Carson. Sinister housekeeper Yvette Rees feeds food scraps to the mindless mutants, while playing "Mrs. Danvers" to a deranged monster that was once Martin Delambre's first wife! Henri Delambre's attitude isn't very encouraging: *"We're scientists. We have to do things we hate!"*

Like many Lippert productions, the film is just too cheap. Although director Don Sharp begins with an intriguing slow motion title sequence of Patricia fleeing an asylum in her underwear, much of the film is flat-lit and unattractive. The mutant make-ups aren't very convincing and even the teleportation scenes fail to excite. The police become suspicious when Henri bounces between Montreal and London without a record of his passport being used.

The conclusion is unnecessarily chaotic. As the cops close in, Brian Donlevy's Henri unwisely decides to teleport his 'mistakes' to London over the objections of Albert, the son manning the London receiver. One would think that disposing of them would be much more difficult there than on the secluded Montreal estate.

Director Sharp's adds a Gothic flavor to the proceedings and the deformed monstrosities locked in their separate rooms recall H. P. Lovecraft's *The Color Out of Space*. In the rush to wrap things up, the cheap production can't quite make it all come together. [3]

The Fly Collection is attractively appointed with clever packaging and a colorful insert booklet. A fourth disc contains most of the extras, including a fine 1997 *Biography* show on Vincent Price. Each film comes with a trailer as well as a full gallery of advertising art. Rare behind-the-scenes stills from the original *The Fly* show Al Hedison sitting patiently wearing his fly head. Chatting amiably with Patricia Owens, he reminds us of "Mant" in 1993's affectionate ode to monster movies, *Matinee*.

Thirty years later David Cronenberg found this story to be the perfect vessel to express his personal themes of biological dysfunction and alienation from the human flesh. But the show that best taps into the moral and philosophical basis of a Langelaan- style matter transmitter is 1990's ten-minute Film Board of Canada short subject *To Be*.

1. In the original short story the cat Dandelo is also lost in limbo. Andre goes through the transmitter again in hopes of un-grafting himself from the fly. He instead comes out a real mess, with cat features mixed in with the fly's characteristics. And the transmitter isn't even under warranty. In the film, therefore, we expect Dandelo's 'stream of atoms' to reappear at any time. When Andre and Helene teleport a magnum of champagne, one half-expects Dandelo to show up crammed into the bottle, like a cat in a Warner Bros. cartoon.

2. Hodgens, Richard. *Film Quarterly 13, no.2* 1959.

3. (spoiler) Henri Delambre disappears into the ether, never to be recombobulated again. I've always wanted him to pop up unexpectedly in a transporter tube on the Starship Enterprise, preferably in B&W: "Pardon me ... my stream of atoms must have wandered your way."

TEENAGE CAVEMAN

Lionsgate Reviewed: May 6, 2006
1958 / 1:37 flat pan-scan / 65 min. / *Prehistoric World*
Cinematography Floyd Crosby. Written by R. Wright Campbell. Produced by Samuel Z. Arkoff, Roger Corman, James H. Nicholson. Directed by Roger Corman

Roger Corman had differences with American-International on this conceptually ambitious cave man story with a clever O. Henry-type twist. The film's original title was *Prehistoric World*; according to the director, producers Sam Arkoff and James Nicholson changed it without even telling him. The edits are visible where Arkoff slugged in the replacement, which actually reads *Teenage Cave Man*. Thus, a potentially thoughtful film was transformed into one of A.I.P.'s teenaged monster movies. *Teenage Caveman* gives us an early look at rising star Robert Vaughn as a primitive intellectual chafing at the restrictions of his uptight community. Vaughn must have fainted dead away when he saw the title change. He needn't have worried, for two years later he'd be nominated as best supporting actor for *The Young Pleistocenes*, I mean, *The Young Philadelphians*.

> A primitive tribe lives in isolation and ignorance. The Symbol Maker (Leslie Bradley) cannot restrain his rebellious son and apprentice (Robert Vaughn) from straying into the forbidden "land beyond" the river, where fearsome monsters, deadly quicksand and the "God with the Touch that Kills" are to be found. As taboo behavior is punishable by death, a malcontent (Frank DeKova) campaigns to make the young Symbol Apprentice pay the penalty. He also covets the Apprentice's blonde girlfriend (Sarah Marshall, aka Darah Marshall). In the land across the river, father and son encounter the living God of the legend.

Viewers venturing beyond *Teenage Caveman's* silly title and pitiful caveman costumes will discover a clever little allegory. R. Wright Campbell's story has relevance even without the last-second twist surprise. Young Robert Vaughn walks through the picture with a permanent smirk on his face, dissatisfied by his society's arbitrary rules. Three symbol keepers guard representations of the "three gifts" that make men what they are. The first two are fire and the wheel. A third keeper repeatedly sculpts and tears down a clay model that represents the human gift for creation and destruction.

Tribal laws set arbitrary limits on curiosity. Vaughn's girlfriend would settle for a quiet life of domestic snuggling but our rebel Vaughn is driven to investigate the unknown. In a telling episode, a horse arrives carrying a wounded man from a forbidden territory called The Burning Plains. He speaks only one word, Peace.

Against Vaughn's pleadings, the villagers obey the law that demands that all strangers from outside the clan be killed on sight.

(spoiler) R. Wright Campbell uses the "forgotten future" idea exploited by the later *Planet of the Apes* series: Robert Vaughn's caveman society is actually post-Apocalyptic! The primitives have forgotten history entirely. "The God that Kills with a Touch" is revealed to be an old man wearing an encrusted radiation suit. Vaughn and his father find a book with mysterious printed images: The United Nations, a mushroom cloud. The surprise is quite unexpected for an exploitation film, making *Teenage Caveman* into a thinking man's creature feature. Roger Corman's thematic preoccupation with breaking barriers and snooping into unknown realms may start right here.

This is one of Corman's leanest productions. Costumes for the twenty or so cave dwellers range from okay fur tunics to what might as well be old bathroom throw rugs. Robert Vaughn tootles through the jungle pathways of the Pasadena Aboretum playing a little homemade flute. As various cavemen, Jonathan Haze and Beach Dickerson take plenty of painful-looking tumbles amid the rocks of Bronson Caverns. Dickerson remembers being killed three times as three different characters ... the blonde caveman who drowns in quicksand, the Man from The Burning Plains, and a bear. Favorite Barboura Morris (*A Bucket of Blood*) is in a handful of shots as well. Stock footage alligators, Tegus and monitor lizards are recycled from *One Million B.C.*. Other shots appear to come from the *Unknown Island* library of anemic Man-in-suit-a-saurs. The incestuous concluding montage uses an outtake of Paul Dubov stumbling out of the radioactive fog of *Day the World Ended*, and a curious broad-daylight shot of *The She-Creature*.

M. Night Shyamalan's 2004 *The Village* is an elaborate thematic remake of *Teenage Caveman*.

I understand that many audiences responded well to *The Village*; at the screening I saw, an audible groan could be heard when its painfully pointless "twist" ending was revealed.

Teenage Caveman on DVD is half of Lionsgate's *Samuel Z. Arkoff Cult Classics Collection* double bill with *The Saga of the Viking Women and Their Voyage to the Waters of the Great Sea Serpent.* Unfortunately, the transfer is a pan-scan of the already cropped Superama (SuperScope) image. Characters are consistently pushed halfway or all the way off the screen. The pan-scan is bafflingly inconsistent. The titles are squeezed, but many stock shots of fake dinosaurs from earlier, pre-widescreen era movies do not look as if they've been cropped!

THE BLOB

Criterion Reviewed: February 24, 2008
1958 / Color / 1:66 widescreen / 82 min.
Cinematographer Thomas E. Spalding. Music Ralph Carmichael. Special Effects Bart Sloane. Written by Theodore Simonson, Kay Linaker, Irvine Millgate. Produced by Jack H. Harris. Directed by Irvin S. Yeaworth Jr.

Independent producer Jack H. Harris made news in 1958 by licensing his monster thriller *The Blob* to Paramount for a terrific profit. Paramount must have been after a socko hit like *Godzilla* or *Rodan*, overseas acquisitions that had done well for Joseph E. Levine and DCA.

The Blob has a unique origin. Harris produced it in rural Pennsylvania with some religious filmmakers making quality 35mm inspirational short subjects. The director at Valley Forge Studios was Irvin S. Yeaworth Jr., an idealist committed to spreading his faith via film. Harris saw an opportunity to turn out commercial color features at a fraction of what it would take in Hollywood or New York.

Criterion's deluxe presentation illuminates all aspects of this drive-in classic. *The Blob* brought Steve McQueen his first starring feature role and reinvigorated the fashion for teen-angst monster films. Its disturbingly simple concept out-shocked movies about shaggy werewolves and gigantic bugs. Twenty years later Steven Spielberg galvanized imaginations by hyping a sea creature that did only three things: swim, eat, and reproduce. What if there came to earth a mindless substance with only one purpose, to dissolve and assimilate human flesh? One can't negotiate with *The Blob*.

> Decent teens Steve Andrews and Jane Martin (Steven McQueen & Aneta Corsaut) encounter an injured Old Man (Olin Howland of *Them!*), whose arm is covered with a gelatinous substance. They rush him to the house of Doctor Hallen (Steven Chase of *When Worlds Collide),* only for the doctor to also be consumed by the blob of protoplasm. Police Lt. Dave (Earl Rowe) wants to understand but Officer Jim Bert (John Benson) thinks Steve's wild story is personal anti-authoritarian harassment. Picked up by their parents, Jane and Steve sneak out again to solve the mystery. Growing as it eats more people, the Blob traps the teens in a supermarket freezer and then infiltrates a movie theater and attacks the audience. It finally lays siege to a diner, trapping Steve and Jane in the cellar. Steve discovers that The Blob is repelled by extreme cold … but can he relay that information to the rescuers outside?

One of the best-remembered 50s movie monsters, *The Blob* has persisted in the public consciousness despite being old-fashioned and paced on the pokey side. The script owes a debt to Nicholas Ray's *Rebel Without a Cause,* and young star Steve McQueen (27 playing 17) is clearly working in James Dean mode. Irvin S. Yeaworth Jr's sincere direction shapes characters as warm as those found in the TV family sitcoms of the day. Steve Andrews and Jane Martin may be slow on the uptake, but unlike the teens of American-International's *The Spider* and *Invasion of the Saucermen,* they're sarcasm and irony-free.

The independent production displays a blend of professional and non-pro qualities. The color cinematography is good but Yeaworth's blocking tends toward static setups. The script dawdles in dialogue scenes. Jack Harris brought promising actor McQueen and future television player Corsaut from New York to play against local theater talent. Some of the film's acting is atrocious, with Jane's little brother Danny (Kieth Almoney) especially hopeless as he shoots at the Blob with a cap pistol holstered over his 'jammies'. Ingenious special effects animate the Blob with clever gags that avoid expensive opticals. Effects man Bart Sloane cut budget corners by photographing the Blob in front of color photo blow-ups. Red-colored silicone oozes slowly and silently, only to suddenly lunge onto Olin Howland's arm. Having just gobbled up the movie audience at the Bijou, it flows into the street like murderous red caramel.

The Blob's scenes of menace unspool at an even pace, often without music; 1958 viewers reported that the film was genuinely frightening. Ralph Carmichael's title theme was substituted at the last minute by a novelty song by Burt Bacharach and Mack David. It's now considered an immortal piece of camp: *"Beware of The Blob it leaps, and creeps, and slides and glides across the floor, right through the door …"*

Why is *The Blob* scary? Its inspirational bloodline traces immediately back to Nigel Kneale's highly influential *The Quatermass Xperiment,* in which a man slowly transforms into a mass of protoplasm. *The Blob's* menace is even more elemental and existential. It's not an intelligent life form; its only instinct is to consume. The Blob has no philosophy and no message; it's irreducible. It's the organic equivalent of Ice-9 in Kurt Vonnegut's novel *Cat's Cradle*, a hard, inert substance that crystallizes all water into more Ice-9. The Blob is an organic solvent that converts all living matter into more Blob. It homogenizes Life. If The Blob consumed the whole world and became sentient, perhaps the earth would be like Stanislaw Lem's planet *Solaris*, a living ocean of protoplasm.

The Blob disturbs at a subconscious level because it negates all human values. Its victims don't just die, they're instantly recycled as raw material for a mindless and Godless 'thing'. *The Blob* brought sheltered American teenagers of the 1950s a taste of existential doom. It isn't about outer space or the future; it's about death in the age of the atom.

Curiously, the film's silly ending has the Air Force transport The Blob to the North Pole. Although it cannot be destroyed the low temperatures will keep it inert and harmless. A final dialogue exchange assures us that the world will be safe, "as long as the Arctic stays cold". Uh oh.

Criterion's DVD of *The Blob* is a dazzling enhanced transfer that replicates the Kodachrome-like colors of original prints. The soundtrack is also of pristine quality. The disc carries two separate commentaries. Host Bruce Eder does his best to corral the garrulous producer Jack H. Harris, and a second commentary offers the thoughts of director Yeaworth Jr. and ex-teen actor Robert Fields. A menu section called Blob-abilia! contains stills from the collection of Wes Shank, and explains how the film's interesting special effects were accomplished.

I MARRIED A MONSTER FROM OUTER SPACE

Paramount Reviewed: September 11, 2004
1958 / B&W / 1:85 widescreen / 77 min.
Cinematography Haskell B. Boggs. Art Direction Henry Bumstead, Hal Pereira. Editor George Tomasini. Special Effects by John P. Fulton. Written by Louis Vittes.
Produced and Directed by Gene Fowler Jr.

I Married a Monster from Outer Space has been praised for transcending its silly title, which imitates the previous year's *I Was a Teenage Werewolf*. Viewers expecting low-grade drek instead found some good acting and okay plotting in Paramount's attempt to poach on the exploitation turf dominated by American-International and Allied Artists.

Feminist film critics of the early 1970s responded strongly to the film's theme of domestic trauma. Poor Marge knows her husband is really a Thing from another world, but who will believe her? Every new wife shares that problem.

The night before his wedding, Bill Farrell (Tom Tryon) runs afoul of a hideous alien on a country road and is enveloped in a sinister black cloud. He goes forward with the ceremony but his new bride Marge (Gloria Talbott) becomes convinced that he's not the man she was engaged to. Naturally nobody will believe her, even after she follows Bill into the woods and finds him consorting with creatures from outer space.

Critics studying sexual politics in genre films have plenty of ammunition in *I Married a Monster from Outer Space*, which lifts ideas wholesale from *Invaders from Mars* and *Invasion of the Body Snatchers*, of which it is a virtual re-think. These kinder, gentler invaders have lost their own females (a scarce commodity in outer space: ask *The Mysterians*) and are here to run a few tests to see if Earth women can bear children with ping pong balls in their mouths and spidery tubes connecting their heads to their bodies.

Instead of killing, possessing or duplicating Earth males these visitors merely suspend them in rows inside their plywood spaceship, using what look like old Nintendo controllers to borrow their appearance and minds as disguises – the M.O. used by the Xenomorphs of *It Came from Outer Space*. Soon eight or nine key males in the community have been taken over, mostly the police, as in *It Conquered the World*. The aliens impersonating married men learn interesting lessons about Earthly carnality – sex is all right, take it from ZxenOth! To identify one other, the aliens can let down their projected disguises and reveal their snarly-twisted faces. Also, lightning storms interrupt the disguise 'broadcast', causing the face of the alien impersonating Bill Farrell to flicker back and forth between Tom Tryon and the icky Outer Space Monster.

Frantic wife Marge finds this out by an interesting means – her "false Bill" eventually confesses all. By imitating a human, the alien has learned human compassion. Instead of going on a rampage, Alien-Bill is disturbed by the unpleasantness of his mission and his deception of the innocent Marge.

This is better treatment than most of Marge's girlfriends were getting. Their human husbands and boyfriends previously hung around Maxie Rosenbloom's bar to gripe about the stifling institution of marriage. Sam Benson's alien marries Sam's girlfriend as well, although we aren't given the physical details of their mating experiments. No babies seem to be on the way, a disappointment for the armada of spaceships waiting patiently in Earth orbit, *Mars Attacks!*-style.

They aliens aren't all-powerful. They must return periodically to their spaceship (hidden in Griffith Park) for injections of their home atmosphere or something. Sam Benson's imposter (Alan Dexter) is accidentally asphyxiated when the kindly Dr. Wayne (Ken Lynch) gives him a poisonous hit of oxygen after a swimming mishap. The other aliens have little choice but to watch the doctor kill their comrade.

The biggest effect of the invasion is the inconvenience suffered by the local wives. Alerted to the mating experiment, Dr. Wayne organizes a score of fathers of proven potency to wipe out the alien nest. Although armed with disintegrating ray guns, the aliens are defeated when a German shepherd pulls their facial tubes apart as if they were made of licorice. Death rays are no match for our puny Earth weapons, as they say on *The Simpsons*.

Paramount's *I Married a Monster from Outer Space* taps the teen monster market with a production polish that only a studio can provide: the imaginatively designed monsters have the appearance of fleshy driftwood. Charles Gemora is said to have played the main alien. Universal optical outcast John Fulton provides expressive ray blasts, glow effects and clouds of smoke. But the cityscape is an unadorned back lot and the rest of the town was clearly filmed in Savant's Paramount-adjacent Hollywood neighborhood. Several road scenes take place on the upper reaches of Bronson Avenue.

B-girl Valerie Allen is disintegrated for accosting an alien daydreaming in front of a maternity store, and the alien-cops murder a pushy gangster in cold blood. Although that scene and an interrupted attempt to contact the F.B.I. appear to be lifted from Roger Corman and Don Siegel, _I Married a Monster from Outer Space_ doesn't aspire to their level of paranoia.

Tom Tryon and Gloria Talbott enjoy showcase roles. Tryon worked for Walt Disney and director Otto Preminger and later became a successful novelist. Talbott had already attained immortality as the ingrate daughter that gives Jane Wyman a television set for Christmas in _All That Heaven Allows_.

Paramount's DVD of **I Married a Monster from Outer Space** looks great, with a perfectly transferred, properly framed enhanced widescreen image. The main titles are no longer surrounded above and below by acres of empty space. The unusually punchy audio track recycles electronic noises from _The War of the Worlds_.

THE TROLLENBERG TERROR

Image Reviewed: December 6, 2001
1958 / B&W / 1:66 widescreen / 84 min. / _The Crawling Eye_
Cinematography Monty Berman. Special Effects Les Bowie. Written by Jimmy Sangster from the teleplay by Peter Key. Produced by Robert S. Baker, Monty Berman.
Directed by Quentin Lawrence

The Crawling Eye is an atmospheric, well-scripted and intelligent thriller with more than its share of genuine chills. Even better, the Image DVD is a fine 16:9 transfer of the original uncut English version, **The Trollenberg Terror**.

Paranormal investigator Alan Brooks (Forrest Tucker) comes to Trollenberg to investigate unexplained decapitations of climbers on the Alpine slopes. The particulars parallel an earlier experience in South America in which extraterrestrials were theorized to be involved. Also drawn to the mountain are performers Sarah and Anne Pilgrim (Jennifer Jayne & Janet Munro). The clairvoyant Anne is driven into a state of near-hysteria by psychic messages from the mountain. Her visions describe climbers menaced by a horrible thing emerging from the mist – which Anne perceives from the thing's point of view. Events come to a boil when more decapitated bodies are found. Then a climber returns as a murderous zombie and tries to kill Anne. She has tapped into the brainwaves of hideous creatures that aren't yet ready to show themselves.

Even before the success of Hammer films, English moviemakers were trying to get a piece of the American science fiction market. Most of the attempts were pretty bleak: *Stranger from Venus, Cosmic Monsters*, etc., but *The Crawling Eye* is a superior surprise. Another teleplay upgraded for the screen, this moody and ambitious chiller benefits from Peter Key's clever story construction. An Alpine chalet welcomes shady scientists, psychics and a reporter who may be a spy. All of them are drawn to a mountain where climbers have been disappearing, or getting their heads ripped off. At the center of the drama is the expressive actress Janet Munro. Her nervous, wide-eyed visions of unseen horrors generate the chill of an expert ghost story.

The movie makes good use of spatial schematics to pinpoint its menace. A hotel in a valley is connected by aerial tram to a heavily fortified observatory. Upward from there is the Trollenberg peak, with its mysterious clouds that shift about as if under their own power. Hiding inside the freezing clouds are the radioactive monsters. When the moving clouds cut off the only escape route from the hotel, every nine year-old knows that it's time to panic.

The Crawling Eye is a good example of an outlandish horror fantasy that uses a rational sci-fi premise. The emphasis is on spooky clairvoyant visions, mutilated bodies and a bloodless killer stalking the night-gowned heroines. When the alien creatures finally show themselves, they freeze the tramway lines to trap the cast in the concrete observatory. Closed-circuit television cameras monitor the onslaught of the horrible invaders.

Unfortunately, the special effects needed for the final battle are beyond the resources of Les Bowie's little unit. *The Crawling Eye* features a really striking monster design, a pulsating tentacled sac of pus. It slides forth with a nervous, pivoting eyeball leading the way. When the chalet doors collapse, revealing one of the bulbous orbs staring in from outside, the effect is awesome. In what is probably the film's only completely successful effects angle, the eye creeps forward at us, waving its tendrils in the smoke and mist. It's a vision out of H. P. Lovecraft.

The nicely designed miniature settings, props, fire and smoke effects are compromised by the absence of slow motion cinematography. It's a wonder that the effects look as good as they do. After seeing a model of a dive-bombing jet zinging in a foolish arc above the observatory, one must admit that that in the same year the Japanese were doing far more sophisticated work in this area. An oft-repeated story has been handed down that the Trollenberg and its cloud were accomplished by tacking some cotton puffs onto a photo, a claim unsupported by the film itself.

Image's DVD of *The Crawling Eye* presents the first acceptable version of the movie since its short theatrical run in 1958. The 'Widescreen European Edition' herein is actually the original UK *The Trollenberg Terror*, complete with its "Certificate X" card and a logo for Eros Films. A bit more gore is restored when a decapitated body is pulled out from under a bed. Sloppy splices marred these moments in the American cut.

The widescreen enhancement is as sharp as a tack, allowing us to enjoy the beautiful close-ups of Janet Munro's anguished eyes. Ms. Munro's standout performance here may have been what attracted the attention of Walt Disney, for whom she appeared in several films beginning with *Darby O'Gill and the Little People*. Disney was keen on all things Alpine; perhaps he fell in love with Janet's screen persona while casting his *Third Man on the Mountain*.

THE RETURN OF THE FLY
(see page 140)

4D MAN

Image Reviewed: March 14, 2000
1959 / Color / 1:37 flat /
Cinematographer Theodore J. Pahle. Music Ralph Carmichael. Special Effects Bart Sloane. Written by Theodore Simonson and Cy Chermak. Produced by Jack H. Harris and Irvin S. Yeaworth Jr.
Directed by Irvin S. Yeaworth Jr.

The Blob returned a terrific profit for Paramount and Jack H. Harris. Harris immediately regrouped with his director Irvin Yeaworth Jr. for **4D Man**, an effective cross between literary science fiction and the traditional Universal horror film. Theodore Simonson and Cy Chermak's screenplay is a dandy construct worthy of close study.

Scientist-brothers Scott and Tony Nelson couldn't be more different. Workaholic head researcher Scott (Robert Lansing) shrugs off the fact that his employer Dr. Theodore Carson (Edgar Stehli) has taken credit for Scott's brainchild Cargonite, a metal with an atomic structure so dense, it is for all practical purposes impervious. Girlfriend Linda (Lee Meriwether) can't motivate Scott to assert his rights.

Younger brother Tony (James Congdon) is a scientific rebel with a reputation for recklessness. Tony claims that he can generate an electrical field that will allow solid objects to occupy the same space. Since all matter is mostly made of empty space, Tony believes that one object can penetrate another without ever touching. Scott arranges for Tony to have a workstation of his own.

When Linda shows signs of attraction to Tony, Scott flips out and hijacks his brother's experiment, with outrageous results. Tony's electrical field transforms Scott into a living 4D object. Able to penetrate anything at will, Scott can reach into locked safes and walk through solid walls. Unfortunately, every second in 4D consumes years of Scott's 'life force', aging him into a shriveled old man. He can replenish his life force only by stealing that of others. Scott's victims grow old and die, while Scott is partially rejuvenated: he has become a fourth-dimensional vampire. Invulnerable while in 4D, Scott discovers that Tony and Linda are plotting to trap him. No walls can shield them from Scott's killing touch.

4D Man's schematic but compelling ideas stand out in bold relief. The passive Scott's impenetrable metal opposes the active Tony's force that pierces without destruction: the film's theme should be the pop song Something's Gotta Give. When Scott jealously steals his brother's invention, he breaks the mechanism of his own personality and spins out of control, like James Mason on cortisone in Bigger Than Life. The Fourth Dimension releases Scott Nelson's

desire for sex, riches and power. In a parody of consumer credit, Scott must kill to replenish his youth ... and is forced to repeatedly enter the 4D state, wasting precious life force in a Catch-22 cycle. Like a drug addict, Scott loses control over everything, even his newfound abilities: his emotions cause him to enter 4D involuntarily. He's both miraculously powerful and a pathetic misfit.

Most tales of deranged scientists establish a jumping-off premise and then devolve into repetitious murders. [1] 4D Man's concept is inseparable from its characters. When the disciplined Scott concentrates his amplified, jealous brainwaves on a problem, what he can do seems limitless. Tony wants to follow his brother into the 4th Dimension but cannot: Tony is brilliant, but his brain just isn't as 'together' as his brother's. Villainous Roy Parker (Robert Strauss) is an exaggeration of the brothers' faults: He's two-faced like Tony and covetous of the things Scott desires, including Linda.

4D Man suggests that Scott succeeds where Tony failed because he taps the creative angst within himself. Since the 4D existence is an unsustainable paradox, it is fitting that Scott's godlike powers be neutralized by the collision of the two halves of his split personality: When the sexually charged 4D power stolen from Tony ("... When an irresistible force, such as you...") plunges back into the 'impenetrable' Cargonite that represents Scott's life-negating sterility ("... meets an old immovable object like me..."), the issue is resolved. Like BrundleFly in David Cronenberg's remake of The Fly, Scott becomes one with his creation. 'What you worship is what you become', just as Lot's wife becomes a pillar of salt in Robert Aldrich's Sodom and Gomorrah, or Mario Bava's Diabolik becomes a golden statue.

4D Man is a model of thematic symmetry but is by no means a classic. Most independent low budget productions are put together like puzzles with missing pieces. Irvin Yeaworth's direction is unsteady and some of his blocking results in odd eye lines. In her first glamour close-up Lee Meriwether somehow ends up cross-eyed!

The photography is glossy, even if the art direction is a bit strange, with altogether too many scenes taking place in blue sets. The imaginative special effects range from good to mediocre. Far more ambitious than Bart Sloane's previous blobby tricks, 4D Man combines traveling mattes and animation to make Robert Lansing walk through walls, an illusion seen previously in Michael Powell's A Matter of Life and Death (Stairway to Heaven). The shots are fairly grainy, with that bane of low-budget effects work, erratic matte lines. Yet all the 4D sequences are successful because the excitement of the story carries them through.

The best effects use low-tech solutions. When Scott penetrates a storefront window to steal an apple, the glass is represented only by a projected line of white light that touches his arm as he reaches through. Another clever shot shows Scott's hand penetrating a mailbox without matte lines. Savant could be wrong, but it looks as if the box had no front panel at all, with the only matted item being the little mail pickup schedule on the front! Of special merit is Dean Newman's ambitious makeup for Robert Lansing's various states of decrepitude. In the impressive final scene it appears to be the cotton build-up kind of job Jack Pierce did for Karloff in The Mummy. Lansing's face wrinkles and furrows while he performs ... It's a fine illusion, and superior to the stiff 'melted candle' look later applauded in Little Big Man.

A trilling Musical Sound Effect is heard whenever Scott enters his 4D state. [2] This sound is often used alone, as when Scott breaks into Linda's boudoir Caligari-style and threatens to rape (kill?) her. Linda runs like blazes for the door, only to find Scott waiting on her front porch, as if he were Tex Avery's unshakeable Droopy Dog. Not one special effect in sight, yet very effective. 4D Man's most radical image shows Scott Nelson reaching into a nuclear reactor, arms outstretched in a blinding blast of fissionable material. The sight sums up 50s attitudes toward nuclear power, and the foolishness of humans that toy with it. [3]

Of course, the actors sell these scenes better than could any effects. When Scott walks *through* Dr. Carson's sofa, the mattes are none too convincing. *"How did you get in?"* Robert Lansing's casual air gives the moment its kick: *"Through the door..."*

The underrated Robert Lansing wisely underplays these moments. He seems to have been chosen for his resemblance to Steve McQueen. Lee Meriwether's 'betrayal' scene is particularly good. As Tony, James Congdon isn't bad but is still the weak link, especially when delivering the occasional clunker dialogue line. The comic Robert Strauss was inseparable from his loutish goofball characters in Stalag 17 and The Seven Year Itch, and elicits some unintentional laughs. Finally, there's tiny Patty Duke in a bit as Marjorie Sutherland, the Little Girl Who Meets A Monster. Boris Karloff's playmate took the plunge in Frankenstein and Richard Wordsworth's teatime girl in The Quatermass Xperiment escaped with just a smashed doll. It's difficult to tell if Scott lets Marjorie go, or victimizes her with his 'touch of death.'

Ralph Carmichael's jazz score often seems overdone. At crucial moments the blaring music backs off to let suspenseful silence take over, or to allow the above-mentioned shimmering Musical Sound Effect to do its stuff. Classic Hammer films often employ overemphatic music ... but not bongo drums.

4D Man became the source of many a playground argument: when Scott enters 4D, does gravity still affect him? If not, why doesn't he float up off the floor? If he still has weight, why doesn't he immediately fall to the center of the earth? Ah, the great debates of the third grade. The kid with the goriest explanation invariably won.

Image's DVD of **4D Man** is a satisfactory no-frills affair. Cropping the flat full-frame image on a widescreen TV restores the compositions to their theatrical tautness.

1 The 1936 *The Invisible Ray* is perhaps the first of the sub-genre of men scientifically given a Touch That Kills: *Man Made Monster*, *The Projected Man* and the little-seen *The Hand of Death* (1961) are other examples. That Scott Nelson must replenish his life force is a new wrinkle, a graft from the Dorian Gray variants in which people steal glands to prolong life: *The Man in Half Moon Street*, *The Man Who Could Cheat Death*, *The Leech Woman*. The concept folded back upon itself in the book *The Space Vampires*, which ended up being made by Tobe Hooper as, appropriately enough, *Lifeforce* (1985).

2 The trilling, oscillating 4D musical sound effect is another of those wonderful science fiction signature 'noises' from the 50s that began with the Theremin used to indicate the presence of the Xenomorphs in *It Came from Outer Space*. The Japanese certainly recognized the appeal of these sound effects; starting with *Gojira*, all of their monsters bear distinctive aural 'signatures.'

3 The visual of Scott Nelson bombarded in an atomic oven also connects to the creation of the Doctor Manhattan character in the eclectic comic book epic, *Watchmen*.

JOURNEY TO THE CENTER OF THE EARTH

Fox Reviewed March 15, 2003
1959 / Color / 2:35 widescreen / 132 min.
Cinematography Leo Tover. Music Bernard Herrmann. Written by Charles Brackett, Walter Reisch from the novel *Voyage au centre de la Terre* by Jules Verne. Produced by Charles Brackett.
Directed by Henry Levin

The engaging and amusing *Journey to the Center of the Earth* is a happy accident for which we can thank Walt Disney. His superior version of *20,000 Leagues Under the Sea* began a brief trend for Jules Verne adventures, including this lavishly mounted epic. Producer Charles Brackett signed James Mason and surrounded him with a capable cast that included teen crooner Pat Boone, who is not at all bad. Best of all, the adroit script gives the fanciful journey a borderline tongue-in-cheek tone. The result is a unique adventure with something for everyone.

A volcanic rock specimen leads freshly knighted professor Oliver Lindenbrook (James Mason) to Iceland to seek Arne Saknussem's secret pathway to the center of the Earth. Menaced by a haughty Saknussem heir (Thayer David), Lindenbrook goes forward into the unknown accompanied by his protégé Alec McEwen (Pat Boone), guide Hans Belker (Peter Ronson) and his rival's widow, the redheaded, single-minded Mrs. Carla Goeteborg (Arlene Dahl).

Nobody had touched Verne's *Journey to the Center of the Earth* since a long-lost silent Spanish version. Except for Tom Sawyer and Becky Thatcher's spooky cave experience in the 1938 *Tom Sawyer*, stories set inside the Earth were of the forgettable kind: *The Night the World Exploded, The Incredible Petrified World*. The show closest to borrowing the Verne concept was 1951's *Unknown World*, an airless adventure about a vehicle called a Cyclotram that drills a path beneath the Earth's mantle.

Jules Verne's tale of spelunkers in a prehistoric world doesn't mesh well with modern science, and the best decision by producer Charles Brackett (Billy Wilder's ex-partner) was to retain the original's period trappings. George Pal had updated H.G. Wells' *War of the Worlds* to great acclaim. Escapist silly-science solves the tough problems. Instead of encountering a furnace of molten rock, our explorers enjoy fresh air, surface gravity and air pressure all the way to the center. Convenient luminous rocks allow the use of Color by DeLuxe, long after the hikers' lamps have rusted away.

Journey to the Center of the Earth is adventure with a capital A, the kind that finds brave souls stepping off into the unknown with no reason-

able expectation of coming back alive. It's the spirit shared by the great explorers: life is short and cities are dirty and dull, so why not go for broke and risk all on a mad quest? The Scots, the Icelanders and even the dastardly villain are all infused with the spirit of adventure.

Journey's characters are firmly established by the time we descend into the crater below Scartarus. Pat Boone has left a girl behind in Edinburgh (the underused Diane Baker). Real life climbing expert Peter Ronson is a non-macho strongman. His pet duck Gertrud is a fob to the Disney audience. The calm Ronson balances Boone's persistent singing and rosy-cheeked optimism: *"Hi Hi! Professor!"*

James Mason's Lindenbrook throws the occasional tantrum but beams at new discoveries and dances a jig upon hearing good news. His commanding voice calms the roughest episodes. When the center of the globe turns out to be an illogical whirlpool in an illogical ocean – which direction is UP? – Mason's, *"This is it! The magnetic center of the Earth!"* provides an appropriate distraction.

Ex-MGM beauty Arlene Dahl was best known for some spectacular red headed close-ups in musicals. The writers contrive an acceptable case for her presence on what was originally an all-male safari into a hole in the ground. Her engaging banter with Mason helps build a light romance, something rare in movies of this kind. And, of course, Dahl also provides excellent screams for the trailer.

Journey is slower than most new action adventures but its characters are more satisfying. Its light mood compares well with the later Spielberg *Indiana Jones* movies, the first of which borrows this film's rolling rock gag. A convenient ending wraps things up with an express elevator ride out of Alice's rabbit-hole – a trick lifted for a yet another *Indiana Jones* adventure.

The final clincher is the thunderous score by Bernard Herrmann, which brings every facet of the journey to life, even when the phony edges of the scenery start to show. Like the earlier *Garden of Evil, Journey* is a Herrmann "music + landscape" picture – the main theme is a dynamic dirge, sinking ever deeper, lower. In its original four-track stereo the opening chords sink lower and heavier than seems possible – making one's stomach rumble like SenSurround!

Fox's DVD of *Journey to the Center of the Earth* is devoid of new extras but the enthusiastic remastering job is gift enough. Color values are excellent. The vistas atop the volcano are awesome, and combined with Herrmann's exultant score, the most powerful thing in the picture. Completeness freaks will want to retain the old laserdisc, which contains alternate scenes from the English version of the movie, where the college lads sing "Gaudeamus Igitur" instead of "Here's to the prof of Gee-ol-o-gee".

The pristine original trailer is quick to name-drop *20,000 Leagues* and *Around the World in 80 Days*. Narrator Mason reads a special billing line for Gertrud the duck, and the big-sell 'see' checklist fills the screen with 'huh?' names for volcanoes and underground grottoes to intimidate the easily impressed. And yes, Arlene Dahl does let loose with an earsplitting Fay Wray at two amiable-looking Dimetrodons. I just hope they didn't harm the lizards – the main concern of my kids when I showed them the film. The spears may be faked, but that fiery oatmeal or whatever that served as molten lava, has Roast Reptile written all over it.

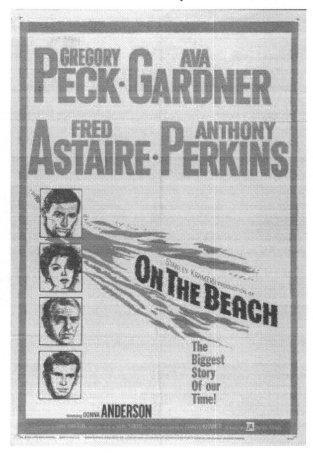

ON THE BEACH

MGM Reviewed November 12, 2007
1959 / B&W / 1:66 flat letterboxed / 134 min.
Cinematography Giuseppe Rotunno. Music Ernest Gold. Screenplay John Paxton from the novel by Nevil Shute.
Produced and directed by Stanley Kramer

Nuclear war was a 1950s buzzword but not a subject that the average American knew very much about. Despite (or because of) official public service films, the factual nature of radioactivity wasn't widely disseminated. Film culture did its part to confuse the issue, by either downplaying radiation's effects or wildly exaggerating them. Even the subversive *Kiss Me Deadly* with its fissionable 'great whatsis' used classical allusions to keep real science at a distance. That same year, the world's first atomic submarine was launched, the USS Nautilus. Nuclear power enjoyed excellent public relations.

> Australian Nevil Shute's enormously influential 1957 novel *On the Beach* chronicles the end of the world from the point of view of a number of atom war survivors in Melbourne, Australia. The date is January 1964. The exact cause of the nuclear exchange is not known, but the entire Northern Hemisphere has been wiped out. Seasonal winds will soon blow the radioactive fallout to the southern half of the planet. In just a few months, most of life on earth will be extinct.

Stanley Kramer's expensive film adaptation creates an odd dislocation that annoyed many critics. Kramer claimed that his anti-nuke film had the noble aim of saving the world. He enlisted the endorsement of the famed scientist Linus Pauling, providing publicity both for the film and for Pauling's campaign to halt above ground nuclear testing. For a simultaneous global premiere, each of the film's stars was dispatched to a different world capitol. If one wants to give *On the Beach* credit for turning public opinion and helping President Kennedy push through 1963's Limited Test Ban Treaty, Kramer's film was an enormous success.

Opposing this noble quest are Kramer's highly developed commercial instincts. He retains the book's fatalistic ending but recasts Shute's 'ordinary people' with glamorous movie stars. Whereas the characters in the novel reacted to doomsday "not with a bang but a whimper", John Paxton's script gives each victim at least one grandstanding soliloquy, a morbid crisis moment. Australian naval officer Peter Holmes (Anthony Perkins) must deal with the necessity of committing suicide with his wife and child. Nuclear scientist Julian Osborne (Fred Astaire, in his first straight acting role) grapples with professional guilt for helping develop the bomb. To combat his feeling of impotence, Julian rejects the advances of beautiful Moira Davidson

(Ava Gardner) and tries to commit suicide with other fanatics in a car race. The desperate Moira begs for comfort from American submarine commander Dwight Towers (Gregory Peck), only to discover that Towers is in denial over the deaths of his family back home. He prefers to join his men in a Captain Nemo-like suicide pact.

Kramer's film did good business despite reviews that emphasized its depressing aspects. *Daily Variety*: "The spectator is left with the sick feeling that he's had a preview of Armageddon, in which all contestants lost." Despite its soap opera construction, *On the Beach* is for the most part sharply directed and has many powerful scenes. With gasoline mostly unavailable, horse drawn buggies and bicycles crowd the roads. The submarine *Sawfish* makes an eerie entrance to the now-dead San Francisco Bay. A homesick sailor (John Meillon) jumps ship at Market Street, preferring to die in the dead city where he was born. [1] The film's most suspenseful set piece occurs in San Diego, where a lone crewmember dons a radiation suit to locate the source of a mysterious radio signal. Composer Ernest Gold grossly overuses the tune *Waltzing Matilda* but provides chilling cues for Captain Towers' submarine voyage to check radiation levels at the Arctic Circle.

On the Beach's reputation has slipped along with that of its producer-director. Stanley Kramer courted controversy as a promotional tool for his talky debate movies that 'resolved' one social issue after another: medical ethics (*Not as a Stranger*), race prejudice (*The Defiant Ones, Guess Who's Coming to Dinner?*), evolution and creationism (*Inherit the Wind*), German war guilt (*Judgment at Nuremberg*). Italian cinematographer Giuseppe Rotunno lends *On the Beach* stylistic refinements not seen in other Kramer pictures. The direction is economical and graphically clean – nobody forgets the long lines of citizens picking up government-dispensed death pills. Dwight and Moira's impassioned embraces carry real power. Rotunno emphasizes the highlight reflections on the water behind their final kiss. Gardner and Peck glint and sparkle in a huge close-up, the filtered backlight visually dissolving the lovers' faces as a visual correlative to the lethal radioactivity around them. The last scene at the windy entrance to Melbourne harbor is a perfect expression of doomed isolation: the camera finds Moira Davidson standing by her Austin-Healy, watching the *Sawfish* sail away.

On the Beach is perhaps Stanley Kramer's best-directed film. It influenced public thinking, altering the perception that nuclear bombs are practical weapons, and helped kick-start the anti-nuke debate of the 1960s.

In retrospect, the desolate oil refinery in *On the Beach* now resonates with *Quatermass 2:* America has been converted into a new land suited only to creatures that can live in highly radioactive conditions. Also, the phrase "When the time comes" keeps cropping up, looking forward to the perverse survival scheme of Joseph Losey's *These Are the Damned.*

MGM's DVD of *On the Beach* is a barely-acceptable flat letterboxed transfer in need of remastering. Some shots are dirty but most look okay; what the picture really needs is an enhanced widescreen transfer and clearer audio. Although UA's vaults hold a wealth of unique publicity material, no extras are included.

1. In the San Francisco sequence, the *Sawfish* sits off the Embarcadero as the sailors take turns looking at the city streets through the periscope. The image drifts slowly up and down as the sub rocks with the tide. The movement matches perfectly across cuts. This was done by 'rocking' the image in an optical printer, moving the 1:66 area up and down on the cut negative. On old 16mm prints the top and bottom frame lines can be seen drifting in and out, while the center 1:66 area remains undisturbed. For its year, this is a very clever optical trick.

NEBO ZOYVOT

Icestorm Region 0 PAL, as *Der Himmel Ruft;* Reviewed January 3, 2010
1960 / Color / 1:37 flat / 77 62 min. / *"The Heavens Call"; Battle Beyond the Sun.*
Cinematography Nikolai Kulchitsky. Written by Mikhail Karzhukov, Yevgeni Pomeshchikov, Aleksei Sazanov. Directed by Mikhail Karzhukov, Aleksandr Kozyr. American version produced by Roger Corman and directed by Francis Ford Coppola

Many American science fiction fans know of 1962's **Battle Beyond the Sun**, an elaborate butchering of the 1960 Russian film *Nebo zovyot* and one of Francis Ford Coppola's earliest screen credits. While gadding about Europe producing movies on a shoestring, Roger Corman bought the rights to several unsold European genre pictures including **Nebo zoyvot**, a sober and moralistic movie about the need for cooperation between the U.S. and the U.S.S.R.. The American version changes the story to omit specific mention of the Space Race, which at the time was practically a public relations adjunct to the Cold War.

The original *Nebo zovyot* is a fascinating propaganda document. Like the East German *Der Schweigende Stern,* the whole point of this picture seems to be to tout the Soviet Union's advantage in the early days of space exploration. The original Goskino movie bears little resemblance to the American recut:

In the present day (1960), Comrade Troyan of the Writer's Union (S. Filimonov) visits a laboratory where dedicated engineers are designing spacecraft of the future. Soviet space scientist-prophet Konstantin Tsiolkovsky's name is mentioned as the leading scientist Yevgeni Petrovich (A Schworin) has his handsome assistant show the writer large models of rockets, satellites and space stations. These miniatures are clearly the same items we'll see later on in special effects sequences. The writer's speculative magazine story then turns into the film's narrative. Brave cosmonauts (the same people the writer has been conversing with) prepare a Mars mission. Sweethearts are left behind as the party blasts off in the large rocket *Homeland.* The ship heads first for a large orbiting space station, which has docking facilities for more than one spacecraft. They're greeted with flowers by the permanent orbiting staff. Taking a break in the station's hydroponic, oxygen-producing greenhouse (twelve years before *Silent Running),* the *Homeland's* commander confides with the station chief that the Mars mission must remain a secret, because of unfortunate international friction.

Then the American spaceship *Typhoon* makes a hasty arrival. Its commander Verst (G. Tonunz) is

an arrogant astronaut-news correspondent on the payroll of the "Mars Syndicate" monopoly back in New York. The pilot Klark (K. Bartashevich) is an unhappy space veteran who bears a large scar from a crash caused when his bosses forced him to take unreasonable risks. The meeting of opposing scientists is an awkward forerunner of a scene in Kubrick's later *2001: A Space Odyssey.* Naturally, the Russians are open and friendly while the Americans are sneaky and dishonest. When Verst reports that the Soviets are going to Mars, the Syndicate orders him to launch *Typhoon* immediately, without proper preparation or clearance. The dedicated Soviet crewmember Gregori Somov (W. Tschernjak) is injured when the Americans fire up their engines without warning.

Back on Earth, we see bits of an elaborate capitalist advertising campaign built around the idea that Verst is racing to Mars in order to open it up for American economic exploitation. A Mars Syndicate announcer says that Martian real estate will soon be offered for sale at ten dollars an acre, while giant neon signs in Times Square advertise a rocket-themed space cocktail that, after the second glass, "will make you feel weightless".

The Russian crewmembers deplore the *Typhoon's* rash action but offer only the heartfelt wish that the Americans stop being so selfish and join the Soviets in the peaceful exploration of space. The *Homeland* takes off as well, but refuses to "race" to Mars; the injured Somov must stay behind.

Sure enough, the foolish Americans navigate their ship toward the sun instead of Mars and send out a panicked S.O.S.. Although their fuel will be depleted as well, the Russians run to rescue them.

From this point on *Nebo zovyot* becomes less coherent as a narrative, with a number of landings and other events referred to only in dialogue. After setting up a couple of romantic relationships, character detail is dropped as well. After rescuing the two Americans, the *Homeland* hasn't enough fuel to proceed to Mars and must instead land on a nearby asteroid. Things look bad when a rescue probe ship with extra fuel crashes on the asteroid, taking the *Homeland's* communications tower with it. Verst responds by becoming depressed, and swearing that Earth can go to hell. The wise Petrovich lectures Verst on his lack of values. We recall that earlier on, one comrade gave another a handful of rich Russian dirt, reinforcing their love of country.

The castaways have little choice but to regard the beautiful planet Mars and wait for their supplies to run out. But the injured cosmonaut Somov has personally piloted a second fuel ship and landed it safely nearby. He sacrifices his life to save the *Homeland*.

Back in the Black Sea port of Odessa, motorboats rush to a giant floating landing platform to welcome the *Homeland* on its safe return. A huge crowd rejoices as the surviving cosmonauts are reunited with their loved ones. The American pilot Klark says he's had a change of heart – thanks to the example of his Soviet rescuers, he likes people now.

Back in the present, Petrovich finishes reading Troyan's tale of future space adventure. Yes, the frontier of space will require a strong commitment to succeed, but it's man's destiny to rule the stars.

Nebo zovyot is competently directed and can boast elaborate, imaginative special effects. The space ships move realistically; Cosmonauts work on the space station's flight deck as a star field spins above. Many shots are set against star backgrounds, and the fact that a few misaligned stars bleed through solid objects is not too disruptive. The color is nicely subdued. One nice moving shot uses a filter to make a (Moscow?) street with Soviet-star decorations look like a magical star-scape slipping by. The acting is straight from the earnest-message playbook. All the Soviets are humanist ideologues, while the American pilot is a bitter malcontent and Verst a hysterical sociopath. The propaganda characterizing the American space effort as a shoddy commercial enterprise rings hollow, after one learns of the reckless, deadly accidents incurred by the Soviet space program.

American producer Roger Corman clearly wanted the film's impressive space scenes, but performed a full ideological overhaul on the film. To make *Nebo zovyot* safe for American children, Corman acolyte Coppola removed all topical references. The action in *Battle Beyond the Sun* is set in 1997, after a nuclear war. The world's competing factions are identified as North Hemis and South Hemis. The *Typhoon* belongs to the arrogant and deceitful North Hemis bloc. With the pasting of optical 'patches' over Soviet insignia, the Russian rocket *Homeland* is now the *Mercury*, the Mars craft of the sane and compassionate spacemen from South Hemis. Soviet stars remain visible on the rocket's fins, and the old name still pokes through in a couple of shots, followed by the telltale letters "CCCP."

Without the Russian-American competition the "new" movie is a politically neutral space opera. *Battle Beyond the Sun* must have run up a substantial optical bill. Besides altering insignia on the rockets, many takeoffs and other shots are duplicated to yield more outer space footage, which occasionally results in the wrong kind of rocket being used. To create a monster to splash across the movie posters, Coppola also filmed new footage of tentacled hand puppets that look like rubbery sea urchins. A single shot of a Cosmonaut reacting to the appearance of the rescue rocket (now unseen) is repeated several times and inter-cut with the monster battle.

Smirking fans have long recognized that Coppola's battling space monsters were cleverly designed to look like exaggerated caricatures of sexual organs; working for Roger Corman evidently required a wicked sense of humor. The original makers of *Nebo zovyot* must have been incensed to see their movie and its message twisted into a kiddie flick about giant space blobs on a Martian Moon.

Icestorm's presentation of **Nebo zoyvot** looks quite good in its original 1:37 aspect ratio. The Soviet color values are often quite striking. The German disc carries a replacement title sequence in Deutsch.

The only version available in region one is Retromedia's graymarket disc of **Battle Beyond the Sun**, on a double bill with a film called *Star Pilot*. The grainy image has slightly faded color; the transfer source was probably a 16mm print. Although tightly cropped, the film is intact and basically in good shape. The only extra is a trailer that uses alternate takes of the laughably gross Martian monsters, printed much more brightly and looking all the funnier for it.

DER SCHWEIGENDE STERN

First Run Films Reviewed: August 18, 2005
1960 / Color / 2:35 flat letterbox / 95 min. /
First Spaceship on Venus, The Silent Star, Milczaca gwiazda, Raumschiff Venus antwortet nicht
Cinematography Joachim Hasler. Production Designer Alfred Hirschmeier. Written by Wolfgang Kohlhaase, Günter Reisch, Kurt Maetzig, Jan Fethke, Günther Rücker, Alexander Stenbock-Fermor from the 1951 novel *Astronauci* by Stanislaw Lem. Produced by Hans Mahlich, Edward Zajicek.
Directed by Kurt Maetzig

In 2000 Image released a DVD of the 1962 Crown-International thriller *First Spaceship on Venus*. First Run Films has come forward with a Region 1 disc of the original East German-Polish version, the colorful **Der Schweigende Stern (The Silent Star)**. Although the film's basic story is unchanged, the original script has a quite different ideological viewpoint. In West Germany the film went under the name *Raumschiff Venus Antwortet Nicht (Spaceship Venus Does Not*

Answer); it was an import of the chopped-down American version. The apocryphal 130-minute cut reported in some texts never existed.

1970. Siberian miners unearth a mysterious artifact in an impact crater formed by a 1908 meteor. Chinese Linguist Tchen Yu (Tang Hua-Ta) and Indian mathematician Sikarna (Kurt Rackelmann) study the 'spool' and decide that it came from Venus. The mission of the Mars rocket Cosmokrator is rerouted to Venus to investigate. The spool code breakers join a crack international team: Russian Cosmonaut Prof. Arsenyev (Michail N. Postnikow) and American nuclear scientist Prof. Hawling (Oldrich Lukes) welcome four more ethnically diverse astronauts. Polish engineer Soltyk (Ignacy Machowsky) has a tank-like robot named Omega. African Talua (Julius Ongewe) is the Cosmokrator's communications expert. Ace East German Cosmonaut Brinkman (Guenther Simon) has a crush on Sumiko Omigura (Yoko Tani), a physician obsessed by nuclear war.

Avoiding a meteor storm, the Cosmokrator lands on the bleak Venusian surface. Brinkman discovers a cave infested with metallic insects that appear to store recorded data. A radioactive forest once functioned as an energy-projecting weapon. Like everything else on Venus, it was damaged when Venus destroyed itself preparing to invade Earth. A living mass of black ooze pursues three spacemen up the spiral ramp of a conical structure. Soltyk fires a ray gun into it, a move that upsets the balance of the giant machines still functioning underground, including a vast power plant that augments Venusian gravity with a force field. To allow the Cosmokrator to blast off, Talua and Tchen Yu enter the plant to reverse the effect. The G-Meter swings to the opposite extreme – negative gravity. The Cosmostrator is being forced off the planet!

In 1960 neither the Soviets nor the US had yet put a man into orbit. Our rockets regularly exploded on the launch pad while the tight lid on information from the USSR made every Russian achievement seem a smashing success. With no small amount of pride this expensive DEFA production imagines an international space program of 'cooperative' nations conquering the heavens while the 'rogue' United States lags far behind.

The source novel by Stanislaus Lem (*Solaris*) apparently had different aims, for the famous Polish author didn't think much of the movie adaptation. By Western standards this original version is 100% Soviet propaganda. Not a scene goes by without comparing the futility of American aggression with the harmony of brother nations working in a common cause. After the hawkish political posturing of 1950s American science fiction, we can see the same phenomenon from the Communist point of view.

Almost every speech not devoted to plot and technical exposition is an expression of party doctrine. The harmonious 'world government' assembles a dream team of international experts but the esteemed American nuclear physicist Dr. Hawling has not responded to the Communist invitation because of objections by New York businessmen. *"My dream is the stars"*, he lectures another Yankee scientist, *"Not your old dream, which was Hiroshima"*. A presumably Jewish German expatriate scientist talks of fleeing Hitler and then being coerced into making bombs. America, the film implies, is the enemy of freedom. Hawling's little boy draws pictures of spaceships going to the stars, but Wall Street's only interest is selling weapons.

Abandoning his capitalist friends, Hawling is flown by the East German hotshot pilot Brinkman to the space center in the mountains of Germany. The original cut gives the beautiful location more screen time – Brinkman and Hawley share a chat in a high Bavarian meadow suitable for the opening of *The Sound of Music*. Brinkman is identified as an American in the Crown re-cut, even though he flies a Russian MIG fighter jet!

During the flight to Venus Hawling plays chess with Soltyk's unbeatable robot Omega, and repeatedly loses. Soltyk obligingly adjusts Omega's circuits to allow the American to win some games. The inference is that those egotistical, competitive Yanks need to maintain the illusion that they're winners.

Brinkman's repeated attempts to ignite a romance with Sumiko elicit tragic memories of her husband's death on a lunar mission. Sumiko is the first to detect what's left of the extinct Venusians – shadows burned into walls by the atomic blast that destroyed the planet. The movie repeatedly cites Hiroshima as proof of U.S. barbarity. Sumiko ruminates on the loss of her family and her inability to have children because of lingering radiation.

The general impression left by *The Silent Star* is that only the Soviets are committed to the noble quest for the stars. In 1960 neither side thought that cooperative joint space ventures were a possibility. Even Stanley Kubrick's *2001: A Space Odyssey* assumed that the Cold War would be a perpetual state of affairs.

The original trailer proudly proclaims that this is the first movie about the exploration of space, which is of course not true. *The Silent Star* rehashes familiar American spaceflight clichés: The meteorite storm, the need for an EVA to repair part of the ship. As Dr. Tchen Yu dies, Sumiko tells him that the seeds he has planted have sprouted, a bit of business borrowed from 1955's *Conquest of Space*. Gender and racial attitudes aren't that much different than in American movies. Pretty Emiko spends most of her time dispensing liquid food to the cranky spacemen. African Talua also fills a 'service-oriented' crew position. The glamorous pilot hero is played by Gunther Simon, an East German actor 'politically approved' for his filmic portrayals of Communist party leaders.

Silent Star mirrors *Forbidden Planet*'s investigation of an alien civilization that overreached and destroyed itself. The aggressive Venusians annihilated themselves with atomic weapons, as did the Martians of *Rocketship X-M*. According to *Silent Star*, Americans are likely to follow suit.

The Silent Star has unique designs: a fanciful four-spired spaceship, the rover vehicles and a hovercraft called an Elasticopter. DEFA artists fashioned awesome miniature landscapes melted and charred by atomic blasts. Groves of drooping gourd-like buildings resemble images of Hell by the painter Hieronymous Bosch. In technique the film is closer to *Metropolis* than *Forbidden Planet*, as there are few if any opticals. The main launch site is an elaborate forced-perspective construction. Careful double exposures are used to superimpose moody oil-smear 'atmospheres' over the eerie Venusian landscapes.

Viewers who have only seen *First Spaceship on Venus* will notice major differences. The original colors are much brighter and the contrast less choked --- Talua's face is no longer a black blot and the surface of the planet now looks like diamond dust instead of black coal. Pre-launch activities are more elaborate. In addition to the expected longer dialogue scenes, we see Sumiko break out a high-tech surgery when Professor Arsenyev is accidentally run over by the robot tank Omega.

A stirring and mysterious music theme under the main title soon gives way to much less interesting *Forbidden Planet*- like electronic tonalities. It's a far cry from the wall-to-wall needle-drop tracks jammed onto the Crown version by import producer Hugo Grimaldi. The original version restores dignity to the character of Talua. Instead of wailing for his friends to return, we last see Talua shouting a noble farewell to the departing Cosmokrator. The American version also removes the original final trucking shot showing dozens of hands joining together in Socialist solidarity. What's so objectionable about that?

First Run Features' DVD of *The Silent Star* is a welcome release with only a few disappointments. The package lists a 16:9 image, when the transfer is actually flat letterboxed. English subs are provided. The liner notes claim that the film was shot in 70mm, which could not be confirmed. The best extras are two newsreel snippets of the film in production, especially the impressive launch site set. Text extras discuss the film (one essay is called *Socialists in Space*) and offer bios for key production personnel. Original set design artwork is included as well.

THE TIME MACHINE

Warners Reviewed: October 2, 2000
1960 / Color / 1:78 widescreen / 103 min.
Cinematography Paul C. Vogel. Art Direction George W. Davis, William Ferrari. Editor George Tomasini. Music Russell Garcia.
Written by David Duncan from the book by H.G. Wells.
Produced and Directed by George Pal

Although not lavishly budgeted, George Pal's 1960 version of the H.G. Wells classic *The Time Machine* was conceived as an A-class family attraction from the get-go. Already famous for his *Puppetoon* short subjects, Pal had inaugurated the science fiction craze with three Technicolor hits. Given the boot from Paramount after the crash of *Conquest of Space*, he moved his office to MGM.

Engaging with Pal's films often means setting them apart from their literary roots. Savant met Mr. Pal at the 1976 Filmex Exposition. Just as everyone says, he was utterly charming and not the sort one might think could survive in Hollywood. His gentle nature and uncomplicated sentimentality equipped him well for fairy tale projects like *tom thumb*, but he was also drawn to dramatic material with complex moral and political ideas. Pal's take on Charles G. Finney's disturbing *The Circus of Dr. Lao* thwarts the book's sardonic purpose.

> 1899. George Wells (Rod Taylor) demonstrates a model of his time machine, hoping that he can inspire men to redirect their energies away from war. Disillusioned by his friends' petty profiteering, George bids them farewell and ventures into the future. Everything he sees is warped by war. His best friend Filby (Alan Young) dies in WW1. A 1966 war with nuclear satellites effectively ends civilization.
>
> When George stops in 802,701 England has become a Garden of Eden. He discovers the Eloi, a strange society of beautiful but passive people, and meets the comely Weena (Yvette Mimieux). Disenchantment sets in when George finds that the Eloi have lost all knowledge of independence, curiosity, and chivalry. George then discovers that this paradise is actually a human stockyard; the Eloi are managed as a food supply for the subterranean Morlocks, a race of hairy green monsters. Seeking to inspire men of his own time, George instead becomes a warrior-emancipator in a remote future world.

The Time Machine is George Pal's best-directed movie, and goes nose-and-nose with *The War of the Worlds* as his best production. Some critics decried Pal's diluting of the underlying message in Wells' 1895 original, the Darwinian idea that Capital and Labor might devolve into separate species of men.

Pal and screenwriter David Duncan retained Wells' framing device of the two 1899 dinner parties before and after the voyage to the future. But they greatly altered the world of the 802nd Millennium. Wells' Eloi are a depressing race of slight and effete midgets that resemble miniature deer on two legs. When trying to communicate with them, the original Time Traveler (he has no given name in the book) barely gets beyond 'hello'. His adventure is a depressing nightmare in a faulty Eden. The Time Traveler has a soft spot for Weena but as she's only quasi-human, the romantic angle is lacking. Although Wells' Time Traveler mulls over the idea of becoming an emancipator, he's still a Victorian traveler in the Third World, and has a tough time coping with anything un-English.

Wells' time tripper finds no great moral lessons, just a despairing future he cannot alter. His fire accidentally burns down the forest, killing many Morlocks and Eloi. Screenwriter Duncan elevates the Time Traveler to the status of a revolutionary Prometheus who brings fire to re-ignite the spark of civilized values.

As an entertainment, most of Pal's *The Time Machine* hits square on the mark. Pal sketches 1899 well and his actors appear to be excited by the material. The under-appreciated Rod Taylor shows considerable charisma. Yvette Mimieux is appropriately fragile and charming. The toothy Morlocks with glowing eyes make excellent villains, and there's something truly uncanny about the use of air raid sirens that hypnotically lure the Eloi to their doom.

A literary discovery? Savant wishes to explain a revelation he had while reading an uncut copy of *The Time Machine* in 1979. I've read several books on Wells since then and have yet to see a mention of this issue, so forgive me if I mistakenly think I've stumbled onto a fresh discovery.

The Time Machine is accepted as the first book that introduced readers to *technological* time travel, a concept later raised to more complex levels by other authors. Everyone is aware of time travel conundrums like the question, "If you go back in time and kill your other self, will you disappear because then you can't have lived into the future to go back in time?" This has pretty much replaced the great chicken-egg debate as the classic schoolyard argument-starter.

Filby (the book's narrator) presumes that the Time Traveler met some calamity in the past or the future, because he never returns to 1900. The story ends in a bitter question mark. Pal and Duncan soften the film's ending with their sentimental 'which three books?' gimmick. The irony is that, although Filby doesn't realize it, in the novel the Time Traveler did indeed return to see him again.

The Silent Man. All of the guests at the first dinner party are identified. At the second dinner gathering, Filby takes note of a guest identified only as The Silent Man. This bearded older fellow is assumed to be someone else's tag-along guest, but Filby does not know whose. The Silent Man (like The Time Traveler, capitalized each time he is mentioned) takes no part in the discussions and simply observes what happens. He stares at The Time Traveler and at one point pours him a glass of wine. The Silent Man never says a word. When the dinner party breaks up he slips away, the perfect party crasher.

The Silent Man is obviously the Time Traveler himself, returned at an advanced age. Older but wiser, he may have attended just to contemplate his younger self. Perhaps the Time Traveler had many adventures and before dying wanted to reflect on his origins. Maybe he's been a tourist observing history, taking pains to be a fly on the wall at all times. Perhaps he finds comfort in being an anonymous man among other men, after his soul-crushing trip to the twilight of existence, the future with the empty beach and the giant crabs.

If this revelation is indeed something new, it alters our impression of the book's conclusion and forc-

es a reevaluation of H. G. Wells. He now seems to have been perfectly capable of conceiving of time puzzles on the Philip K. Dick scale, even back in 1895. Perhaps Wells thought his Victorian audience wasn't ready for such complications.

Be forewarned that not all copies of *The Time Machine* include this material. The original book had several lives, serialized in periodicals and under separate cover; the reference may have been edited out for later versions.

Turner/Warner's enhanced DVD of **The Time Machine** looks great in its proper screen shape, with its many effects scenes carefully transferred. The expressive Russell Garcia score is an active and dynamic surprise in stereo. The packaging claims an isolated music track that does not appear.

The main extra is the 50-minute documentary *The Time Machine: The Journey Back*, which tells the tale of the film's title prop. The throne-like machine was rediscovered in a thrift store and reconstructed by dedicated effects fans Bob Burns, Tom Scherman and Gene Warren. The haste of the 1960 filming process can be judged by the fact that as soon as the prop had finished shooting, it was sawed apart to film inserts of its control panel. Producers nowadays would make three sturdy props with breakaway variations; the original Time Machine was a delicate construction that barely lasted through filming.

The docu also stages a scene with guest stars Alan Young and Rod Taylor reprising their characters. It makes us wonder why sequels to *The Time Machine* were never made. With all the principal actors alive and kicking, it would seem a natural, especially in the early 70s when Pal was in a slump and Fox was mining pay dirt with its *Planet of the Apes* franchise. One reason might have been the notion that shows like the *Apes* series and television's *The Time Tunnel* had made Pal's film seem obsolete. It remained for Robert Zemeckis and Bob Gale's clever *Back to the Future* movies to re-popularize time travel for general audiences.

They fought for the Ultimate Prize!

THE LAST WOMAN ON EARTH

NEW
Eastman 52-50
COLOR
VISTASCOPE

Starring
ANTONY CARBONE / BETSY JONES-MORELAND / EDWARD WAIN

Produced and Directed by ROGER CORMAN
A FILMGROUP PRESENTATION

LAST WOMAN ON EARTH

Retromedia Reviewed: January 6, 2006
1960 / Color / 1:85 flat letterboxed / 71 min.
Cinematography Jack Marquette. Music
Ronald Stein. Written by Robert Towne.
Produced and directed by Roger Corman

Roger Corman didn't plan to make his now-legendary *The Little Shop of Horrors* in two or three days. According to star Jackie Joseph, he rushed the production so filming could finish before December 31, 1959. On the next day a new Screen Actor's Guild residuals policy went into effect, forbidding the director to hire actors on a flat buy-out basis.

Thus was born Corman's Filmgroup producing label. While other cheapjack outfits making drive-in fare simply folded their tents, Corman took his film crews outside Guild jurisdiction. His first haven was the Caribbean island territory of Puerto Rico. He arrived expecting to make two pictures back-to-back but slipped in a third to further amortize his costs. Corman's industriousness was matched by his frugality. *Last Woman on Earth* could afford the luxury of color but Corman saved airfare by insisting that his screenwriter Robert Towne double as the second male lead, as "Edward Wain".

Robert Towne's storyline recaps the previous year's *The World, The Flesh and The Devil*, minus that picture's glossy production values. On a working vacation in Puerto Rico, sharp businessman Harold Gern (Antony Carbone) enjoys dominating his alcoholic wife Evelyn (Betsy Jones-Moreland) and bossing around his meek lawyer Martin Joyce (Robert Towne, billed as Edward Wain). While the three are scuba diving, an unexplained disaster depletes the oxygen from the air for a number of minutes, killing every breathing thing on Earth save our three survivors. By the time their scuba tanks are spent, the trio has returned to the greenery on shore, where the plants have exuded enough oxygen to sustain them. Calmly accepting their isolation, the three make only one foray back to the city. Harold continues to behave as if Eve were his private property, an attitude that worsens when Eve and Martin are drawn to each other. It soon becomes clear that two men will enter into a violent competition. The desultory ending takes place rather symbolically in a church.

Last Woman on Earth comes off as arty and pretentious. Towne's script bears the influence of Michelangelo Antonioni, with oblique dialogue and lapses of communication that emphasize each character's personal isolation. The pace is slow and "Edward Wain" is at best an awkward actor. Carbone carries most of the scenes while the statuesque Jones-Moreland serves as an attractive center of attention.

Corman uses the absolute minimum of resources to tell his story, an approach that sometimes yields a good scene but more often gives the impression of marking time. After the fatal oxygen kill-off and its equally abrupt restoration, the science fiction element is mostly dropped. Only three or four brief shots suggest the spooky "empty world " vibe that fascinates in thrillers like *Five* and *Target: Earth*. The film does have expressive moments, as when Eve demonstrates her opinion of Martin by writing his name in the sandy beach, and then wiping it out. The best script content examines Eve's predicament as an object of desire. Martin and Eve try several times to make Harold understand that the concept of monogamy needs to be abandoned.

After disappearing from television, **Last Woman on Earth** became practically a lost picture, with terrible prints circulating on gray market VHS tapes. It was most often seen in B&W; color prints were faded to a monochromatic brown. Retromedia's copy is an okay transfer of a surviving 35mm print. The color is variable yet gives a good indication of the show's original appearance. The encoding is flat letterboxed: the "Vistascope" credit on the posters is Filmgroup hype for ordinary matted widescreen.

A commentary features Fred Olen Ray interviewing Antony Carbone and Betsy Jones-Moreland, 45 years later. Neither is bitter about the experience but both sound eager to tattle on Corman's legendary cheapness. Jones-Moreland worked eighteen-hour days while taking care of her wardrobe and doing her own makeup and hair. She also did her own stunts, including perching on the balcony railing of the high-rise hotel room. The actors' analysis of the film isn't very useful. I don't think anybody watches *Last Woman on Earth* and feels, as the commentators claim, that Antony Car-

bone's character is being lauded for having high moral standards.

Also included are a tasty stack of Corman trailers, including one for *Last Woman*, and a separate section of flat, full frame B&W-only scenes filmed for later television sales by Monte Hellman, Corman's go-to guy for re-shoot padding. The three stars, all looking a bit heavier, take part in new scenes in a bar and on a Southern California beach.

SPECTACULAR ADVENTURE BEYOND TIME AND SPACE... AS **CINEMAGIC** TAKES YOU TO THE **ANGRY RED PLANET** IN MAGNIFICENT COLOR

THE ANGRY RED PLANET

MGM Reviewed: December 8, 2001
1959 / Color / 1:37 flat / 83 min.
Cinematography Stanley Cortez. Written by Ib Melchior from a story by Sid Pink. Produced by Norman Maurer & Sid Pink.
Directed by Ib Melchior

The major claim of the colorful but tame space saga **The Angry Red Planet** is an impressive visual effect billed by its producers as "Cinemagic".

A Mars mission returns, minus a crewmember. Only Dr. Iris Ryan (Nora Hayden) recovers consciousness to tell her story: "Irish" explored the red planet with Colonel O'Bannion (Gerald Mohr), Professor Gettell (Les Tremayne) and Warrant Officer Sam Jacobs (Jack Kruschen),

confronting several horrible life forms before escaping. She also made contact with one of the rulers of the planet, a multi-eyed insect creature.

Although testimony from writer Ib Melchior and producer Sid Pink would have us believe that *The Angry Red Planet* is an outer space classic, it simply isn't so. The complaints are typical: flat direction, a dull script, cheap sets and too much stock footage. Good music has animated many a genre picture worse than this one, but *The Angry Red Planet* is shortchanged in that department too.

What's left is the imaginative Cinemagic process, described by inventor Norman Maurer as a complicated lab manipulation involving printing with negatives. It resembles the solarization so often seen in later '60s psychedelic imagery. The makers stated that the detail-leeching visual effect was used to make live-action photography look like hi-contrast line art, like a cartoon. The face of Naura (Nora) Hayden certainly gives this effect, with barely more than her eyes and lips resolving in the tinted red glow. In practice the process reveals budgetary side benefits: flat artwork and crude props look better than they would under normal photographic conditions.

The film's other effects are inconsistent. The rocket in space is tedious cel animation. The fantastic Martian monsters range from a humdrum carnivorous plant, to the interesting giant amoeba, to the nicely designed but poorly executed Bat Rat Spider Crab. We learn from Robert Skotak's book *Ib Melchior, Man of Imagination* that all of these scenes were done in great haste, mostly at Howard Anderson's optical shop. The monsters were delivered to the studio before Melchior discovered that miscommunication had resulted in effects he didn't want, like the rotating eye on the jellyfish-like amoeba. The Bat-Rat creature was a marionette that proved difficult to operate.

One almost subliminal effect looks like a flaw in the print. A binocular view of the futuristic city seen across the motionless lake reveals a half-hearted attempt at animating a Martian flying saucer. A random-looking dot in the background reappears as a little oval shape that zips by in front of the futuristic building. One's DVD player needs to be set at a slow rate to perceive this feeble bit of animation.

As with their *Reptilicus* and *Journey to the 7th Planet*, the real fun regarding *The Angry Red Planet* is the long-running feud between its makers Ib Melchior and Sid Pink. Sid's autobiography makes bogus claims to greatness for these sub-par pictures while identifying every facet of their production as his personal doing. Ib defends himself while playing the blame game as well. *The Angry Red Planet* was their first cooperative venture, entered into with high spirits and some good ideas. The really good input seems to have come from the inventive Norman Maurer, cameraman Stanley Cortez (*The Night of the Hunter*) and the Howard Anderson special effects staff. Press-shown late in 1959, the film was obviously an investor's disappointment. The Cinemagic gimmick wasn't enough to overcome the fact that the sci-fi space cycle had waned, and the only distribution offer came from AIP's Sam Arkoff.

MGM's disc of **The Angry Red Planet** is unfortunately not the refreshing revisit to a nostalgic favorite we hoped it would be. It's essentially the same flat transfer as the old Orion video and what's shown on cable television. Good original elements have gone missing, making a full film restoration impossible. The picture is grainy and soft, with scratches and film damage; the DVD mastering adds excessive digital grain to some of the Cinemagic Mars scenes. Their color is an orange-red; Savant remembers them as blood red, but could easily be mistaken.

VILLAGE OF THE DAMNED & CHILDREN OF THE DAMNED
Warners Reviewed July 6, 2004
B&W 1:85 widescreen

These superior chillers continue England's commitment to science fiction as a serious film genre. Based on a popular book by John Wyndham, the films employ a realistic atmosphere and present their fantastic elements in a logical manner. The first film was considered shocking on two counts: It presents a virgin birth from outer space, and features "innocent" children as demonic villains.

VILLAGE OF THE DAMNED

1960 / 77 min.

Cinematography Geoffrey Faithfull. Written by Stirling Silliphant, Wolf Rilla, Ronald Kinnoch from the novel *The Midwich Cuckoos* by John Wyndham. Produced by Ronald Kinnoch. Directed by Wolf Rilla

These are the eyes that HYPNOTIZE!

Like an invisible dome, an unexplained black-out surrounds the hamlet of Midwich for several hours. A few weeks later the town's entire population of fecund females turns up pregnant. The children develop quickly and when born continue to grow faster than normal. Local researcher Gordon Zellaby (George Sanders) studies the children, who include his own "son" David (Martin Stephens). The tots all look similar and band together like a gang against the normal village kids. Gordon's inquiries discover that they possess a communal mind, which can telepathically force its will on humans.

One of John Wyndham's best novels, *The Midwich Cuckoos* is almost as popular as his groundbreaking post-apocalyptic *The Day of the Triffids.* Wyndham's narrative logic is impeccable. Weird scientific mysteries are followed by further impossibilities that overturn everything dear to the English heart: order, propriety, and the traceability of bloodlines. Instead of meteor showers and deadly flora, this time it's a mysterious "Sleeping Beauty" blackout of an entire town followed by the pregnancy of every woman capable of bearing children. Cuckoos are birds that lay their eggs in the nests of another species so that other mothers can be tricked into raising them. "Life will find a way", but it's an unethical jungle out there. Movie aliens are forever searching for human females for mating purposes. In this show there's no chase, just the Blessed Event.

In 1960 church authorities were uncomfortable seeing normal pregnancies depicted in movies, and the perverse ideas here (called "sick" by *Daily Variety*) conjure visions of females raped by men from outer space. Even more commercially daring is that ordinary-looking children represent the alien menace. The play *The Bad Seed* explained its murderous moppet in *Alraune-* like terms, namely the superstitious notion of inherited evil. The wanton murders committed by *The Village of the Damned's* little devils were contrary to acceptable public taste. [1]

Juvenile delinquency as a modern problem emerged in both the U.S. and the U.K. in the middle of WW2. Unsupervised middle-class adolescents got into trouble and formed unauthorized associations outside of the family ... to wit, gangs. The kids in *Village of the Damned* are a little mob of pre-Droog, pre *X-Men* mutant freaks. Half of their chromosomes are designed to implant a dominant alien consciousness in whatever life form they encounter – identical blonde hair, calm rounded faces, dark eyes. The children wear identical black raincoats with the cool fashion conformity that has become a given in neo-sci-fi.

The childrens' communal instincts evoke fears of Communism and the enforced conformity engendered by *Invasion of the Body Snatchers*. Their super-intelligence is a byproduct of their communal mind; as George Sanders' Zellaby puts it, they're *"one mind to the power of twelve"*. They are a multiple organism, much like the composite alien of *Quatermass 2*. Young David's loyalty to his comrades is far stronger than his affection for his mother.

Like the giant children in H.G. Wells' *Food of the Gods*, the Midwich Cuckoos consider themselves a different species in competition with humankind. *Food of the Gods* ends with the beginning of a war between humans and giants, and Wyndham's book goes a lot farther than the movie in showing the military quarantine of Midwich. In both books, the idea seems to be that anything living will fight to survive and prevail – "Life will find a way" is really a variant of "Dog Eat Dog." [2]

Village of the Damned's visual gimmick is to superimpose glowing irises over the eyes of the children when they use their telepathic powers. The necessity of freezing the frame results in eerie static visuals with the staring children arranged in disturbing compositions ... visuals echoed in Bergman's *Persona*. Silent film expressionist imagery is used to illustrate Gordon Zellaby's mental effort to deflect the childrens' piercing telepathy. Director Rilla simply dissolves from Zellaby's worried face to the literal image of a brick wall, slowly crumbling.

The Cuckoos betray a terrifying aptitude for sadism. They calmly compel a man to crash his car, and another to blow his own head off with a shotgun. *Village of the Damned* is also not a good screening choice for an expectant mother. The pregnancy panic is covered only by the town doctor's reports of attempted suicides. The women of Midwich suffer in medium shot here and there, but their anguish is felt mostly through their husbands. When the going gets tough the men abandon their spouses and go to the pub.

Gordon's wife Anthea (Hammer horror favorite Barbara Shelley) is a major character but her scenes are limited. Her name suggests that she's another rose in Gordon's garden, a trophy wife. One of the few "female" traumas in the film is the powerful shock cut to Anthea plunging her arm into scalding water, accompanied by an explosion of music. With most of the characters exhibiting calm and reserve, the sight of Anthea flailing in pain is the movie's most violent moment. Poor Anthea Zellaby easily gains our sympathy. Her husband is a wet noodle and her mystery child rejects her unequivocally. Then hubby goes and sacrifices himself without so much as consulting her first.

An unintentional laugh comes when the Midwich women line up at an aid station. Just as the idea sinks in that every Jane and Jill in town is pregnant, there's an abrupt cut to Zellaby's large German Shepherd dog. Gee, is the dog preggers too? Will we see puppies running around with blonde wigs between their ears?

The film hints that the Midwich children are aware of their status as alien invaders. Zellaby's students avoid his probing questions and soon form into a sealed-off conspiracy. The necessity of exterminating them is unambiguous. The only question is, how? The book is less clear on this issue. Like the Boll Weevil lookin' for a home, the aliens spread their seed around the galaxy, starting new colonies and outposts that do not necessarily know their origin. Every terrestrial species does this to the full limit of its capability. Wyndham's book maintains this doubt, whereas *Village of the Damned* falls back on the invasion idea, adding hints of "demonic evil" via the disembodied eyes that appear to survive the fire.

Little Martin Stephens is unforgettable in the role of David Zellaby, a child with an intelligent poise far beyond his years. The same (female?) talent as in *The Innocents* dubs David, conveying a large part of his eerie character through the precocious calculation in his voice.

CHILDREN OF THE DAMNED
1963 / 89 min.
Cinematography Davis Boulton. Written by John Briley. Produced by Lawrence P. Bachmann.
Directed by Anton M. Leader

These are the eyes that PARALYZE!

Scientists Tom Lewellin and David Neville (Ian Hendry & Alan Badel) are studying a multinational group of super-intelligent children. The children's respective governments are treating them like Cold War scientists: Brain Trust resources to be carefully controlled. When the children band together in an old church and use their telepathy to aggressively defend their turf, the authorities counter with force. Surrounding the church with guns and mining it from beneath, they argue among themselves whether the children are a genuine threat or simply misunderstood.

Children of the Damned is often thought of as superior to *Village*; but it is little more than a pacifist sermon with a dull edge: sci-fi lite. Everything in the movie is tilted toward the innocence of the children victimized by militaristic Cold Warriors.

Screenwriter John Briley has a gift for smooth dialogue and brisk pacing. His liberal reworking of the original *Midwich Cuckoos* concept changes the alien-fathered genetic mutations into home-grown prodigies described breathlessly as "mankind advanced a million years". The concept is

similar to that of Marvel's *X-Men*. Briley's beautiful children live in London but are unrelated in origin. One mother (Sheila Allen) claims that hers was a virgin birth. The supposedly open-minded scientist heroes scoff at that one.

The political authorities assume that controlling a few brainy children will not be a problem. Just as scientists are expected to build bombs and keep their pacifist mouths shut, the various governments want these kids separated to work on new weapons systems back in their home countries.

When the politicos discover that the children have the power of telepathic communication, they react like Chinese Communists pulling the plug on the Internet. Writer John Briley's logic isn't faulty; it's just that the story arc insists on a harsh political interpretation. *Children of the Damned* is a Little Golden Book of pacifist platitudes.

The corrupt adults constantly bicker while the children remain in calm accord with one another. But the kids also lack a personality, even an aggregate one. That's why *Children of the Damned* doesn't appeal as much as does the first film. Briley and director Leader work an anti-nuke message into their ending by illustrating how an innocent fumble can result in the sending of an erroneous attack signal. Sure, when meddling scientists and dissenters are rampaging through command headquarters, anything can happen.

Ian Hendry and Alan Badel form a close pair, even to the point of their eventual split on the controversy of what to do with the children. The emotions between them play like a lovers' tiff. In his commentary John Briley claims that the relationship between the two scientist partners is not intended to be homosexual. What did Briley expect people to think when he made them adult roommates without female interests, arguing over domestic issues?

Ian Hendry would figure in small roles in several genre efforts to come (*Repulsion*, *Journey* to the Far Side of the Sun) and Alan Badel takes a welcome break from playing ethnic villains. This time around none of the children, even the young actor playing lead kid Paul, makes an impression.

MGM marketed the film as a continuation of the original's horror concept. The trailer and print ads ignore the pacifist theme, making the children even more diabolical than those of the first film.

Warner's DVD of **Village of the Damned** and **Children of the Damned** is a beauty. The films have always been in good condition and this enhanced transfer only improves it. The first film includes a commentary from author Steve Haberman, who explains that the "blasphemy" issue stalled the movie's production for years. The commentary on the semi-sequel is by its screenwriter John Briley, who later wrote *Gandhi* and *Cry Freedom!* Briley praises England's tolerance of blacklisted American Communists. He's less clear about his own background as an American who worked almost exclusively in England.

1. The idea of children as perverse demons is now a horror staple. In the Spanish *Who Can Kill a Child?* moppets on a sunny island band together to murder their parents. The reason remains unexplained, as in *The Birds*. The message is that, in an age of riches and leisure, children are more neglected than ever.

2. When the Beatles came along three years later and millions of kids started growing their hair longer, Establishment backlash criticized the Fab Four for starting a fashion that emphasized group conformity. We 60s kids were really after an *alternate* conformity so we could be 'different' but not isolated. I've also often wondered if the identical blonde wigs worn by the Eloi in George Pal's *The Time Machine* of the same year were hand-me downs from *Village of the Damned*.

GORGO

VCI Reviewed: September 7, 2007
1961 / Color / 1:85 flat letterbox / 74 min. Cinematography Freddie Young. Original Music Angelo Francesco Lavagnino. Editor Eric Boyd-Perkins. Written by John Loring, Daniel Hyatt (actually Robert L. Richards, Daniel James). Produced by Frank and Maurice King. Directed by Eugène Lourié

Renowned French art director Eugène Lourié's *The Beast from 20,000 Fathoms* was the first 50s movie about a prehistoric monster on the loose. Lourié's efforts to extend his directing career stalled in *The Colossus of New York*, a cheap Paramount picture about an unhappy cyborg. The English producer of his next film, *The Giant Behemoth (Behemoth, Sea Monster)* rejected a more abstract, invisible blob monster before production began, so Lourié simply re-structured the *20,000 Fathoms* story into a tale about another dinosaur jolted from suspended animation by nuclear radiation.

Anyone would have thought that would be enough, but the prolific King Brothers decided to make their next film yet another story of a monster attacking a city. They hired Lourié to essentially undertake the same challenge for a third time. The big difference was that the King Brothers saw *their* monster movie as an expensive Technicolor production.

Gorgo is the monster movie equivalent to *Ben-Hur* or *El Cid* – its main title towers on the screen in giant stone letters to the crashing chords of Angelo Francesco Lavagnino's symphonic score. The cinematography is by Freddie Young, who would soon dazzle the world with *Lawrence of Arabia.* Claiming that their new show was a personal ode to mother love, Frank and Maurice King spared no expense. Filming commenced in 1959 in both England and Ireland. *American Cinematographer* devoted an article to the film's enormous River Thames miniature set, with its realistic model of the Tower Bridge.

Marine salvage partners Joe Ryan and Sam Slade (Bill Travers & William Sylvester) almost lose their ship to an enormous underwater disturbance. Looking for repairs on the Irish island of Nara, they are given a cold welcome by McCartin (Christopher Rhodes), an archeologist who profits from valuables found on the sea bottom. Tipped to McCartin's illegal cache by orphan Sean (Vincent Winter), Joe and Sam conduct their own search for ancient gold. They instead find Gorgo, an oversized sea monster with red eyes and dragon-like ears. Joe descends in a diving bell, the beast is netted and the ship heads to London to take advantage of a lucrative deal with the Battersea Park circus run by Dorkin (Martin Benson). Sam and Joe restrain little Sean from setting Gorgo free. They ignore

the advice of professors Hendricks and Flaherty (Joseph O'Connor & Bruce Seton), even when the experts calculate that Gorgo is a relative infant. Sure enough, a towering 200-foot parent monster rises from the deep, stomps Nara Island flat and sets a course for London, to liberate its offspring!

The screenplay by John Loring and Daniel Hyatt (actually Robert L. Richards and Daniel James) introduces a powerful ecological theme, As in the earlier 'save the elephants' epic *The Roots of Heaven*, civilized man is the villain. Joe and Sam exercise their business rights by strong-arming the competition and ignoring government experts blocking their path to a fast profit. As in *King Kong*, Gorgo is exploited as a circus attraction. The pint-sized Sean predicts disaster, being a believer in the pagan sea fairies later celebrated in *Local Hero*. Sure enough, Gorgo's mother comes to the rescue.

Gorgo is the first monster movie to clearly understand that kids root for the beleaguered monsters and couldn't care less about the handsome hero and his girlfriend. Joe finds Sean grinning in delight as he watches Gorgo's mother pull half of London down around them: *"You little knothead!"* He yanks the kid to safety, but we're with Sean all the way. Not only that, an editorializing radio reporter intones a stirring (if unlikely, considering the suffering all around him) epitaph to the whole affair:

"Yet, as though disdaining the pygmies under her feet, she turns back, turns with her young, leaving the prostrate city, leaving the haunts of man. Leaving man himself to ponder the proud boast that he alone is Lord of all creation."

Thanks to the King Brother's generous budget *Gorgo* is truly spectacular. Gorgo rises determinedly from the sea with water pouring over its glowing red eyes, but retreats with howls of protest when Joe leads the Nara fishermen in pelting him with firebrands. Clever camerawork makes Gorgo's mama appear suitably enormous as it wades upriver, smashing through "London's oldest landmarks" and ripping a path right through the city center. One breathtaking shot shows mother Gorgo approaching the Houses of Parliament under a blazing sky of purple and red smoke. In the awesome finale the monster's giant foot flattens the circus enclosure, and we see the once imposing Gorgo dwarfed by his colossal parent. The cacophony of music and destruction subsides for a moment as the creatures exchange squawks that sound like the trumpeting of elephants. It's a fairy tale saga of Mother Nature triumphant.

This was reportedly a troubled production that may have stalled for over a year; scenes showing Hammer's *The Mummy* playing in Piccadilly Circus date back to 1959. The cutting of the movie suggests a major rescue by the creative editor Eric Boyd-Perkins. An opening scuba diving sequence is broken up into two separate dives to slow the pace and stretch out the running time. Boyd-Perkins works feverishly to assemble sometimes-inadequate special effects and stock shots into acceptable sequences. Scenes with the main characters barely seem to cover the story essentials, suggesting that filming was curtailed before the entire script was filmed, or that Boyd-Perkins kept only those scenes that moved the action forward.

The editing really cooks in the core city destruction scene. As panicked crowds flee in terror from the monster's onslaught, editor Boyd-Perkins employs cutting patterns that emulate and improve on the rhythmic montage in Menzies' *Things to Come*. We alternate between views of the monster approaching Piccadilly Circus and frantic fast cuts of terrorized victims in full flight. One frenzied flurry of cuts perfectly expresses H.G. Wells' *War of the Worlds* quote about "the rout of civilization, the massacre of mankind".

Gorgo did well thanks to strong distribution by MGM; reviewers prone to snubbing genre films found merit in its surprise ending – the monsters aren't destroyed. Seen on a big screen in Technicolor, the film is a marvel. Unfortunately, rights reverted away from MGM and the film fell into legal limbo. Existing video transfers are from less-than-adequate source material. Transfers from actual Technicolor prints have clogged blacks and a lack of detail that in no way replicates the theatrical experience. VCI's special edition is a flat-letterboxed presentation artificially pumped to lighten scenes. We can see the darker action now, but most of the film's traveling mattes look terrible, especially the roving reporter shoehorned into the film in post-production. Colors are washed out and the editor's manipulations are painfully visible. We now can clearly see the Tower Bridge lying wrecked in shots *before* Gorgo's mother attacks it!

MOSURA

Sony Reviewed: August 4, 2009
1961 / Color / 2:35 widescreen / 101 min. /
Mothra
Cinematography Hajime Koizume. Written
by Yoshie Hotta, Shinichiro Nakamura, from
a story by Takehiko Fukunaga. Produced by
Tomoyuki Tanaka.
Directed by Ishiro Honda

The colorful and enchanting *Mothra* is especially noteworthy for its political attitudes. The
shortened American version omits some of the
flavor of this unique monster fairy tale about the
giant insect god of a mysterious lost civilization.
In keeping with the genre's newfound ecological theme *Mothra* is the first Japanese *Kaiju* in
which the monster is the hero and villain is modern society itself. Mothra blows cities to rubble

with the force of its giant wings, yet retains the
full sympathy of the audience.

A scientific team is dispatched to investigate a
mysterious radioactive isle. Thought to be unin-
habited, Infant Island supports a tribe of reclusive natives. Dr. Sinichi Chujo (Hiroshi Koizumi) meets the tribe's twin fairy princesses, called
"Shobijin" (Yumi & Emi Ito, aka "The Peanuts"),
tiny women that communicate telepathically.
Stowaway reporter Senichiro Fukuda (Frankie
Sakai) also befriends the Shobijin, but sneaky
Rolisican gangster-entrepreneur Clark Nelson
(Jerry Ito) returns to the island, murders a number of natives and kidnaps the princesses to sing
in his stage show back in Tokyo. Official efforts
fail to force Nelson to relinquish the princesses.
The Shobijin tell Senichiro that they are sad, not
for themselves, but for Tokyo: Mothra will rescue them. And indeed, as the natives back on Infant Island dance, a giant egg hatches an equally
monstrous larval moth, which immediately sets
sail for the Japanese capitol.

Mothra is a charming monster tale with spectacular special effects. The giant larva plows
through the ocean waves and leaves a wake of
destruction across enormous miniature sets.
Kids react positively to the psychic connection
between the princesses and the monster, and
the metamorphosis from caterpillar to colorful moth is an affirmation of nature's triumph
over man's petty politics. The giant flying insect is an impressive screen presence, despite
the fact that it is little more than a fuzzy marionette. Its mighty wings blow down buildings
like a modern-era Big Bad Wolf.

Yuji Koseki's wonderful musical score includes a great title tune sung by the tiny
twins during a command performance similar to the exhibition of *King Kong*. In the uncut
Japanese version, the Peanuts perform a second song in kimonos on a little cherry blossom set. It is interesting that the huge audience watches the tiny princesses sing in rapt

attention, when nobody beyond the first two rows could possibly get a good look at them.

The giant larva climbs Tokyo Tower to spin its cocoon. When the fairy princesses are removed to a foreign country called Rolisica, the newly hatched giant moth files halfway around the world to rescue them. In the context of the movie "Rolisica" is clearly an amalgam of Russia and the United States. Roliscia denies the hard evidence that Infant Island, which they once used as an atomic blast site, is inhabited. The Rolisican bad guy Clark Nelson is an exploitative combo of Carl Denham and Al Capone, committing theft and mass murder against a native population. Clark dodges kidnapping and slavery charges by claiming that the tiny princesses are merely merchandise. They like to sing and dance, so he's making them happy! The Rolisican government is complicit with Nelson's efforts to loot the world, at least until Mothra arrives to wipe out "New Kirk City." The dubbed American version retains only the bare bones of this anti- U.S. fervor. The Russian aspect of Rolisica can be seen in the combination of symbols on the flag of the Rolisican Embassy and the Russian-looking uniforms of the Rolisican generals helping to fight Mothra.

Toho assembled all of its usual Anglo actors to play Rolisican citizens. New Kirk City has skyscrapers, the Golden Gate Bridge and Los Angeles' Harbor Freeway. We also see a short clip of the row of hotels where Santa Monica reaches the bluffs over the beach. Nelson's gangster thugs occasionally speak in English. He and his main crook pal laugh themselves silly: *Mothra is dead! Now we can be happy and filthy rich! Ha ha ha ha!*

Clark Nelson's last ten lines are the same: *"Shut up!"* Nelson's final act is to knock the cane out from under an old man! I think there were some happy subversives at Toho that year.

The loveable Frankie Sakai's nickname "Snapping Turtle" was changed to "Bulldog" for the American dub version. He never lets go, see, and is a master of the obscure martial art of slapping bad guys on the head with folded pieces of paper.

Mothra has been seen on American television and VHS tapes only in a severely cut Pan-scanned version. Little kids react to the bright color and wonderful music as a monster fairy tale. The 1990s revival series doesn't recapture the original magic.

Steve Ryfle and Ed Godziszewski's commentary for Sony's DVD of *Mothra* offers a full run-down on an unused back story and an alternate ending. A wealth of production detail includes the information that the crawling larva monster costume was twenty feet long and operated by several men, Chinese Dragon style: at that scale, some of the "miniature" landscapes are enormous. The commentary also gets deep into the film's political context, and lists some topical protest-oriented material that was left out. The movie indeed shapes up as a P.C. fairy tale about superpower arrogance.

VOYAGE TO THE BOTTOM OF THE SEA

Fox Reviewed: June 7, 2007
1961 / Color / 2:35 widescreen / 105 min.
Cinematography Winton C. Hoch. Original
Music Paul Sawtell, Bert Shefter. Written by
Irwin Allen, Charles Bennett.
Produced and Directed by Irwin Allen

Irwin Allen sold cheap goods in his early sci-fi
fantasies. *The Lost World* (1960) is a colorful disappointment and *Five Weeks in a Balloon* a real
stinker. **Voyage to the Bottom of the Sea** never
earned much respect but it possesses an indel-
ible charm thanks to a goofy story and colorful
special effects. With its incredibly cool submarine *Seaview* gliding under the ocean surface,
the Fox CinemaScope production was the perfect air-conditioned summer popcorn matinee.

Allen forced his name cast to wade through a
soggy script riddled with logical and scientific
holes. Ten year-old kids didn't mind a bit.

On its shakedown voyage at the North Pole, the
super-scientific research ship U.S.O.S. *Seaview*
(the kind with nuclear weapons) surfaces to discover that the Van Allen radiation belt has ignited and is roasting the Earth below. The ship
rushes to New York to allow Scientist Admiral
Harriman Nelson (Walter Pigeon) and his co-
hort Commodore Lucius Emery (Peter Lorre)
to present the assembled United Nations with
a radical solution: shoot a nuclear warhead into
the belts and blast them away from the Earth.
When the U.N. science chief (Henry Daniell) rejects the idea, Nelson commandeers the *Seaview*
on his own authority to save the planet, with the
world's navies out to sink him. As the temperature soars, the ship races across half the globe.
Harriman battles sea monsters, pursuing submarines and a mutiny to reach his objective in
the Marianas.

For all of his crass idiocy, Irwin Allen was an
early proponent of upscale genre pictures,
which only became the norm after *Star Wars* a
generation later. *Voyage to the Bottom of the Sea*
interrupted the flow of low-budget exploitation movies with a studio effort boasting color,
flashy special effects and star names well past
their prime. Irwin Allen and Charles Bennett's
'kitchen sink' screenplay modernizes its Jules
Verne / Captain Nemo rip-off with an end-of-
the-world ecological catastrophe. Apparently
designed in Detroit, Admiral Nelson's glass-
nosed excursion craft sports late-fifties tail
fins. The 'scientists' on board do double duty
as Naval officers and stand by the triggers of a
nuclear arsenal ... in case The Bottom of the Sea
won't talk, I suppose.

Variety called the film "a crescendo of mounting jeopardy", a fair description of the way the
script piles one emergency onto another. We al-

most expect Peter Lorre to throw his arms up in despair, howling, *"Not an een-describable sea monster attack <u>now</u> ... we just ee-scaped a nuclear sub attack!"* The on-board drama re-hashes a ten-cent version of *The Caine Mutiny*, when the Admiral is accused of losing his marbles. While the obnoxious psychiatrist (Joan Fontaine) offers ignorant, unsolicited diagnoses, ship's Captain Lee Crane (Robert Sterling) maintains a gotcha list on the Admiral's eccentricities and bad decisions, waiting for an actionable 'Strawberries Incident' to seize command. Somebody is messing with the nuclear pile, setting staterooms on fire and rattling the Admiral so that he makes real mistakes, like cruising into an underwater minefield. It's interesting that the sub has a picture-window front end, but no lookout posted to actually watch where the *fershlugginer* boat is going.

Fussy Peter Lorre is wasted in a role that has him ad-libbing his dialogue while trying to elbow his way into other people' scenes. Barbara Eden serves coffee and struggles to pass through those raised port-ways in a skirt three sizes too small. Director Allen shows his opinion of Eden's acting talent by saving his only non-eye level, non-boring interior shot for a CinemaScope close-up of her derrière gyrating to goldbrick Frankie Avalon's trumpet music. Eden's off-screen husband Michael Ansara wanders about cradling a puppy and mumbling deranged prophecies about the end of the world. The annoying radio announcer with the Jersey accent is none other than our producer Irwin, saving a buck.

The sets look pretty cheap, with a swimming pool for sharks on board even though the sub frequently cruises at a 30-degree down angle. The electronics on the bridge are just a lot of blinking lights that include the matter transmitter from Fox's *The Fly*, itself inherited from *Desk Set*. Yes, it does shoot sparks while the crew lurch and stagger about, as if unaware that a boat might pitch and roll. They must surely experience additional *mal de mer* whenever the *Seaview* does its show-off, give-everyone-the-bends crash surface maneuver, lurching a hundred feet into the air.

L.B. Abbott's effects include some marvelous master shots: the sub cruising majestically under the fiery surface, or nearing the U.N. building on an East River roasting in temperatures upwards of 135 degrees (the mercury eventually climbs to 173°). Technicolor expert Winton Hoch helped light the effects setups to get the beautiful color contrasts. The big sub model had plenty of problems, the basic one being that its cool-looking manta ray- like 'wings' up front weren't particularly hydrodynamic. The sub had to be pulled on wires not to steer 'up' and as it filled with water it tended to list to port. It looks great anyway. The sub chase scene isn't very convincing (Eiji Tsuburaya's implosion effect in *Atragon* is far better) but the scene in the minefield with the tiny mini-sub is rather well done. Unfortunately, the big climax is botched because the crucial missile launch is under-visualized. The movie ends far too abruptly.

Anybody familiar with *Voyage to the Bottom of the Sea* will choke at the idea of the film making a serious ecological statement. This is the movie where ICE SINKS, which tells us how scientific it is. The Van Allen belts are tiny particles far out in space, where there's no oxygen to let anything burn. And the crew's radiation badges are a real hoot – by the time they glow red, the bearer has already received a lethal dose.

All of these inanities enhance the film's charm – but I doubt that Al Gore will endorse the Global Warming tie-in for this DVD release.

Fox's *Cinema Classics Collection* **Voyage to the Bottom of the Sea: Global Warming Edition** is a reissue masquerading as a special edition with a purpose. The previous release was a double bill with *Fantastic Voyage*, a film that lends itself much better to Sp. Ed. exploitation. *Voyage* has a slightly improved transfer and a welcome isolated music track.

Author Tim Colliver provides an uncritical feature commentary, offering comparisons between the script and its pocketbook novelization. He's a fan of the movie and TV series and likes to explain special effects in detail. I fondly remember the old *Mad* Magazine spoof, entitled *Voyage to See What's on the Bottom*. I wish that were included!

The featurette *Science Fiction: Fantasy to Reality* is a hasty examination of the Global Warming phenomenon that makes only tangential use of clips from shows like *Voyage* and *The Day After Tomorrow*. Looking like a million and still perky enough to be a genie, Barbara Eden appears for a lengthy series of interview responses. She offers nice-talk generalities about her *Voyage* experience and her lunches with Lorre and Pidgeon: *"They were so funny!"* The art and photo extras include some less interesting visual concepts for the *Seaview*. The insert liner notes are 100% original publicity baloney. *Voyage to the Bottom of the Sea* was the perfect infantile undersea adventure. With two or three thousand minor changes, it really ought to be remade for today's kiddies.

YOSEI GORASU

Not on Region 1 DVD Reviewed: September 20, 2007
1962 / Color / 2:35 Tohoscope / 89 & 73 min. / *Gorath*
Cinematography Hajime Koizume. Special Effects Eiji Tsuburaya. Written by Takeshi Kimura, Jojiro Okami. Produced by Tomoyuki Tanaka.
Directed by Ishiro Honda

The success of *The Mysterians* for Japan's Toho Films begat a spirited semi-sequel entitled *Uchu Daisenso (Battle in Outer Space)*, another martial confrontation between the Earth Defense Force and sinister invaders. In the next couple of years Toho's fantasy output would literally explode. In addition to orchestrating the return of Godzilla, the studio released several genre mysteries about men that melt or transmit themselves like television signals. Toho then returned to outer space for its epic *Yosei Gorasu (Gorath)*, an ambitious variation on the astral collision idea exploited in George Pal's *When Worlds Collide*. Takeshi Kimura and Jojiro Okami's screenplay takes a can-do attitude to celestial disaster. Instead of responding with riots and religious hysteria, Japan comes up with a practical method of saving the world.

Rocket ship JX-1 is diverted from a Saturn mission to examine a large object entering the solar system: the star Gorath, only ¾ the size of earth but six thousand times its mass. Realizing that his ship cannot escape Gorath's immense gravitation, Captain Sonoda (Jun Tazaki) prepares his men for the selfless job of sending crucial data back to earth, before they are destroyed.

Back at the Mount Fuji Interstellar Exploration Agency, eager cadets chase girls while awaiting orders from Captain Endo (Akihiko Hirata). The bureaucrats bicker about the loss of the expensive JX-1 until Drs. Tazawa (Ryo Ikebe) and Kono (Ken Uehara) tell them that Gorath is on a collision course with the earth. Nations unite behind Tazawa's plan to build thousands of rockets in Anarctica to push earth out of harm's way. Tazawa forms a relationship with Sonoda's daughter Kiyo (Yumi Shirakawa). Kiyo's girlfriend Taiko (Kumi Mizuno) mourns her fiancée lost on the same mission, and rejects the advances of another rocket cadet Tetsuo Kanai (Akira Kubo). As construction gets underway for 600 square kilometers of rockets at the South Pole, Gorath 'collects' a comet, augmenting its mass and gravitation. The JX-2 is dispatched to investigate. Kanai mans a probe ship to approach Gorath, and has a nervous breakdown. He's rescued but remains unable to speak.

At the South Pole, the project awakens a colossal hibernating walrus monster, which threatens to wreck one of the rocket fields. The project leaders have no choice but to kill the animal. The huge network of rockets at the South Pole is ig-

nited, and the earth begins to shift from its orbit. Anxious and stressed, Tazawa is comforted by Kiyo. In space, Gorath passes Saturn, 'eating' its rings.

As Gorath nears the earth, Taiko accepts the mute Kanai and takes him to Kiyo Sonoda's house. Gorath consumes the moon and huge tidal waves smash into cities. But the earth is spared, as Gorath passes by in a near miss.

The most surprising thing about *Gorath* is its relatively mature attitude. Although Eiji Tsuburaya's space effects are technically better than ever – the shots of the JX-2 leaving earth orbit are beautiful – the emphasis is on a varied group of characters reacting to an extraordinary situation. Sonoda's spacemen do their duty, sending back a crucial warning and shouting a spirited 'Banzai!' as they plummet to their deaths. Dr. Tazawa nearly cracks under the responsibility for expending all of the world's resources on a rescue plan that might not work. On a nighttime taxi ride Kiyo's uncle Kesuke (Takashi Shimura) observes Tokyo's complacent citizenry shopping as usual. Can humanity even conceive of total annihilation?

Gorath takes on an eerie tone not shared by any of Toho's previous sci-fi films. The giant walrus monster (referred to outside the film as Magma) is an inoffensive beast accidentally disturbed by man. The South Pole Operation's jet planes are forced to kill the beast, leaving a huge dismembered hulk in a smoky Antarctic canyon. Kaiju monsters are never dispatched so summarily, and the creature's death creates a feeling of sadness. As with the previous years' *Mothra*, we want to see everyone saved, even the monster.

Not all of the visuals are convincing. The South Pole project uses impressive, enormous miniatures, but too many shots of toys intercede, including shiny bulldozers manned by stiff plastic drivers. Gorath itself looks like a glowing candy apple; even accompanied by crashing music chords, it isn't very threatening. Shots of the rogue planet pulling away Saturn's rings are accomplished with obvious cel animation. The idea is so strange, the effect works anyway.

The few American viewers that remember *Gorath* have probably only seen the mercilessly edited version distributed by Brenco in 1964. Brenco's cut is sixteen minutes shorter and contains added shots of a map of the solar system to explain Gorath's progress toward earth. Most dialogue scenes are shorter and the two romantic relationships are so abbreviated that Dr. Tazawa appears to be in Tokyo and at the South Pole at the same time. Material excised includes the bulk of a dance number, a sing-along in a helicopter and the entire episode with Magma, whose attack is now reduced to a simple cave-in. The jet mission to kill Magma is now just a check-up on volcanic activity. Although the daytime construction effects are not altered, Brenco darkened almost all of the nighttime miniatures, obscuring the flooding of the city. At the South Pole, the rows of propulsive jets are so darkened that only the flames are visible.

Voice specialist Paul Frees dubs at least five or six separate characters in addition to providing narration, resulting in a surreal aural dislocation. The American dubbing script alters many story details. The JX-1 is now investigating disturbances in the Van Allen radiation belts, indicating that the screenwriters were fresh from a matinee of *Voyage to the Bottom of the Sea*. Instead of colliding with a comet, Gorath's gravity is said to be breaking up a satellite. The mission to re-assess Gorath's gravitation has become an attempt to destroy it with an atomic bomb. We're told that the nations of earth have disbanded their armies to see the Antarctica project through. Otherwise, the dubbing is embarrassing. A drunk at a bar remarks, *"No reason to save the booze – Gorath will be drinking it in three months."* Greeting Kanai at her doorstep

wearing a towel, Taizo snaps out *"You just got me outta my nice warm bath you clown"*, as if this were Woody Allen's *What's Up Tiger Lily?*

The dumbed-down and dramatically impaired American cut ends identically to the Japanese original, with a scientist quipping, *"We thought that was difficult. Now we have to start thinking about getting earth back into its proper orbit!"* As will soon be demonstrated in *The Day the Earth Caught Fire*, that's easier said than done.

THE CREATION OF THE HUMANOIDS

Dark Sky Reviewed: April 15, 2006
1962 / Color / 1:85 widescreen / 75 min.
Cinematography Hal Mohr. Written by Jay
Simms. Producers Wesley E. Barry, Edward J.
Kay.
Directed by Wesley E. Barry

The Creation of the Humanoids is a visionary
opus hiding behind a threadbare production
and stilted performances. This curiosity is said
to have been one of Andy Warhol's favorite
films. Its technological prophecies will fascinate
hard-core science fiction aficionados, while others may find it difficult to stay awake!

The film's thematic complexity goes far beyond
the norm for 1962. The cerebral script by Jay
Simms (*Panic in Year Zero!*) layers enough talky

exposition to fill three movies. It's really like no
other science fiction film: the humanoid robots
called "Clickers" stare through stainless-steel
ball bearing eyes and speak in monotones familiar from later *Coneheads* parodies on *Saturday Night Live*.

The near future after a nuclear war. Kenneth
Cragis (Don Megowan, the Gill Man from *The
Creature Walks Among Us*) belongs to The Order
of Flesh and Blood, a secret society dedicated to
the suppression of robots. The Order illegally
monitors the activities of the robot "Clickers"
and engages in terrorist activities. Cragis is attracted to Maxine Megan (Erica Elliott) and
is shocked when informed that his own sister
Esme (Frances McCann) is "in rapport" (cohabiting) with a Clicker named Pax (David Cross).
Cragis tries to shame Esme into breaking off
the relationship but she scoffs at his reactionary
ideas. The robots are here to stay.

Meanwhile, Clickers Acto and Lagan (George
Milan and Dudley Manlove) are supervising
subversive doings at The Temple, the robot's recharging headquarters. The Clickers are circumventing the law that prohibits the manufacture
of robots more than 70% human. They bribe humans to pilfer new humanoids from the assembly line so that renegade scientist Dr. Raven (Don
Doolittle) can upgrade them to the 96th percentile level. Raven cosmetically alters the "R-96's"
to perfectly match recently deceased humans.
He then performs a "thalamic transplant" from
human to robot, causing the dead human to be
'reborn' in an artificial body, unaware that he is
no longer made of flesh and blood. Cragis' illegal anti-Clicker squad uncovers the conspiracy,
but will his intervention make a difference? As
Acto says, *"Why is it the more we become like Man,
the more some of them hate us for it?"*

The Creation of the Humanoids is wildly uneven.
An ugly title sequence backed by shots of nuclear explosions is followed by an amateurish
prologue explaining how computers evolved

into R-21 humanoid Clickers at the same time that human reproduction plummeted. Among several cardboard robots wiggling their arms is the alien costume from *Earth vs. the Flying Saucers*.

The actors playing the bluish, bald Clickers wear huge silvery contact lenses. The Clickers speak without looking at each other, move stiffly and wear jumpsuits similar to the Metalunans of *This Island Earth*. Writer Jay Simms gives them a number of provocative dialogue zingers: *"I know who created me. You (humans) have to accept your creator on faith."*

The movie has only five or six major scenes and perhaps fewer than a hundred camera setups. The tacky painted backdrops were probably rented from a scenery dock. Legendary cameraman Hal Mohr's strong color contrasts become a little hard on the eyes after a while. The actors are blocked as if in a static one-act play; almost everything is spoken instead of being visually dramatized. The show could easily be performed as a stage play – but it might be criticized as being too talky!

The central theme is the riddle of human identity. Robots so perfect that they cannot be distinguished from humans pop up frequently in the books of Philip K. Dick but took twenty years to fully reach the screen in *Blade Runner* and *Star Trek: The Next Generation*. References are made to humans having their memories "dispersed", in the same way we now might erase a computer's hard drive.

The film's politics have definitely become more relevant. The Order of Flesh and Blood is a radical minority that wields undue political power. It espouses a chauvinist definition of "human-ness" and seeks to outlaw robotic imitations. Members of The Order wear Civil War Confederate uniform pants and caps, suggesting the Civil Rights issue; the word "Clicker" is a demeaning epithet. Members

carry ceremonial daggers as did the Nazi elite, use thug tactics to intimidate policemen and plant bombs like modern terrorists. Cragis' worst nightmare is mechanized miscegenation, mixed marriage between human and robot.

The distinction between man and machine is disappearing. Clickers merely want to serve man and be accepted by him, and the R-21s marvel at unknown emotions experienced by the 'improved' R-96s. Dr. Raven sees nothing wrong with his *Invasion of the Body Snatchers*-like substitution of robots for people. In return for upgrading prototype R-96's with transplanted thalamus glands, the Clickers have promised to revive him after death as an R-96. Like Dr. Frank in *The Revenge of Frankenstein*, Dr. Raven gives humankind the possibility of immortality. We can all be reborn in new synthetic bodies. When that body wears out in 150 years, we'll simply move to another, like a hermit crab trading shells: *"Build me more stately mansions, o my soul…"* [1]

The Order of Flesh and Blood considers robots a threat to the idea of God as the sole creator of life. *The Creation of the Humanoids* doesn't equate faith with superstition, as the Clickers have developed a religion of their own. They consider the central controlling computer their "father-mother" and the recharging facility is called The Temple. Do all self-conscious beings share the need for a belief system?

Director Wesley Barry paces the dialogue so that every line is given the kind of earnest, hollow reading heard in instructional films. In the future, humor no longer exists. Only Pax the Clicker laughs, and his is a pretty feeble display. Some shots hold for the better part of a minute while the Clickers stand like talking statuary, droning away. Little or nothing is told visually and few details of futuristic life are given – Clicker hubby Pax serves some drinks at one point, and that's it. Dr. Raven toys with a disembodied arm, in a trick that wouldn't fool a five-year-old.

The actors playing humans never really get a handle on the thick dialogue, placing the dramatics at an artificial remove. The actors playing Clickers combine good vocal skills with the stamina to wear those scary contact lenses – just looking at them makes our eyes itch. George Milan has the most to say, while Dudley Manlove (memorable as the alien who throws a hissy-fit in Ed Wood's *Plan 9 from Outer Space*) is equally adept in his vocal mannerisms.

The Creation of the Humanoids has a reputation as a static non-movie, but it's also a treasure trove of speculative and challenging social ideas. Concept-starved science fiction fans will love it.

Dark Sky's DVD of ***The Creation of the Humanoids*** is a beauty, with vibrant color. Hal Mohr's gaudy images give us close looks at the Clicker makeup by the legendary Jack Pierce. The excellent enhanced transfer exposes every flaw in the original film, like the misaligned main titles that pop on late for every cut, and the inconsistent color of the Clickers' plastic skin. The original negative is in great shape overall with just a few dings and weak splices here and there. The soundtrack features "Electronic Harmonics by I.F.M." that bear a strong similarity to the "tonalities" from *Forbidden Planet*, with an added wailing vocal.

Republished by permission of Turner Classic Movies.

1. Of course, Dr. Raven's bid for immortality may be a cruel joke. Does his Thalamus operation transplant human consciousness, or only the blueprint for human consciousness? Is the new robot Raven, Raven himself or just a "guiltless copy" as in John Weldon's 1990 film *To Be*?

THE DAY THE EARTH CAUGHT FIRE

Anchor Bay Reviewed: May 15, 2001
1961 / B&W / 2:35 widescreen / 99 min.
Cinematography Harry Waxman. Special Effects Les Bowie. Writing credits Wolf Mankowitz and Val Guest. Produced by Frank Sherwin Green and Val Guest.
Directed by Val Guest

The average citizen and his problems are the last concern of science fiction spectaculars focusing on mass disasters. The common man is usually an anonymous victim fleeing in panic from some threat bearing only a symbolic relation to anything real. Val Guest's *The Day the Earth Caught Fire*, one of the best science fiction films made anywhere by anybody, gives us a 'future shock' glimpse of what might transpire if the world turned topsy-turvy. The film still resonates for audiences forty years after it was released to critical acclaim and good box office. As governments persist in protecting 'economic interests' in the face of ecological disasters, the dysfunctional world pictured here is a very familiar one.

> Depressed over his divorce, cynical reporter Peter Stenning (Edward Judd) is drinking too much and letting his job go to pot. Colleague Bill Maguire (Leo McKern) covers for him as best he can. News of catastrophes and climatic aberrations begin to gel into a disturbing pattern. Verification leaks out through Jeannie (Janet Munro), a government office worker who has fallen for Peter: Simultaneous nuclear blasts at the poles have knocked the Earth off its axis and pitched it from its orbit – in the direction of the sun. Civilization begins to crumble as the Thames dries up and cyclones hit London. Jeannie and Peter find romance ... while the temperature climbs to the 140-degree mark.

For once, the credibility of a wild premise is not the only issue in a science fiction movie. Two bombs jolting the Earth out of kilter is treated as just another official secret the newspaper heroes must ferret out of uncooperative government officials. Actual London editor Arthur Christiansen serves as technical advisor in addition to playing a major role, while Judd and McKern's unflappable newsmen twist the truth from uncooperative sources just like the reporters of *All The President's Men*. The necessity of a free press has never been as well expressed, and this movie can join *President's Men* and Sam Fuller's *Park Row* as epitaphs for the journalistic profession.

Wolf Mankowitz' snappy writing style would be welcome in any genre. His newsmen have jobs and families and quietly lust after the bartender's wife. Bill Maguire helps his alcoholic best friend hold onto his job with a veiled affection reminiscent of Edward G. Robinson in *Double Indemnity*. Hero Peter Stennings' advances toward fetching working girl Jeannie are met with a complex mix of reproach, good humor, and adult teasing.

Good production values and Guest's fluid direction make every bizarre new phenomenon believable. An unseasonable heat wave in London precedes a strange mist, itself interrupted by a destructive typhoon. Effects man Les Bowie makes use of mattes and large painted cycloramas: CGI artists should study what can be done with so few resources. With the exception of one shot of a mist rolling up the Thames, the views of empty riverbeds, fog- enshrouded cities and scorched landscapes are superb. Stock footage of fires and storms are utilized to excellent effect; one gets the feeling that pandemonium is indeed breaking out all over the world. The newspaper editor responds to the doomsday news from the Russians by saying he doesn't see what they have to gain by lying.

Once a prime candidate to play James Bond, Edward Judd handles the often-racy dialogue well and is a good match for the wonderful Janet Munro, here graduating from Disney features into an adult role. Leo McKern is best at delivering the wisecracking, overlapping patter in an ensemble cast that maintains a pace as fast as *The Front Page* – without sounding artificial or forced.

Although underreported here, England in the late 50s witnessed massive 'Ban the Bomb' rallies. Director Guest put Edward Judd in the middle of one. It's surprising to see the 'peace sign' we associate with Vietnam protests ... our peaceniks lifted it from the banners of English peaceniks, it seems. Guest and Mankowitz envision the breakdown of society as beginning with the rationing of water, which is definitely not science fiction to those who have endured gasoline rationing. Scarcity encourages hoarding, and black-market H_2O spreads an epidemic of typhus.

It's a cliché of doomsday scenarios that mass populations are unruly mobs waiting to create social havoc at the drop of a scare headline. Some shows revel in exploitative chaos to the detriment of making a coherent point: *No Blade of Grass* comes to mind in this context. Here we have a water riot backed by Monty Norman's Dixieland 'beatnik music'. The fighting and disorder work well without turning Edward Judd into an action hero or the movie into a show of brutality.

The Day the Earth Caught Fire uses a flashback structure framed by bookend scenes tinted a strange orange-yellow. The tinting expresses the idea that London has become a furnace that melts the rubber on typewriter carriages. Wolf Mankowitz's final words should be up there with Robert Scott Carey's soliloquy at the end of *The Incredible Shrinking Man* as classic science fiction poetry:

"So Man has sown the wind, and reaped the whirlwind. Perhaps in the next few hours there will be no remembrance of the past and no hope for the future that might have been. All the works of man will be consumed in the great fire out of which he was created. But perhaps at the heart of the burning light into which he has thrust his world, there is a heart that cares more for him than he has ever cared for himself. And if there is a future for man, insensitive as he is, proud and defiant in his pursuit of power, let him resolve to live it lovingly, for he knows well how to do so. Then he may say once more, 'Truly the light is sweet, and what a pleasant thing it is for the eyes to see the sun.'"

Because it focuses on people instead of wholesale slaughter, this is the most thoughtful and persuasive of the doomsday films. Val Guest's earlier *Quatermass 2*, Joseph Losey's *These are The Damned* and this film are the top classics of British science fiction.

Anchor Bay's DVD of **The Day the Earth Caught Fire** looks stunning in its proper aspect ratio.

The wide Dyaliscope screen is always crowded with characters and visual interest. Film historian Ted Newsom hosts a fine commentary with Val Guest, who is clearly proud of this film that he produced as well as directed. They point out scores of actors in small parts, including a young Michael Caine. A trailer and several television spots are included that amusingly alter McKern's word 'bastards' into 'bunglers'.

A clean Certificate 'X' card is displayed at the front of the show. The commentary implies that this uncut English version is longer than the American release. The changes must be minor, for the scenes with Janet Munro don't seem more explicit. She makes perspiration look as sexy as anything in *Body Heat*. The stills section includes color cheesecake shots of Munro standing in front of a set that looks identical to Mark Lewis'es setup in *Peeping Tom*, made the year before.

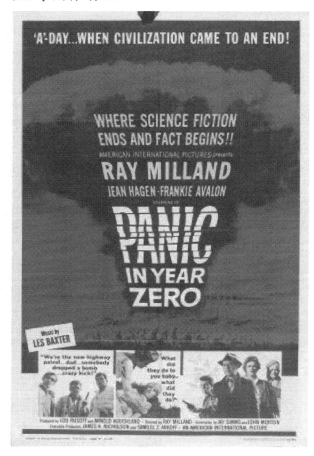

PANIC IN YEAR ZERO!

MGM Reviewed: April 8, 2005
1962 / B&W / 2:35 widescreen / 92 min.
Cinematography Gilbert Warrenton. Music
Les Baxter. Written by John Morton, Jay
Simms. Produced by Samuel Z. Arkoff, Arnold
Houghland, James H. Nicholson, Lou Rusoff.
Directed by Ray Milland

The atom-scare film **Panic in Year Zero!** goes
beyond *On the Beach's* solemn sermonizing to
depict the immediate aftermath of a nuclear
strike. After a decade of public service films
predicting order and optimism in a Civil defense emergency, this American-International
film was one of the first to suggest that an attack
would precipitate an immediate breakdown of
society. Framing its story within an "average
American family", writers John Morton and Jay
Simms can't wait to depict civilization revert-
ing to one simple rule: Every Man For Himself.

The Baldwin family receives a shock as they leave
for a camping vacation in the Sierra Nevadas –
behind them, multiple mushroom clouds hang
over Los Angeles. After shaking off his initial in-
hibitions, Harry Baldwin (Ray Milland) marshals
his wife Ann, son Rick and daughter Karen (Jean
Hagen, Frankie Avalon & Mary Mitchel) to grab
up supplies before rural shopkeepers know what
has happened. They hide at a remote campsite to
avoid the chaos that will surely result when civilization comes to an abrupt halt.

The nearly hysterical *Panic in Year Zero!* would
play much better if its script and acting were a
bit smoother – the film is just too cheap-looking
to endure as any kind of classic. Just the same,
its premise is as gripping now as it was in 1962,
when the undertaker living on Savant's street
was building a backyard fallout shelter. The
Baldwins' station wagon and trailer endlessly
crisscross the same narrow roads north of Los
Angeles, and the same five or six cars are recycled to represent a flow of panicky Angelenos
heading for the hills. In one supremely unconvincing setup, the station wagon is blocked at a
rural intersection by an unbroken flow of zooming traffic – represented by grainy, mismatched
shots of an L.A. freeway!

The visuals may sag but actor-director Ray Milland keeps the dramatic tension high. Jean Hagen (*Singin' in the Rain's* Lina Lamont) is fine as
the mother slow to accept the idea that ruthless survivalism is now the name of the game.
Frankie Avalon fails to convince as a teenager
but is handy at riding shotgun for his pistol-tot-
ing father. As the original *Variety* review pointed out, sister Mary Mitchel and pretty refugee
Joan Freeman (of *Tower of London* and *Roust-
about*) share a first for a mainstream American
release – both become the targets of rapists.

Survivalism as a major American industry didn't start until a little later, with magazines dedicated to helping one store food and ammo for the impending (desired?) apocalypse. *Panic In Year Zero!* impressed millions of wide-eyed young males wondering how they'd protect Ma and Sis in the universally hostile future. There's little moral distance between guarding one's own bomb shelter with a shotgun and the marauding scavenger-rapists of movies like *No Blade of Grass*. Harry Baldwin takes advantage of a greedy grocer (O.Z. Whitehead) unaware of the crisis. A greedy gas station owner tries to enforce a price hike – up from 34 cents to $3 a gallon! For 1962 America, the notion of gas that expensive would indeed indicate that civilization was coming to an end.

Harry feels compelled to rob decent hardware retailer Ed Johnson, who figures later in the story as another unfortunate refugee. Milland holds a gun on Johnson, a shocking act for an "average American father" in a 1963 movie. Even more ironic is the fact that Johnson is played by Richard Garland, the reformed sniper spared by Quaker Gary Cooper in the pacifist *Friendly Persuasion*.

Ray Milland's atom war is represented by reports on the Conelrad radio station. We're given only a sampling of the kinds of trouble that could occur. A township puts up roadblocks against the human scum prowling the roads, a development with a precedent. Small municipalities were overrun by motorcycle 'clubs' in the early '50s – the Brando film *The Wild One* is based on one such incident. But the limitless possibilities of lawlessness are distilled into three minor-league punks who murder and rape on a small scale. Perennial juvenile delinquent Richard Bakalyan plays their leader. The film infers that the Baldwins (especially their ravaged daughter) would have been better off if Harry had executed the rogue hoods at the first opportunity.

A beacon of hope comes in the form of martial law. The moral delivered by Willis Bouchey's doctor/author's spokesman is that America needs martial law *now*. While the Baldwins hid out in the hills, drug addicts have been running wild, stealing and killing. Atomic war getting you down? It's those darn junkies!

Panic in Year Zero! avoids scenes requiring more than minimal production values yet manages to deliver on its basic promise, allowing the imagination of the audience to enlarge what's actually on the screen. It was certainly shocking in 1962, and its exploitation thrills easily trumped other more pacifistic efforts. *The Day the Earth Caught Fire* was for budding flower people; *Panic in Year Zero!* could have been made as a sales booster for the gun industry.

MGM's disc of **Panic In Year Zero!** is a flawless enhanced transfer from prime elements. Half the enjoyment will be seeing this title in its proper 'Scope aspect ratio, as older pan-scanned VHS tapes were terrible. The sound track replicates Les Baxter's jazzy but overstated music score. The one extra is a trailer that bears text titles in an exaggerated font that might be called 'Hysteria.'

CHILDREN OF ICE AND DARKNESS...
THEY ARE THE LURKING, UNSEEN EVIL YOU DARE NOT FACE ALONE!

COLUMBIA PICTURES PRESENTS

these are The Damned

MACDONALD CAREY · SHIRLEY ANNE FIELD · VIVECA LINDFORS · ALEXANDER KNOX

Come at your own risk ... if you come alone!

THE DAMNED

Sony Reviewed: July 4, 2007
1961 / B&W / 2:35 widescreen / 77, 87, **96** min. / *These Are the Damned*
Cinematography Arthur Grant. Production Design Bernard Robinson. Music James Bernard. Written by Evan Jones from the story *The Children of Light* by H.L. Lawrence. Produced by Anthony Hinds.
Directed by Joseph Losey

In the 1950s runaway radiation created monsters, raised the dead and turned people into midgets and giants, effects that only alluded to the real-life dangers of nuclear power. Blacklisted American director Joseph Losey struck much closer to the truth with this chilling fantasy from Hammer films. Completed in 1961, the film wasn't seen until 1963 in Eng-land and 1965 in the United States, and both releases were drastically edited. Even *Variety* wondered openly if it had been suppressed. *These Are the Damned* (original English title, *The Damned*) is a radical thriller about artists and bureaucrats, juvenile delinquency and sinister top-secret government projects: a catalogue of ideas guaranteed to inflame the guardians of England's public image. Its source is a book by H.L Lawrence, *The Children of Light*.

The seaside town of Weymouth is overrun by a pack of unruly Teddy Boys, biker hoodlums led by King (Oliver Reed), a sullen thug with incestuous designs on his sister Joan (Shirley Anne Field). The gang uses Joan as bait to mug Simon (MacDonald Carey), an American tourist disenchanted with modern life. Simon meets the bohemian artist Freya (Viveca Lindfors, in her best role), a free-spirit sculptress of statues that resemble the charred remains of Hiroshima victims. Freya is the mistress of Bernard (Alexander Knox), a stuffy executive in charge of a classified military experiment. It is so secret, Bernard says, that should he tell Freya about it he *"might be condemning her to death"*.

Simon defies King's gang and escapes on his boat with Joan, who seeks to break free of her brother's control. King pursues them near Bernard's secret project, a heavily guarded compound reminiscent of Hammer's earlier *Quatermass 2*. Simon, King and Joan end up in a futuristic bunker hidden below the sea cliffs, with a group of imprisoned children. The sheltered and polite children wear tidy school uniforms and are being raised by remote control. The only contact with their 'keepers' is a television screen, through which Bernard condescendingly promises that their many questions about life and the world will be answered, *"When the time comes"*. The children are a mystery to Simon until Joan discovers that their body temperature is ice cold. Bernard is rearing a breed of radioactive people to continue the human race in a post-nuclear radioactive world.

These Are the Damned takes a completely anti-establishment view of the nuclear arms race. Bernard justifies his atrocious experiment with the conviction that nuclear annihilation is inevitable. Freya goads him with loaded libertarian questions: why is a public servant permitted to have secrets from his master, the public? Freya suspects that Bernard is up to no good in his secret lab, yet worships oblivion in her own way, through her morbid statues. Screenwriter Evan Jones is quick to choose sides; as in Anthony Burgess' *A Clockwork Orange* the motorcycle hooligans mirror the institutionalized brutality of society at large. The Teddy Boys' outlaw disenchantment is a direct reaction to the warped values of the adult generation. As Bernard puts it, *"The age of senseless violence has caught up with us too"*. James Bernard's Teddy Boy theme *Black Leather Rock* is an anthem for a new era of anarchy.

Joseph Losey's prowling Hammerscope camera uses landscapes to heighten his dramatic contrasts. The sleepy holiday town gives way to the barren cliffs of Weymouth. The concrete and steel warrens of Bernard's inhuman project lie just below Freya's cliff-side studio, implying a direct relationship between political art and society's hidden agendas. The violent climax sees huge helicopters pursuing King's sports car down the seaside highway like ominous Orwellian watchdogs.

All bets are off when the bunker doors open and the children stumble out into the daylight. As a rubber-suited goon threatens, Joan introduces a liberated little girl to the joys of a tiny flower, expressing perfectly the later pacifist motto, "War is Not Healthy for Children and Other Living Things". Freya and Simon should be running for their lives instead of confronting Bernard with the obscene truth of

his atrocious project – the "graveyard bird" helicopters are already closing in for the kill.

By Hammer's standards *These Are the Damned* is a lavish production that uses extensive location shooting and some extremely convincing stunts. The cast is uneven, with MacDonald Carey an unappealing American playboy and Shirley Anne Field awkward at best. Losey overplays the tension between Joan and her brother King, but every scene with Viveca Lindfors is golden. Her Freya enjoys the luxury of pursuing her artistic goals unaware that everything around her, even her lover/patron, is an abomination to her values. The emotion of the final scene justifies its theatricality: *"Is that your great project, Bernard, to set these children loose in the ashes of the world?"*

Joseph Losey's career is blessed with the kind of symmetry that film critics love. *These are the Damned* extends thematic elements in the director's first movie *The Boy with Green Hair*, another plea for human tolerance in the face of war. *Green Hair's* ghostly "war orphans" are very much like *Damned's* prepubescent guinea pigs, innocent victims lost in an insane world they didn't create. Both groups of children beg for help and understanding. A bona fide subversive classic, *These are the Damned* increases its grip on the audience as it speeds to one of the most doom-laden finishes in science fiction: "Help us! Help us! *Please help us!"*

Never really properly released, Losey's film was cut by nineteen minutes for one version, removing many of its sharp philosophical speeches and a handful of interesting character confrontations. An encounter between Freya and King was cut in half, inadvertently suggesting that a rape occurs. Losey reportedly objected when the studio insisted that the Bernard character personally commit one of the final murders, as the director's plan was to assign that role to the faceless helicopters. If released in a timely fashion, *These Are the Damned* might have been a key film of the Ban the Bomb years. It was instead shelved, cut up and discarded for reasons that were never made clear. Did Hammer and Columbia think the film too talky and insufficiently horrific? Or was Britain simply worried about its potential effect on tourism?

Sony/Columbia restored the film to its original 96-minute length in the early 1990s, and it has been greeted with enthusiasm at film festivals ever since. What was once considered one of Joseph Losey's weakest efforts is finally being recognized as the very best of British science fiction filmmaking.

THE DAY OF THE TRIFFIDS

Not on authorized DVD Reviewed: October 29, 2005
1963 / Color / 2:35 flat letterbox / 93 min.
Cinematography Ted Moore. Special Effects Wally Veevers. Written by Bernard Gordon (uncredited) from the novel by John Wyndham. Produced by George Pitcher, Philip Yordan. Directed by Steve Sekeley (and Freddie Francis)

John Wyndham's 1951 novel *The Day of the Triffids* is a favorite. Its central innovation of an intriguing post-apocalyptic setting has become a screen staple. An unforeseen calamity stops civilization dead in its tracks, pitting humans against monsters in a fight for survival. This 1962 film version is no classic in either script or execution, and yet its story remains irresistible.

Wildcat screenwriter Philip Yordan was in Europe fashioning highly profitable blockbusters for Samuel Bronston. His production of *The Day of the Triffids* is something of a fascinating bust. Bad production management and poor writing sidetrack a potential classic. Blacklisted screenwriter Bernard Gordon's screenplay was never fully filmed. Just the same, the big-scale CinemaScope show has its ardent fans.

> Recovering from an eye operation, ship's engineer Bill Masen (Howard Keel) must miss 'the aerial light show of the century', a dusk 'til dawn meteorite shower that fills the skies with brilliant flashing lights. He soon learns that he's in a lucky minority, as all who observed the event are now blind, and that's almost every human being on Earth. Adding to the grief is the sudden proliferation of giant walking plants called Triffids. Blinded citizens have no defense against the monsters' poisonous killing whips. Bill joins another sighted person, a young school runaway named Susan (Janina Faye of *Horror of Dracula*) and with her crosses the channel to France. They become lost in the countryside outside Paris and happen upon a school for the blind run by

Christine Durant (Nicole Maurey), who also can see. Masen isn't optimistic about a future in a world overrun by Triffid monsters, especially when fellow survivor Mr.Coker (Mervyn Johns) shows him a field where millions of the plants are growing from spores.

The Day of the Triffids has been filmed only twice but its spirit has been replicated in countless post-apocalyptic thrillers. The original novel makes sense in ways that this monster-oriented adaptation does not. Wyndham's original Triffids are already a daily reality before the meteorite shower that blinds most of the world; they are raised in controlled farms where their poisoned whips are carefully trimmed to allow the harvesting of fine oils useful to industry.

The book concentrates on communal efforts to survive after the collapse of mankind, with the monsters as a side threat. Their origin is a critique of Cold War business competition. The Triffids were genetically developed behind the Iron Curtain as a source of oil for perfumes. Smugglers stole a quantity of Triffid spores but competitors shot down their jet plane. Millions of spores were released into the stratosphere and blanketed the Earth.

The film flattens the Triffid concept to conventional monster movie dimensions. The meteors that blind also stimulate the growth of the Triffids, overnight. This unlikely coincidence makes the pesky Triffids an immediate threat. In a world suddenly gone blind, almost anything could be a deadly menace – wild dogs – anything.

The early scenes are the best. Bill's eye surgeon kills himself upon realizing what has happened. Bill cannot help the hundreds of sightless people in the street. Trains and ships are left unguided. Unable to land, an airplane runs out of fuel and crashes. With London in flames, Bill and Susan leave by boat to answer radio news of a conference in France.

The monsters encounters are at first limited in scale. A Triffid in a greenhouse kills a night watchman and Bill sees one on the street. An encounter on a foggy country road has the best atmospherics – the hazier these monsters are, the better. Dozens of Triffids mass in the woods near Miss Durant's chateau and thousands march against an electrified fence in Spain.

Somewhere in France, the film's production budget and script give out at roughly the same time. The book's ideas about competing groups in the post-disaster world are dropped in favor of a poorly staged episode in which convicts invade Miss Durant's school. The criminals force the women to sing, dance and drink, until the Triffids attack. The story then shrinks in scale to allow Bill, Susan and Miss Durant to form a ready-made new family. Blind Bettina (Carol Ann Ford) tries to entice Bill into staying, a remnant from a book scene in which one group of scavengers barters for Bill's loyalty with the offer of a willing, blind sex partner. The Triffid onslaught ruins any ideas Bill might have about becoming a new Hugh Hefner.

Post-apocalyptic stories offer the morbid appeal of an egocentric survival fantasy. With civilization dismantled and the law dissolved, we can imagine ourselves as lucky 'winners' given a chance to prevail in a world operating under new rules. We can apply our own practical imaginations to the specific problems confronting the hero.

Whether standing still or in motion, the movie's Triffids are never as interesting as the ferocious creature in the film's memorable ad art. Prop Triffids pulled by wires look exactly like what they are, clunky rubber mannequins that couldn't negotiate a step. Their stalks are almost always tied together on top, probably because they'd fall apart otherwise. A wide angle uses a model Triffid that moves far too smoothly. Later in the film we see walking plants played by men in ill-fitting suits, shuffling along trying to look alive. Even with some angles cut very short, we can still see human legs stepping at the bottom of shots. If ever there were a movie concept in need of Computer Generated Imagery, this is it.

Even if they looked perfect, Wyndham's Triffids would be a tough sell. The book's description doesn't make an individual plant sound particularly threatening. It's just a round bole at the bottom with three leaf-like feet that shuffle along like a one-legged man on crutches. The stalk above waves about wildly as the thing jerks forward. Triffids find something warm, sting it, and then sit on it 'til it rots. They communicate by rattling dry, twig-like appendages. The movie at least gets that part right by providing an effectively creepy sound effect.

The last section of the film is very bitty. Wally Veevers' special effects become a desperate succession of smeary mattes. Illusions are ruined when smoke disappears behind matte lines. The script simply evaporates, leaving Keel and Maurey to exchange weak exposition. Keel was quoted more than once as saying that the production fell apart, forcing him to make up his own dialogue. A Spanish couple with terrible accents is glad to see the foreigners arrive to help deliver their baby. Expensive-looking but poorly filmed sets match poorly with real locations.

The film's first cut lacked an acceptable conclusion. After Susan discovers that the plants are attracted to sound, Bill uses a 'Pied Piper' music truck to lead a group of Triffids over a cliff, like lemmings. Writer Bernard Gordon explained that when a rough cut eliminating ineffective monster footage came in at only sixty minutes, the film sat dormant for more than a year before director Freddie Francis was hired to film new scenes with a second unit. This accounts for the completely separate subplot situated in a remote lighthouse. Husband and wife acting team Kieron Moore and Janette Scott fret and struggle to keep the Triffids out, a process broken into sections and inter-cut with the

rather dull progress of Keel, Maurey and Faye. To provide a conventionally dramatic ending, Moore discovers in the nick of time that ordinary seawater dissolves the Triffids into green soup. This "God saves humanity" scientific breakthrough makes no sense whatsoever. The monsters attacking the lighthouse matured on the rocks outside, which are constantly being soaked in sea spray.

The 1981 BBC teleseries of *The Day of the Triffids* is more faithful to Wyndham's book but this imperfect theatrical spectacle retains a nostalgic attraction. Back around 1990 Image released a pricey letterboxed laserdisc but as yet no decent DVD version exists.

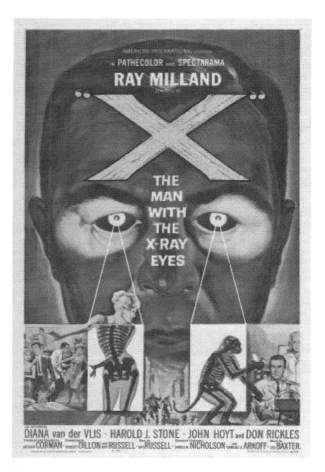

"X" (THE MAN WITH THE X-RAY EYES)

MGM Reviewed: July 10, 2001
1963 / Color / 1:78 widescreen / 79 min.
Cinematography Floyd Crosby. Production
Designer Daniel Haller. Writing credits
Robert Dillon and Ray Russell. Produced by
Samuel Z. Arkoff, Roger Corman & James H.
Nicholson.
Directed by Roger Corman

Italy's Trieste Science Fiction Film Festival pre-
viewed a number of international films in 1963,
including *Ikarie XB 1* from Czechoslovakia,
Omicron from Italy, *La Jetée* from France and *The
Amphibian Man* from the Soviet Union. Roger
Corman's **"X"** stood out from the crowd. Described as a semi-religious sci-fi parable, it uses
vision as an analog for human curiosity.

Dr. James Xavier (Ray Milland) self-tests a se-
rum that allows him to see through solid matter. Xavier hopes to better cure the sick, but his
friends Dr. Brandt and grant representative Diane Fairfax (Harold J. Stone & Diana Van Der
Vlis) are alarmed when Xavier's eyes mutate
into super-sensitive organs. Xavier's new sight
becomes a curse instead of a blessing. Com-
mittees scoff at his claims and end his funding.
Xavier proves that a colleague's diagnosis is
incorrect by forcibly taking over an operation
and saving a small girl's life. But his behavior
convinces all that he is insane. Hiding first as
a carnival attraction and then as an inner-city
faith healer, Xavier becomes a fugitive from
the law. He sees deeper into the universe but
cannot recognize people sitting in front of him.
Seeing through his own eyelids and a pair of
leaden glasses, Xavier begs to be able to find
darkness again...

Roger Corman began the 1960s by surprising
the industry with quality adaptations of Edgar
Allan Poe. This mystical science fiction movie
proved him a director who could juggle high-
powered ideas. Known commonly as **"X"**, *The
Man with The X-Ray Eyes*, "X" is Roger Corman's best and most mature science fiction film.

Not as self-destructively cheap as the director's
50s sci-fi output, "X" fully realizes every eerie
chill and conceptual horror in Robert Dillon
and Ray Russell's clever screenplay. Unpredictable time jumps and scene transitions impart a
strange sense of temporal displacement. Feet
tumbling down a staircase cut directly to a POV
of a whirling Ferris Wheel. Xavier stares off-
screen, and we cut not to what he sees but to a
detail in another room weeks or months later.
Xavier's exile as a *Nightmare Alley*- like carnival attraction is a model of narrative economy.
Comic Don Rickles shines in what is probably
his best screen role.

"X" actively courts weirdness. It begins with a
60-second shot of a staring eyeball backed by
unsettling, wailing music. Ray Milland's commitment to his role is total. Corman exploits
the expressive power of the human face with
genuinely frightening close-ups of Xavier's anguished countenance. The obsidian orbs that
his eyes have become stare blindly as Xavier
gnashes his teeth in pain.

The film analyzes the act of seeing but is not an
essay on voyeurism like Michael Powell's *Peeping Tom*. Dr. Xavier is a surreal hero on a journey into the unknown, with no idea where his
obsession will take him.

Robert Dillon and Ray Russell's screenplay
neatly develops the idea of relative forms of
vision. Xavier's doctor friend Brandt worries
that the X formula is affecting other parts of his
brain and suggests that his experiences might
be hallucinations. As Xavier's perceptions are
expanded, his personal relationships begin
to break down. He finds that trying to bring
anything new or challenging to his peers is extremely difficult. Novel ideas are rejected and
the messenger is treated as a menace.

"X" has been likened to a critique of LSD research theories. It was claimed that mind-altering drugs could unlock mental doors to resources hidden within the human brain, enabling the perception of greater truths. But Xavier's every advance in "vision" constricts his relationship to the real world around him. He sees people only as "living, breathing dissections" and buildings as skeletons of steel "dissolved in an acid of light." It's difficult to relate to people that no longer have faces. When one's consciousness can penetrate to the center of the universe, it's impossible to concentrate on petty interpersonal matters.

Dr. Xavier achieves the status of a persecuted guru, or a cursed Demigod. Timothy Leary welcomed the coming of a New Kind of Man but "X" shows Dr. Xavier as a tragically unappreciated visionary. Russell and Corman were acutely aware of 1950s non-conformists pilloried and vilified by the culture at large. That decade saw plenty of idealist adventurers political and otherwise who either lived in isolation from society or were brought down by it. Lenny Bruce's crime was merely to openly state things that society denied.

Xavier's psychological isolation warps his judgment. He can see, but he can't "un-see". Once enlightenment is granted it can't be gotten rid of, only denied. Xavier seeks the light of truth while yearning for a moment of darkness; even Jesus may have envied the lesser state of enlightenment of those around him. Hoping to transform human existence with revolutionary truths, Xavier instead becomes a pariah. He's not a mad tyrant like *The Invisible Man*. Arrogant and flawed, Xavier fumbles his journey from the first step and never regains control.

As Dr. Brandt warned, Xavier cannot distinguish his revelations from what may be hallucinations from within. Xavier may be seeing to the center of the universe or he may be seeing to the center of his own soul. All he finds there are frightening visions and harsh self-judgment.

Corman's special effects combine prismatic color separation with the axial smearing of diffraction gratings. Inadequate as they are to a literal representation of X-Ray vision, the effects are perfect for this film. A colored iris, various shots of innards and even clumsy paintings of dissections serve as placeholders and our imaginations fill in the gaps. Convincing illusions wouldn't have improved Corman's thesis. We saw perfect living X-Ray images in Paul Verhoeven's *The Hollow Man*; they simply distracted our attention from the rest of the film.

Robert Dillon's original screenplay has unused dialogue that makes Xavier's experiences much more literal. When Xavier tells the revival congregation "what he sees," he elaborates further:

"There are great darknesses ... as far off as time itself – and they are coming ... coming to destroy all our world ... Larger than the stars – than galaxies of stars, they're coming..."

In the script, the fiery vision of the center of the universe is revealed as a literal *"shimmering eye of light"* that *"great darknesses threaten to blot out."* What we see in Corman's movie is no more distinct than the effect that results from squinting at a pulsing light bulb. It succeeds by NOT being literal.

(Spoiler) In the Dillon screenplay, Xavier responds to the cry to "pluck it out" with a scream, and the screen jumps to darkness. The screams of the congregation fade out as well. Corman added a stark optical freeze-frame that seeks, for a fraction of a second, to show Xavier with empty eye sockets. The jolt is unforgettable. A rumor has persisted that Ray Milland once spoke a traumatized line of dialogue from the final darkness: "But I can still SEE!"

This notion came from Stephen King in his non-fiction book *Danse Macabre*, as his inspiration for a zinger that would have upped the horror quotient at the film's conclusion. In older interviews Corman repeatedly denied that he filmed the line, but he's apparently heard the rumor so often that he's no longer certain. On the disc's commentary he first says definitely No. Then he pauses in mid-sentence and suggests that perhaps the line was recorded after all. Discussion boards and eager fans will now take his remark as Gospel, and compare the "censored" ending of *"X"* to the end of Corman's *The Trip*, which AIP did indeed alter to add an anti-drug message.

MGM's DVD of *"X"* is a knockout. The clean 16:9 image shows much more accurate color than I've seen in this title before, and I didn't put any drops in my eyes. The original trailer identifies the film as simply *"X"* but it must be said that the original print advertising added the *"The Man With the X-Ray Eyes"* sub-line. The disc also offers a prologue cobbled together to pad the film out for longer TV slots. It's a ragged montage of unrelated images backed by some weak narration.

In his commentary Roger Corman says that Robert Dillon and Ray Russell "were a team," which seems odd. The script I have is 90% the finished film, and carries only Dillon's name.

See the JUGGERNAUT of Destruction Challenge the Incredible EMPIRE Beneath the Sea!

KAITEI GUNKAN
Media Blasters Tokyo Shock
Reviewed: January 21, 2006
1963 / Color / 2:35 widescreen / **96** 89 min. / *Atragon*
Cinematography Hajime Koizumi. Special Effects Director Eiji Tsuburaya. Music Akira Ifukube. Written by Shigeru Komatsuzaki, Shinichi Sekizawa from the novel *Kaitei okaku* by Shunro Oshikawa. Produced by Tomoyuki Tanaka. Directed by Ishiro Honda

Atragon (Kaitei gunkan) is perhaps the last of Toho's lavish 60s fantasies not to center on giant *Kaiju* monsters. It's based on an eclectic Japanese novel about a multi-phibian warship that reflects long-standing trends in Japanese *Manga* and Anime. Although filmed in great haste, *Atragon* represents the studio's fantasy output at its creative peak.

The colorful *Atragon* also marks the entrance of post-war militarism as an overt theme in Toho fantasy. Media Blasters' uncut original Japanese version restores the film's original attitudes about re-armament and military honor. The film was Toho's big Christmas movie for 1963.

> The fabled Mu Empire, a lost sunken civilization in the center of the Pacific, broadcasts its claim that the dry-land nations are its colonies. Commanding a fleet of submarines armed with death rays, the Mu Empress (Tetsuko Kobayashi) threatens to devastate nations that do not capitulate. A suspicious journalist (Kenji Sahara) tails fashion photographer Susumu Hatakana (Tadao Takashima) and Makoto Jinguji (Yoko Fuji), the daughter of famous Navy captain Hachiro Jinguji (Jun Tazaki), who hasn't been seen since the 1945 surrender. Along with ex-Admiral Kosumi (Ken Uehara) they accompany one of the Captain's old sailors to a secret island where Jinguchi commands a crew of Navy holdouts preparing the fantastic super-submarine Atragon, aka Gotengo. Jinguchi is intent on using the sub to reverse the outcome of WW2, but changes his mind when Mu agent #23 (Akihiko Hirata) sabotages Atragon's hidden underground silo. Although is buried in rubble, the sub can still escape: in addition to sailing undersea, on the surface and through the air, the mighty ship can bore through solid rock.

Atragon expands on the notion that Japanese soldiers are still living on remote islands, unaware that the war has ended. Captain Jinguji has not only survived, he's managed to build an amazing underground shipyard – without visible resources. The visitors from Tokyo ride an elevator down to a tremendous naval dry dock in a steel-braced cavern. Like John Ford's Ethan Edwards, Jinguji never acknowledged the surrender on the battleship Missouri. His hardy sailors still observe Imperial Navy formalities.

Toho's *The Mysterians* imagines the Japanese military channeled into the Earth Defense Force, a fighting wing of the United Nations that re-turned in *Battle in Outer Space* and *Gorath*. Mothra sees Japan as a peace-loving nation living in the shadow of an arrogant superpower that's an obvious amalgam of the USSR and America. *Atragon* sticks with a world similar to the one we know. Japan is militarily neutral while America's atomic submarines prowl the oceans. [1] The wise Admiral Kosumi is now a shipbuilder in the post-war economic recovery. Jinguji brands Kosumi a traitor for betraying the Emperor and Admiral Yamamoto, and insists that Atragon will only be used to reestablish Japan as a military power. Kosumi implores Jinguji to reconsider. Japan's key to peace and honor is to build strong economic and diplomatic ties with former enemies.

Every jingoistic fantasy needs an implacable enemy, and *Atragon* proposes the Mu Empire, a nation of pagan savages with multicolored hairdos. Yet they cruise the Pacific in porcelain submarines with ray guns mounted in dragon sculptures! As in George Pal's *Atlantis, the Lost Continent*, the Mu warriors dress like Phoenicians and carry spears, but have engineered a futuristic undersea empire. [2]

With his daughter kidnapped and Gotengo sabotaged, Jinguji narrows his eyes and issues terse orders to clear away the debris. It's the Japanese macho version of Popeye's "That's all I can stands, 'cause I can't stands no more!"

The Mu Empire looses submarines, weird flying bombs and a platoon of silver-suited frogmen that pose on the ridge of a crater identically to the Ninja spies in the Bond film *You Only Live Twice*. Mu then hits Tokyo with an underground sneak attack: half the city's center collapses, undermined from below. The high priest's flagship surfaces in Tokyo Bay and proceeds to set ships aflame with its heat ray.

In answer, the super-sub Atragon reconfigures itself like a Transformer toy and drills its way out of its own ruined dry dock; it levitates into the air on air jets and rockets across the sky at supersonic speed. Jinguji wastes no time in attacking the Mu Empire's undersea, underground power center, but must first fend off a colossal aquatic dragon, the "messenger" of the Mu deity Manda.

A dorky marionette cousin to *Reptilicus*, Manda is a traditional pop-eyed Chinese dragon shoe-horned into the proceedings to create a monster for the poster art. But overall *Atragon's* special effects belie the fact that Toho reportedly "threw the film together" in just a few months. The ship looks appropriately huge, especially its initial appearance rising into the air from the surface of a lake. Stop motion animation is used for shots of it breaking through rocks and rubble. Its fanciful drill-head nose and crawler tractors are reminiscent of the Cyclotram, the digging vehicle from the 1951 *Unknown World*. The effects composites are a distinct improvement over similar work in, say, *Mothra*.

The only place the haste shows is the script. The large cast eventually becomes unwieldy – there are enough back stories here for a three-part saga. Just how did Jinguji and fifty lost sailors manage to build Atragon with their bare hands? We're surprised that shipbuilder Kosumi didn't secretly underwrite Jinguji's project.

The last third of the show gets a big lift with the entrance of the Mu Empress. With her red hair and cross attitude, the Empress is like an irate valley girl. (And who's that six-foot Viking woman to the left of the Empress's throne? She looks like Herman Goering's sister.) From an American point of view, the ancient empire ruled by a leader worshipped as a god has similarities to Jinguji's own semi-medieval militarist Japan. The Mu congregation shouts "Manda!" identically to the Japanese cheer of "Banzai!"

Atragon is a fable about the rehabilitation of an intransigent militarist – that also celebrates the old fighting spirit. The underlying message is that Japan is uncomfortable as a pacifist bystander in the Cold War. Prevented from battling America, Jinguji redirects his rage onto a pack of primi-

tive upstarts living at the bottom of the ocean. As in *Our Man Flint*, no tears are shed as an entire civilization is wiped out in colorful flames and bubbles. Jinguji plays the generous conqueror by allowing Tetsuko Kobayashi's Empress to leap into the burning sea, like that princess of old in *Kwaidan*. *Atragon* might have a slightly different feeling if, at the end, Jinguji told his crew, *"So much for those seaweed-eaters! Lock and load, and set a course for the Golden Gate Bridge!"*

Media Blaster's DVD of *Atragon* is a beauty, a colorful enhanced transfer displaying little or no visible damage. The effects match much better than they once did – the blends between live action, painted mattes and miniatures are greatly improved. Even the paintings representing Mu warriors frozen by the subzero rays now look reasonable. On the other hand, the increased sharpness finally allows us to see the wires holding the craft in the air. But only if one looks for them ...

Akira Ikufube's thunderous martial score is one of his best. The super-sub's heavy-duty march theme transforms a floating toy into a colossal juggernaut. Audio is offered in both mono and 5.1 Dolby for both English and Japanese. The English track is not the original 1965 AIP dub job; Sam Arkoff cut the show by about seven minutes for American release.

The disc comes with an "Exciting!" trailer, but the real treat is a good Japanese commentary with Ishiro Honda's chief assistant director Koji Kajita, subtitled in English.

1. *Atragon* has an amusing sequence on board a Polaris-type submarine. Ishiro Honda's interpreters awkwardly direct American actors apparently plucked from the streets of Tokyo. Their dialogue sounds like old Sansui stereo instructions. One of the sailors is obviously a Frenchman ... his accent is hilarious.

2. The 200 or so massed natives in the court of the Empress are said to be dance students. The poorly rehearsed crowd never gets fully into step. Half of them go in the wrong direction and a few can be seen struggling to avoid tripping over their unfamiliar costumes. Some of the dancing looks like a slowed-down version of the Hully Gully.

CHILDREN OF THE DAMNED
(see page 171)

IKARIE XB 1

Filmexport Region 0 PAL, Reviewed: March 7, 2006
1963 / B&W / 2:35 widescreen / 83 78 min.
Cinematography Jan Kalis, Sasa Rasilov.
Production Designer Jan Zázvorka. Special
Effects Jan Kalis. Music Zdenek Liska Written
by Jindrich Polák and Pavel Jurácek.
Directed by Jindrich Polák

One of the more delightful fringe benefits of the DVD revolution is the growing access to previously unavailable Eastern-bloc science fiction cinema. The Cold War gave Western governments and film distributors the opportunity to block the wide release of over four decades' worth of films from Eastern Europe. The few movies from East Germany and the Soviet Union granted respectable American releases tended to be exceptional art-house fare such as *The Cranes are Flying* and *War and Peace.*

Some Eastern-bloc imports, as we've seen with *Nebo zoyvot* were reworked to excise Soviet propaganda. The American distributors did their best to make the films look American in origin, as when a prologue by Art Linkletter was added to the animated fairy tale *The Snow Queen.* Many critics came into contact with pictures like *The Magic Voyage of Sinbad* without knowing they were made in Moscow. If they found out, as happened with the release of the epic fantasy *Illya Muromets* (aka *The Sword and the Dragon*) their reviews invariably stressed the propaganda angle.

Science fiction was one of the easiest genres to sell in the West. Cut by twelve minutes, the Czechoslovak space odyssey **Ikarie XB 1** appeared in 1964 as the American-International release ***Voyage to the End of the Universe***. It's one of the best movies about space travel ever made. What follows is a full synopsis of the original version, with spoilers.

In the 22nd century the Earth spaceship *Ikarie* departs for a satellite of the star Alpha Centauri known only as "The White Planet." A mixed crew of forty will make the two-year round trip, although when they return, Earth will have aged fifteen years. The Engineer (Radovan Lukavský) regrets that his pregnant wife chose to remain behind. He won't see his daughter until she's a teenager – if he returns at all. Another married couple on the expedition is expecting a child. The ship's Science Officer (Frantisek Smolík) has brought along a useless but friendly robot companion that he tinkered together a hundred years before. At a dance social, two crewmen compete for the attention of the attractive Bridget (Irena Kacírková). They're dismayed to learn that Bridget has a husband back home.

The *Ikarie* pauses to investigate the *Tornado*, a derelict military spacecraft from 1987. The ancient corpses inside include gamblers still holding their cards and two officers with ray guns. The spacemen theorize that the crew fought among themselves; the ship is packed with live weapons. One of the investigators accidentally trips a mechanism. Before they can escape, *Tornado* self-destructs with an atomic bomb.

The ship encounters strange radiation from a Dark Star. Receiving heavy exposure while on an EVA, Svensen and Michael (Jirí Vrstála and Otto Lackovic) break out in ugly burns. Michael becomes deranged and threatens to destroy the ship. The Dark Star's radiation causes the crew to fall into a deep sleep. The Captain (Zdenek Stepánek) talks the Engineer out of aborting the mission as both lose consciousness.

The crew reawakens less than a day later, and discovers that the ship has been shielded from the radiation by a force field projected from The White Planet: an intelligent civilization has reached out to protect the voyagers. The crew of the *Ikarie*, including the newborn baby, waits before the view-screen to see what miracles await them on the welcoming new world.

The sophisticated *Ikarie XB 1* betters anything filmed in the West until Stanley Kubrick's *2001: A Space Odyssey*. The exterior design of the *Ikarie* resembles a cross between a flying saucer and an upside-down Hostess Twinkie. The interior's impressive hexagonal corridors closely match those of *2001*, made a couple of years later. Instead of Kubrick's modular plastic and fiberglass, a close inspection of the Czech ship interior reveals a lot of woodwork covered by contact paper!

The Czech filmmakers invent the trappings of an entire future civilization, a thriving space community that will remind *Star Trek* fans of the *The Next Generation* TV series. A young crewman visits a sweetheart's private sleeping quarters carrying a space-grown sunflower as a romantic gift. The main bridge is a large hall dominated by a view-screen. Deck chairs resemble the furniture in Exteter's ship in *This Island Earth*. Large sets represent a dining hall / recreation center (with a carousel food dispenser), and a gymnasium / bathhouse.

Some of the visual gimmicks are very up to date. Coordinated rear-projections on view-screens show a space shuttle moving outside from multiple angles. A matte of a little spaceman in a capsule porthole doesn't quite align; it was possibly composited in-camera. Cameraman Jan Kalis handled effects as well and worked with Polák on several other films. The investigation of the derelict craft is a terrific horror set piece. In one grisly image, a spaceman touches the dead Captain's face and the dry flesh drifts away from the skull as if it were underwater. The mood on the eerie ship is enhanced with funereal music, which becomes more pronounced as the spacemen run (in slow motion) to escape the nuclear blast.

The space suits are more carefully crafted than those in *Der Schweigende Stern*. The soles of the space boots light up with each step, a helpful feature when walking in darkness. Uniforms have unusual collars and the women don attractive formal gowns for the dance party. The couples perform what looks like a subdued techno minuet. When a fast song with an Italian-Latin flavor comes up, we see more elaborate dance moves, all invented for the film.

The long Czech cut offers a fascinating throwaway detail. Partygoers swap and sniff little tubes that look like Chapstik, as people might share a treat or use cigarettes. The tubes evidently contain pleasant odors (or more complicated "experiences"?) from back home. The only dialogue hint is in this exchange:

Man, offering a tube: *"November?"*
Woman, smiling as she smells: *"Earth!"*

Dare you take the incredible...

VOYAGE TO THE END OF THE UNIVERSE

DENNIS STEPHENS · FRANCIS SMOLEN · AN AMERICAN INTERNATIONAL PICTURE

American-International's re-dubbed and cut version *Voyage to the End of the Universe* made major changes. The *Ikarie* becomes an alien craft from an unknown planet on a one-way pioneering trip. Although we recognize the derelict space ship as being from Earth (the playing cards, numbers written on bulkheads) the voyagers merely theorize that it's a primitive craft from some unnamed warlike civilization. In *Voyage* the spacemen seek a "Green Planet," which in a surprise ending turns out to be Earth. The view screens display a ratty-looking stock shot of the Statue of Liberty. American-International repeated this ploy for Mario Bava's 1965 *Planet of the Vampires*. Its "peaceful" aliens arrive in New York as parasitic invaders.

As in other Eastern-bloc space movies, *Ikarie XB 1* makes a direct reference to war crimes, name-

dropping Hiroshima and Ourador. Little else is heard about conditions on Earth, and we don't know what kind of government is in power. No mention is made of organized religion, which some viewers may take as political comment by omission.

The Czech original contains added subplots that flesh out and individualize the characters. The derelict space ship sequence presents many more dead soldiers and capitalist gamblers than are shown in the U.S. re-cut. The film's sharpest political barbs were removed from the U.S. version entirely. We see the nerve gas guns that killed the crew; they are painted like toys and bear English-language labels reading, "Tigger Fun". Behind the Captain's chair is a full rack of guns – "Tigger Fun" for the whole family! The added details characterize Americans as decadent and hostile.

In the 'sleeping sickness' sequence, Bridget retreats alone to her cabin and records a Last Testament before slippinginto unconsciousness. It is to be read by future Earth astronauts, should the *Ikarie* become another derelict wreck.

The birth of the baby becomes a hopeful event in the wondrous conclusion, which builds to a rapture similar to the finale of Steven Spielberg's *Close Encounters of the Third Kind*. The astronauts react to the glorious revelation of the White Planet, as Zdenek Liska's score reaches its emotional climax. There's even a heart-tug on the cut to the baby, who likewise seems to be staring in awe ... a classic bit of Kuleshov-Pudovkin cutting. The American version trims away the majority of the beatific faces, dulling the emotional impact. The image of the curious baby is also an uncanny foreshadowing of *2001*'s staring Star Child, so much so that we wonder if Stanley Kubrick appropriated it from this Czech production.

Filmexport Home Video's PAL Region 0 DVD of *Ikarie XB 1* is an enhanced transfer of a fine

B&W source in mostly good condition. Definition and contrast are good. The image has some dirt here and there and a couple of instances of minor momentary unsteadiness. The audio is bright and sharp; the menus offer a choice of removable subtitles.

The extras are not translated into English. Film historian Pavel Taussig lectures in one featurette. Other extras are illustrated with interesting stills. Of immediate interest are pan-scanned clips from the beginning and ending of *Voyage to the End of the Universe* showing the Statue of Liberty and the ridiculous Anglicized credits: "Directed by Jack Pollack."

More Czech-only text extras are available on DVD-ROM files. A helpful correspondent looked at them and forwarded these (slightly rewritten) notes in English:

"... Director Jindrich Polák talks about his 1961 visit to see Stanislaw Lem, as the film was inspired by one of the famous author's books. The director also went to the Russian rocket institute to get approval for his designs. Neither Lem nor the Russians were particularly interested in the project. Lem didn't like being asked stupid questions by nosy filmmakers, and with the Titov mission in progress the Russian scientists were concerned about information leaks. Polák had to get space agency approval, and a 'no' answer would probably have meant the end of his movie!"

In 1965 Robert Lippert produced an inferior British knock-off called *Spaceflight IC-1*. The weak production has a carbon-copy space voyage plot. The hack script has the ship's captain put down a feeble mutiny while trying to make one of the women passengers give up her unborn baby for medical reasons. It shows occasionally on cable TV and is recommended only for curiosity's sake.

FIRST MEN IN THE MOON

Sony Reviewed: March 21, 2002
1964 / Color / 2:35 widescreen / 102 min. Cinematography Wilkie Cooper. Special Visual Effects Ray Harryhausen, Les Bowie, Kit West. Original Music Laurie Johnson. Written by Nigel Kneale and Jan Read. Produced by Charles H. Schneer.
Directed by Nathan Juran

Just as real Gemini and Apollo space missions were making fanciful space adventures obsolete, Ray Harryhausen and Charles Schneer came forward with this spirited version of H.G. Wells' classic *First Men In the Moon*. Filled with turn-of-the-century charm and awesome imagery, it has a first-rate script from English

Quatermass creator Nigel Kneale. Lionel Jeffries is an endearingly daffy Professor, the inventor of a miracle goo that 'severs the magnetic ties of gravitation'.

> 1896. Too lazy to work, wastrel playwright Arnold Bedford (Edward Judd, *The Day the Earth Caught Fire*) strings along Kate Callender, (Martha Hyer), a fine woman he doesn't deserve. Bedford becomes excited when his neighbor, eccentric inventor Joseph Cavor (Lionel Jeffries) shows him his new invention, antigravity paste. Fired with the spirit of adventure (and eager to dodge his creditors), Bedford joins Cavor on an expedition to the Moon. Kate becomes an inadvertent extra passenger as the trio zooms across the heavens to the Moon's dead surface – only to find that an entire alien civilization thrives in its cavernous interior.

H.G. Wells really hit his stride with *First Men In the Moon,* the best written, perhaps, of all his science fiction work. Told from Bedford's point of view, the novel flows as a semi-surreal fever dream, with Bedford trying his best to describe one incredible situation after another.

The poster for the movie adaptation reveals that a *girl* has been included on the voyage. But there is nothing to fear, as Martha Hyer's stowaway does not interfere with the classic storyline. Wells' drug-like depiction of lunar weightlessness is missing, but as soon as the explorers meet spear-carrying Selenites on the underground cliffs, we know that the show is on the right track.

A bombastic music score by Laurie Johnson kicks off an arresting title sequence. The majority of the film plays in the quaint Victorian mode familiar from earlier H.G. Wells and Jules Verne adaptations. The sight of Cavor's capsule launching skyward cues a nonstop flood of special effects.

Unlike some of Harryhausen's earlier films,

First Men In the Moon doesn't arrange its effects into episodic vignettes. A rather disappointing caterpillar called a Moon Calf is the only standard monster among a horde of insectoid Selenite creatures. Some are animated via stop-motion but most are not. The colorful moon world is imaginatively designed: galleries of pathways and stairs crisscross immense subterranean grottoes.

This is Harryhausen and director Nathan Juran's most polished film overall. Although relatively little standard animation is on view the design and creation of the effects is clearly Ray's. His wavy-glass tricks with the Grand Lunar are quite effective, along with some self-mummifying ant creatures. Nigel Kneale rarely saw his writing brought to life with such technical artistry, but he gives Ray what his films have always needed, a script that adds up to something more than a string of monster encounters.

First Men In the Moon is Harryhausen's only effects feature in the anamorphic format Panavision. In Germany, *Moon* was blown up to 70mm and marketed as a Cinerama attraction with multi-channel audio.

Martha Hyer is both sensible and sympathetic as the girl written into a boy's adventure. Edward Judd's irresponsible lout Bedford eventually becomes a take-charge guy, making for a nice change of tone. Lionel Jeffries' Cavor begins as a silly twit but by the end is the conscience of the human race. He has the boyish fervor we associate with English hobbyists – Michael Powell was said to be this kind of impulsive, buoyant man.

Nigel Kneale and Jan Read's script is exemplary. A bit too much kiddie humor crowds the front (*"Madame, please leave the room!"*) but Lionel Jeffries is quite endearing when he bids farewell to his beloved gaggle of geese. With Wells' story outstripped by current events, Kneale cleverly frames his narrative as a flashback from the present. The moon landing is similar to the real one that would happen five years later. A United Nations capsule touches down only to find that a desiccated Union Jack preceded them. Kneale's script uses a shock cut from feet touching the lunar surface to a ticker tape parade back on Earth, an editorial device copied twenty years later in *The Right Stuff*.

Now ninety years old and confined to a rest home, Arnold Bedford is all too eager to tell his story to the assembled press. The charming ending allows for a bit of irony, working a reversal of the famous conclusion of Wells' other hit, *The War of the Worlds*. Nigel Kneale invariably envisions his alien encounters as a disastrous biological mismatch.

First Men In the Moon doesn't quite fit in with the vogue for family films based on Verne and Wells stories, a subgenre cheapened by A.I.P. and Irwin Allen. The alarming assassinations and wars of the 60s led science fiction to take on more mature themes. From then on, many serious sci-fi pix would involve threats and conspiracies with an ecological or political basis. The abstract paranoia of the 50s became a given state of affairs. *First Men In the Moon* is all the more endearing for its retro optimism.

Columbia TriStar's DVD of *First Men In the Moon* is a welcome sight. It's presented for the first time in stereophonic sound, thanks to a four track magnetic element secured at Columbia a few years back – the stereo mix engineered for West Germany's Cinerama release was remixed with an English dialogue stem.

One moment in the movie has always drawn unintentional laughter: the iron moon capsule striking the surface of the moon at what must be over a hundred miles an hour. The railroad shock absorbers don't fool anyone, as the violent impact should have reduced Hyer, Jeffries and Judd to Lunar Jelly. It's all part of the fun.

ALPHAVILLE

Criterion Reviewed: July 6, 2002
1965 / B&W / 1:33 flat / 99 min. / *Alphaville, une* étrange *aventure de Lemmy Caution*
Cinematography Raoul Coutard. Editor Agnès Guillemot. Music Paul Misraki. Written by Jean-Luc Godard and Paul Éluard. Produced by André Michelin.
Directed by Jean-Luc Godard

More than a few sci-fi addicts were excited to catch up with *Alphaville*, only to be confused when confronted with their first Jean-Luc Godard movie. *Alphaville* appears woefully under-produced, but only at first glance. Because this gray comic strip *Alphaville* uses familiar pulp conventions as a springboard for Godard's poetic mode of expression, it's a good advent into the cinematic world of the idiosyncratic French director.

Following in the failed footsteps of Dick Tracy and Flash Gordon, secret agent Lemmy Caution (Eddie Constantine) arrives in Alphaville. The city is ruled by Alpha-60, a gravel-voiced central computer that has regimented humans into strict classes and split the city into zones of night and day, cold and warmth. Alpha-60 has ambitions to conquer the rest of the world – Nueva York, Tokyorama – and rule all under its cold eye of logic. Lemmy contacts his immediate predecessor Henry Dickson (Akim Tamiroff), who has become a hopeless drunk in a seedy hotel. Dickson steers Lemmy toward Professor Von Braun, a.k.a. defector Leonard Nosferatu (horror icon Howard Vernon), the brains behind the super-brain Alpha 60. Lemmy also commences a weird romance with Natasha Von Braun, the mastermind's daughter (Anna Karina). When interrogated by the all-controlling computer, Lemmy plays semantic games. But when he's had enough, he lashes out with a .45 automatic – and the power of poetry.

Jean-Luc Godard's genre movies are intellectual, joking meditations that express his free-associative political ideas. They go beyond the merely self-referential, and they aren't spoofy or camp. They avoid styles and trends to instead reveal the structural underpinnings of film itself. Godard refuses to stage conventional scenes. His staging of a fight scene merely cuts to several shots of the combatants in extreme poses, as if posing for still photos.

Alphaville is constructed like unrepentant beat poetry. Bald messages are inserted in the form of "signage visuals": neon signs, drawings, traffic signals, etc. They signify the complexity of the omniscient Alpha-60 computer, a menace represented by whirring fans, crude flashing lights and mechanical noises. The voice of Alpha-60, as has been pointed out, is the 'dead voice' of a man with no larynx, who has learned to speak artificially by making croaking sounds.

Godard declares traditional production values irrelevant. The film's only optical special effect is an occasional negative inversion of the image – to perhaps represent the malfunctioning of Alpha-60? Raoul Coutard's handheld photography is frequently very smooth, even beautiful. Other scenes are as crude as anything in a no-budget exploitation movie. Godard's artistic tone says, "This is Jazz. Read between the images. It's not my job to put a manicured commercial picture in front of your faces at all times".

Godard's themes are pure pulp: poetry versus the inhuman computer future. One title under consideration was *Tarzan versus IBM*. With the SuperSpy subgenre in full swing, Godard co-opted the established tough guy Lemmy Caution, a hardboiled French hero played by expatriate American GI-turned movie star Eddie Constantine. Lemmy is the ultimate secret agent, a vengeful angel. *"Reporter and Revenger start with the same letter,"* he deadpans. Like any two-fisted hero, Caution carries a big gun. His only other gadget is a pitiful Kodak Instamatic, a mass-produced camera with a flashcube on top that took low-quality photos through a cheap lens.

Lemmy Caution's hardboiled voiceovers contradict what we see: a flight through inter-sidereal space in his 'Galaxie' is a simply Caution arriving by freeway in a Ford Mustang. Industrial installations stand in for the workings of Alpha-60, and the interrogation rooms look like ordinary recording booths. Futuristic Alphaville is simply the modern structures of 1965 Paris, which Godard implies are already architecturally oppressive.

Poetry and literature are at the center of the story. Alpha-60 is erasing human consciousness one word at a time; dictionaries are replaced daily as more words and their underlying concepts are eliminated. Played beautifully by Anna Karina, Natasha Von Braun doesn't recognize the word 'tenderness' and has forgotten what it means. The poetic conceit has teeth: our culture 'forgets' concepts as quickly as it creates new ones. At one point the bad guys distract Lemmy with a verbal joke – words are all-powerful in Godard's world.

Alpha-60 murders the condemned dreamers of Alphaville in an indoor pool ritual that combines a Nazi execution with an Esther Williams-style aquacade. Each victim shouts out his last words as he dies. One of them talks about moving straight toward one's goal instead of in circles, a theme that echoes throughout *Alphaville*. The circles hide everywhere to entrap the individual, in the computer's logic and in the circular stairways. The citizens of this 'Nowheresville' move in pointless circles because Alpha-60 has drained the meaning from their lives. In contrast, Lemmy Caution steers straight to the things he loves.

Alphaville is a bizarre, unfeeling *Capital of Pain*. Natasha attends a class on the basics of mind-control and mass murder. Lemmy shuns the prostitutes that appear whenever he approaches his hotel room. Scientists Heckle and Jekyll (played by a pair of film critics) labor in a think tank, staring at a pretty girl in a trench coat. Another female works as living statuary behind glass near a well-traveled stairway.

Lemmy Caution voices hardboiled sentiments: *"Not bad for a veteran of Guadalcanal"*; *"Let this be a lesson to all those who would take the world for their private hobbyhorse"*. But his pockmarked face and sad, dead eyes are repositories for the conscience of the world. Lemmy and Natasha share a 'poetic duet' in his mundane hotel room with its jukebox and darkened salon. They pose before a mirror as the camera exposure racks up and down, erasing the textures of their skin, darkening into murk, and then brightening again. The words of their love poem include more references to 'going straight to what you love'.

Lemmy Caution is prepared to destroy Alphaville without batting an eye. When Alpha-60 melts down, its entire empire collapses, leaving the populace without guidance or control. "La Zone" of Cocteau's *Orpheus* is revived in the lost, unbalanced way the now-disoriented citizens stagger and cling to the walls. The lovers escape into outer space (the freeway again) as Alphaville self-destructs. The Paul Misraki score becomes transcendent as Lemmy prompts Natasha to speak the word 'Love'. If she can remember what it means, the concept of Love can return.

Criterion's DVD of *Alphaville* is a good rendition of the film, as good as the theatrical prints I've seen and far better than the awful dubbed and mangled messes once shown on television. The flat 1:33 looks appropriate, although I'm certain that theatrical screenings were slightly wider.

Andrew Sarris' brief liner notes sum up the film's charm and significance. This early entry in the Criterion Collection has no other extras, and is certainly due for a new edition.

THANK GOD IT'S ONLY A MOTION PICTURE!

Science miscalculates... underground Atom Bomb explodes earth's core... and the world totters on the brink of destruction!

TODAY'S TERRIFYING LOOK INTO WHAT MIGHT HAPPEN TOMORROW!

CRACK IN THE WORLD
TECHNICOLOR

Starring DANA ANDREWS · JANETTE SCOTT · KIERON MOORE · ALEXANDER KNOX
BERNARD GLASSER and LESTER A. SANSOM · ANDREW MARTON
JON MANCHIP WHITE and JULIAN HALEVY · JON MANCHIP WHITE · PHILIP YORDAN

CRACK IN THE WORLD

Olive Films Blu-ray Reviewed: August 17, 2007
1965 / Color / 1:66 widescreen / 96 min.
Cinematography Manuel Berenguer.
Production Design & Special Effects Eugène Lourié. Music Johnny Douglas. Written by John Manchip White, Julian Halevy (Zimet). Produced by Bernard Glasser, Lester A. Sansom, Philip Yordan.
Directed by Andrew Marton

Prolific writer, producer and dealmaker Philip Yordan followed his weak but successful *The Day of the Triffids* with another ambitious science fiction project, this one filmed by associates who worked with him on Samuel Bronston's Anthony Mann and Nicholas Ray epics.

One of the first convincing ecological nightmare movies, *Crack in the World* doesn't use a giant monster to make its point about human meddling with Mother Nature. A group of idealistic geologists accidentally open up devastating fissures in the earth's crust that threaten to tear the world in two.

In East Africa, terminally ill Dr. Stephen Sorenson (Dana Andrews) goes forward with Project Inner Space despite the misgivings of his younger assistant Dr. Ted Rampion (Kieron Moore). Inner Space plans to drop a nuclear warhead into a deep well shaft, to punch through a final barrier deep within the earth. If superheated core magma rises to the earth's surface, mankind will gain an unlimited power source. Rampion predicts that a blast that deep will weaken fault lines in all directions, causing a potentially cataclysmic geological reaction. Sorenson forges ahead out of pure hubris, determined to become mankind's savior before he dies. Stephen also wants to impress his young wife Maggie (Janette Scott), who was once Rampion's lover.

The blast is an initial success. But earthquakes and volcanic eruptions open up the Macedo Fault, which extends from near the Inner Space lab out into the Indian Ocean. Ted Rampion tries to stop the moving split by using a second nuke to blow a stopgap in an island volcano. The crack instead doubles back along another fault line, forming a giant circle that will close back at the project. The scientists evacuate the subterranean lab but Sorenson refuses to leave. Ted and Maggie take the two-mile elevator ride down to try to change his mind.

Crack in the World's outlandish concept widens into an ever-escalating spiral of excitement and jeopardy. Although advances in geological theory have made its science obsolete – *Crack in the World* precedes the adoption of the Plate Tectonic theory – most of what happens in the movie is unique and original. A deep-sea submarine finds a fiery rupture in the bottom of the ocean. Scientists descend into an active volcano with a bulky nuclear bomb, trying to properly position it before their special suits melt from the intense heat. The film's only truly silly image is a conventional missile rather foolishly positioned upside-down over the Inner Space bore hole.

Brilliant Technicolor printing allows Eugène Lourié's clever art direction and superb special effects to look their best. The movie has spectacular scenes of destruction – several chapters end with the detonation of something BIG. At the climax, the sense of claustrophobic panic is overpowering: whichever way the hero and heroine turn they're confronted by towering volcanic eruptions and the collapsing remains of the Inner Space headquarters. Several shots attain the feeling of uncontrolled planetary apocalypse missing from movies like *When Worlds Collide* and *Deep Impact*, culminating in the awesome spectacle of a 20,000 square-mile slice of East Africa hurled into the sky. John Douglas's majestic music score adds greatly to the sight of billions of tons of fiery rock and earth exploding into outer space.

Screenwriters John Manchip White and Julian Zimet are definitely 'having us on' – their story structure is really about SEX. The impotent, dying Sorenson can't impregnate his wife Maggie or stave off the rugged competition represented by scientific rival Rampion, so he sublimates his sex drive into his work. Sorenson's upside-down phallic missile 'impregnates' the earth like an atomic sperm plowing into a terra firma ovum. The symbol for the 'Inner Space' project just happens to be a red triangle piercing a blue globe. At one point the masculine Rampion alerts his staff that his bomb needs extra insulation – to prevent a premature explosion!

Sorenson imagines himself a sexual Prometheus, bringing unlimited power (potency) to our energy-starved (flaccid) male-dominated world. He instead precipitates a global cata-

clysm: Mother Earth has her own agenda. The sterile Sorenson succeeds in fathering a new moon, although like most useless drones, he perishes after fulfilling his function. *Crack in the World* concludes with a powerful image of the chastized couple, standing tattered but still alive in a fiery volcanic landscape. The message seems to be that men are the despoilers of the earth, and that even their most noble efforts are based on vain dreams of power and immortality. Either that, or the movie is about the need to invent Viagra.

CURSE OF THE FLY
(see page 141)

TERRORE NELLO SPAZIO

MGM Reviewed: December 19, 2001
1965 / Color / 1:85 flat letterbox / 88 min. /
Planet of the Vampires
Cinematography Antonio Pérez Olea, Antonio
Rinaldi. Music Gino Marinuzzi Jr.. Written
by Mario Bava, Alberto Bevilacqua, Callisto
Cosulich, Louis M. Heyward, Ib Melchior,
Antonio Román, Rafael J. Salvia from a story
by Renato Pestriniero. Produced by Fulvio
Lucisano, Samuel Z. Arkoff, James H. Nicholson.
Directed by Mario Bava

For **Planet of the Vampires** Mario Bava redirected his unique visual sense to the space opera genre. American movies about interplanetary travel were scarce in 1965, but Italy was having a mini-boom, mostly through the work of prolific director Antonio Margheriti. With their over-lit sets and emphasis on flashy action, pictures like *I criminali della galassia (Wild, Wild Planet)* play like Sword 'n' Sandal pix transplanted to rocket ships. Going in another direction entirely, Bava's stunning Gothic variation weaves a weird tale of flying saucers, ray guns and alien zombies.

> Twin spaceships Argos and Galliot land on the dark and foggy planet Aura. Captain Mark Markary (Barry Sullivan) and Sanya (Norma Bengell) can barely restrain the Argos crew from maiming each other in inexplicable fits of violence. They discover that the Galliot's entire compliment is dead, apparently from a similar orgy of murder. Repairs to the Argos are under way when Mark and Sanya detect a derelict alien craft nearby. It contains the grotesque skeletal remains of alien creatures. The mystery becomes clear when the hastily buried casualties begin rising from their graves. Spectral beings on Aura are taking possession of the spacemen's dead bodies, hoping to escape to a new world.

Planet of the Vampires has almost nothing in common with similarly plotted space thrillers like Curtis Harrington's *Queen of Blood*. In the standard space epic, hardware is everything. On the ghastly planet Aura it takes second place behind Mario Bava's signature lighting and atmospheric effects.

The action takes place in two very unnatural locales. The gloomy interior of the Argos is similar to that of *Ikarie XB 1*. The spacemen sit at uncomfortable stations in a cavernous piloting room. The rest of the craft is dominated by heavy bulkhead doors and industrial-sized machinery.

But the Argos is cozy compared to the rocky, boiling hell-scape outside. Volcanic activity and bizarre gases allow Bava to conjure all manner of weird lighting schemes. Glowing rocks and phosphorescent mists bathe the characters in reds and greens; after a few minutes of unmotivated lighting schemes the most strangely colored key lights seem perfectly natural.

Bava's Future Gothic designs are similar to the comic book look of his next film, *Diabolik*. The images have a direct affinity with shots in *Black Sabbath* or *Blood and Black Lace*: huge scarred faces are soaked in green light and spidery figures creep along hallways or struggle out of shallow graves. Bava fans don't need to be persuaded that a pleasing movie can be made from visuals alone.

According to author Robert Skotak,[1] this is a true international co-production headed by Italy's Fulvio Lucisano, with additional money from Spain. American-International valued Bava (then still obscure in the US) and hooked him up with writer Ib Melchior, the writer deemed the positive factor behind A.I.P. moneymakers *The Angry Red Planet*, *Reptilicus* and *Journey to the 7th Planet*, as well as Paramount's impressive *Robinson Crusoe on Mars*. The cast is mostly Italian, with the aging second-stringer Barry Sullivan providing an American name. Representing Spanish investors, the Rio-born Norma Bengell was already an established star in South America.

Working at the height of his Italian popularity, Bava adhered to his personal style of production – a small crew and a low budget. Almost all of Bava's effects are done in-camera. When the visuals in *Planet of the Vampires* fall within Bava's bag of tricks, the results are marvelous. But many specific illusions come off much less successfully. Most angles on the spaceships in flight suffer from an insufficient depth of focus, making them look like what they are, miniatures attached to the front of the camera. Some of the physical trappings, like the unconvincing ray guns, also don't make the grade. On the plus side, the sleek leather-vinyl costumes are both attractive and interesting. They must have given Bava's costumers a trial run at the remarkable rubbery costume later perfected for *Diabolik*.

Ib Melchior's script is an unfortunate bore made worse by undeveloped ideas. Interesting concepts, such as the spacemen being able to momentarily see the Auran phantoms in their extreme peripheral vision (corner-of-the-eye ghosts, so to speak) are insufficiently supported by the visuals. The onscreen action remains a repetitive series of fights and disappearances among interchangeable spacemen. Keeping track of who is possessed and who is not is unrewarding. Cutting between the two spaceships is also confusing. Melchoir's script intended for the Galliot to be a crashed wreck, but making the two ships identical simplified the production schedule.

The exploration of the derelict alien spaceship is by far the best sequence. The monstrous occupants are desiccated skeletons but their still-functioning machines trap the heroes inside. This very spooky scene is the film's best transposition of the Gothic into outer space, and is noted as the inspiration for a major section of Ridley Scott's 1979 *Alien*. Unintentional comedy breaks the eerie mood when Barry Sullivan grabs a glowing disc that not moments before delivered a shock to Norma. He's doltishly surprised when the disc shocks him as well.

MGM's DVD of **Planet of the Vampires** is not 16:9 formatted; European disc releases are reportedly better looking. The otherwise sharp transfer shows off Bava's compositions in their full 1:85 aspect ratio. Shots that on VHS cropped characters out of frame and made symmetrical compositions look lopsided are now balanced and complete.

Unable or unwilling to investigate the legal status of the music tracks on a number of European A.I.P. titles, Orion Pictures replaced a handful of them in the middle '80s with dull synthesizer scores. MGM's disc restores Gino Marinuzzi Jr.'s moody original score, an electronic jumble of strange sounds and tones.[2]

1. **Ib Melchior, Man of Imagination** by Robert Skotak. (see bibliography)

2. Savant wrote an article on the restoration of this film for the September 2001 issue of Video Watchdog (#76).

THE WAR GAME

New Yorker / Project X Reviewed: July 16, 2006
1965 / B&W / 1:37 flat / 48 min.
Cinematography Peter Bartlett, Peter
Suschitzky. Design Tony Cornell and Anne
Davey. Editor Michael Bradsell. Action
sequences Derek Ware.
Written, Produced and Directed by Peter
Watkins

The War Game is a semi-documentary Nuclear
Aftermath movie, one of rebel director Peter
Watkins' controversial BBC programs that combine fictional storytelling with You-Are-There
newsreel techniques. A two-way scandal erupt-
ed when the supposedly independent BBC
refused to air Watkins' film, reversing its own
policies for reasons never made clear. The filmmakers claimed that the BBC suppressed the
film under pressure from the government.

The program was banned from British television for decades, but the BBC had no power to
limit theatrical screenings, and *The War Game*
became the next year's liberal cause movie.
Critics and politicians voiced approval despite
the film's tone of outrage toward government
civil defense policy. American media would
not catch up with Watkins' vision for eighteen
years, with the Ronald Reagan "Star Wars"- era
miniseries *The Day After*.

Handheld news cameras capture telling details

of a national crisis interrupted by stark infor-
mational maps, inter-titles and authoritative
quotes. Tensions in Vietnam lead to a battlefield nuclear exchange in Germany followed by
nuclear war. Focusing on county Kent, we witness pitiful attempts at evacuation in a country
where a defense target is never more than thirty
miles away. Areas not directly hit feel the blast
and heat effects and are swept by firestorms.
Law and order vanishes as the post-attack suffering begins. The numbers of horribly injured
overwhelm the filthy and shell-shocked survivors. The police must resort to brutal tactics. In
just one afternoon, all of English civilization has
been destroyed.

When shocked BBC officials (and the government representatives 'invited' to make political evaluations) tried to shelve *The War Game*,
they found that they had no legal basis to reject it for airing. Peter Watkins had produced
his film under BBC guidelines; everything in
it is well-researched truth. The government's
official policy stated that a Nuclear War would
be like the Blitz, with the citizenry bracing itself in an orderly response. Watkins uses direct quotes from politicians and civil defense
manuals to demonstrate that England has no
coherent policy on the issue. His convincing
newsreel-like recreations use non-actors to
good effect. Citizens are hustled onto evacuation buses and forced into already packed Kent
households. "Man in the street" interviews
point up the fact that the public is almost totally ignorant about nuclear war and the effects of radiation. Given only a few hours or
minutes to prepare, citizens either cannot find
materials to build a shelter or cannot afford
them. Pundits parrot American propaganda
about defending shelter space while a foolish
citizen brandishes a shotgun and pronounces
himself ready for anything that comes.

It's true that nothing could have prepared Brit
audiences for what follows: a nuclear blast
blinds a teacher's children and the shock wave

caves in their house. Closer to the blast area, survivors and the firemen trying to help them are cremated alive when a firestorm raises temperatures to 2,000 degrees. The narration stresses that these facts were gleaned from the experience of bombing German and Japanese cities in WW2.

Watkins keeps his camera views intimate – there are few spectacular scenes – but we're completely convinced. His 'stunt arrangers' provide excellent images of panic and bodies tumbling in the 100 mph firestorm winds. Gritty B&W photography shows pleasant neighbors reduced to grimy refugees with smashed teeth and horrible wounds and burns. Exhausted police officials block the camera's view of terrible scenes, such as the mass burning of corpses. In some ways it's a ghostly revisit of WW2, with buckets of wedding rings collected to allow later identification of the dead. The conclusion shows a gaggle of orphaned, filthy children. They stare into the camera with numbed eyes and mumble that they don't want to be anything when they grow up.

The War Game succeeds marvelously at its task, and was suppressed on the grounds that it would compromise national morale. No specific reason was given why the British public should be denied access to the truth about their security situation. It's impossible to know where that path might lead – people might start asking questions.

The ultimate result was that Peter Watkins was no longer welcome at the BBC even though most there agreed that he was its most brilliant and relevant social documentarian. Watkins' next movie *Privilege* would be political science fiction offering the idea that British despots might manufacture a messiah-like Rock Star to control and subdue youth rebellion. Since then, Watkins' brand of social criticism has been tolerated mostly in Scandinavian countries.

It's an underappreciated fact that all one need do to make a memorable film, fiction or non-fiction, is to tell the truth. *The War Game* is an interesting alternative to the glamorous extermination soap opera *On the Beach*. It follows through on the dark promises of *These are the Damned* and *The Day the Earth Caught Fire*, and of course the black comedy *Dr. Strangelove*. Nobody who sees *The War Game* forgets it; it has more impact than the masochistic post-apocalypse miniseries *The Day After* and *Threads*. Watkins told an unpopular truth and was officially branded as an Enemy of the People. Perhaps that's what makes him an angry artist.

Project X and New Yorker's handsome DVD of **The War Game** is presented in its original B&W full frame television format. The transfer is in fine shape if marred by a few imperfections. The film has a high contrast look, with official-looking scrolling inter-titles similar to the ones seen in *Dr. Strangelove*.

The War Game is accompanied by the very pro-Watkins commentary of Senior Lecturer Patrick Murphy of York St. John University College in England. Murphy also contributes a lengthy insert essay reprinted from a 2003 issue of *Film International* magazine. It details the exact chronology of the bureaucratic conspiracy mounted to prevent *The War Game* from 'harming' the British public.

LA DECIMA VITTIMA

Anchor Bay Reviewed: May 19, 2001
1965 / Color / 1:85 widescreen / 92 min. / *The Tenth Victim*
Production Designer Piero Poletto. Writing credits Ennio Flaiano, Tonino Guerra, Giorgio Salvioni and Elio Petri from the short story by Robert Sheckley. Produced by Carlo Ponti. Directed by Elio Petri

This playful Italian satire was made famous by a provocative still photo of a bikini-clad Ursula Andress symbolically cutting a necktie from her prey amid applauding nightclub patrons. Anchor Bay's disc is the first time American viewers have been shown *The Tenth Victim* in its original language, a factor that elevates its clever script a few notches in the science fiction sub-genre of satirical, dysfunctional futures.

The dominant worldwide cultural interest of the 21st century is The Big Game, an organized murder system with hunters, victims and prizes. The promoters insist that wars will be avoided by channeling mankind's violent tendencies into a regulated sport. The strict rules impose a 30-year prison sentence for killing the wrong person. After many successful kills, Italian Marcello Polletti (Marcello Mastroianni) and American Caroline Meredith (Ursula Andress) square off in a battle of wits. She's a cold-blooded pro who felled her last opponent with a double-barreled brassiere; he's in the throes of an annulment while fending off marriage demands from his longtime *amore*, Olga (Elsa Martinelli). Advertisers approach both contestants in the hope of arranging for a 'kill' to become the centerpiece of an ad campaign. Caroline tries to lure Marcello into a live television trap just outside the Coliseum. Marcello plots to have Caroline eaten by a crocodile in a swimming pool, while he recites his sponsor's product slogan.

The farcical *The Tenth Victim* has its amusing points. Police congratulate a hunter over the body of his victim, and then give him a parking ticket. Streets are named after Fellini and Rota. A public announcement at Big Hunt headquarters repeats, "A killing a day keeps the doctor away". Caroline executes her latest victim in the Masoch Club, a kinky dive just off Wall Street in NYC. Comic books are great literature and a player complains that killings are no longer allowed in nursery schools.

The tone would be as sardonic as Ed Neumeier's *RoboCop* if not for some softening touches. The victims die minus the bloodshed or trauma that might spoil the party atmosphere. Pains are taken to establish that the Vatican is still in full operation and doesn't condone the hunt. The Italian ban on divorce is also carefully preserved. Marcello secretly takes care of his parents when society demands the elderly be put into homes or euthanized. Caroline doesn't have that problem as she was born in the Hobo-ken Fertilization Center! Marcello's day job is leading a sun-worshipping cult ("I get 20%") that hasn't been paying well lately. With the entry of advertising money into the hunt, murders for fame and cash have been raised to a higher level of deception.

The fast-paced script is from a Robert Sheckley short story extrapolated from *The Most Dangerous Game*. The excellent concept slumps in the second act, when the two killers' double-crossing loses its novelty. Marcello and Caroline's romantic flirtations don't convince in such a cynical world, and the sexual chemistry isn't there either. As if to compensate, comedy elements broaden *The Tenth Victim* into "Homicide, Italian Style".

There are other drawbacks. The movie features good costumes and locations but indifferent camerawork. The intention is clearly to create comic-book atmospherics, but the sparse music and harsh sunlit lighting defeat the creative set design. This is the 21st century but the cars remain vintage 1965. Yet excellent individual set pieces linger in the memory: Caroline's dance in the Masoch Club, the assassination that springs from the middle of a television commercial. Director Elio Petri had more success with his creepy horror film *A Quiet Place in the Country*, and his famous thriller *Investigation of a Citizen Under Suspicion*.

Anchor Bay's DVD of **The Tenth Victim** is a welcome surprise. The enhanced image looks good, if not great, due more to lackadaisical original photography than any transfer flaw: lots of ugly shots in direct sunlight, with dark faces. The film comes with both Italian and English tracks, and English subtitles. Andress' voice isn't used in either version, so the Italian is preferable. The only extra is the creative American trailer.

FAHRENHEIT 451

Universal Reviewed: April 17, 2003
1966 / Color / 1:78 widescreen / 112 min.
Cinematography Nicolas Roeg. Music Bernard Herrmann. Written by Francois Truffaut & Jean-Louis Richard from the book by Ray Bradbury. Produced by Lewis M. Allen, Miriam Brickman.
Directed by Francois Truffaut

Fahrenheit 451 is usually examined as a science fiction film or a Francois Truffaut movie, as if the two were mutually exclusive. sci-fi enthusiasts point to unconvincing details in Truffaut's future Utopia while Truffaut aficionados think it a misstep away from his intimate relationship stories – and outside of his native language, to boot.

A bit rigid in form and dramatically muted, *Fahrenheit 451*'s substitution of poetic immediacy for futuristic hardware went against the science fiction trend in 1966. But it still remains the best adaptation of a Ray Bradbury story.

A conformist future society has banned reading. Montag (Oskar Werner) is a disillusioned fireman in an elite squad whose job it is to locate and burn books. Montag faces a dictatorial supervisor who pretends to be his friend (Cyril Cusack) and an openly hostile co-worker (Anton Diffring). Montag's wife Linda (Julie Christie) is a model citizen, a docile, consumer-obsessed fan of inane television shows. Like most citizens, Linda thinks so little of the past that it doesn't really exist for her. Everything is convenience in the here and now. Montag meets the spirited Clarisse (Julie Christie again) on the monorail, and she awakens the rebel in him. He plays hooky from work to help Clarisse deal with losing her job as a teacher. They watch a citizen on the street betraying a neighbor to the authorities. Montag begins to hoard books to read at home, knowing it's only a matter of time before someone, perhaps his own wife, will turn him in.

In the 1960s some top-name directors were attracted to fantastic science fiction subject matter. Stanley Kubrick caught the brass ring but others included Jean-Luc Godard, Joseph Losey and, if one counts *The Birds*, Alfred Hitchcock. All made memorable films and then returned to more conventional material.

Truffaut was interested in the poetry of Ray Bradbury's fanciful book, which reacts to the spirit of *1984* with an irony expressed in a single phrase: his firemen don't save houses; they burn books. Bradbury's love of literature is everything. He's less concerned with the oppressive dictatorship than he is the loss of all that great literature.

Truffaut's movie is an ode to books, as Samuel Fuller's *Park Row* is a valentine to the free press. Effective art direction and superior cinematography by Nicolas Roeg create a future of anonymous houses and sinister red fire stations, with curbside Judas boxes for citizens to inform on their neighbors. In familiar Orwellian fashion, we see a populace tamed by drugs and dulled by television and consumerism. Linda believes that she's an active part of the Reality Shows on her flat screen television. She obediently throws products away so that she can buy new ones.

Truffaut shows an entire populace emotionally stifled to the point of psychosis. People on the monorail exhibit little neurotic behaviors. Linda can't relate to her own body. Montag 'expands his mind' with books, an experience that doesn't make him unhappy, as his boss claims, but instead inspires a reckless nonconformist streak. Montag concocts a plan to frame his co-workers by planting books in their houses and informing on them, but he lacks a flair for subversive tactics. After he flagrantly reads a book in front of his wife's friends, his fate is sealed.

Medicine bottles only have numbers and colors on them, and ID photos and the Sunday comics are likewise text-free. But inconsistencies easily evaded in print leap from the movie screen. If books have been forgotten, how does the chief know so much about them? Does he read the covers to memorize all those authors' names, or has an elite class retained access to the taboo literature?

Perhaps other book criminals were secretly taught their literacy, but where did Montag learn to read? At one point we see him consulting a contraband dictionary. Do the schools teach only math? Even mathematics must introduce concepts best expressed in words. Since the society has no history or news except the drivel dispensed by 'the family' on the TeeVee, what's to teach? In this dull society, it's surely not art or anything creative. The technology on view seems too complicated to be sustained solely through oral communication.

Truffaut directs the film away from these literal issues. He uses interesting masks to block out sections of the screen. A textless main title sequence makes *Fahrenheit 451* seem a product of the society on view, as if constructed from a different set of aesthetic rules. He finds poetic solutions to many problems. Unfortunately, the climactic vision of people wandering in the snow reciting the text of their book-identities grates on a first viewing, when we're looking for a more practical conclusion. Earlier, Montag berated his houseguests by calling them zombies. In visual terms, the book people are also somewhat zombie-like.

What keeps the film vitally alive even for non-fans of Truffaut or science fiction is Bernard Herrmann's incomparable music score. The main love theme finally makes its full statement at the conclusion with the onset of falling snow. Its emotions transcend the film – one wants to weep, but not for Clarisse or Montag.

Oskar Werner is an interesting sad hero and Julie Christie has some good moments as the two women in his life, but the drama is tentative at best. Truffaut does not engage his proven talent for creating vital romantic characters. The result is odd and cold, at least for 1966.

Cyril Cusack is excellent as the offensive martinet, offering medallions with his picture on them and berating two fire cadets like bad dogs. Anton Diffring (*Circus of Horrors*) does his usual sinister act; it is interesting that both hero and villain here are Germanic. Diffring also shows up in a weird cameo as a woman in Clarisse's school, just to keep us off-balance. Bee Duffell is compelling as a doomed Book Lady. Truffaut's treatment of actors is so tender that when we see Duffell walking with Julie Christie, we don't think of them as opposites of beauty and plain-ness. Actor spotters will have no trouble identifying little Mark Lester (*Oliver!*) in two scenes.

Fahrenheit 451 doesn't land on many favorites lists, which makes Universal's extras-packed, bargain-priced disc a special delight. The transfer easily supersedes the previous flat matted DVD release. Laurent Bouzereau's battery of docus includes a focus on the Bernard Herrmann music and a sit-down with Ray Bradbury.

The producer and editor are on hand to discuss how a French 'auteur' came to make a film in a language he couldn't speak. Thom Noble has a great story to tell about being a reluctant bilingual intermediary between the director and the composer. Lewis Allen explains why Julie Christie ended up in a dual role. Both marvel at Truffaut's visual inventiveness, but neither explains why crack cinematographer Nicolas Roeg (or someone) muffed the ragged blue-screen monorail interiors.

Also included are a photo & poster gallery, an unused title sequence and a trailer. The commentary is by Julie Christie and a number of crew people and contributors.

KONEC SRPNA V HOTELU OZON

Facets Video Reviewed: January 3, 2006
1967 / B&W / 1:37 flat / 87 min. / *The End of August at the Hotel Ozone*
Cinematography Jirí Macák. Written by Pavel Jurácek. Produced by Czechoslovak Army Studios.
Directed by Jan Schmidt

The End of August at the Hotel Ozone has been a difficult-to-see title for almost forty years. *Variety* caught it at a New Czechoslovak film festival in 1967 and was so unimpressed with its commercial prospects that it waited a month to post its review. The similarity of descriptions in sci-fi film journals suggests that many were written not by seeing the picture but from reading that one *Variety* notice.

Variety was correct in terms of the film's overall appeal – this slow, arty combo of *On the Beach* and *Lord of the Flies* dwells on disturbing animal cruelty that would surely raise hackles today and provoke an outright ban in England. But *Hotel Ozone* is interesting as a missing link between sober nuclear doomsday movies and the later escapist post-apocalyptic thriller genre.

Years after a nuclear holocaust, a group of young women roam the forests, led by an "Old Woman" (Beta Ponicanová) in military garb who keeps the less stable members in line. The women have little sense of purpose and while away their time in senseless cruelty to the animals they catch. The novelty of a small hotel run by a harmless old man (Ondrej Jarichek) charms the group into a sense of tranquility – momentarily.

The End of August at the Hotel Ozone's band of bored females forage on horseback through thick woods and dead cities overgrown with vegetation. The movie is all distant observation with little dialogue. Having reverted to a semi-feral existence, the all-female Lost Patrol relates to the environment mostly through knives and guns. Although one girl enjoys reading a found love letter, what most excites them is locating untouched stocks of kerosene, ammunition and liquor. The platoon is a cross-section of physical types. Although some are beautiful (second-in-command Magda Seidlerová) all are dirty and unkempt.

Little conventional storytelling takes place. We're never really introduced to the girls as individuals. The old woman tries to keep order but her troops can be hard to manage, especially when an animal appears. One young woman shoots both a cow and a dog with a high-powered rifle, incidents that do not look faked. In another disturbing animal cruelty scene, a girl catches a small snake and rips it to pieces while it struggles. Distributor interest in *Hotel Ozone* probably vanished when buyers saw this content. It's front and center and there's little else to think about.

An extended sequence shows the old woman following a series of chalk marks on some buildings to find one of her girls trapped in the crumbling gallery of a long-abandoned church. The rest of the group watches from below, accompanied by one of their white horses, which makes for some unforced and eerily evocative imagery.

The picture perks up in the last two reels. After fording a river the troop encounters a man, something most of them have never seen. The old codger welcomes them to his home, the 'Hotel Ozon' of the title. The girls consume his sit-down meal like a pack of animals. The old woman is charmed when the Old Man brings her flowers – he remembers the old way of things. With most of the world's population dead from leukemia, the Old Man assumes that the girls are in search of young men to impregnate them. The old woman doubts his interpretation. The girls don't seem interested in the idea, either.

The bleak and violent ending imparts the conservative message that the younger generation will destroy what they don't understand and cause an abrupt break in civilization. The women kill to possess a wind-up gramophone that to them represents a magic talisman. It comes with only one 78rpm polka record, *Roll Out the Barrel*.

Director Jan Schmidt stages the drama with standoffish neutrality, never imposing symbolism or significance onto the material: the killing over the gramophone is tragic, not ironic. There's none of the feeling of later post-apocalyptic movies that revel in junkyard anarchy (the *Mad Max* films) or satirical inversions of present-day political systems. Schmidt and Jurácek show humanity calmly devolving into savagery, living off the stored canned goods of a previous era. They use hand grenades to catch fish. The gritty B&W cinematography keeps the screen alive with naturalistic compositions and handsome telephoto pans.

The acting is fine as well, although only Ponicanová and Jarichek are standouts. There's a tiny bit of non-exploitative nudity. The movie is a Czech Army Production and considering the rough duty on view, the actresses may be soldiers. They ride bareback and handle weapons with expertise. After shooting the cow, the group immediately begins to gut it, like a pack of happy Amazon butchers.

Facets Video's DVD of *The End of August at the Hotel Ozone* is a good transfer of a satisfactory source element. The movie is originally 1:37 so the flat screen ratio is correct. The first reel is a tad scratchy but most of the film accurately renders the hazy feeling of the forest scenes. An arresting title sequence begins with an audio jumble of international voices reciting a missile-launching countdown. The balance of the film studiously avoids flashy effects.

The accompanying literature makes use of enthusiastic critical quotes that overstate the film's general appeal. It's only tangentially comparable to *Mad Max* or Tarkovsky. *The End of August at the Hotel Ozone* is a must-see title for fans interested in the creative margins of the genre.

Republished by permission of Turner Classic Movies.

FORCE MORE POWERFUL THAN 1,000 H-BOMBS UNLEASHED TO DEVASTATE EARTH! WORLD IN PANIC! CITIES IN FLAMES!

QUATERMASS AND THE PIT

Anchor Bay Reviewed: December 5, 1998
1967 / Color / 1:78 flat letterboxed. / *Five Million Years to Earth*
Cinematography Arthur Grant. Screenplay & Story Nigel Kneale. Produced by Anthony Nelson-Keys.
Directed by Roy Ward Baker

Quatermass and the Pit, Hammer Film's third adventure featuring the Bernard Quatermass character is front-rank science fiction overflowing with ambitious concepts. As *Five Million Years to Earth*, it was released in the U.S. in the same year as *2001: A Space Odyssey*. Concept-for-concept it is less pretentious and more coherent than that landmark Kubrick epic.

A London subway excavation yields humanoid fossils and a buried space ship that lead Professor Quatermass (Andrew Keir) to an expanding circle of theories: unexploded bombs, Nazi propaganda weapons, Poltergeist-style occultism, alien invasion, genetic manipulation and demonic possession. Quatermass soon finds himself battling government and military bureaucrats over the mystery ship, the meaning of which proves to be too disturbing for public acceptance: human evolution may be the result of intervention by ancient alien visitors.

Pit unspools like the granddaddy of all *X-Files* episodes. All three of Hammer's *Quatermass* films were originally multi-chaptered BBC television serials written by Nigel Kneale. The first two film versions were re-written by Val Guest but Kneale personally adapted this third saga for the big screen, somehow packing three hours' worth of plot into 98 minutes. The film's breakneck pace can leave casual viewers in the dust; I confess that on my first viewing I was swamped by the rush of intellectual twists.

As with many color Hammer films, the production is on the anemic side. To compensate for smallish sets and limited extras director Roy Ward Baker (*A Night to Remember*) shoots far too much of the film in close-up. The dead Martian insects are feeble props and some of the special effects with the frightening spaceship aren't so hot even by pre-*2001* standards. And a gadget that turns mental thoughts into television images is both unconvincing and detrimental to the story line, being one Big Idea too many. If such a miracle machine existed, it would be just as important as Kneale's story about aliens; Wim Wenders made a four-hour movie about just such an invention, 1991's *Until the End of the World*.

As a fantasy thriller *Quatermass and the Pit* really cooks, something few effect-laden yawners can boast. The demonic riot at the finale is a chilling highlight, and the superior acting of Keir and Hammer star Barbara Shelley keep the tale involving at a personal level. Particularly effective in the frightening climactic action is top-billed James Donald, a familiar face from *The Bridge On the River Kwai* and *The Great Escape*.

Pit is often compared to *2001*, which is especially interesting because Nigel Kneale's superlative thriller bears similarities to Arthur C. Clarke's mind-blowing earlier novel *Childhood's End*. Both tales hinge on racial memories of devilish alien visitations that redefine human identity.

Anchor Bay's DVD of **Quatermass and the Pit** looks and sounds quite good, although the image is not widescreen-enhanced. Director Baker and writer Kneale share a commentary track. The trailers and TV spots allow a comparison of the Brit and Yank ad campaigns, neither of which lets on that the film has so many compelling ideas.

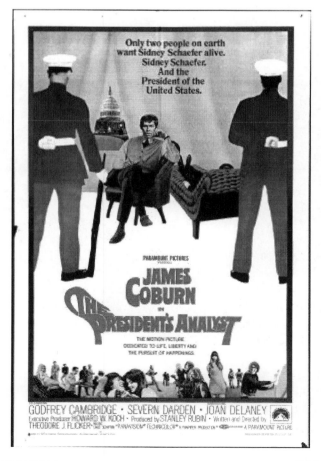

THE PRESIDENT'S ANALYST

Paramount Reviewed: June 3, 2004
1967 / Color / 2:35 widescreen / 103 min.
Cinematography William A. Fraker.
Production Designer Pato Guzman. Produced by Howard W. Koch, Stanley Rubin.
Written and Directed by Theodore J. Flicker

Perhaps the best all-round political satire of the '60s, *The President's Analyst* soared over the heads of its audience – and probably still does. The talented Theodore J. Flicker directed this studio picture and the independent *The Troublemaker* using talent from Chicago's Second City Theater Group. What might have been a collection of stand-up routines coheres into an uncannily prophetic spy spoof. The fall-down funny show makes good points about espionage, hippies, high technology and government intrusions into our privacy.

After his star breakthrough as *Our Man Flint* James Coburn threw himself into some interesting offbeat projects. *The President's Analyst* shows an intelligent star letting a brilliant writer-director run loose with a good idea.

Psychiatrist Dr. Sidney Schaefer (James Coburn) is hired to tend to LBJ, but finds the President's daily problems too much for his own psyche to bear. Ethan Allen Crocket of the CEA (Eduard Franz) and his professional associate Dr Lee-Evans (Will Geer) try to help but the diminutive FBR director Henry Lux (Walter Burke) disapproves of Sidney's living with his girlfriend Nan Butler (Joan Delaney). Sidney becomes paranoid and goes on the run, hiding out with the Quantrills (William Daniels, Joan Darling), an "average American family" that prove to be gun-toting wackos. But when teams of international spies indeed try to kidnap Stanley, midget FBR agents are ordered to kill him as a security risk! Luckily, Sidney has loyal friends on his side: CEA hit man Don Masters (Godfrey Cambridge) and

Russian agent V.I. Fydor Kropotkin (Severn Darden).

Skit comedies based on talent gathered from theatrical comedy groups had a pretty spotty record in the '60s; Philip Kaufman' *Fearless Frank* comes to mind. That under-funded, unfocused mess cast this film's Severn Darden and Joan Darling with Jon Voight in an Al Capp-style comic strip plot about gangsters and a super-cyborg. In *The President's Analyst* the stand-up is sublimated into a spy satire that moves like a house afire. A parody of competing security agencies in Washington segues to White House jokes and from there to a devastating lampoon of extremism in suburbia. The script jumps to the next level before its ideas become stale, working its way to a genuinely profound science fiction ending.

Coburn flexes his screen persona to play a gong-ringing good-guy shrink, an amiable straight man to a cast of crazies. This is Godfrey Cambridge's best role; we're in his pocket right from his sympathetic soliloquy about childhood racism. He's best pals with his opposite number in the KGB, the garrulous, sociable Severn Darden. Darden's endearing top spy turns out to be in need of Dr. Schaefer's soothing psychoanalysis.

The script provides good opportunities for a score of comedians. Joan Delaney comes on like a submissive love object and then balks at the perceived constrictions of marriage. Barry McGuire's hippie guru impersonation is priceless, as is Jill Banner's love child. Best of all are William Daniels and Joan Darling as pistol-packing, karate-chopping liberals that think lethal gas is too good for their "fascist" neighbors. Their son taps Sidney's phone calls and alerts the FBR; when the first spies attack, Sidney escapes because the Quantrills retaliate as a coordinated killing team.

The President's Analyst asserts that the American government illegally spies on its own citizens.

Sidney's zinger line, *"The sanctity of a psychiatrist's office is like a confessional"* always gets a gasp because of the Daniel Ellsberg/Pentagon Papers break-in that happened a couple of years later. The CEA is presented as a liberated Ivy League think-tank staffed by a co-ed group of collegiate spies smoking pipes and sitting on the floor. A midget zealot runs the repressive FBR, hiring only agents shorter than he. In perfect Joe Friday cadence, FBR agent Arte Johnson tells his victims that he's only following orders, while his "squire" assistant advises young Bing Quantrill not to use ethnic slurs. [1]

Spies chase spies as if Antonio Prohias were in charge; in a bucolic musical number an international selection of killers wipes each other out trying to get to Sidney first, as he and his hippie girlfriend are getting acquainted in a field. [2]

Just when we wonder when the show will run out of steam, Flicker produces his science-fiction trump card, a *Great Moments with Mr. Lincoln* – like robot named Arlington Hewes (Pat Harrington). The condescending Hewes explains to Dr. Schaefer why it's imperative that he helps The Phone Company implant a 'cerebrum communicator' into the brain of every newborn child. Not only does *The President's Analyst* skewer the corporate mentality seen in the Disney *Tomorrowland* shows, it prophesizes cell phones and The Internet. We're very close to seeing personal communicators implanted in our bodies, as in *The Outer Limits'* episode *Demon with a Glass Hand*.

Flicker sagely sees Cold War rivalry as a secondary distraction. His primary villain is a corporation set on "improving" humanity by insinuating itself deep into our lives, in this case, reorganizing our biology to include corporate-controlled assets.

A key moment in *The President's Analyst* occurs when Severn Darden offers Sidney an M16 to hold off The Phone Company's private army.

Pacifist Sidney refuses until Darden insists: *"You wanna change the world? Take the gun!"* The joke acknowledges that effecting social change in America is a frustrating process that makes do-gooder liberals appear impotent: The opposition is more likely to use force as a first option. As it is, non-violent Sidney embraces his machine gun and becomes an instant Che Guevara.

Theodore Flicker's funny-but-chilling conclusion is great science fiction. In an *It's a Wonderful Life* setting of celebration and harmony, more Phone Company automatons share the joy and shed sincere robot tears for our Yuletide happiness. It's a wonderful satire of the Brave New World.

Paramount's DVD of **The President's Analyst** is a stunner, with great color and clear audio. The enhanced widescreen images make sense of compositions previously sliced up in flat TV presentations. Cinematographer Bill Fraker's style switches between slick New York normalcy and psychedelic spy paranoia without a stumble.

1. A not-so secret fact is that *The President's Analyst* originally identified the FBI and CIA by their real names. Producer Stanley Rubin confirmed to the author that pressure was brought to rename them after the film was completed. Thus every line where 'FBR' and 'CEA' are heard has been re-dubbed, often very audibly. If you watch the actors' lips, they're really saying FBI and CIA. Movies can spoof the Army, the Navy, Congress and even the President (if it's in certain interests) but our secret police organizations can enforce a ban on criticism.

2. This is backed by the hilariously apt Barry McGuire song *Changes*, which was replaced for some TV versions of the film. It's intact on this disc.

PLANET OF THE APES

Fox Blu-ray Reviewed: November 6, 2008
1968 / Color / 2:35 / 112 min.
Cinematography Leon Shamroy. Makeup John Chambers. Music Jerry Goldsmith. Written by Rod Serling, Michael Wilson from the novel by Pierre Boulle. Produced by Arthur P. Jacobs. Directed by Franklin J. Schaffner

Stanley Kubrick's *2001: A Space Odyssey* is now acknowledged as *the* science fiction film of the 1960s, the experimental epic that changed the genre. But this genre thriller opened at almost the same time and was a much bigger popular success. Fox's *Planet of the Apes* came out wide in April of 1968 and was still playing as a second feature when we went back to school in September. Unlike the puzzle picture with the "giant space baby", *Planet of the Apes* connected with audiences on intellectual *and* emotional levels.

Not since *Forbidden Planet* had Hollywood made a major movie about the exploration of an alien planet. Rod Serling and Michael Wilson's screenplay overturns expectations from the very beginning, when the female astronaut set up to be Charlton Heston's love interest fails to make it through the first scene. The three earthmen never get a chance to point ray guns at alien monsters. Before they've caught their breath, they're imprisoned by a topsy-turvy society that switches the roles of man and monkey in the evolutionary pecking order.

What follows is a brilliant mix of realism and farce, as *Planet of the Apes* sidesteps audience derision by providing its own jokes. Heston's George Taylor comes upon the local humans, mute and ragged, foraging like sheep, and figures that he'll be running things in less than a year. Then they're attacked by the actual dominant species on this new world. Wounded and silenced, Taylor watches dumbfounded as screenwriters Rod Serling and Michael Wilson show us a barbaric inversion of our own society, reworked to place monkeys in control. Ape society's class divisions are based on species, with lighter Orangutans on a higher level than Chimpanzees, and the darker gorillas an uneducated working class. The theocratic government will not tolerate science that challenges official dogma. The existence of Taylor, a talking man, is a threat to the authoritarian Dr. Zaius (Maurice Evans), who has been suppressing the archeological findings of Chimpanzee Cornelius (Roddy McDowall) because they contradict religious texts. Taylor not only challenges Zaius's status quo, he fulfills a dread holy prophecy that a New Man will come and destroy ape civilization.

Audiences were fascinated by John Chambers' clever ape make-ups, which transform noted actors Evans, McDowall, Kim Hunter

and James Whitmore completely yet permit a wide range of facial expression. The apes become angry, laugh out loud and kiss one another. We accept them as characters interacting with Charlton Heston, who single-handedly reverses the "science fiction curse" on actors by delivering one of his best performances. An expert at sustaining one-dimensional epics, Heston recites mouthfuls of exposition in a way that makes us listen to every word. He communicates vulnerability, desperation and humiliation even in long shot. And Heston is never upstaged, even when surrounded by fascinating monkey-men.

Taylor befriends the Chimpanzees McDowall and Hunter; both actors are extremely effective under their simian muzzles. The lone earthman finds a possible mate in Nova (Linda Harrison) and with the help of his new friends avoids the vivisectionist's scalpel, not to mention an appointment to be gelded. Unlike his fellow astronauts, Taylor is a loner cynic who doesn't like civilization. He seems not the least upset to be cut off from Earth, never to return. Taylor believes in self-reliance. He's a fighter, and more than a little arrogant.

Planet of the Apes is a movie of the 60s, when film companies had no reason to fear liberal messages. Serling and Wilson seize the opportunity to put the naked Taylor on trial before a society determined to prove that he doesn't exist. In a combination McCarthy witch hunt and Scopes Monkey Trial, Taylor is officially "disposed of". It's all very much like Joseph Losey, Bertolt Brecht and Charles Laughton's notorious production of *Galileo*, a late 1940s theater piece aimed squarely at the evil of blacklisting. The satirical "funny monkey" context allows *Apes* to pursue political issues more dangerous than *Dr. Strangelove's* atom war theme. Everybody's against nuclear war, but few other mainstream movies of the day openly challenged the existence of God.

Allegory was the perfect format for TV's *The Twilight Zone*, where each episode would end with Rod Serling's God-like voice delivering his liberal "Author's Message". The saving grace of Serling and Wilson's didacticism is that they don't claim final victory for liberalism. Zaius is a functional hypocrite but is also acting in good faith to forestall a terrible fate. He wants Taylor eradicated because Man by his very nature is naturally evil: arrogant, violent, destructive. And he's right. Zaius plays dirty and hides behind a show trial because he fears what Taylor represents – humans destroyed their own world and are perfectly capable of doing the same to the Ape planet.

Planet of the Apes may be more accessible than *2001* but just because its messages are obvious doesn't mean that they've been "dumbed down". Reviewers picked up on the Rod Serling / *Twilight Zone* connection, with the result that people normally discussing John Wayne or Julie Andrews were suddenly talking about *Planet of the Apes* in connection with evolution and civil rights. This was 1968, when national leaders were being assassinated and the country was aflame with race riots. Discussing *Planet of the Apes* at the dinner table was an acceptable way of addressing real issues. No other "lowly science fiction movie" had quite the same impact.

Fox's **Blu-ray** of *Planet of the Apes* will thrill fans of the popular sci-fi franchise. Producer Arthur P. Jacobs dragged the concept on for four sequels, advancing the story to Armageddon and then backtracking into time travel stories and budget-challenged battle epics.

This first chapter holds up as great filmmaking, demonstrating director Franklin Schaffner's flair for efficient visual storytelling. The desert landscape around Lake Powell never looked so alien, and marvelous sets on the Malibu Ranch (we keep expecting a fly-by of *M*A*S*H* helicopters) sketch an amusing simian culture.

Schaffner's action direction is nothing less than brilliant, perhaps because of his and Charlton Heston's previous experience on the impressive medieval epic *The War Lord.*

The Blu-ray brings the film's faded colors back almost all the way to normal. Faces occasionally seem too light; otherwise the presentation is a visual beauty. The famous ending shot, an extreme optical zoom, looks better than ever before. The exceptional audio provides a fine showcase for Jerry Goldsmith's eccentric score, with its strange sound effects incorporated into the composition.

The extras replicate the long list of early special edition items. A commentary track features Roddy McDowall, Kim Hunter, Natalie Trundy and makeup artist John Chambers; Jerry Goldsmith has a second track all to himself.

Two new docus have been produced in HD. *The Impact of the Apes* interviews fans of the movie, most of which were too young to have seen it new in theaters. For many kids of the early 1970s, the *Apes* movies were their first exposure to time travel, post-apocalyptic worlds, mutants, alternate futures, etc.

The Evolution of the Apes gets off to a promising start by investigating the backgrounds of the writers and producer. Serling's original script was rewritten by Wilson to take place in a more primitive setting. The movie identifies The King Brothers as holders of an early option on the Pierre Boulle novel. It slams them as makers of "cheap crime and monster movies" – like the expensive, well-regarded *Gorgo*, and imagines an unmade cheap King Bros. *Apes* by showing a still from Fox's silly *Gorilla at Large!* The best disc content remains the fascinating older featurette material on John Chambers' makeup, and the extensive galleries of ad materials.

An epic drama of adventure and exploration

2001: A SPACE ODYSSEY

Warners Blu-ray Reviewed: October 27, 2007
1968 / Color / 2:20 / 141 min.
Cinematography Geoffrey Unsworth.
Production Design Ernest Archer, Harry
Lange, Tony Masters . Art Direction John
Hoesli. Film Editor Ray Lovejoy . Special
Makeup Stuart Freeborn, Graham Freeborn,
Charles E. Parker. Written by Stanley Kubrick,
Arthur C. Clarke.
Produced and Directed by Stanley Kubrick

2001: A Space Odyssey is one of the most written-
about films of all time, a visionary science fiction
epic that still holds up under deep-think analysis. Arthur C. Clarke tells us that Kubrick had
little patience with previous sci-fi movies, and
scorn for most of them. When Kubrick dismissed
Things to Come as naïve, he had a point. Thirty

years after its premiere much of H.G. Wells' film
seemed like an ancient fossil. Forty years have
now passed since the arrival of *2001: A Space Odyssey*, and only a few of its technical details have
dated. Pan-Am no longer flies and we don't yet
have commercial space stations or gigantic interplanetary vehicles. The Cold War has thawed, at
least in terms of Yanks vs. Russkies.

After the film's initial "Huh?" impact – it took a
great many reviewers by surprise – *2001* became
a regular Rorschach Inkblot Test for filmgoers.
Literal types looked for a concrete meaning for
the mysterious monolith, while impassioned art
film adepts claimed to have accompanied astronaut Bowman "beyond the infinite". The words
'mind-blowing' and 'psychedelic' were added to
the vocabularies of a few more million filmgoers. [1]

THE DAWN OF MAN. A mysterious monolith
suddenly appears before a group of prehistoric
ape-men, and inspires an Alpha-male leader
(Daniel Richter) to improvise a weapon to assert
his territorial imperative. Thousands of years
later, man is building space stations and a giant
moon colony. Space bureaucrat Dr. Heywood
R. Floyd journeys to Moon Base Clavius to in-
spect an extraordinary find, a second monolith
buried below the surface of the crater Tycho.
When sunlight strikes the object, it sends a radio
signal aimed at Jupiter. JUPITER MISSION, 18
MONTHS LATER. Astronaut Drs. Dave Bowman and Frank Poole (Keir Dullea & Gary Lockwood) pilot a vast atomic-powered Jupiter craft
called *Discovery*. Helping them care for three
other scientists in suspended animation is the
HAL-9000 computer (voice of Douglas Rain).
Programmed to manifest a personality, HAL
takes a spirited interest in Dave and Fank's welfare – until he begins to show very un-comput-
erlike signs of fallibility.

Every Kubrick film from 1953's awkward *Fear
and Desire* forward marked a quantum career
leap for the director, taking him from amateur

status to the top rank of his profession in less than a decade. When Kubrick's films weren't moneymakers they were huge prestige successes. Most of them courted 'dangerous' subject matter – war crimes, the nuclear stalemate, a novel deemed un-filmable. With *2001* Kubrick spent unheard-of sums on a fuzzy story about man's relationship to the universe. Before 1968's *Planet of the Apes* science fiction films had been middling performers at best, and more often than not juvenile in appeal.

Few space films had actually attempted an illusion of photo-reality. Kubrick wanted nothing to do with visible wires and fluctuating matte lines. Drawing talent as much from the scientific world as from movie back lots, he gave his crew the mandate to make everything as authentic and real as possible. Elaborate spaceship interiors are seen for only a few seconds and massive sets cleverly create the illusion of zero gravity. The views of outer space are done as much as possible 'original negative', avoiding opticals that degrade the image. The entire picture was filmed in expensive 65mm, from enormous spaceship models to microphotography of lacquer smears mixing in water. To film the elaborate Dawn of Man sequence, giant front-projection plates of African locations were matched on English sound stages.

Across a hard cut, a bone becomes a nuclear weapons satellite. Michael Powell's *A Canterbury Tale* beat Kubrick to the draw with this particular editorial idea, but Kubrick's cut from man's first weapon to his newest killing tool is a stunner, an impressive cosmic joke. We'll skip those millennia of world history, say Kubrick and Clarke; the important issue is that mankind is still murderously aggressive. Dr. Floyd's nonchalance regarding rumors of a bizarre moon epidemic keeps the Russians off guard, but even he seems incapable of appreciating the full import of the buried monolith. His fellow space executives appear equally excited by their ham sandwich lunches. Space travel has become

such a routine that even evidence of intelligent life is taken as a matter of course.

Unimaginative viewers were tickled by the film's futuristic hardware – all shiny and clean, with many video status readouts – but wondered when the outer-space thrills would show up. Previous space travel movies had featured near-disasters with meteors, dramatic intrigues on board and confrontations with dangerous aliens. *2001's* space jocks Poole and Bowman play chess and exercise while maintaining an even strain of bland efficiency.

When HAL turns traitor *2001* becomes a strange antiseptic battleground. Many see the show as an epic struggle of man's destiny, as determined by his weapon-tools. Insecure ape-men sought an advantage to prevail over their enemies; the space program is as dedicated to warfare as it is to exploration. HAL's mutiny shows Man to be losing control over his own weapon-tools. His murder of the crewmembers, destroying the mission in order to save it, is a horrible joke on mankind, like the Doomsday Machine in *Doctor Strangelove*. A more cold-blooded massacre cannot be imagined; anybody with a feeling brain senses the tragedy as the life functions of Man's best and finest are terminated. Perhaps the most chilling 'what's wrong with this picture' moment in films occurs when Frank Poole's pod pivots to attack him. We sense HAL's growing paranoia when he reads the astronauts' lips and discovers their plans to disconnect him. Mankind's perfect artificially intelligent helper flexes its newfound instinct for self-preservation.

That 'take' on *2001* works beautifully until the final chapter. I remember a nervous sensation flowing through the audience when the title "JUPITER – AND BEYOND THE INFINITE came up: what possible miracle would Kubrick put before us? A second interpretation is less Homo Sapiens-centric and more in line with Arthur C. Clarke's uncredited stories *The Sentinel* and especially *Childhood's End*. That novel shows the final generation of human children reincarnated as a new super-entity, much like *2001*'s Star Child.

In the second interpretation, the specifics of the Bowman vs. HAL duel on board *Discovery* are as inconsequential as the rest of human history. By leaving his planet, Man has proven himself a resourceful and intelligent species worthy of entrance into the league of galactic beings. Chasing the cookie-crumb trail of monoliths to the rendezvous amid the moons of Jupiter is sort of a graduation exam, not all that different than assembling the Interociter in *This Island Earth*.

As soon as the expedition to Jupiter begins, *2001* becomes another of Kubrick's sex-based jests. The *Discovery* resembles – what else – a giant Spermatozoa, and the keepers of the monolith need only one human to (for lack of a better analogy) fertilize mankind's transition to its next evolutionary level. Like the myriads of Spermatazoa that don't reach the egg, the rest of our race is now irrelevant.

But the space executives have sent five living humans on board *Discovery*. To eliminate all but one (and prove him worthy of his prize), the aliens *cause* HAL's 'major malfunction'. Poor Poole is lost and Dave Bowman must continue the mission alone. Like Odysseus, Bowman uses his wits to survive, but the end of his quest is a dead end for his personal identity. When he finally succumbs in the alien 'holding room', Bowman is replaced by a new being, a Star Child with god-like powers. In Clarke's scheme of things, individual humans don't have souls, only a generic racial spirit with the potential to evolve to a new plane of god-like omnipotence.

Interpretation #2 is cold and anti-humanitarian at its core, but it's basic Stanley Kubrick. Arthur C. Clarke's fiction stressed great wonders for the future of mankind, but Kubrick the director repeatedly imagined human endeavors tripped up by fate and political folly.

Warners' *2001: A Space Odyssey Two-Disc Special Edition* fulfills the promise of earlier editions. MGM's 1998 disc was a fairly ugly non-enhanced transfer. This new disc rights previous wrongs; the overture and exit music play over appropriately blank black screens. Audio is in English and French with subs in English, French and Spanish.

On their commentary Keir Dullea and Gary Lockwood discuss their experience with Stanley Kubrick but can offer few insights as to the workings of his mind; Kubrick kept most normal kinds of on-set communications to a minimum. Dullea does remember suggesting the business with the broken glass for the last scene of Bowman in captivity. A theatrical trailer is present on the first disc as well.

The Making of a Myth is a docu overview produced in 2001 for England's Channel 4. Douglas Trumbull is interviewed on a California beach lamenting the fact that manned space exploration was curtailed after the Apollo moon landings. Sir Arthur C. Clarke speaks from the garden of his home in Sri Lanka, where a local monkey plays on a full-scale monolith! New featurettes interview a range of personalities, from Barry Diller to Keir Dullea. One features testimonials from latter-day filmmakers and another examines the accuracy of the film's prophecies.

Especially interesting for Kubrick fans is a photo-filled piece on the director's first job as a photographer for *Look* magazine. Also good is Jeremy Bernstein's 1966 audio interview with Kubrick. We're surprised when Stanley sounds like an ordinary New Yorker!

The director was often at a loss to visualize an alien world with 'unseeable sights' and 'new colors'. Some of his psychedelic images no longer work as well as they might, especially the solarized views of alpine glaciers, ocean waves and Monument Valley. Kubrick ran out of time and money just like many another ambitious filmmaker; the unique and puzzling 'Dorchester Hotel' ending was apparently considered a compromise. By coming up with the knockout punch of the Star Gate sequence, Douglas Trumbull truly was the picture's savior. The effect blew away audiences in 1968, prompting the film's reissue tagline 'The Ultimate Trip' and finding a commercial niche for a movie that hadn't gained a grip on the general audience.

Within three years Hollywood's Cinerama Dome was reviving *2001: A Space Odyssey* whenever a new booking under-performed. Dalt Wizzy's dizzy marketers repackaged the 1940 *Fantasia* as a similar 'head trip' movie. For either title, we'd all trek to The Dome to take in the 'light show.' Whenever I see *2001* on a screen, I can still remember the smell of marijuana in the air!

1. MGM Culver City's head negative cutter Mike Sheridan told Savant that Stanley Kubrick made editorial changes to *2001* even as he crossed the Atlantic on an ocean liner. After its premiere, Kubrick cut the film by 15 -20 minutes and ordered the chapter title cards – "The Dawn of Man", etc. – which Sheridan added in Culver City. Kubrick controlled the negative and all outs were returned to him, so the extra content of the deleted 20 minutes are locked in the memories of those who saw it. The revisions caught up with the movie less than a week after it opened in its reserved seat engagements. Future producer Jon Davison recorded his reaction in a 1968 letter. He was floored by the movie and went to see it only a day or two later – to be confronted with the shorter cut. The same thing happened to the next year's *The Wild Bunch*, only done without its director's knowledge or consent. It played only a few days before being trimmed by over ten minutes.

DER GROSSE VERHAU

Edition *filmmuseum* *(Region 0 PAL)* Reviewed:
August 30, 2007
1969 (71) / Color / 1:37 flat / 90 min. / *The Big Mess*
Cinematography Thomas Mauch, Alfred Tichawsky. Art Direction Achim Heimbucher, Hannelore Hoger.
Written and Directed by Alexander Kluge

How obscure must a film be to be obscure? Alexander Kluge's *Der große Verhau* is a long-awaited West German art effort that piqued my interest because of enthusiastic coverage in the Phil Hardy Sci-Fi Encyclopedia. Hardy lauds it as a counter-culture rebuttal to *2001: A Space Odyssey*, offering an alternate vision of space as a frontier of commercial exploitation by warring corporations. *Variety* caught *Verhau* at the '71 Venice film festival and called it an anti-film, saying "its chances for the regular market are practically zero". With an endorsement like that, how could anyone resist?

Der große Verhau is a political statement from an intellectual German filmmaker. It is best suited for fans of visionary radical concepts, or science fiction fans motivated to see everything in the genre.

2035. It's a hot time in the Krüger star system, where small entrepreneurs strive to eke out a living on the edge of civilization. Big sections of the galaxy have been deeded outright to large corporations to exploit raw materials. Unlicensed operators are pursued as pirate outlaws. Two families in a tiny spaceship search for a planet where they can work away from the domination of aggressive Suez Canal Company. Where corporations compete for territory, *bürgerkrieg* or civil war results. The Suez Corporation extends its influence with a vast space fleet. Some ships sell protection to new territories while others carry out anti-insurgency operations. We see the construction of a new cruiser called the *En Cascade*. Admiral Von Schaake (Hark Bohm) cannot get his vendors to make the ship's systems operational, and fire breaks out on its first trial run. Von Schaake is distracted from emergency and rescue efforts by agents eager to win the salvage contract for the ship's scrap metal. Elsewhere the fleet is beset by multiple mutinies and fragging incidents.

Senior citizens Vincenze and Maria Starr (playing themselves) buy a small spacecraft and go into the 'accumulating' business, wrecking other ships for scrap and items of resale value. Their latest haul nets $87 million from a fence operating on a small asteroid. When arrested, they give the following accounting: They keep 25% of the loot. 35% goes to their bank loan and 25% to the rebels. The Starrs say they like the rebels because "they still honor many human rights and will let you get ahead".

Unlicensed space pilot Douglas (Siegfried Graue) works for Fraü Fürst's Joint Galactical Transports (JGT) an illegal independent outfit. Fürst (Henrike Fürst) hires anybody who can fly and serves routes where the monopoly's influence is not strong. Douglas tries to steal client contact information that could allow him to set up his own business. Fürst catches him each time, but lets him off because good employees are hard to find. Douglas shoots down and raids some ships on his own, and spends his earnings on liquor and drugs in a space brothel with Sylvie Szeliga (Sylvia Forsthofer). Meanwhile, Suez seizes JGT and forces Fraü Fürst to sell out. Douglas steals some plans from a Suez Company outpost and is pursued by a tank. To quell an insurgency, the corporation inaugurates an unending bombardment of the planet Krüger 60. Millions are forced to live in bunkers. The final scene has Mr. Hunter, 'the last American', eager to go into space. He asks for landing instructions on a corporate fleet ship and arrogantly orders a fancy meal to be prepared for his arrival. The warship instead blasts his capsule to bits.

The synopsis makes *Der große Verhau* sound like a grandiose anti-establishment space epic. Although we don't know if George Lucas ever saw the film, the similarities between the all-devouring Suez Canal Corporation and The Empire are rather striking, what with smugglers and scavengers representing the only 'free' activity in the star system. Some sources claim that the film is based on a 1966 book, *Monopoly Capital* by Marxist economists Baran and Sweezy, but that book is apparently about dry economic theories. *Der große Verhau* is a big anti-capitalist joke. Outer space is just another territory to be exploited for profit.

Much of *Verhau* consists of text inter-titles. Little of the sweeping storyline is visualized and almost no action of any kind takes place. Endless voiceovers and title cards chart the politics of the conflict, or list particulars about the activities of the space fleets. The amateurish spaceship models look like random auto parts assembled in odd patterns and the costumes are mostly crude improvisations. Space-ship interiors are ordinary rooms or industrial spaces filled with clutter and random equipment. The space pilots work in tiny compartments surrounded by garbage, and even Admiral von Schaake suffers in cramped meeting rooms. The *En Cascade* dry dock appears to be an ordinary shipyard.

Der große Verhau plays like an elaborate sophomoric skit with most of the humor missing. Everything is archly comic but only once or twice does the film actually become funny. The episode with the senior-citizen scavenger pirates could be taken as a conceptual joke on the interview-driven documentary style. The fleet security agent (a woman in a leather trench coat) calls for absolute secrecy, even as a press agent with a video camera continues to film everything that happens. In the film's defense, its view of corporate colonialism reaching to the stars now seems much more accurate than Stanley Kubrick's orderly investigation of space. But the film is a political statement, not an entertainment.

When *Der große Verhau* was shown in Venice, even *Variety*'s reviewer was impressed with director Alexander Kluge's reputation as the most intellectual of the new German directors. Others may think the whole movie is an incoherent trifle, or that it was produced under the influence of controlled substances.

The Filmmuseum's Region 0 PAL DVD of *Der große Verhau* is an acceptable transfer of a project that may have been filmed in 16mm. The image is sharp but colors are variable and some scenes are grainy; the lighting is nothing to write home about. Of course, if we accept this as an anti-movie, such concerns are by definition irrelevant. Subtitle options are included for English and several other languages.

The opening titles appear to be video-generated, indicating that the film originally may not have had any. Credits details differ from records in print (Sigi Graue instead of Siegfried Graue, etc.) The 2-disc set includes three other Alexander Kluge short films and one feature, *Willi Tobler und der Untergang der 6. Flotte* from 1972. It's a followup set in the same galaxy in the same time period; a clever man loses his family and becomes a press agent for the Admiral of the 6th Fleet. It's equally intellectual and just as frustrating. The disc cover illustration resembles nothing in either feature.

The Future is here.
THX 1138

Warner Bros. presents THX 1138 · An American Zoetrope Production · Starring Robert Duvall and Donald Pleasence · with Don Pedro Colley, Maggie McOmie and Ian Wolfe · Technirama® · Technicolor® · Executive Producer Francis Ford Coppola · Screenplay by George Lucas and Walter Murch · Story by George Lucas Produced by Lawrence Sturhahn · Directed by George Lucas · Music by Lalo Schifrin

THX 1138

Warners Blu-ray Reviewed: September 21, 2004
1971 / Color / 2:35 widescreen / 95 min.
Cinematography Albert Kihn, David Myers.
Editor George Lucas. Music Lalo Schifrin.
Written by Walter Murch and George Lucas.
Produced by Francis Ford Coppola, Lawrence Sturhahn.
Directed by George Lucas

THX 1138 was once a darn good movie, the dream of every 1970 film student. George Lucas expanded his USC film into a 35mm feature in color and 'scope, a movie with a great look on a minimalist budget. The intense young filmmaker pulled off a heady blend of *1984* and *The Great Escape* told through visual montages of buttons, flashing lights, television screens and complex audio montages

invented by his eager fellow student Walter Murch.

Unfortunately, Lucas has retro-vised his 1971 feature for a new 2004 release, augmented with extensive CGI computer work. Movies can become Clockwork Oranges too.

THX (Robert Duvall) and LUH (Maggie McOmie) are cheerless proles confined to an underground city where all citizens are controlled via Orwellian monitoring and Huxley-style sexless breeding. THX and LUH defy the ban on sex. They also commit the crime of drug avoidance – the use of stimulants and depressants is mandatory. Under stress, THX causes an accident on a radioactive materials assembly line. Meddling admirer SEN (Donald Pleasance) manages to get LUH arrested so he can have THX to himself. Both THX and SEN end up in a featureless space that serves as a kind of detention limbo. That's when THX decides to flee the city to the unknown world outside.

THX 1138 was a superior product of its day, and it's too bad that it's no longer available. In its place, George Lucas has given us a revised, CGI-augmented version. Once downright Spartan and featureless, the film now has giant factories assembling golden robots that look like *Star Wars'* C3PO. Escher-like tangles of high-speed roadways have been added where once stood monotonous views of the same BART tunnels. And every previously vacant space is now packed with crowds, dozens of vehicles, etc. It's like those street scenes in *Star Wars* where a couple of original pedestrians are now joined by enough aliens to fill a page in *Where's Waldo?* THX's lonely escape in a sole vehicle has been replaced by a full-scale Grand Prix of zooming Formula One cars. And a short skirmish with some dwarf denizens of the city's outer shell is now a full-on attack by a pack of mutated monkey creatures.

In other words, *THX 1138* has gone the way of *Star Wars*, with its extensive revisions and up-datings. We can't see a simple image of an or-dinary lizard sitting on some computer wires without the addition of CGI moth antennae. What ever happened to old-style film direc-tors, who were too busy with new projects to screw around with old ones?

New viewers of *THX 1138* will be able to fol-low the film just as well. They'll also enjoy the sound design, which isn't appreciably changed from the original even with the ad-dition of 5.1 audio. LUH's disappearance was once a tragic shock, but now too much is hap-pening for her to really be missed. Robert Du-vall's controlled performance hasn't changed, but the extra cars, screaming monkeys and teeming crowds distract from the focus on his character.

The basic structure of *THX 1138* is still there, like a good layer cake with too much frost-ing. Duvall's soulless worker recovers his identity once he gets off drugs and becomes determined to leave the city, as LUH had hoped to do. When we originally saw THX burst through to the surface, to be confronted with his first view of an orange sunset, it was a wonderfully ambiguous finale. Where is he going to go now? Is the environment topside an ecological wasteland or the preserve of a lucky ruling elite? The final shot seems to have been processed to put more of a visual distortion on THX's tiny figure silhouetted against the sky. That distracts from the final joke of the original, in which a bird few by and we imagined THX thinking, "What the heck was that?" With all the unnecessary visual additions to the film, THX's triumph now plays like a letdown.

For audiences unaware of film history, War-ner's two-disc set of *THX 1138* will certainly not be the cultural outrage described above. The beautifully mastered image looks far bet-ter than it ever did projected, where all those featureless white rooms showed every tiny scratch and piece of dirt.

The extras are plentiful. A nice transfer of the original USC student film is included, along with a vintage featurette that focuses on all the actors having their heads shaved. Lucas and Walter Murch offer commentaries and participate in docus. Special effects whiz Dennis Muren seems bored with it all, while Murch delights in detailing his sound design theories. Murch also takes credit for the mu-sic score – he says that Lalo Schifrin simply transcribed the 'notes' produced by Murch's classical records taped backwards and at 1/4 speed. The best docu is an overview of the early years of the Zoetrope Company and its unfulfilled creative promise. Nowhere do the extras mention the extensive CGI revision. Does Lucas intend to rewrite movie history to fit his personal agenda?

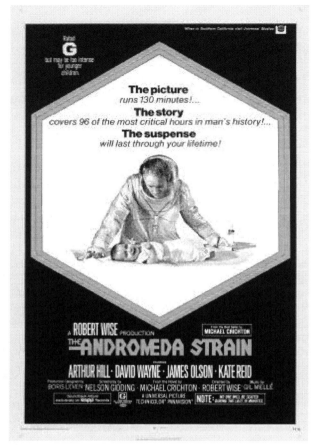

THE ANDROMEDA STRAIN

Universal Reviewed: April 16, 2003
1971 / Color / 2:35 / 130 min.
Cinematography Richard H. Kline. Production
Designer Boris Leven. Special Effects James
Shourt, Albert Whitlock, John Whitney Sr.,
Douglas Trumbull. Music Gil Melle. Written
by Nelson Gidding from the novel by Michael
Crichton.
Produced and Directed by Robert Wise

The one big tech-oriented sci-fi movie to succeed in the immediate wake of Kubrick's *2001:
A Space Odyssey*, Robert Wise's **The Andromeda
Strain** thrilled audiences by flattering their intelligence. The suspenseful doomsday film is
composed of roughly two solid hours of uninterrupted technical exposition, yet is consistently entertaining. Writer Michael Crichton

blends themes from classic sci-fi and ventures
some political content that proves once again
that movie science fiction is a good barometer
of America's Cold War stance.

A space-age disaster threatens when the residents of Piedmont, New Mexico foolishly retrieve and open an off-course satellite. Something the capsule picked up in outer space kills
everyone in town within minutes. The military
activates Project Wildfire, an expensive secret
desert lab built specifically to fight the danger of
contamination from extraterrestrial organisms.
Top personnel are assembled: Dr. Jeremy Stone
(Arthur Hill) and Dr. Mark Hall (James Olson)
enter Piedmont in isolation suits, locate the capsule and discover that the mystery substance
brought back from space turns human blood
into a fine dry powder. A drunken old man
and a crying baby are the only two unaffected
survivors. Can Wildfire isolate and identify the
unknown contagion, and concoct a medical defense against it?

A tale that relies for its thrills on the unfolding
of a technical enigma, *The Andromeda Strain* can
at least claim to have more than silly gimmicks
on its agenda. As in the convincing source book,
following the four scientist heroes into a Sher-
lock Holmes mystery has its own rewards, and
minor drawbacks. It's a serious attempt at intelligent science fiction, a welcome rarity.

The relentlessly literal film spends its first hour
rounding up four researchers and getting them
to the bottom level of a secret lab in the Nevada
desert. As with the tech-happy *2001*, most of the
interest is in the hardware: the lab's color-coded levels, each more sterile than the next; the
up-to-the-minute (or fancifully extrapolated)
scientific equipment. As envisioned by crack
production designer Boris Leven most of this
looks terrific, if a bit dated now. *Star Trek* has
overdone the spacey corridor look, and trying
to work in an environment painted fire engine
red would drive people crazy.

The film makes an admirable attempt to humanize the proceedings. The military men and politicians carry just as much procedural exposition as do the lead characters. Nurse Paula Kelly is charming and the adult survivor of Piedmont, George Mitchell, does a nice spin on the jolly drunk everyone remembers from *Them!*, right down to bargaining for booze and cigarettes. His comic asides into the TV monitors are a welcome respite from the sober tension.

The four leads attack the alien germs with cold reasoning. As the old crank on the payroll, David Wayne has the lightest exposition burden and comes off the best. Kate Reid's cynical remarks carry most of the comedy, but she lets the team down with her epilepsy problem. Another actor makes excuses for Reid by blaming the non-disclosure of her ailment on prejudice and fear, but the fact remains that Kate's main plot contribution is to jeopardize the mission. James Olson and Arthur Hill are better than the film's detractors say they are, but poor Hill's expository responsibilities prevent him from doing much more than explaining things non-stop to the other characters. Olson's confusion regarding the purpose of his red nuclear key ("No, no, you don't set off anything – all you can do is stop it!") is unintentionally ironic. One hopes the keepers of our nuclear arsenal have a better understanding of their duties.

The chilling sequence in the dead town of Piedmont tops previous doomsday depictions of mass slaughter through gas or biological agents. Like the rubber-suited man in *On the Beach*, Olsen and Hill search the town and find only corpses. Wise and editor Stuart Gilmore use split screens for this sequence, with men looking into windows next to stills of what they see. A couple of brief full screen setups make interesting use of held frames, reminding us that Boris Leven worked on the visually quirky *Invaders from Mars* 18 years earlier. Of all the late 60s attempts to do split-screen work (*The Boston Strangler* etc.), this one works the best. [1]

The two doctors rescue an orphaned baby and take it to the lab. This is Crichton's best plot gimmick. Audiences with whom I saw *The Andromeda Strain* in 1971 couldn't have cared less about 64 dead Nevadans, and probably weren't really worried about the world being depopulated by a Space Germ. But one cute, crying baby grabbed them at the personal level.

Michael Crichton's medical knowledge lends the story an air of authenticity. The film touches on concepts from classic-era sci-fi movies but its biggest debt is to the *Quatermass* films, two of which involve biological colonization from Outer Space. There's also a generous lift from the humble *Kronos*. Exactly as in that movie, the heroes demand that the government nuke the Piedmont location, only to discover that Andromeda 'feeds on energy'. Several dialogue lines are practically direct quotes from *Kronos*.

Project Wildfire is a more impressive version of the super-secret desert labs seen in sci-fi films from *GOG* onward. A similar facility in *The Satan Bug* is in fact a germ warfare development station, one with really pitiful security. *Destination Moon* came right out with the statement that American space exploration was really a military issue, and Crichton has one of his scientists make the blunt accusation that the Wildfire Project is a hoax, that Project Scoop's mission is to find new biological weapons in space. That potent idea was dropped for a decade, until *Alien* suggested that Earth's weapons researchers might welcome space monsters exploitable for military purposes.

The film's biological threat peters out in a limp non-conclusion when Andromeda becomes harmless all on its own. To provide a conventional climax Crichton cleverly updates the tense bomb countdown from *Invaders from Mars*. Audiences bought this rude narrative sidestep and enjoyed the extra kick provided by James Olson's desperate attempt to reach the nuclear disarm station. [2]

The computers in *The Andromeda Strain* instantly analyze every situation and are unusually efficient for 1970, or 2010 for that matter. What we never see is how the instant data is collected and digitized, whether it involves measuring growth on Petri dishes or the instant analysis of blood. No matter what the question, our dauntless heroes plink a few keys on a keyboard and the facts they want simply leap into view. Is *The Andromeda Strain* the dawn of the lazy writer-brilliant computer syndrome? The scientists here pluck vital info out of the air as nonchalantly as do the space men of *Star Trek*.

The fact that audiences didn't recoil at the illogic of certain scenes says a lot about the film's basic effectiveness. Project Wildfire's highly trained personnel balk like ignorant peasants at the possibility that Kate Reid might carry the Andromeda germ. At least they're not a bunch of lily-livered crybabies, like the astronauts in the now-hilarious *Marooned*.

After wiping out Piedmont the Andromeda organism mutates to a form that no longer co-agulates blood, but instead dissolves human flesh and certain plastics. A jet pilot and his polychron oxygen mask are reduced to bones and some metal fittings. When David Wayne is later exposed, he is spared because the virus specimen in the lab has mutated to Andromeda 2.0 as well. It attacks the polychron plastic of the lab's isolation seals, dissolving them as it did the pilot's mask. But what about Andromeda 2.0's habit of powder-izing human flesh as well? Wayne looks pretty untouched to me.

Andromeda's post-mortem is also a bit on the pat side. If it spontaneously mutates from a deadly form to a deadlier form, which form is drifting into the Pacific Ocean? It's eventually neutralized by acidic seawater, a gag associated with feeble monster movies like *Day of the Triffids*. How do we know Andromeda won't mutate again, and learn to tolerate a wider range of Ph?

Other plot gripes are less critical but point up some of Crichton's short cuts. Using the paper wedge in the Teletype feed to conveniently put the whole lab out of contact with Washington is a desperate plot gimmick. Even if the doofus in the radio room didn't hear a bell, he'd certainly hear and see the reams of Teletype paper spilling out onto the floor. Has no one heard of backup systems?

Finally, Kate Reid's epilepsy problem is used to delay the discovery of the obvious means for killing Andromeda, allowing James Olson to intuit it at a more dramatic moment. This one's *sort* of character-related, but is still a yawning plot hole. Crichton's dodges show how dumb accidents can foul up any mission. They also make it seem that, if Wildfire had but a smidgen of proper organization, Andromeda would have been defeated before lunchtime.

Universal and Robert Wise are to be commended for their attempt at quality sci-fi so soon after *2001*. Universal buried an equally visionary but politically more interesting film called *Colossus – the Forbin Project* for almost two years, a big commercial mistake considering how prepared audiences were for a new computer menace. *The Andromeda Strain's* politics have a martial-law flavor. 1971 audiences gave approving laugher when armed soldiers pick up the scientists and block phone calls from their relatives. The government spies don't bother with civil liberties. It all now seems rather sinister. Perhaps when our leaders exhaust other sources of fear, we'll be informed that our rights are being suspended to protect us from germs from space ...

Universal's deluxe disc of **The Andromeda Strain** belies its low price. The transfer favors the movie's aluminum rooms and shiny white lab instruments. The audio is in Dolby Digital 2.0 mono, and there are English and Spanish subtitles. The disc cover art looks like a *Dianetics* pocketbook. A text blurb predictably exploits the Crichton-*Jurassic Park* connection.

The docu is a tour of the film guided by Robert Wise and writer Nelson Gidding. Wise hasn't much to say beyond the old 'it's not science fiction but science fact' nonsense. Crichton is on hand to volunteer stories of his first movie deal. Douglas Trumbull sketches the details of his and Jamie Shourt's brilliantly achieved effects. They used custom-built high-resolution television screens in ways that predict concepts later developed to record computer images onto film. The film was Trumbull's entry into real film industry effects (not the dream-factory, sky-is-the-limit situation of *2001*) and he acknowledges his admiration for the experts who preceded him. Trumbull named one of his daughters Andromeda after this movie, by the way.

Choking the Monkey

A number of lab animals are seen being very realistically killed in *The Andromeda Strain*. Jon Bloom, a director's assistant on *Andromeda*, told me the whole story.

The ASPCA was present during filming and approved the procedure. It was shot on a set that was sealed airtight and filled with carbon dioxide. The monkey's glass cage was also airtight – it contained oxygen. The mechanical arm put the cage on the table, and opened the door. The monkey immediately could not breathe, and fell unconscious in only a few seconds, just as we see in the film. Assistant director James Fargo was just off camera breathing through a scuba outfit and holding a second oxygen source. As soon as the monkey was still for a couple of seconds, he rushed in and fed it oxygen while carrying it out of the set. The monkey revived immediately. There was only one take.

Jon suspects that the ASPCA wouldn't allow this sort of thing to be done today. As is obvious from the movie, the monkey did suffer for a traumatic few moments. Jon feels that the scene was necessary because audiences had only

heard *talk* about deadly germs and needed to see something that looked undeniably real. The monkey and the crying baby depict the consequences of an invisible 'monster' that was impossible to show directly. [3]

I myself am not sure where the line should be drawn with the killing of living things for movies, as we do it so much everywhere else in daily life. Thousands of that monkey's cousins may have been sacrificed for significant medical research – or perhaps frivolous cosmetics testing.

1. Arthur Hill later has a chilling dream of Piedmont's corpses that adds an additional split-screen image of his wife dead back in Washington. It is presumably what he fears will happen if Project Wildfire fails.

2. The chase scene on ladders leading out of a secret lab didn't work so well when adapted for the ending fizzle of 2000's *Hollow Man*.

3. Telephone interview with Jon Bloom, April 14, 2003

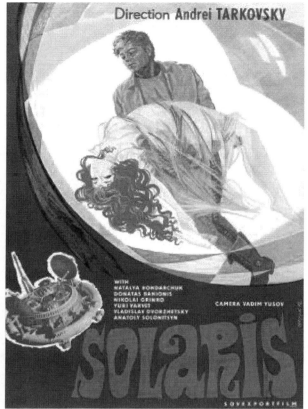

SOLYARIS

Criterion Blu-ray Reviewed: November 23, 2002
1972 / Color, B&W / 2:35 / 169 min. / *Solaris*
Cinematography Vadim Yusov. Editor
Lyudmila Feiginova. Music Eduard Artemyev.
Written by Fridrikh Gorenshtein, Andrei
Tarkovsky from the novel by Stanislaw Lem.
Produced by Viacheslav Tarasov.
Directed by Andrei Tarkovsky

On its American release, Tarkovsky's **Solaris**
carried the critical tagline, 'The Soviet Answer
to 2001.' The film's achievement wasn't immediately recognized – the American premiere at
the 1972 Filmex in Los Angeles played to an audience that had difficulty making sense of this
epic-length science fiction tale. [1]

Psychologist-cosmonaut Kris Kelvin (Donatas
Banionis) journeys to the planet Solaris to de-

cide whether to shut down an orbiting observation station. Although the scientific investigation called *Solaristics* has reached a number of
conclusions about the liquid planet – all agree
that the ocean of Solaris may be a gigantic living being – the objectivity of the research team
is in doubt. All that have gone to the station
have suffered from hallucinations, including
Berton (Vladislav Dvorzhetsky), who claims to
have seen miraculous plastic 'communications'
formed by the ocean in the form of huge liquid
sculptures.

Kelvin expects to find three scientists at the station but his old friend Dr. Gibaryan (Sos Sarki-
syan) has killed himself. Dr. Snauth and Dr. Sartorius are living with what may be humanoid
simulacra created by the ocean below. Neither
scientist will discuss the phantom beings. Before
Kelvin can fully grasp the situation, a mysterious visitor of his own appears out of nowhere.
She's identical to his own wife, Hari (Natalya
Bondarchuk), who committed suicide millions
of miles away on Earth. Kelvin doesn't know
how to react to this living, breathing synthetic
copy. She can't drink or eat, and wears a dress
with no provision for unfastening. And she's
desperate not to be separated from Kelvin.

Twelve years before, author Stanislaw Lem had
been critical of the East German-Polish simplifi-
cation of his first novel *Astronauci*, made as *Der
Schweigende Stern (The Silent Star)*. He wasn't
pleased with Tarkovsky's film either, complaining that the Russian director had substituted
his own humanist theme for the original's scientific riddle.

U.S. filmgoers weren't prepared for a sci-fi
movie conceived as a philosophical meditation,
and the film remained a strictly art house release. Despite some impressive sets Tarkovsky's
show is no technical challenge to Kubrick's
2001: A Space Odyssey. But the Russian movie is
a remarkable look at the same cosmic mystery
from a radically different perspective.

2001: A Space Odyssey spends almost all of its time celebrating futuristic hardware and conceives of the human race as the pawn of god-like extra-terrestrials with a master plan for our *Childhood's End*. In *Solaris*, man's search for intelligent life in the galaxy has reached a dead end before the gigantic psychic mirror of Solaris' sentient ocean. Communication and understanding are impossible for humans that insist that all phenomena fit neatly into our sphere of reference, and cooperate with our instruments of observation. 'Alien' means different in more than just form.

If *Solaris* were a straight science fiction movie it might follow the pattern of *The Martian Chronicles* or even *Journey to the 7th Planet*, stories about alien intelligences defending their turf from Earthly incursion by conjuring up hallucinations from our own minds. But *Solaris* ignores adventure thrills to instead challenge the basis of our motivation to seek out other life forms. [2]

At first glance, Tarkovsky's viewpoint might seem the conservative idea that man is fundamentally unprepared to deal with the truly unfamiliar and should therefore stay close to his womb planet. The narrow-minded scientists in Berton's interrogation video assume that because Solaris crewmembers report inconsistent and irrational phenomena, their research is worthless. But the miracles witnessed by the space station scientists cannot be hallucinations. Gibaryan's 'visitor' is a young girl whose image is recorded on videotape. Snauth and Sartorius' visitors (mostly unseen) are troublemakers that physically abuse their hosts – every scene shows the scientists suffering from a new injury. The sentient Ocean is trying to communicate with the aliens in the only way it knows: creating living beings out of thin air.

(spoilers) Kelvin undergoes a traumatic experience with his 'visitor'. The new Hari clone (Hari #2) appears when Kelvin is asleep, as if he had to be unconscious for the Ocean to access the

Hari blueprint in his mind. This bears a similarity to the organic invaders of *Invasion of the Body Snatchers*, which could copy humans only during sleep. The original Hari committed suicide, apparently distraught over her relationship with the unemotional Kelvin. Hari #2 has little memory beyond her love for Kelvin, and cannot bear to be apart from him. When a metallic door gets in her way, she rips through it. She seriously cuts herself, but her wounds heal in a matter of minutes. Convinced that she's a *lamia* up to no good, Kelvin shoots Hari #2 away in a rocket. But a Hari #3 soon appears out of nowhere, as in a Tex Avery Droopy cartoon. Each new Hari remembers the previous copy, and is capable of more advanced human reactions, as if Hari's psychological pattern were slowly emerging. Hari is a product of Kelvin's mind, yet not a phantom – when the first dupe is disposed of, he's left with an extra shawl and dress.

The other two scientists are dealing with their own phantoms, which they theorize might be manifestations of personal guilts that haunt them, like ghosts. Sartorius's visitor is briefly glimpsed as a dwarf. Perhaps the Ocean goofed in its first attempt at creating a human child.

Kelvin is confronted with the dilemma straight from *Vertigo*. He feels responsible for the original Hari's death, but murders her a second time when 'she' returns. Just as Scotty Ferguson fashioned a new Madeleine, Solaris gives Kelvin several chances to recreate his lost relationship. His conversion from calculating scientist to a simple seeker of truth and happiness is the film's most positive aspect.

(spoilers continue) As viewer-voyeurs, we're entranced by Hari, who would be welcome in any man's life whether she were real or not. Sartorius refuses to address Hari directly and tries to explain to Kelvin that he's sharing his bed with an illusion, essentially masturbating. The character of Hari is one of the better female roles in science fiction. She's a benign spirit and a breathing, loving woman who dies and is reborn. Her rebirth scene is simultaneously jarring and erotic at the same time, as we watch the frozen woman thaw back to life in a jerking, spasmodic frenzy. Kelvin warms to Hari and is willing to accept her for what she is, ignoring Snauth's warning that she'll cease to exist if he tries to take her back to Earth. But Hari #3 eventually recovers all of Hari #1's traits, including the original's disillusion and despair.

Solaris perhaps gathers a few too many authors' messages. There are allusions to *Don Quixote* when the Cosmonauts quote Cervantes on the subject of sleep. The Ocean, a communal mass of shared intelligence, is teaching itself to interrelate with us individualized humans. Some of the cosmonauts advocate blasting the Ocean with lethal X-Rays, just to see what the effect might be. The Ocean proves to be a far less destructive researcher.

Tarkovsky's production is short on gee-whiz effects but creates convincing, credible settings (although we wonder where the fresh fruit and flowers on the space station come from). After a few minutes, the sets undergo sublte changes, like something out of a Philip K. Dick book. Artifacts from Kelvin's Russian home show up, including a religious Icon accompanied by *Andrei Rublev*- like music. When Kelvin hallucinates, anything goes: a painting of the snow becomes confused with his memories. Old movies from home are projected on the ship's widescreen television, which glares down at the Cosmonauts like the haunted map of *I Bury the Living*.

The Russian actors playing scientists do a fine job of withholding key information. Just what does Snauth have hidden in his room – a giant toad? Brigitte Bardot? Donatas Banionis is soulful and sober as Kris, although we would feel better if he smiled just once or twice. Natalya Bondarchuk is completely compelling as a devoted zombie that evolves into a woman with a

full personality. Hari's male-oriented character arc is justified because she is a mental creation taken from Kelvin's brain.

The visuals in *Solaris* are better than adequate, even though the only spaceship depicted is the Solaris orbiting station. The views of the Ocean look like high-speed photography of swirling oils in a large pool. The ending of one Ocean shot includes the camera slowdown flash frames, an unnecessarily sloppy error.

To be sarcastic, *Solaris* is not what you'd call fast-paced. Scenes play out in uncut takes, often minutes in length. On Earth, Kelvin stares endlessly as underwater reeds sway like Hari's hair, mirroring the rhythms of the liquid surface of Solaris. We watch Kelvin sleep for more than a minute in one scene. The most noted (or

criticized) sequence is Berton's rainy drive back 'into town', a gratuitous scene represented by a series of lengthy shots taken on what looks like a Japanese freeway. Apparently Tarkovsky liked the tedium and puzzlement engendered by the sequence.

Criterion's DVD of **Solaris** maintains the company's high standards with an impeccable transfer of this Russian classic. Even the sometimes-irritating cuts to sepia and B&W are attractive.

The insert booklet contains an essay on the film and a reprint of an article written by Akira Kurosawa on his trip to Moscow to see Tarkovsky. A commentary by Tarkovsky authors Vida Johnson and Grahame Petrie points out dozens of production details and puzzling inconsistencies. Then there are interviews with key creatives and actress Natalya Bondarchuk. A too-brief excerpt from a Polish docu on Stanislaw Lem shows the author shoveling snow and griping about the film's liberties with his book. The gallery of deleted or altered scenes is somewhat confusing. It's hard to tell what the differences are in some of them; the only obvious one is a text opening that Tarkovsky deemed unnecessary.

1. Savant was at the Filmex premiere, albeit as an *usher* ... The audience was intrigued, yet frustrated by its poorly translated subtitles. After the birthday party scene, the screen went dark and the curtains closed, and the audience of 1800 puzzled sci-fi fans rose to leave – until a Filmex official ran down the aisle saying, "Come back, there's still another reel to go!" People laughed and the film resumed, but many chose to walk out at that point.

2. Sid Pink's *Journey to the 7th Planet* predates the publication of *Solaris* and plays like an infantile version of the same basic story. Astronauts on Uranus are confronted with landscapes that suddenly transform into idyllic imitations of the Danish countryside 'back home', complete with buxom Nordic women created from the Astronauts' own brain patterns. A glowing brain in a cave is the dream-weaving culprit. Critic Raymond Durgnat in *Films and Feelings* noted the un-cinematic graces of the 'turnip' *Seventh Planet*, with its brilliant central concept.

A BOY AND HIS DOG

First Run Reviewed: December 11, 2003
1975 / Color / 2:35 flat letterboxed / 91 min.
Cinematography John Arthur Morrill. Film Editor Scott Conrad. Music Tim McIntire, Jaime Mendoza-Nava. Written by L.Q. Jones from a story by Harlan Ellison. Produced by L.Q. Jones, Alvy Moore.
Directed by L.Q. Jones

There had been sober and not-so-sober post-apocalypse pictures by 1975, but none took on this independent show's cynical attitude. The survivalist-fatalist philosophy seen here would soon become the standard for a wave of movies depicting the nasty future after World War Three. Or Four.

A Boy and His Dog premiered at the 1975 Filmex Science Fiction Marathon and became the hit of the show. It could boast two things missing from most 70s sci-fi: the voice of a science fiction author with something to say, and, even more rare, a sense of humor.

2024. Vic (Don Johnson) and his dog Blood (voice: Tim McIntire) share the ability to communicate telepathically. They scavenge the desert wasteland eking out a violent living. Vic fights for food, and in return, Blood helps Vic locate females to rape. Blood wants to search for a less hostile place to live, but Vic is distracted by the beautiful Quilla June Holmes (Suzanne Benton). Quilla June wants Vic to join her in an underground Utopia of survivors, a new Topeka. Only problem: no dogs allowed.

A Boy and His Dog would be just another derivative rags 'n' shotguns post-nuke story if it weren't for the unique relationship between its human and canine heroes. The dialogue may have been rewritten, but the bickering exchanges between Don Johnson's somewhat thickheaded Vic and his intellectual mutt are pure Harlan Ellison. The disdainful, mocking Blood is practically the voice of the brilliant author with the short-fused temper. Blood constantly nags Vic about his relative stupidity, lack of perspective and one-track search for 'female companionship': i.e., female victims of any stripe to ravage.

The ugly premise is legitimized because *A Boy and His Dog* matches its apocalyptic theme with an appropriate warping of values. The earlier doomsday *Panic in Year Zero!* and *No Blade of Grass* films endlessly debate whether the threat of extinction excuses bending the polite rules of society regarding property rights and due process for criminals. The few audiences that saw Cornell Wilde's *No Blade* likely ignored its preachy ecological message, preferring to enjoy his world gone wild, where theft and murder were prerequisites for survival.

Ellison's story begins with that situation already firmly established. Vic is interested only in finding some canned peaches and his next female partner. Ironically, the dog is the repository of historical knowledge. If not for Blood, Vic would have long forgotten that there were two nuclear wars that put an end to the 'normal' world.

The talking Lassie joke is a boy-dog relationship unlike any other. Blood's psychic ability to scan for danger enables him to provide the gun-toting Vic with information needed to prevail in fights. In one scene Blood must wait while Vic makes love, and passes the time by sussing out the derivation of the word 'copulate'.

Vic engages in a series of savage skirmishes against competitors in the wasteland. They avoid the 'Screamers', ominous blue-glowing monsters (unseen) that are presumably some kind of post-nuke mutation. Then a girl enters the picture. Comely Suzanne Benton's corn-fed princess causes Vic to risk his symbiotic partnership with Blood. He follows her into a legendary underground world of supposed luxury: Topeka.

Topeka turns out to be a trap. An authoritarian troika called The Committee (Alvy Moore, Helene Winston and Jason Robards) maintains a strict retro society modeled to imitate pre-industrial Middle America. The girls wear schoolmarm clothing and curtsey, etc. The underground world is played for broad satire. Vic's dream of performing super-stud duty for an entire race of women goes sour when The Committee's robots hook him up to a mechanical semen-extracting machine. The episode would be in extreme bad taste if it weren't such a logical part of the story.

Quilla June hopes Vic will use his guns to stage a revolution, but all he wants is to return to the surface and resume his nomadic lifestyle. Again, the underplayed cynical ending is too central to the theme to be a cheap twist. It carries the bond between Vic and Blood to a logical end that in 1975 was a little bit beyond public expectations. Ten years later, the same finale was used for the (more glamorous) *Prizzi's Honor*, where it was hailed as sophisticated black comedy.

Director L.Q. Jones is an actor best known for his Sam Peckinpah westerns, often playing scavenger outlaws similar to this film's Vic. The Mojave Desert locations are dressed mostly with random junk and a few key props. The perpetually dark underground society is achieved via night exteriors in ordinary, sterile-looking modern buildings. The costuming in Topeka is a little severe, but the dozen farm girls dressed in wedding gowns make for a strangely disturbing image.

Blood's handlers do a superb job making the trained animal appear to be communicating with Vic. Some of the dialogue must have been tailored to the shots, as when Blood speaks, walks a few steps, speaks again, and so forth. We accept the Dr. Doolittle situation faster than you can say *Francis the Talking Mule*.

Don Johnson was at the time known as the star of rather cheesy exploitation pictures like *The Harrad Experiment* and *The Magic Garden of Stanley Sweetheart,* a fact that makes Vic's ambition to be a big stud seem a critique of his previous filmography. It's tempting to think that Jason Robards came to this show through Sam Peckinpah, but L.Q. Jones was a well-connected actor before his association with his definitive director. The no-nonsense casting extends to stalwart Charles McGraw as a preacher in the underground world.

First Run Features' DVD of **A Boy and His Dog** is an unspectacular flat letterboxed transfer of a clean print given only a so-so encoding. This minor classic deserved better. The DVD includes two trailers, a stylistic rip-off of the trailer for

A Clockwork Orange and a more conventional montage with a barrage of drooling critical accolades. Both exhibit superior marketing savvy.

L.Q. Jones, cameraman John Morrill and critic Charles Champlin provide a lively commentary. The talkative Jones exaggerates wildly, claiming that 500 auditions were made for Blood's voice, that the dog was almost nominated for an Oscar, etc..

David Bowie
The man who fell to Earth

THE MAN WHO FELL TO EARTH

Criterion Blu-ray Reviewed: January 9, 2008
1976 / Color / 2:35 / **140** 119 min.
Cinematography Anthony B. Richmond.
Production Designer Brian Eatwell. Film
Editor Graeme Clifford. Music John Phillips,
Stomu Yamashta. Written by Paul Mayersberg
from the novel by Walter Tevis. Produced by
Michael Deeley, Si Litvinoff, Barry Spikings.
Directed by Nicolas Roeg

The year before *Star Wars*, a science fiction movie appeared that appealed to an entirely different kind of audience. Made from the thinnest
of sci-fi premises, *The Man Who Fell to Earth*
is the kind of mysterious cinematic collage we
expect from director Nicolas Roeg. The sensual
story of a stranger in a strange land carries a big
appeal for lovers of artsy puzzle pictures.

Thomas Jerome Newton (David Bowie) falls from
the sky in New Mexico. He has a British passport,
thousands in cash and a fistful of gold rings to
barter. He's soon presenting New York lawyer
Oliver Farnsworth (Buck Henry) with the opportunity to develop nine separate basic patents.
Farnsworth quickly develops Newton's futuristic
knowledge into a corporate empire. The reclusive
alien takes to the New Mexico back roads, gathering up a lover, Mary-Lou (Candy Clark) along
the way. Newton doesn't reveal that his purpose
is a mission of life and death for his home planet.
Far across space, the lonely voyager's wife and
children are slowly dying, waiting for him to return with needed water.

Poor Thom Newton hasn't an extraterrestrial's
chance in Area 51 – no sooner does he alight on
our planet than a shop owner cheats him by un-
derpaying for a solid gold ring.

The Man Who Fell to Earth is a frustrating, fascinating mystery. In his first film role, cadaver-
ous David Bowie is a natural alien. His amphi-
sexual looks, feathered red hair and soft British
voice go far to persuade us that he is indeed
from outer space. Although a number of fantastic events occur, most are from Newton's weird
POV – his eyes can apparently see into the past
and across the vastness of space. We don't have
to take Newton at his word that he's from beyond the stars, because he eventually does reveal himself in his earless, genital-challenged
alien form. [1]

The film quickly reveals its unconventional
aims. The only space gadgetry on view is seen
in a wishful-thinking daydream sequence. And
the actual 'plot' makes little effort to flesh out
Newton's abortive space mission. Newton isn't
a lost *E.T.* who wants to phone home; he's a
post-modern Baron Munchausen who never
ages, watching the rest of the cast grow old
around him.

The liner notes of an earlier Anchor Bay disc

pointed out that any civilization that can transport a man across the universe faster than the speed of light should be able to derive water from hydrogen one way or another. Newton comes well-equipped to start a gigantic corporation, but his alien comrades give him no way to get back, other than by encouraging Earth scientists to invent a vehicle for him. Why doesn't he just hand over the blueprints for whatever device projected him to Earth in the first place?

Obviously, Paul Mayersberg's trippy screenplay is concerned with themes of a more ethereal nature. Newton is literally alienated, but he also experiences a profound need for companionship and forms several very human bonds. Alas, the more human he becomes, the more faulty becomes his judgment. By foolishly revealing his identity to the hearty but corrupt Nathan Bryce (Rip Torn, again playing Judas as he did in *King of Kings*), Newton surrenders all hope for his mission.

Newton eventually finds himself checkmated by institutions that even Klaatu and Gort would have a hard time besting. Oliver Farnsworth is a reliable choice to run Newton's businesses but the corporate competition that muscles in on Newton's World Enterprises is a boardroom version of Murder, Incorporated. In the (paranoid) real world, persistent buyers urge resistant sellers to "take the wider view", employing the same methodology used by big nations to impose their will on smaller ones – polite inquiry, followed by brute force.

The Man Who Fell to Earth lets the conspiracies fester in the background while Newton, unaccustomed to a sensual existence, flounders in his awkward relationship with Mary-Lou. Newton's skewed perceptions require watching a dozen televisions at the same time, a situation that gives poor Mary-Lou grief. All that video enables editor Graeme Clifford to weave bizarre montages, which are not always inspired – Mary-Lou and Nathan Bryce's discussion about betraying Newton is inter-cut with parallel material from the conclusion of *The Third Man*.

Most of the classical science fiction elements in Mayersberg's script are used as borderline irrelevant background material. As in *This Island Earth*, ultra-advanced aliens arrive and then unaccountably expect humans to "do the science" for them. Like the alien of *The Man from Planet X*, Newton is captured and destroyed by men more concerned with profit than study or communication. *The Man Who Fell to Earth* is best when it expresses interior states, when it visualizes Newton's cosmic despair. Thomas Jerome Newton behaves more like Howard Hughes than a monster from outer space. When the powers that be decide to study him like a lab animal, they don't give a damn that he's from outer space. His enormously profitable companies have upset too many established monopolies.

Nicolas Roeg is one of the more successful directors at using the 70s freedom of the screen to present sexual behavior. Much of the show's R-rated content was cut from the film's first American release, and there's plenty of full-frontal, full dorsal, and full-on-everything nudity. Yet even when it goes far beyond what the MPAA (or most actors) would now permit, none of it seems exploitative. Rip Torn's dalliances with a series of interchangeable college girls play as if the actor repeated the same script pages with several actresses just for the extra fun to be had. Bowie and Clark's bedroom abandon goes beyond anything in a David Lynch film. Even Bernie Casey's corporate villain is given a sensual scene with a loving wife (Claudia Jennings). Director Roeg can ask his actors to disrobe without making all involved look foolish.

First-time viewers may be thrown for a loop by the editing, which makes use of the time-slip fragmentation tricks of earlier Roeg collaborations *Petulia* and *Don't Look Now*. Combine

Newton's strange sense perceptions of what's happening back on his home planet with a time logic that leaps about at will, and linear-minded people will quickly throw in the towel. At one point, Newton's limo suddenly leaps back 100 years for a brief and bewildering encounter with a pioneer family. The scene seems to be a completely gratuitous throwaway.

Just as Newton's plans crumble we're suddenly given an imagined vision of success. Newton prepares to board his completed spaceship for the return flight, accepting the congratulations of a jubilant mob that includes the real Jim Lovell from Apollo 13! Instead of being gratuitous the scene provides an emotional cliff from which Newton's hopes can plunge, Icarus-like: yet another of Mayersberg's long list of classical references.

Viewers expecting the tinsel & Plexiglas eye candy offered by the same year's dismal *Logan's Run* may be sorely disappointed. Newton's home planet is pictured as an ordinary desert. The aliens wear tight plastic suits with water piped through tubes that remind us of aquarium accessories. Just as space travel is pictured with stock shots and flashes of light, the hardcore sci-fi content here is merely representational. The only one of Newton's nine patents pictured is his instant camera, which seems an improved Polaroid. Instead of throwing inadequate resources at slick realism, as in *Zardoz*, *The Man Who Fell to Earth* stays in virgin minimalist territory, hewing closer to the poetic artificiality of Godard's *Alphaville*.

Thomas Jerome Newton ends up much like Henri Dickson in *Alphaville*, a psychic burnout forced to abandon his mission ages ago. But Mayerberg's Newton will never age, and is doomed to linger in a dissipated stupor for all eternity, like the man who can never die in *The Asphyx*. Newton's betrayer has no guilt, and Newton is not bitter, even though he will never again make contact with his home planet. Earth

becomes a strange purgatory for an ultra-chic rock star in a camel's hair coat and black fedora.

Criterion's Blu-ray of **The Man Who Fell to Earth** upgrades a two-disc DVD set that came packed in a fancy box with a reprint of Walter Tevis' original novel. The extras are retained but the book is not. The beautifully mastered feature looks extraordinary, especially the razor-sharp New Mexico locations. The audio track (2.0 stereo) recreates the film's sophisticated sound mix. Buck Henry and David Bowie join Nicolas Roeg on a wide-ranging audio commentary. The director makes a solid effort at communicating his directorial aims and methods.

Interesting interview featurettes dominate. Screenwriter Paul Mayersberg is precise in what he wants to convey, a quality that Candy Clark and Rip Torn could use a bit more of. Audio interviews with the production and costume designers are included, as is an archival radio interview with author Walter Tevis (*The Hustler*). He and Mayersberg draw apt parallels between the two stories. William Shatner narrates one of several UK and US trailers and teasers.

1. A limey from space? It makes perfect sense, as Michael Rennie proved without a doubt in *The Day the Earth Stood Still*. Newton is a sort of Son of Klaatu, and shares with him an unusual interest in trains. He should have brought Gort along as backup.

CLOSE ENCOUNTERS OF THE THIRD KIND

Sony Blu-ray Reviewed: December 8, 2007
1977 / Color / 2:35 / 135, 132, 137 min.
Cinematography Vilmos Zsigmond.
Production Designer Joe Alves. Film Editor
Michael Kahn. Original Music John Williams.
Produced by Julia Phillips and Michael
Phillips.
Written and Directed by Steven Spielberg

Close Encounters of the Third Kind was Steven Spielberg's first personally initiated blockbuster hit. He allowed free rein to his childhood interest in all things wondrous, reinventing the flying saucer invasion movie as a visitation by enlightened beings. If movies about people from space are really about us, Spielberg's aliens reflect the spirit of Man at his most benign.

An international team of UFO experts struggles to connect with extra-terrestrials that are contacting groups and individuals all over the world, communicating in musical tones and implanting psychic suggestions as to the location of their imminent rendezvous with mankind. French scientist Claude Lacombe (Francois Truffaut) prepares a secret group of volunteers for 'The Mayflower Project', a human/alien exchange program. But he becomes aware that the aliens are conducting a volunteer project of their own, mentally impregnating sensitive individuals the world over with the impetus to seek out a curiously shaped mountain. One of these contactees is Jillian Guiler (Melinda Dillon), an artist whose son Barry (Cary Guffey) has been abducted by the lights in the sky. Roy Neary (Richard Dreyfuss) is a Johnny Paycheck who throws wife and family aside in a mad quest to find out what his personal close encounters mean. It all ends in a cross-country race to Devil's Tower, Wyoming. Lacombe's interpreter David Laughlin (Bob Balaban) has discovered that the location will be ground zero for the biggest event in human history.

Savant has a special lump in his throat for *CE3K*, a movie that turned out to be a classic. What seemed during production to be a lopsided, over-ambitious remake of *Earth vs the Flying Saucers* became a cultural event that made UFOs credible and aliens benign. It also marked the height of Spielberg's first wave of directorial achievement, establishing his visual strengths and signature effects: the unabashedly manipulative use of music and his transcendent camera moves into the awestruck faces of cosmic converts. The *Collector's Edition's* extras cover all the known bases: I'll try instead to relate some personal perspectives on the show.

This new 3-Disc set presents all three *Close Encounters* versions (1977, 1980, 1997) separately, allowing us to choose a preferred cut. The differences are a little more complicated than just choosing whether or not to see inside the giant alien mothership.

CE3K was scheduled to come out much earlier but was pushed back several times to allow its special effects to be finished. Steven Spielberg says he was forced to finish *Close Encounters* in a rush, and that the 1980 *Special Edition* with its expensive re-shoots was his chance to 'fix' the film. The big compromise for the *Special Edition* is the scene of the Mothership interior. Misled by focus groups wanting to see where Roy Neary goes when he enters the giant alien black box, Columbia unwisely decided to address the issue in the re-do. The *Special Edition* honors only the letter of the request, taking Neary about twenty feet further into the ship and putting on a glittery light show.

The tendency toward literal thinking happens whenever abstract ideas hit the committee rooms. Disney's fiasco *The Black Hole* fizzles when the amazing dimension beyond the title vortex turns out to be an image from a Sunday school rendering of Hell. Three years later *Brainstorm* fell into the exact same trap when it pictured the Great Beyond as a greeting-card vision of Heavenly Angels. *The Special Edition* cuts from Richard Dreyfuss being showered with Tinkerbell dust in the mothership interior, to a new-type alien emerging from the ship and communicating with François Truffaut. I always thought that the shot order inadvertently implied that the alien *is* Neary, transformed by the pixie dust!

The 1977 *Original Theatrical Version* differs in more important ways. Roy Neary clearly screws up at work, going AWOL and proving himself undeserving of the trust put in him by his superiors. In the later versions Spielberg abridged several early Neary scenes, substituting the effective 'shower breakdown' moment.

After screenings in 1977 I remember complaints that Neary's arts 'n' crafts madness, throwing things in his window and chasing geese around the neighborhood (fluttering birds = madness) was too long. Spielberg must have thought so too because he cut most of it. The original version is the only one that fully addresses the tension between Neary, the helpless victim of alien brainwashing, and Neary the irresponsible dope. When Neary goes on his cross-country quest, he's already been reduced to a total loser in the grip of an infantile obsession – an insecurity that science-fiction addicts surely identify with.

Spielberg tailored *The Special Edition* to audiences that had already seen the first version. The director re-shot a number of small effects moments, making previously subtle hints grindingly obvious. Before we get a good look at the flying saucers, the first version showed a single star shadowing Neary's truck. In the revision, the star is replaced by the giant shadow of a large flying saucer, literalizing what Neary is up against and undercutting the suspense. The other changes are all details, like the cute dialogue of the hillbilly-ish Roberts Blossom. The one I really miss is the bit where National Guardsman Carl Weathers advises Neary, *"We got orders to shoot looters, Smith."* It's important to establish that Neary is going out on a limb when he defies the mass evacuation.

Of the other new material, the really successful scene is the discovery of the Cotopaxi ship found aground but intact in the middle of the Gobi Desert. It's the mystery that kicks Monsieur Lacombe's investigation into high gear, the kind of jaw-dropper that would convince the Washington bean counters to approve massive funding for Lacombe's Devil's Tower base camp. But we can see that in the space between the first release and the *Special Edition* Spielberg's directing taste has already altered. The Cotopaxi sequence begins with a flurry of unnecessarily hyped action shots. Large vehicles vault over sand dunes *Rat Patrol* -style and helicopters inexplicably hug the ground and *follow* the trucks. This comic book sensibility is way out of line with the rest of the film.

Douglas Trumbull's company Future General produced the film's effects in 65mm. A clever plan to blow up the 35mm feature footage and mate it with the effects in the larger format was abandoned in the rush to complete the film. All of the 65mm effects were taken to MGM and reduction-printed to 35mm, and then RE-EN-LARGED to 70mm with the rest of the show, a process that sounds ridiculous, but at least made the footage match better. Unfortunately, all those hero 65mm final effect take negatives have since disappeared, making the new special editions of *CE3K* an editorial nightmare for Columbia.

In the grandeur of 70mm, *CE3K* was one impressive picture. Crowds exited the theater in a daze, always with a few claiming they'd seen God. Spielberg had out-Disney'd Disney. Just as Universal had engineered word of mouth that made 1975 a banner year for shark attacks, 1977 saw a rash of flying saucer sightings that Savant thinks must have been snowballed by *CE3K's* publicity brains. Even President Carter copped to having seen a UFO. *Time* lost all credibility but sold a pile of magazines with a full color cover of the Mothership and the words "The UFOs Are Here!"

Close Encounters still carries an emotional kick. Spielberg has the miracle of little Cary Guffey behind his sentimental scenes. Roy Neary is an undistinguished man who throws his life away to run happily into some abstract kind of eternity. The fact that the aliens have hypno-suggested Neary's erratic behavior doesn't mean that they're completely responsible for breaking up his family. As in Nicholas Ray's *Bigger Than Life,* the childlike Neary is simply following his true character. Neary's rush to 'become one with the universe' is an ultimate

escape from the responsibility of mundane human problems.

The *Close Encounters of the Third Kind 30th Anniversary Ultimate Edition* is an impressive disc set. The movies are on separate discs. The 1977 version is a thing of beauty with accurate color values and good detail: I wish that George Lucas would treat his *Star Wars* originals with equal respect. Each disc has closed captioning and subs in seven languages. Tracks are in Dolby Digital in English, French and Spanish; and in English in DTS.

A long 1997 making of docu by Laurent Bouzereau is still the last word on the film, with great interview input from practically everyone who worked on it. A smartly designed chart plots the differences between the three *Close Encounters* versions.

Spielberg returns with more perspective and analysis in a new interview featurette. He explains that after facing darker aspects of the world while raising his family, *Close Encounters* no longer reflects his personal philosophy. The movie remains an ambitious, audacious and *worthwhile* epic – how many science fiction films make us feel this good?

STAR TREK: THE MOTION PICTURE

Paramount Blu-ray Reviewed: November 16, 2001
1979 / Color / 2:35 / **136** 132 min.
Cinematography Richard H. Kline. Editor
Todd Ramsay. Music Jerry Goldsmith, Gerald
Fried. Writing credits Harold Livingston.
Produced by Gene Roddenberry.
Directed by Robert Wise

Star Wars made big-time Hollywood do a flip-flop. Formerly obscure special effects techniques became the toast of the town. The so-called wizards that jump-started George Lucas' space epic were suddenly in hot demand, because everyone wanted to do space movies and crummy standard effects would no longer do.

Paramount had pettifogged for a decade, unsure whether their *Star Trek* television series merited a big screen revival. Complicating the issue were the original actors from the show, all industry veterans who had been scraping around the periphery of fame and fortune for decades, and who weren't about to let their services go for a pittance. The studio snared famed director Robert Wise, hired all the originals, and then proceeded to take their franchise effort into one of the most expensive post-productions in Hollywood history.

The DVD revival of *Star Trek: The Motion Picture* as "The Director's Edition" reworks a number of effects scenes, some that were skipped in the panic to finish, and others that the new producers have deemed 'not good enough'.

A colossal cloud of space gas threatens Earth, and the necessity of stopping it allows a determined Captain Kirk (William Shatner) to retake command of a newly refurbished Enterprise. This irks the ship's Captain Willard Decker (Stephen Collins), but once old pals Doc McCoy (DeForest Kelley) and Spock (Leonard Nimoy) rejoin the trek, things perk up. Communications with the menace are impossible until the cloud disintegrates the Enterprise's Lieutenant Ilia (Persis Khambatta) and replaces her with a robot simulacrum. It seems something called V'ger is at the center of the cloud, and is looking for its creator on Earth. Desperate, Kirk enlists Decker's assistance to make an emotional connection with the 'false' Ilia, who may still retain the memories of the human original. Ilia is the only hope for communicating with V'ger, whose stated intention is to rid Earth of its infestation of 'carbon units'.

Star Trek: The Motion Picture was an enormously popular hit, mainly because the fan base for the franchise turned out to be bigger than anyone's estimates. The happy turn of events allowed Paramount to continue a series of films, learning some lessons in economy and common sense along the way. Overlong, bloated and unexciting, this first Trek movie has a dull script that gives its lively and beloved television regulars little to do except react to overblown and repetitive effects. That said, Trek fans will find enough here to hold their interest.

The show gets off to a good start with a socko John Dykstra sequence in which V'ger evaporates a trio of Klingon cruisers. Then comes the rush to launch an unfinished Enterprise Mark II, with some variable-quality matte paintings of San Francisco. A rather grotesque transporter accident obliterates a new science officer, creating the need to spring Spock from retirement and allowing us to witness some ponderous views of a ritual in a weird valley on the planet Vulcan. The new Enterprise is introduced in a long, reverently scored series of slow approach shots, waiting in its orbiting dry dock. Everything is pageantry, with far too much awe and no sense of humor. The one real laugh is supplied by Doc McCoy when he tells Spock that the ship "just happened to be going his way". The series would later abuse this cozy over-familiarity with the characters, but *Star Trek: The Motion Picture* could do with more of it.

The story revolves not around our regulars, but Ilia and Decker's cosmic romance. It begins as a problem relationship, as Ilia has taken a vow of celibacy. All turns out okay when, to be eternally with his love, Decker proves quite willing to give up his human form and become a noncorporeal set of atoms.

Star Trek: The Motion Picture cribs ideas from *2001* (the Star Child & species evolution) and shoehorns them into the original series' philosophies of human passions vs. cold computers, etc. Unfortunately, all of this is represented quite literally on the screen, first in dead-serious speeches, and then through the Ilia / Ilia V'ger Probe character. Not that there's a solution to the problem, but having Ilia talk in an emotionless monotone imitation of a computer voice is a cliché that has dragged down science fiction movies since time began. When Ilia calls

human beings 'carbon units' she might as well be one of the Coneheads on *Saturday Night Live*.

V'ger itself is nothing more than the 'enormous Space Wedgie' gag from the most memorable radio parody of the original Trek series. The proceedings bog down constantly. The big revelation about V'ger's true identity is a word game straight from *Zardoz*. The climactic merging of Ilia/Decker into a new dimension does have an emotional effect, but as our regulars are not directly involved, it leaves them standing around with nothing much to say. This first *Trek* movie is indeed an elaboration on a television idea; the later films would more wisely develop the series' real strength, its beloved characters.

This new DVD incarnation is yet another revision of an older movie to improve its effects scenes. Updating some of the visuals doesn't alter the fact that their conception was never very interesting in the first place. Most are from the 'awesome vista' school of boredom, stuff that used to work well when Bernard Herrmann's music was behind it. Investigating V'ger originally took forever, with a tendency for symmetrical forward-tracking shots along the surface of the giant space object (a *Rendezvous with Rama* rip-off if ever there was one) that made it seem as if Douglas Trumbull thought only in terms of Kubrickian compositions and variations on the Star Gate sequence from *2001: A Space Odyssey*.

The documentaries on this special edition disc leave out elements of the production story that were the talk of Hollywood in 1979. Media Genius Bob Abel was originally tapped to do the special effects. After several months of R&D his company was dumped in favor of Doug Trumbull, who reassembled the team from *Close Encounters*. John Dykstra, who had put together the first Industrial Light and Magic for *Star Wars*, took on a number of sequences with his new company, Apogee. Facing a hard release date, Paramount threw huge amounts of money at *Star Trek's* complicated special effects.

Dozens of already top-salaried experts worked practically around the clock for months.

When the series moved on, the lessons of this first effort were certainly taken to heart – nearly every complaint mentioned above was rectified three years later in *Star Trek: The Wrath of Khan*. To leave on a positive note, something that can't be faulted is Jerry Goldsmith's inspiring score, especially when it introduces the new Enterprise.

Paramount's DVD of *Star Trek: The Motion Picture* throws in everything but the kitchen sink. A commentary gathers Robert Wise, Douglas Trumbull, John Dykstra, Jerry Goldsmith and Stephen Collins.

Three separate documentaries give franchise-friendly accounts of the filming. *Redirecting The Future* shows how some of the movie's effects were redone using digital animation. The result is that the original *The Motion Picture* will be obscured. Yes, there were a lot of explosions and composites (and particularly matte paintings) that weren't all that great in the original. But they were original, and these are not. Will a 2021 revision redo all the effects over again? Using this logic, why not replace the fake airplane models in *Casablanca* or erase the visible wires in *War of the Worlds?*

A voluminous set of unused scenes is offered. *Star Trek: The Motion Picture, The Director's Edition* is heavily billed as being the studio's generous effort to allow Robert Wise to finally finish the movie the way he wanted it finished. When will Hollywood realize that such a casual attitude toward revisionism reveals that they don't value their movies for any purpose but cash flow?

LA MORT EN DIRECT (DEATHWATCH)

BLADE RUNNER
Warners Blu-ray Reviewed December 9, 2007
1981 / Color / 2:35 / 117 min.
Cinematography Jordan Cronenweth,
Production Design Lawrence G. Paull, Written by Hampton Fancher, David Webb Peoples from a novel by Philip K. Dick, Produced by Michael Deeley.
Directed by Ridley Scott

Blade Runner wasn't a success at first, and disappointed Harrison Ford fans knew why. Unlike Indiana Jones, the humorless future detective Rick Deckard spends the entire movie looking down in the mouth. Perhaps to compensate for the lifeless hero, someone added poorly written tough-guy voiceovers. The film's Dystopian future displays Film Noir stylistics, but Harrison Ford is no Philip Marlowe. The sci-fi ground rules are established through a glut of expository dialogue, with Ford and the cops discussing topics they should already be familiar with. Although the film touches on fascinating sci-fi concepts, the story boils down to a series of pursuits and shoot-outs in the rainy streets of a futuristic Los Angeles. Ridley Scott's commitment to textures and surfaces epitomizes the eighties' triumph of style over content: a simplified storyline backed by terrific visual thrills.

The film's reputation grew steadily in the decade that followed. Interest in author Philip K. Dick increased, and it was rumored that the theatrical version had been compromised by the studio marketers. After a number of years pan-scanned on VHS and cable, *Blade Runner* was one of the first discs to be released on widescreen laserdisc. Then in 1990, lightning struck. A couple of theaters in San Francisco and Los Angeles (the Fairfax) capable of running 70mm screened a series of forgotten Road Show prints from the studio vaults. Many of these Road Show cuts were different than the final 35mm versions, making it thrilling to see something like *In Harm's Way* with an intermission, and maybe even an extra scene. When the series organizers projected Warners' vault copy of *Blade Runner* the audience went nuts. The 70mm print was a one-of-a-kind preview version of the film before the studio's final changes. It had only a few hardboiled voiceovers and skipped the happy ending altogether.

Since then the film has twice been restored in a 'director's cut', with Ridley Scott (or his designated editors) being allowed to rework scenes and in some cases add new material. This release's new *The Final Cut* has been a 'stop & go' project for more than ten years.

> Police supervisor Bryant (M. Emmet Walsh) coerces ex-policeman Rick Deckard (Harrison Ford) back to work. The exploitation of alien worlds has been made possible by the production of 'replicants', genetic-synthetic workers

difficult to distinguish from humans. They're used as slaves and soldiers and are forbidden to come to Earth; when they do, 'blade runners' like Deckard are dispatched to kill them. Bryant has determined that four dangerous replicants are at large in Los Angeles. One (Brion James) has already killed a man during a test with a replicant-detecting device called a Voight-Kampf machine. Deckard interviews replicant manufacturer Eldon Tyrell (Joe Turkel) and discovers a good reason for the revolt: replicants have a built-in life span of only four years. The fugitive leader Roy Batty (Rutger Hauer) leaves a trail of corpses in his search for a genetic technician who can 'give him more life.' Meanwhile, Deckard falls in love with Tyrell's beautiful secretary Rachael (Sean Young), who sympathizes with the doomed replicants.

Just as his *Alien* transformed a deep space freighter into a new kind of haunted house, the visually oriented Ridley Scott creates in *Blade Runner* a compellingly tactile portrait of a 'used future'. Los Angeles in 2019 is a rainy mess of the trendy new and the crumbling old. Genetic labs share kiosk space with fast food sushi. New-age cops in flying squad cars police multilingual streets where English speakers are in the minority. Huge animated billboards play music and advertising pitches over public address systems. Giant advertising blimps float above, promising a new future for unhappy city dwellers in the glorious off-world colonies.

These details are hints to themes in other Philip K. Dick stories, several of which involve an overpopulated future in which excess 'human resources' are cajoled into emigrating to miserable hovels on far-off planets. Nobody can expect a two-hour film to fully embrace Philip K. Dick, and *Blade Runner* only skims the surface of the author's mind-altering concepts. Simply by taking itself seriously, the film has gathered an intensely loyal following.

Blade Runner certainly looks good. Its best material is not the detective story, which tries too hard for a neo-noir angst. To cozy up to Joanna Cassidy's snake dancer, Deckard badly replays the bookstore scene from *The Big Sleep*. Better than the predictable chases and violence are a few choice moments that exploit new ideas. We learn that 2019 photographs can be put in a viewer that allows us to 'enter' the space in the photo and look in different directions. The film's most affecting scenes present the quiet, sad realization that one of the main characters is a replicant and doesn't know it. Replicants are cruelly implanted with fake childhood memories that give them an illusion of the human experience.

The film's quiet passages are a meditation on the meaning of personal identity. Nobody talks about God but the revelation that one is a synthetic 'thing' is a fall from grace comparable to Adam and Eve being expelled from Eden. By most measures the replicants are superior to living humans. They're stronger and more durable – replicant Leon can stick his hand in liquid oxygen without ill effects. The abusive treatment of replicants reads as species jealousy – 'racism' pure and simple.

Tycoon Eldon Tyrell lives high above the squalor in an Olympian pyramid. Roy Batty's visit is a clear case of Frankenstein meeting His Monster. Batty appeals for fatherly protection but Tyrell sees his creation only as an expression of his pride – and something to suppress. For *Star Wars* fans unaware that sci-fi can transcend spaceships and monsters, *Blade Runner* is an introduction to the possibilities of speculative fiction. For fans already attuned to such things, the film just scratches the surface. [1]

Seen 25 years later *Blade Runner* is a visual marvel, with the top effects wizards of its day working in support of superior art direction. Harrison Ford may not be perfect for his role but the players around him are consistently interesting. Joe Turkel is a lonely industrial Demigod. Rutger Hauer does indeed suggest an unhappy soldier back to ask for a new life. It's touching when Roy proves to be more than just a killer. Edward James Olmos maintains an impenetrable 'cool' throughout, and the other players are effective in even sketchier parts. Daryl Hannah's flaky concubine android Pris airbrushes paint onto her closed eyes, an intimate, disturbing touch. Joanna Cassidy's replicant Amazon has only one scene but makes a lasting impression. A substantial part of Sean Young's performance is provided by a killer hairstyle and exaggerated Joan Crawford shoulder pads. Ridley Scott imposes his elaborate patterns of stylization on the characters too – especially the women.

In Young's case we learn that Rachael is 'shallow' for a definite reason. Rutger Hauer may be a replicant, but he's the most soulful person we see. The idea persists that Rick Deckard might unknowingly be a replicant as well, a notion deliberately salted with a few narrative hints and unconsciously encouraged by Harrison Ford's dispassionate performance. Curiously, even the movie's main artistic contributors are in conflict on this question – some claim it was wholly intentional but one of the screenwriters insists that any such interpretation ruins the film's concept!

All the above will be but quibbling to the legions of devout *Blade Runner* fans. Warner Home Video's offerings include packages in DVD and Blu-Ray. The new transfer replicates (hmm...) the dark, rich look of the original theatrical experience. People indifferent to sci-fi concepts will be entertained just by the clouds of cigarette smoke artfully obscuring Sean Young's all-too-perfect face.

The Final Cut Two-Disc Special Edition is the basic item. It has The Final Cut with three commentary tracks: Ridley Scott alone, one with the writers and producers and a third with the film's art directors, designers and special effects people. Some scenes are extended while some dialogue has been changed. A few special effects shots have been improved, and we're told a couple of them are new. The second disc contains *Dangerous Days*, an exhaustive docu that considers *Blade Runner* the culmination of 20th century culture.

But wait, there's more! The *Blade Runner 4-Disc Collector's Edition* packs two more discs with additional material. Disc three contains three separate film versions. The 1982 *Theatrical Cut* allows one to assess the original's happy ending and added voiceovers. As is to be expected with any film in multiple versions, many viewers prefer this cut and love Deckard's stilted noir speeches. The 1982 *International Cut* is a slightly longer unrated version with a bit more violence; it's what appeared on cable and later home video releases. The 1992 *Director's Cut* is Ridley Scott's first crack at a renovation initiated by the wave of publicity that followed the 70mm preview cut screening. *Blade Runner* was swept up in the brief flurry of major restorations that followed *Lawrence of Arabia* and *Spartacus*. New opportunities for home video revenue made possible the notion of reworking a ten year-old picture that hadn't turned a profit.

Disc Four is called the *Enhancement Archive*. It carries a long list of featurettes on and about the film's designs and fashions, cameraman Jordan Cronenweth and even the poster art. Philip K. Dick is covered with three extras, including Paul Sammon's audio interviews. The controversy of whether Deckard is organic or plastic is addressed as well. The Archive also contains screen tests, the expected trailers, teasers and TV spots and a big stack of deleted and alternate scenes. We also see an alternate title sequence.

After all that, the pricey *Ultimate Collector's Edition* has yet another hook to lure the Blade

Runner completist. It comes in oversized packaging resembling Deckard's briefcase, with a lenticular film clip, an origami unicorn, a toy spinner flying car, stills and a note from Ridley Scott. The *Ultimate Edition's* fifth disc contains a transfer of a work print (the old preview cut) that amounts to yet another distinct version of the film. The work print has been tweaked in transfer but is still fairly ugly compared to the restored versions. It comes with a commentary track by author Paul Sammon, an intro by director Scott and a featurette called *All Our Variant Features*. The producer of The Final Cut relates its long, interrupted gestation period and shows how new digital effects were used to alter scenes. Joanna Cassidy returned to help replace a stunt double's face with her own for the big gun-down scene. Harrison Ford's son serves as a 'mouth double' to correct some of his father's wildly out-of-sync dialogue. In contrast to the effects revision job on *Star Trek: The Motion Picture*, the new material is nigh invisible. Some continuity mistakes were corrected and others retained as 'desired flaws' from the original filming process.

1. *Do Androids Dream of Electric Sheep?* was reportedly written in 1966, although Philip K. Dick probably worked with the same concepts much earlier. The truly groundbreaking *film* on the subject of synthetic humans and the robotic future is Jay Simms' 1962 *The Creation of the Humanoids*.

VIDEODROME

Criterion Blu-ray Reviewed: August 26, 2004
1983 / Color / 1:85 / **89**, 87 min.
Cinematography Mark Irwin. Art Direction
Carol Spier. Original Music Howard Shore.
Produced by Pierre David, Claude Héroux,
Victor Solnicki.
Written and Directed by David Cronenberg

In *Videodrome* director David Cronenberg hit
his pace as a purveyor of bizarre intellectual
concepts. The film presents the movies' first
fully realized virtual reality world, and accompanies it with more dangerous ideas than had
ever seen major distribution: insidious technology, underground video, porn, violence, sado-
masochism and snuff movies.

They're all in the service of a film concept that
in its maturity is light-years ahead of the com-

petition. Readers of fare like Philip K. Dick's
The Three Stigmata of Palmer Eldritch possibly
felt right at home, but most of the 'normal' 1983
audience was lost, lost, lost.

Soft-core cable entrepreneur Max Renn (James
Woods) is hot for new programming content
when he taps into an illegal satellite transmis-
sion of an all-torture, all-murder TV signal called
Videodrome. Max dispatches porn agent Masha
(Lynne Gorman) to find it for his cable channel,
and follows the trail to Bianca O'Blivion (Son-
ja Smits), the daughter of cult video visionary
Brian O'Blivion (Jack Creley). The techno-guru
exists only on videotape, dispensing weird wisdom about a future in which people will physically merge with the virtual video world. Max
also becomes attracted to radio psychologist
Nicki Brand (Deborah Harry), a sensationalist
who introduces him to mild S&M. When Nicki
finds out about Videodrome, her response is to
immediately seek out the video horrorshow – to
become a 'contestant'.

David Cronenberg's films before *Videodrome*
were a string of exploitative shockers with
strong core ideas that overshadowed their
grind-house content. *Shivers* is a gloss on *Invasion of the Body Snatchers*, and *Scanners* hit the
jackpot with super-powered telepaths that
could invade the minds of others. *Videodrome*
recycles previous Cronenberg ideas – strange
new body orifices, exploding bodies, technological conspiracies to transform mankind
– and adds the Dickian idea of altered reality.
We experience Max Renn's disconcerting hallucinations as his mind is invaded by the Videodrome signal. Max becomes the classic surreal
hero of Buñuel, an *Archibaldo de La Cruz* or *Horrible Dr. Hichcock* exploring new conceptual territory with his eyes wide open. An evolutionary mutation is changing Max from the inside
out, and he must learn to embrace an unknown
future he calls 'the new flesh'.

Cronenberg really hits his directing stride with

Videodrome. His actors are all top-rank. The effects don't overpower the story and the story doesn't rely on a chase to sustain its thriller framework. We accept some truly weird happenings as matters of fact. A television is transformed into a veined and pulsing sexual organ; Max Renn pulls an organic pistol from a vagina-like slit in his stomach.[1]

James Woods' sympathetic character is also a voyeur and soft-core smut peddler. Deborah Harry makes a terrific initial impact and then exits the film early, which probably sparked resentment among the fan-base that knows her as Blondie. One of the few convincing masochists in movies, Harry's Nicki Brand completes the erotic connection that Cronenberg needs. A surreal heroine, she aims straight for the center of her obsession and never looks back.

Cronenberg breaks with standard genre rules. Excellent supporting player Lynne Gorman, a woman older than fifty, is allowed to exhibit a sexual appetite. At one point Max Renn tries on a pair of dark-framed glasses, "transforming" for a second into a substitute David Cronenberg. During an alley escape, Renn passes workers moving a series of doors. Are they a visual pun for the doors of consciousness?

But the most memorable bizarro moments merge technology with erotic taboos. Max Renn is able to have physical sex with a pair of lips on a television screen, and his 'stomach vagina' hides weapons. Some of the concepts aren't as well established as others. In one scene Renn's obscene gun-arm (shades of *The Quatermass Xperiment*) is meant to shoot instant-growing cancerous tumors.

In the gross ending Max Renn is shown the next step in his personal evolution by a virtual Deborah Harry, who might as well be speaking to him from *The Matrix*. His crossover is accomplished by imitating something he sees on television. Cronenberg's movie ideas in these early films are *way, way out there* in the best possible meaning of the term: they're always driven by a coherent interior logic.

Criterion's exhaustive special edition of *Videodrome* is laden with behind-the-scenes docus and galleries. Interviews, commentaries and essays offer more conceptual riches. The commentators are Cronenberg, his cameraman Mark Irwin and his stars Woods and Harry. All are verbally articulate about the film and their work. Disc one also includes a short Cronenberg film from 2000.

Disc two has more docus and audio interviews. A section called *Bootleg Video* includes the complete footage of Max Renn's soft-core *Samurai Dreams* cable show and seven minutes of Videodrome torture sessions, including 'notorious' material cut from the film. Topping off the extras is a 1981 roundtable interview with Cronenberg and fellow directors John Carpenter and John Landis, at the time all involved in fantastic filmmaking. The least demonstrative of the three, Cronenberg seems the only one with "something to say."

1. In *Alien* it was difficult to accept a space creature that combined organic materials and chrome steel. In *Videodrome* Renn's organic melding with a steel gun is a kind of practical evolution, and the changing of a man's hand into a hand grenade is like a gag from a Looney Tunes cartoon. In *The Fly*, Seth Brundle becomes partially fused with his own invention, dragging the steel door of his teleportation pod behind him like an albatross. Cronenberg sees man fusing with his obsessions, like the morbid car fetishists in *Crash*.

Beings from Another Dimension have invaded your world. You can't see them...but they can see you.

Your only hope is Buckaroo Banzai.

THE ADVENTURES OF
BUCKAROO
BANZAI
ACROSS THE 8TH DIMENSION!

THE ADVENTURES OF BUCKAROO BANZAI ACROSS THE 8TH DIMENSION

MGM Reviewed December 3, 2001
1984 / Color / 2:35 widescreen / 102 min.
Cinematography Fred J. Koenekamp.
Production Designer J. Michael Riva. Art
Direction Richard Carter, Stephen Dane.
Written by Earl Mac Rauch. Produced by
Sidney Beckerman, Neil Canton, W.D. Richter.
Directed by W.D. Richter

A conscious attempt at the cult pantheon, *Buckaroo Banzai* has grown a small but fanatically loyal following in the years since its 1984 box office flopparoo. Had this first feature succeeded writer Earl Mac Rauch would have been on the top of a mountain of sequels, tie-ins and merchandising – its franchise hero is a combination of Doc Savage, The Lone Ranger and a rock star. Often laboring too hard at its inside jokes, *Buckaroo Banzai* nevertheless shapes up as a fun adventure along the lines of a Republic Serial – but with a hip attitude.

Surgeon, rock musician, particle physicist and leader of the Hong Kong Cavaliers, Buckaroo Banzai (Peter Weller) returns from an excursion to the 8th dimension with the ability to see the villainous Red Lectroids who have come from that alternate reality and are living among us. They've taken possession of Doctor Emilio Lizardo (John Lithgow) who now goes by the name of Lord John Whorfin. Together with Red Lectroids John Bigboote (Christopher Lloyd) and John O'Connor (Vincent Schiavelli), they steal the oscillation overthruster invented by Professor Hikita (Robert Ito) to return to the 8th dimension. Unfortunately, the benign Black Lectroids don't want them back. Black Lectroid John Parker (Carl Lumbly) brings a threatening message from leader John Emdall (Rosalind Cash): Earth will be destroyed unless Buckaroo stops the Red Lectroids in time. Buckaroo alerts stalwart Cavaliers Reno (Pepe Serna) and Rawhide (Clancy Brown) and enlists new members New Jersey (Jeff Goldblum) and Penny Priddy (Ellen Barkin) into the crusade to make the Earth safe from the Red Lectroid scum.

What makes a cult film? *Buckaroo Banzai* certainly qualifies, even if its makers planned for such status from the beginning. The Hong Kong Cavaliers are a collection of jocks, nerds and pretty boys devoted to their leader and the United States of America, in that order. Perhaps Buckaroo's time has come, although I think America is probably more ready for DC Comics' *Blackhawks* to strut their quasi-fascist stuff.

Director W.D. Richter animates Rauch's world with energy and commitment, embracing every awkward situation (the discovery of Penny Priddy crying in a cabaret audience) and making sure every cornball dialogue line is delivered as if it were the most serious utterance ever heard in a movie theater. Even the manic Emilio Lizardo is played straight. The wackiness is unified into something we can care about – a consistently earnest tone, the maintenance of which is no mean feat.

Deadpan Peter Weller puts just enough irony into his delivery to have fun with his role; he's also sufficiently vulnerable to be an interesting hero. His Cavaliers are nicely orchestrated personalities with varying combinations of the cool and the klunky. Actors like Pepe Serna and Clancy Brown can be distinctive without reams of 'character color' written into their dialogue. Jeff Goldblum is amusingly green and Ellen Barkin interestingly waiflike, even when striding about in a scarlet cocktail dress.

The villains on view are a pack of clowns led by John Lithgow's Lizardo. A tight bundle of goofy mannerisms and extreme facial expressions, Lizardo is wonderful working with the tight-ass Christopher Lloyd and sub-moron Red Lectroids Schiavelli and Dan Hedaya.

The imaginative special effects include organic spaceships, giant flying seashells that look as if they were grown instead of constructed. Going against the *Star Wars* trend, the effects and special makeup augment the show without overwhelming it. Some barely make the grade, yet seem just perfect.

The only real letdowns in *Buckaroo Banzai* are the action scenes and the settings. Without a budget for large sets, too much of the film takes place in (yawn) derelict factories, with endless games of tag being played in nondescript corridors and hallways. The movie also seems a bit shortchanged for rough stuff. It doesn't pay off on the action promised by all the guns, martial arts and samurai hardware

brandished by the Cavaliers. On the other hand, this may be a plus for fans sick of so-called 'science fiction' movies that are really lame action films.

The self-conscious cornball factor is a big plus. Scooter Lindley (Damon Hines) rushes out to tell his father Casper (Bill Henderson) that Buckaroo needs help, and receives a response that brings down the house. Obnoxious Perfect Tommy (Lewis Smith) needs constant assurance that he is, after all, *perfect*. When the Cavaliers function as a working unit, blending their technical expertise towards a common goal, the picture becomes a kind of Utopia for young adult males: coolness, hi-technology, guns and rock music. You can imagine the Fox executives sweating when screenings were greeted with mostly smiles and chuckles instead of belly laughs. Word of mouth was good but this isn't the kind of crowd-pleaser that studios understand, then or now.

MGM's DVD of **Buckaroo Banzai** presents an enhanced transfer of the standard 1984 cut. Some of the special effects shots are shown to have optical dirt printed in. This Special Edition has a number of unusual extras that will either thrill or frustrate *Buckaroo* fans.

One extra restores a prologue (starring Jamie Lee Curtis) that explains Buckaroo's name and heritage, the genesis of the overthruster, and the relationship between Penny Priddy and Buckaroo's dead wife. Losing this background info (which was presented in a fairly exciting manner) robs Buckaroo of needed depth while alienating literal-minded viewers who prefer plot details to add up to an even number.

Richter and Rauch use the Special Edition to promote new life for their one-shot 'franchise'. The extras are produced with a tongue-in-cheek tone that pretends that

Buckaroo is an historical figure and that the movie was made to popularize a small fraction of his many exploits for the big screen. Earl Mac Rauch pretends to be the real-life Reno on the main commentary track; hopefully it won't be taken as too taxing by those expecting a straight approach. In addition to looks at the film's effects, the extras include deleted scenes that explain Buckaroo's back story and introduce the all-important unseen character Hanoi Xan.

Savant still finds *Buckaroo Banzai* to be amusing and diverting; his kids think it's great. It's certainly out of the ordinary, which in these cookie cutter days of entertainment is high praise.

DUNE

Universal Blu-ray Reviewed: February 11, 2006
1984 / Color / 2:35 widescreen / 137 & 177 min. Cinematography Freddie Francis. Production Designer Anthony Masters. Editor Antony Gibbs. Music Brian Eno, Roger Eno, Daniel Lanois, Toto. Written by David Lynch from the novel by Frank Herbert. Produced by Dino De Laurentiis, Raffaella De Laurentiis.
Directed by David Lynch

David Lynch's **Dune** has three things in common with Fritz Lang's *Metropolis*. It has an unwieldy storyline that, no matter how it's filmed, leaves one with the impression that big pieces of the plot are missing. The marvelous settings, costumes and creatures evoke fantastic worlds and visions previously unseen in movies. And the public by and large rejected both films. *Dune* premiered as Universal's 1984 Christmas release and was met mostly with indifference, as if it were yet another *Star Wars* copycat like the Japanese *Message from Space*. It was also called "a two-hour trailer for a twelve-hour movie". The Frank Herbert literary faithful resented omissions and changes to the original book.

Just the same, *Dune* sets the imagination in motion with a feudal struggle that makes one crucial planet the battleground for galactic domination. Better still, David Lynch's superb casting of at least twenty unique characters is some of the best ever done for a fantasy. And his director's "vision" is as exciting here as in his more celebrated films.

The planetary status quo is threatened when the Emperor Shaddam IV (José Ferrer) conspires with Baron Vladimir Harkonnen (Kenneth McMillan) to destroy the clan of Duke Leto Atreides (Jürgen Prochnow) while taking over the mining of the spice Melange on the isolated planet Arrakis. Leto's son Paul (Kyle MacLachlan) is revealed to be a prophesized super-being, who will restore order to the galaxy.

"For he surely IS the Cuisinart Hat Rack!"

Dune sprawls as only a novel with dozens of characters can; the original books included glossaries for names, phrases and organizations within a galactic empire. Viewers that attended the original release of *Dune* were handed a mini-glossary cheat sheet defining twenty or thirty of the film's colorful terms, like Gom Jabbar, Mentat and Bene-Gesserit. (Some or all of this list is included as a paper insert with this disc.) Unfortunately for David Lynch, he felt it necessary to include all of this terminology in his movie along with exact explanations for all of the exotic characters and their tangled relationships. There is also an entire back-story cosmology to be explained, how a dominant sisterhood of telepathic witches has been struggling to breed a super-being over the course of 90 generations, yadda yadda. And don't forget the present political conflict in which a galactic emperor and the Harkonnen clan hatch a conspiracy to crush the Atreides clan. But wait, there's still the over-arching power represented by the Spacing Guild and its mutated navigator creatures (giant Eraserheads in forty-foot aquariums) that need the spice of Arrakis to enable intergalactic commuting.

All that information to dispense means that at least 50% of *Dune* is a lecture, whether it comes from a narrator or from the mouths of each and every screen character. David Lynch had shown excellent judgment when he moved up from *Eraserhead* to the more conventionally challenging *The Elephant Man*, but the sheer size of *Dune* perhaps got the better of him. The film has too much, and also not enough, exposition. Viewers get tired of listening to characters explain things that they don't want to remember. The who, how, and where of the basic setup (in the theatrical cut) are repeatedly declaimed, while the "why" is often buried in a half-heard sentence somewhere. We don't discover the story, it's explained to us.

Not being a reader of the books, I remember seeing *Dune* new and understanding practically nothing of what I was seeing. Lynch insists on leaping ahead with his story so quickly that we can't tell which planet is which. The film's visual dazzle gives us no time to absorb the dense storyline. A giant space navigator with an obscene gash for a melange-sniffing nose has the right idea: *"I see plans within plans"*.

The irony is that Lynch's excellent cast handles much of this constant exposition extremely well, especially when engaged in relevant activity we can see for ourselves, like spice mining. But the rest of the story is doomed. When we can't tell the teams or the players apart, Lynch's eerie "prophecy" montages become an annoying redundancy. [1]

That said, after one's third or fourth viewing *Dune* starts to look like a much better movie. Characters still talk as if reading from the Bible but they also begin to show uncommon richness. Jürgen Prochnow's doomed Leto seems less powerful. Kenneth McMillan's nasty Baron Harkonnen is a memorably foul villain who pulls heart-plugs from shivering flower boys. He keeps a doctor to cultivate hideous facial blemishes ("My diseases") to help him maintain a foul temper. Max von Sydow's Dr. Kynes exudes quiet wisdom and authority, and each of three royal tutors (Patrick Stewart, Freddie Jones, Dean Stockwell) has a sharply defined character. Sting and Paul Smith are perverse meanies under Kenneth McMillan. Jack Nance's tremulous Harkonnnen captain and Brad Dourif's eccentric mentat assassin make excellent impressions. Dourif's stylized gestures are brilliant: *"It is by will alone that I set my mind in motion."*

There's design, and then there's *design*, and this show has settings, props and costumes that inflame the imagination. Little things like back-collar epaulets contrast with rich tile work and carved wall decorations made from exotic materials. Francesca Annis' erotic *hairstyle* is a wonderment that's simultaneously antiquated and futuristic. Objects and spacecraft are an intriguing blend of technologies and cultures. The space navigator's *Rendezvous with Rama*-like spaceships serve as mass-transport cannisters from one end of the galaxy to another. The little Arrakis hovercraft looks like a boxy DIY kit, similar to vehicles seen in ancient sci-fi like 1929's *High Treason*.

I remember my friend Mark Sullivan once dismissing *Dune* because (in 1987) he was "sick of idiotic Luke Skywalker movies about Princes inheriting their rightful kingdoms". I understood exactly what he meant, as George Lucas' hit franchise was based on a fantasy guaranteed to appeal to under-achieving teenaged boys: a glorious Galactic Entitlement Program. *Sure, you're failing in school / lazy / ignorant and proud of it ... but you're a dreamer. The universe really is about YOU and nobody else. If the rest of the *&%@! world would just get its act together, it would recognize that YOU are the fabulous furry frog prince.* In *Star Wars* Luke does very little except have a good attitude and a healthy ego. He doesn't listen to his mentors or work much at anything ... by invoking his magical heritage he becomes an instant Master of the Universe. Experience teaches us that grand opportunities really come only when one prepares. Aggressive kids instead demand unearned rewards.

The eclectic *Star Wars* borrows heavily from Frank Herbert to fashion a highly entertaining (at least the first two installments or so) fantasy machine. Beyond that, the mystique of Jedi Baloney is not particularly profound. *Dune's* Paul Atreides (19 year-old Kyle McLachlan) is a dedicated student who has earned the right to stand and fight next to his teachers, and has the potential to become a great leader.

I don't know if *Dune* the book gives forth with the same ideas, but *Dune* the movie now looks like a metaphor for war in the Middle East with giant outside civilizations fighting to control a crucial resource. All the verbal imagery is Arabian, and the struggle of the Fremen is referred to as a Jihad.

Dune's feudal setup also carries a primitive misogynistic streak. Female perfidy is at the center of the political struggle, with the Bene-Gesserit sisterhood conspiring to overthrow the natural order of things by creating and controlling a super-being. Unfortunately, true love intercedes to create a male messiah in the form of Paul, with some added help from special training and drug-induced mental implosions. Paul's attitude toward women is that they need to be silent and stay that way. Those uppity dames with no eyebrows will no doubt be sent back to the kitchens where they belong. In one cut scene Paul screams out his disapproval of his mother, invoking a masculine right to put even the woman who created him in her place.

Every so often a rumor arises that *Dune* will be rebuilt and re-edited by David Lynch, an outcome devoutly to be wish'd. The original 137-minute movie confused many fans that had glimpsed other scenes in promo materials. *Dune* should have been split into two 2.5-hour movies, as the Salkinds had done with *Superman* and *The Three Musketeers*, a ploy that recently turned into a fabulous success with the *Lord of the Rings* trilogy.

An unwieldy compromise version, "A Alan Smithee Film" (sic) turned up syndicated on TV stations in 1987 or 1988, adding new material, albeit pan-scanned. Lynch was unavailable or uninterested in tinkering with the picture; it's not likely that Universal was offering much money for the privilege. "Alan Smithee" greatly expanded the storyline, restoring dialogue to scenes that had been mercilessly cut to a minimum and fleshing out material that was too rushed to make a proper impact. "Smithee's" editors also reinstated several scenes deleted in full, including one with Patrick Stewart's warrior-balladeer playing a stringed instrument. Additional detail abounds, and several performances are now much more satisfying. Richard Jordan's Duncan Idaho is no longer a passing blip and Linda Hunt's Shadout Mapes gets to do more than deliver a couple of expositional telegrams. Underground with the Fremen, we witness an extra knife fight and a burial. In a bizarre blend of sci-fi and Lynchian imagery, we witness the milking of "The Water of Life" from a baby Sandworm.

Unfortunately, this Extended Cut also flattens out much of David Lynch's poetry by plastering clarifying visuals and redundant exposition over previously mysterious imagery. Princess Irulan (Virginia Madsen) had provided a hopelessly confusing expository monologue-prologue for the Theatrical Cut, but Universal couldn't/didn't rehire her services, so a male voice takes us on a mind-numbing rehash of Dune politics that adds eight minutes to the running time. It's still followed by the redundant lesson that Paul watches on his laptop. The new male voice pops in throughout the Extended Cut, adding and restating information over introductory scenes of new planets, thus spoiling the mystery of Lynch's visual transitions.

The Extended cut also opens up every time some character travels from one world to another. Since there aren't enough shots of spaceships to go around, they're repeated ad infinitum. Some arrivals are highly suspicious, as if the wrong planet were being pictured – is this the Emperor's home orb, or planet Caladan? Worse, the editors just plain cheat. When the Reverend Mother Mohiam (Siân Phillips) arrives on Caladan, one cockpit view is stolen from a later scene of Paul and Jessica being taken out to the desert to die ... we can plainly see mother and son bouund and gagged at the

bottom of the frame! Toward the end, various effects shots unfinished in the film proper are replaced with bad flat artwork placeholders. It's quite a mish-mosh.

It's almost too bad that Universal released this DVD, if they could have interested Lynch in revisiting the movie as a theatrical event. After the success of Lord of the Rings, a three-hour Lynch cut might have been a practical possibility. And with twenty years to think about the problem, Lynch might have figured out an editorial solution to the puzzle. We'd happily accept a completely obscure 'impressionist' version of Dune, if it were Lynch's doing.

Universal's DVD of the **Dune Extended Edition** is a great way to catch up with this ambitious David Lynch epic. Both versions of the show are present, and both are 16:9 enhanced at 2.35:1. Lynch's theatrical cut flows better visually and has a much better sound mix, starting with the fact that music cues are heard only once, where they were meant to be heard.

The Extended Cut has been re-transferred in its full Panavision width. The TV version anomalies have been left intact, including the choppy titles, a blackout or two, and several annoying censor cuts that should have been restored. Baron Harkonnen doesn't kill the flower boy by pulling his heart plug out, or spit on Lady Jessica (although Piter de Vries still wipes the spittle away). Rabban doesn't crush a little creature in a hand-juicer and then suck its fluid through a straw.

Several new and unattributed docus are welcome additions. International designers and model makers display the wonderful designs and effects, with a good explanation of foreground miniatures provided by the Spanish art director Benjamín Fernández. Impressive location and production footage seems to have been repurposed from older featurettes. As the new shows have no input from cast or main production crew (and no bites from Lynch or Freddie Francis) we wonder just how tenuous the relationship between Lynch, Universal and the de Laurentiis people really is. There is also a selection of stills (favoring producer Raffaella, hmmm...) but no trailer.

Compensating is a "deleted scenes" extra. Rafaella de Laurentiis introduces it with a suspicious speech stressing the fact that no long Lynch cut exists, and that the film went straight from a 4.5 hour rough assembly interrupted by many "scene missing" place holders for effects not filmed. Raffaella shows us a nice selection of work print material, some of which is just dailies of characters staring and spouting more mind-numbing exposition. But we also see wonderful unseen bits like Paul's final wedding plans and the fate of Thufur Hawat (Freddie Jones). I didn't realize until now that Thufur disappears right in the middle of the final throne room confrontation.

1. Walt Disney had the obvious solution to this problem: Two weeks before the premiere, have a *Dune* Christmas TV special, with a half-hour adventure about a back-story issue from the film, something that was filmed but can't possibly fit into the movie itself ... like Duncan Idaho searching for Fremen desert people and seeing a worm from afar. The rest of the hour can be David Lynch standing in front of artist's renderings, explaining Frank Herbert's world of imagination and drilling the basics of the *Dune* "set-up" into the public consciousness. Follow this with liberal sprinkles of exciting film clips, and voila!, instant public awareness!

EXPLORERS

Paramount Reviewed: November 20, 2004
1985 / Color / 1:85 widescreen / 106, 109 min.
Cinematography John Hora. Production
Designer Robert F. Boyle. Special Makeup
Effects Rob Bottin. Film Editor Tina Hirsch.
Music Jerry Goldsmith. Written by Eric Luke.
Produced by David Bombyk, Edward S.
Feldman, Michael Finnell.
Directed by Joe Dante

Luis Buñuel described *Metropolis* as two movies glued together by their bellies; Joe Dante's ***Explorers*** is a similar case. The first two thirds is a wonderful tale of young teens on a mysterious quest, and the last third is a *Looney Tunes* riff on our culture as seen by two blobby aliens obsessed with TV commercials and Rock 'n' Roll. Dante does both styles exceedingly well. His later *Matinee* is a minor masterpiece deeply in need of special edition consideration. *Explorers* is far too charming to be dismissed but it is true that its two halves don't mesh as well as they could – the promise of wonder and imagination in part one doesn't pay off in the 'what the heck' dizziness of the final chapter. But it's still a great movie about something Dante knows better than anyone else, the culture-specific sci-fi obsessions of our 50s-60s generation, the group that read *Famous Monsters* and dreamed of gloriously elaborate space fantasies long before *2001* and *Star Wars*.

Viewers unfamiliar with the film will be intrigued to find River Phoenix and Ethan Hawke playing perfectly realized nerdy teen heroes.

> Teen sci-fi fan Ben Crandall (Ethan Hawke) and boy genius Wolfgang Müller (River Phoenix) share dreams they can't account for, dreams of a giant circuit board landscape. When Wolfgang copies the schematic in the dream into a program for his computer it produces a blue bubble unaffected by inertia, and that can be moved by computer command. Soon thereafter the two lads team with disaffected friend Darren Woods (Jason Presson) to build a homemade craft. Riding inside the bubble, they make a flight that local papers report as a UFO. Further dream revelations provide their bubble with an unexplainable oxygen supply. When an outside force takes control of their craft, Wolfgang realizes that their dreams have been planted by aliens that want to make human contact. The trio packs their gear and some junk food for a fantastic trip into space and the unknown.

In the late 50s I read a children's book about some neighborhood kids that make their own antigravity ship and fly to Saturn. I think the story turned out to be a dream. *Explorers* takes that basic idea and weds it with other ideas generally similar to *Close Encounters* and *E.T.* [1]

Dante and his writer Eric Luke fill *Explorers*

with childhood references. Besides clips from *The War of the Worlds* on TV, we see the unforgettable cover of the *Classics Illustrated* comics version with its beautifully designed Martian war machines. The boys go to Charles M. Jones Junior High school. Ben relates to all events through sci-fi favorites like *This Island Earth*. Dante references every bad space opera ever made when an atrociously funny film-within-the-film called *Starkiller* screens at a drive-in.

What makes *Explorers* special are the kids, who are given personalities and speech patterns that actually resemble real young teens, not After School Special clones or some aged writer's conception of adolescence. Kids at the awkward age of 13 or so are almost never portrayed with this kind of simple sincerity, and *Explorers* makes them middle class types with a range of responses to their environment. Ben is the dreamer and the least mature; he's also the most foolhardy and awkward, and already slightly girl crazy over the dreamy blonde in his homeroom, Lori Swenson (Amanda Peterson). Pleasantly subdued prodigy Wolfgang tries to pull Ben down to Earth but is equally as excited about the adventures to come. Darren is the proto- hood from the wrong side of the tracks, already drifting toward a grim future when he finds inspiration with his geeky new pals. This odd trio becomes absorbed in a fantastic adventure, a dramatic feat that *Explorers* masters 100%. *Close Encounters'* Roy Neary spent two hours deciding whether or not to take the big step into space with a bunch of pint-sized bug-eyed aliens. Our boys lack the restraint of adulthood and leap into the unknown on general principle.

Their spaceship is an old Tilt-a-Whirl ride from a junkyard. The alien program does all the technical heavy lifting, freeing their flying joyrides to become pure fun. Wolfgang drills through the Earth while floating in a bubble, much to the consternation of an irate gopher. Ben uses the bubble to peep into Lori's bedroom, a familiar teen fantasy that *Explorers* embraces along with some non- PC beer drinking.

The delicate balance between suburban reality and wondrous fantasy is highlighted when the boys' secret space program is investigated by a middle-aged space fan, played by Roger Corman/Joe Dante acting icon Dick Miller. He's left behind like Joe Wilson in *This Island Earth* or the dog Nana in *Peter Pan*. Miller alone understands their dream, although he's too old to share it. Wondrous dreams are the central theme of *Explorers* and childhood is seen as a magical, fleeting opportunity. Lori eventually joins Ben in the dream flights, completing the promise of this pubescent fantasy. All of this first section of the film is a rousing success, every bit as touching and inspired as *Matinee*.

The film's last act can't be discussed without spoilers. *Explorers* changes into an entirely different animal. Surrendering themselves to the summons of an alien intelligence, the boys find not an intergalactic war (*This Island Earth*) nor a *2001* star-trap but characters straight from the Chuck Jones cartoon universe, the other big Dante theme that made his *Gremlins* franchise so entertaining. Wak and Neek turn out to be dizzy teenaged space aliens very much like the grab-bag xenomorphs encountered by Duck Dodgers and Porky Pig in old cartoons. Wolfgang chats with Neek, who affects a Marilyn Monroe voice and arranges her eye and mouth tentacles into an eye-batting seduction mode. Wak (played by Robert Picardo, Dante's all-purpose wonder actor) is the boastful kid down the block who tries to impress the boys with his stand-up comedy. Wak eventually admits that he and his sister have 'invited' them to visit as a caprice because their parents are away.

Explorers is dazzling filmmaking and a visual delight, showing a full command of Industrial Light & Magic's pre- CGI effects techniques and the talents of monster maker Rob Bottin. But our reaction is understandably similar to that of the three adventurers. This is it? This is the magic of the cosmos? Wak Wak dismisses the issue with an aside, *"Gee, too bad you have to leave before we could tell you the secrets of the universe,"* and we're a little sad too. It's kind of odd when a splendid cartoon can derail the sense of wonder built up so beautifully. We're left with a collage of old TV images of Earth behavior that the aliens fear – war footage and movie clips showing aliens and anything else 'different' being blasted out of the sky with ray guns. We weren't looking for such a pat moral.

But 98% of *Explorers* is thrilling. The goofy aliens are a marvel to behold, and Picardo's antics are undeniably funny. My kids, now in their twenties, will happily watch the show again just to hear Wolfgang's little mouse say "Go to Hell" and watch the way Ethan Hawke gets over-excited about his own enthusiasm. *Explorers* captures the joy and wonder of being a kid, and that's no small accomplishment.

Also notable in the cast are James Cromwell (*L.A. Confidential*) as a ditzy father and Mary Kay Place as a protective mother.

Paramount's DVD of **Explorers** is one of their plain-wrap discs, albeit at a friendly bargain price. The enhanced widescreen image makes this the first video version of the film in its correct aspect ratio, and the compositions improve the look of all the mattes and motion control special effects. The humble homemade spaceship, with a glued-on plastic model of the space shuttle as a masthead, has a back yard grandeur.

1. *The Abyss* is another film where a terrific story (an undersea adventure) is sidetracked in the last couple of reels by a gear change (to a sci-fi flick). In the depths of a bottomless ocean canyon, Ed Harris comes across a gigantic alien colony that might as well be Santa's village from *The Polar Express*. The aliens communicate by showing Harris (groan) edited clips from TV displaying man's inhumanity to man (groan), dragging out Dante's idea in a much more pretentious context. I like *The Abyss* a lot, but my eyes just glaze over at that ending ... I don't think I've seen a film where a sci-fi element is more unwelcome.

THE QUIET EARTH

Anchor Bay Reviewed: June 11, 2006
1985 / Color / 1:85 widescreen / 91 min.
Cinematography James Bartle. Production
Designer Josephine Ford. Editor Michael
Horton. Music John Charles. Written by Bill
Baer, Bruno Lawrence, Sam Pillsbury from the
novel by Craig Harrison. Produced by Sam
Pillsbury, Don Reynolds.
Directed by Geoff Murphy

The Quiet Earth followed up its quiet American theatrical release in 1985 with a short life as a curiosity on cable TV and VHS, where its arresting key art attracted fantasy fans. The recent *The Road Warrior* had contemplated a violent post-apocalyptic world friendly to the needs of the gross-out action genre, but this calm little thriller offers relatively few thrills beyond its intriguing premise: A man suddenly discovers he's the only person left on Earth. It's hardly a new idea but it hadn't been exploited to any great degree since the early 1960s and episodes of TV shows like *The Twilight Zone*.

This product of the then-budding New Zealand film industry has a refreshing Kiwi sensibility combined with a stellar central performance from the always-interesting Bruno Lawrence (*Smash Palace*). Although *The Quiet Earth* invents some interesting pseudo-science to motivate its premise, it suffers the same dramatic problems experienced by earlier American attempts at the "Last Man Alive" science fiction subgenre.

> Scientist Zac Hobson (Bruno Lawrence) awakens one day to find he's the only person left in the world. Zac adjusts to solitude by raiding consumer goods and stocking a fancy apartment, but loneliness causes him to turn first eccentric and then delusional. Then it appears that Zac is not entirely alone after all.

Fifties science fiction movies were quick to discover the morbid thrill of the 'depopulated Earth' concept, in which humanity has mysteriously disappeared or been driven away by a cataclysmic atomic war, a plague or even an alien invasion. The basic fantasy is an attractive one. "We" are the lucky survivors who inherit an empty city. A place built for millions now has only one or a few inhabitants. With all the people gone, the hero indulges our daydream fantasy of an unlimited consumer shopping bender. Like good materialists, nobody takes advantage of unrestricted access to the public library. The survivors instead grab new cars, fancy clothes and the best penthouse apartment in town. People may go fuzzy on the details in pictures like *The Omega Man* or *Dawn of the Dead*, but they don't forget images of people raiding shopping malls, or Charlton Heston driving a new car through a plate glass showroom window.

Strange antecedents like RKO's 1933 *Deluge* mined the initial idea of rag-tag survivors living in a world ruined by a natural disaster, while 1950s movies like *Five* revolved around the specter of atomic war. The expense needed to empty city streets for scenes of this nature gave the advantage to large studio efforts like George Pal's *The War of the Worlds*, although a few minutes at the beginning of the otherwise unimpressive *Target: Earth* did the same on a nothing budget. In 1959 came *The World, The Flesh and The Devil*, a full-blown fantasy that stranded Harry Belafonte in an empty New York City. Its 'deserted & devastated' look was established by clever camera angles and early Sunday morning shoots.

The Quiet Earth closely follows *The World, The Flesh and The Devil*, at least at the outset. Zac Hobson wakes up naked on his bed to discover he's inherited an empty world, with all of New Zealand at his disposal. Previous fantasies made excuses for the absence of unpleasant rotting corpses; in *On the Beach* a character theorizes that dying people hide themselves to die, like dogs and cats. *The Quiet Earth* has it in mind that living things just disappear, leaving empty planes to crash (Zac comes upon a convincing wreckage site) and cars to collide. People vanish from their beds and babies from their bassinets, leaving their blankets wrapped around nothing at all.

The movies in this subgenre are most effective in the early stages, where the lost individual roams among the empty streets and abandoned vehicles of his new environment. *The Quiet Earth* is better than most thanks to Bruno Lawrence's intriguing performance. He starts to flip out, imagining that he's God. He goes nuts for a while and dresses in a woman's clothes, perhaps having slipped his gears on the notion of never seeing a living woman again. We eventually discover that his anguish over what has happened is more complicated than first presented.

(spoiler): Zac is a dissenting member of a scientific team that cooked up "Project Flashlight," an alignment of satellite dishes to produce some undisclosed chain-reaction effect. In a development anticipating elements of Wim Wenders' *Until the End of the World*, Zac's colleagues forge ahead even though their American 'partners' have been withholding information. Fearing that the balance of matter and energy in the universe will be disrupted, Zac retreats to his house to commit suicide rather than find out what will happen.

Project Flashlight shifts the entire universe into a new dimension, leaving everything alive behind, even bugs. Zac is the only living creature around because he was *in the process of dying* just as the 'reality shift' took place. Although it looks as if his team has obliterated all life on Earth, everyone else has taken a divergent fork into an alternate reality.

At this point *The Quiet Earth* has little choice but to follow the story path that didn't work well for earlier movies. In *The World, The Flesh and The Devil* Harry Belafonte finds first a surviving female (Inger Stevens) and then a male competitor (Mel Ferrer) and the rest of the movie becomes a competition for the twin crown of Alpha Male and Racial Winner. The next year, Roger Corman envisioned a similar love triangle as a struggle to possess voluptuous Betsy Jones-Moreland, *The Last Woman on Earth*. In both instances the science fiction aspects were dropped in favor of philosophical speechmaking.

The Quiet Earth continues to develop its sci-fi premise, with mixed results. Post-apocalyptic Tarzan Zac finds a Jane in Joanne (Alison Routledge), a good-looking blonde who happened to electrocute herself with a hair dryer just as the Flashlight effect disturbed the time-space continuum. They enjoy a celebratory fling together. Then a third wheel shows up in Api

(Pete Smith), a Maori truck driver who was in the process of being strangled at the appointed cosmic event. Just as in *The Last Woman on Earth*, a love triangle forms, but Zac opts out of the competition when he sees the need to alter the big experiment. Instruments tell him that the experiment's reality shift will either correct itself or shift once again, at a predictable moment only a few hours away. He decides that setting off a big explosion at the lab would have a beneficial effect; we don't learn much more than that. The plot sputters to a finale with some unsatisfying action and murky character complications.

The conclusion comes straight from the *Twilight Zone* playbook, leaving us with a conceptual tease and no real answers. Zac walks on a weird beach with bizarre clouds and unfamiliar planets rising in the heavens, leading us to conclude that the experiment's second burp has skipped reality into yet another cosmic groove. If logic follows, both Joanne and Api have either been destroyed or been left stranded in another alternate limbo. Zac prevails because he was again at the point of death when the shift occurred. Reality can be a real bummer when the eggheads screw around with stuff they don't understand, you know; Zac's lonely fate reminds us of the bleak beach at the end of H.G. Wells' *The Time Machine*. It also has similarities with the supernatural conclusion of Lucio Fulci's *The Beyond*.

(spoilers finished) *The Quiet Earth* is clever and spectacular but essentially unsatisfying as a drama. There aren't that many revelations in Zac's solitary adventure, although it's fun to see him graduating from toy trains to a real one to satisfy his urge to play engineer. The underwritten dramatic triangle contains no great discoveries either. The show plays like a version of the creaky old play *Outward Bound*, minus character conflicts. Zac, Joanne and Api might as well be lost souls in limbo; instead of a ship in a foggy sea between Earth and Heaven, these characters find themselves in a cosmic penalty box.

Director Geoff Murphy moved to the U.S. in the '90s to shoot mostly sequels; he's the credited Second Unit Director on the three *Lord of the Rings* films.

Anchor Bay's beautiful presentation of *The Quiet Earth* looks far better than old flat TV and VHS copies; the enhanced 1:85 transfer has rich color in the New Zealand exteriors. Writer/Producer Sam Pillsbury provides a thoughtful and informative commentary, letting us know that it's a lot easier to *empty* scenes than it is to creatively fill them up, so the "empty Earth" look wasn't as tough to achieve as one might think. We're also informed that in Craig Harrison's source book the depopulation of the Earth had something to do with fruit fly genes instead of radio physics.

ALIENS

Fox Blu-ray Reviewed: March 19, 2009
1986 / Color / 1:85 / 137 & 154 min.
Cinematography Adrian Biddle. Music James
Horner. Written by James Cameron, David Giler,
Walter hill from characters by Dan O'Bannon,
Ronald Shusett. Produced by Gale Anne Hurd.
Directed by James Cameron

After the success of *Star Wars*, producer Roger
Corman went against his general principles
and invested in filmmaking infrastructure, utilizing an old lumber yard in Venice to serve as
a special effects shop for a number of space-
oriented movies. James Cameron, a technically
minded miniature maker hired to help with effects for *Battle Beyond the Stars*, moved quickly
up to production designer for subsequent films,
stepping in to finish *Piranha II: The Spawn-*
ing when the original director left. Cameron's
breakout picture *The Terminator* was relatively
inexpensive yet outclassed major studio films
with much bigger resources. He proceeded to
fashion the sequel for Ridley Scott's 1979 *Alien*,
the phenomenally successful haunted house
movie set among the stars, "where no one can
hear you scream".

Alien's insectoid monster has been much imitated but not improved upon. Benefiting from
a larger budget, James Cameron crammed his
lavish action sequel with elaborate future hardware and weaponry. Instead of one implacable
space monster, the hapless humans must fight
against hundreds.

Fifty-seven years after the events of the first
movie, Ellen Ripley (Sigourney Weaver) is
found drifting in her space "lifeboat". Her welcome home is ruined when the corporate own-
ers blame her for scuttling the spaceship *Nos-*
tromo with a nuclear bomb. Company rep Carter
Burke (Paul Reiser) asks Ellen to accompany
him back to planet LV-426, where the first alien
eggs were found; contact has been lost with the
colonists there.

Ellen and Burke depart for LV-426 with a platoon of Colonial Space Marines led by Lt. Gorman (William Hope). The soldiers include the
braggart Pvt. Hudson (Bill Paxton), quiet Cpl.
Hicks (Michael Biehn), gung-ho Pvt. Vasquez
(Jenette Goldstein) and tough sergeant Apone
(Al Matthews). Ripley is upset to learn that an
additional crewmember Bishop (Lance Henrick-
son) is an android.

No sooner do the Marines land than the mission
goes awry. The colony has been wiped out save
for little Rebecca "Newt" Jorden (Carrie Henn),
found hiding in a tiny space. The insect monsters immediately wreck the platoon's landing
vehicle and confused orders from Gorman result in a massacre. Retreating to the colony's lab,
the soldiers prepare to wage a near-hopeless last

stand against the hordes of aliens. That's when Ripley discovers that Burke has been lying all along. As in the first movie, the corporation wants to retrieve alien specimens to breed as a weapon. Burke tries to use Newt and Ellen as live incubators for monster eggs. Ellen and the surviving Marines confront the alien creatures – and then the Alien Queen itself – in an escalating series of battles.

Aliens is the payoff movie for fans dreaming of spacemen battling monsters at the end of the universe. The screenplay by David Giler, Walter Hill and director Cameron jams together action situations and motifs from classic space operas in literature and film, forming a satisfying, if exhausting, monster combat tale. Cocksure Space Marines, their fingers itching at the triggers of their pulse rifles, take on steel fanged, acid-filled insect monsters: *"Is this going to be a stand-up fight, sir, or another bug hunt?"*

After their initial defeat, the human fighters must cooperate, compromise and sacrifice to achieve their goal. The sinister-looking android Bishop is revealed to be a loyal comrade, evoking an interesting sentimental reaction that points back to HAL in *2001: A Space Odyssey*. Forced to rely on their own resources, the Marines rise to the challenge. Green Lieutenant Gorman and the spitfire Private Vasquez grow as characters, taking personal, *fatal* responsibility for the success of the mission.

Sigourney Weaver's beleaguered Ripley also grows in stature from a bystander to the provisional unit leader. By the conclusion she's become a symbol of feminine power, protecting little Newt and facing down the horrid Alien Queen. Ripley's key dialogue line: *"Get away from her, you* bitch!*"*

James Cameron masters the spooky scenes and excels at injecting a maximum of excitement into frenetic battle action. Just as importantly, as an effects expert Cameron knows exactly what props and settings must be fabricated for close-up inspection, and what futuristic décor can be rendered as miniatures or faked with scenic backings and even mirrors. *Aliens* is not a cheap movie, but it looks several times more expensive than it really is. To unify the live action and special effects, Cameron decided on a slightly grainy look overall, with subdued color. The result, accomplished before the advent of Computer Generated Imagery, is almost completely convincing. Every scene introduces a new mechanical marvel or fanciful vehicle, any one of which would have broken the budget of a 1950s genre production.

Cameron's compressed scripting had a significant impact on all violent action films, not just science fiction thrillers. He works *Aliens* into a frantic climax at the beginning of the third act, and then extends the movie thirty or forty minutes longer with several more climaxes, each more intense than the last. Every time we think the havoc will subside, *Aliens* kicks once more into "sudden-death overtime" mode.

The genre's traditional opposition of scientists, soldiers and politicians no longer counts in *Aliens*, as economic interests have trumped all other values. We see very little of the future Earth but realize that even the armed forces are controlled by monopolies that have extended their hegemony to the stars, as in Alexander Kluge's *Der grosse Verhau*. James Cameron's cynical corporation ruthlessly sacrifices an entire space colony in the search for a new biological weapon. Their lackey Burke is expected to smuggle research specimens through a mandated "alien life form quarantine". Ripley has harsh words for this treachery: *"I don't know which species is worse. You don't see them fucking each other over for a goddamn percentage"*.

Fox Home Entertainment's *Special Edition* DVD of *Aliens* is a remastering of an expensive laserdisc boxed set from 1991. The expanded version extended the film's running time by seventeen minutes, adding, among many other scenes, an impressive sequence in which Newt's family of colonists rediscovers the derelict ship from the first film.

An enormous extras section includes eight detail-oriented making-of featurettes, a director interview, a trailer and packed sets of photo, art and storyboard galleries. Almost every visual in the film involves clever engineering and filming tricks, most of which are as good or better than later CGI-based effects.

THE FLY

Fox Blu-ray Reviewed: April 3, 2009
1986 / Color / 1:85 / 95 min.
Cinematography Mark Irwin, Music Howard Shore, Producer Stuart Cornfield, Written by David Cronenberg and Charles Edward Pogue from a short story by George Langelaan.
Directed by David Cronenberg

Canadian David Cronenberg spent the 1970s fashioning obsessive films about disturbing personal themes: the split between the intellectual and the animal, and our fear and loathing of our own bodies. Human ignorance of its own physicality is such that Cronenberg need only offer a few pseudo-scientific speeches about telepathic evolution or psycho-plastics to give his fantastic transformations credibility. Cronenberg's first successful exploitation pictures were lurid tales about artificial glands, strange parasites and bizarre mutations. Custom-bred "pleasure parasites" turn apartment residents into sex fiends in *Shivers (They Came from Within)*. In *Rabid* a mutated "stinger" appendage turns a woman into a disease-spreading vampire. Cronenberg's *The Brood* and *Scanners* add more science fiction elements to his repertoire but the emphasis remains on our basic squeamishness about the mysterious tissues and organs hidden just under our skins.

1986's **The Fly** proved to be a mainstream hit that made stars of its leading players. Significantly, it's the one modern remake of a classic-era sci-fi that improves upon the original in almost every way. Audiences accepted *The Fly* as a highly intelligent scare show that tapped directly into their fears. Its most memorable bit of dialogue became an instant buzz: *"Be Afraid. Be very afraid"*.

The trim screenplay expands the structures of genre, as opposed to Cronenberg's earlier, more exploitative films. His leading players this time out are not rebels or criminals but attractive young professionals. Science journalist Veronica Quaife (Geena Davis) interviews Seth Brundle (Jeff Goldblum), an eccentric but likeable lone-wolf inventor. As with Andre Delambre in the 1958 original, Brundle is perfecting a matter transmitter. A scientific shut-in, he foolishly uses the machine to entice Veronica away from her "macho schmuck" publisher boyfriend Stathis Borans (John Getz). Brundle's fatal error of teleporting himself before the machine is totally proven can be chalked up to drunken sexual hysteria. He will later try to describe to Veronica the total brutality of "insect politics", but the unfortunate love triangle that precipitates Brundle's disaster stems from another uncontrollable "primitive" instinct – sex.

The masterstroke of Cronenberg's adaptation is that the matter transmitter isn't utilized as a facile monster-maker. Only later, when he begins to suffer troubling side effects, does Brundle task his computer to trace what's gone wrong. Unlike the original film, the flawed teleporter doesn't rearrange body parts like Tinkertoys; Brundle has inadvertently combined himself with a common housefly on the "genetic-molecular level". He is now a Brave New Species from the blueprints up: Brundle-Fly. Suffused with a 50% insect "heritage", his body will quickly metamorphose into … what? As Bela Lugosi might howl, *"Not man, not beast – Thing!"*

The Fly takes an immediate and very cerebral left turn into the unknown; Seth Brundle is the ultimate surreal voyager. In the short run he's invigorated by a new insectile strength and purity of purpose that he confuses with mental clarity; he gets the notion that he's *refined* his tissues. But while his internal organs undergo violent changes, redundant Seth Brundle tissues rot and fall away, sloughed off like a snake shedding skin. Brundle first imagines that he's going mad, mumbling allusions to Kafka's *Metamorphosis* and collecting a "museum" of obsolete body parts in his medicine cabinet:

"What's this? I dunno."

As with H.G. Wells' *The Island of Dr. Moreau*, Cronenberg's *The Fly* reaches beyond the usual concern about scientific tampering to question basic assumptions of human existence. What makes us human, and what separates us from the lower species? Brundle has becomes his own Dr. Moreau, grafting "beast-flesh" into every living cell in his body. In the process of transformation he undergoes the ultimate in alienation from the physical self. At times we all feel like strangers to our own bodies, residents in uncooperative and even treacherous flesh and bone. Brundle's entire body is an alien, cancerous mutation, dragging his mind and soul into another kind of existence. He becomes aware of a shared consciousness with a new entity. Is it his insect half, or is he just going mad?

But the film's main sensation is a creeping morbidity that connects directly with our basic fear of death. Brundle must witness the corruption of his body, an accelerated version of a process that comes to every person who falls victim to the ailments of old age. Suddenly aware of the rotting of his tissues, Brundle is horrified in the same way a hypochondriac might react to a startling new symptom: *"Is this how it begins? Am I dying?"*

To his credit, Cronenberg pushes his concept to its logical extreme. In *Scanners* he imagined his telepathic hero "hearing" psychic communications from an unborn fetus, direct from its mother's womb. In *The Fly* Veronica is traumatized by uncertainty over whether her new pregnancy was conceived before or after Seth's genetic reconfiguration. In a brief tangent into *Rosemary's Baby* territory, the film makes a strong, if extreme, case for a woman's pro-choice rights. The shock sequence that results is a remnant of Cronenberg's previous exploitation mindset.

Brundle-Fly is a wholly original movie monster

given several generic attributes – hideous but superhuman, he has an insect's strength and gymnastic ability. A classic misunderstood outsider, Brundle-Fly loiters on rooftops like Quasimodo. He smashes through a wall to kidnap the female of his choice, as has every self-respecting monster in film history. From *The Cabinet of Dr. Caligari* forward, the midnight kidnap has been a generic substitute for rape.

In *The Fly* the implied rape fantasy is given a futuristic twist: Brundle-Fly wants Veronica to enter the matter transmitter with him, fortifying his genetic structure with her own, and presumably that of her unborn baby. He reasons that this process would lessen the "fly" component of the resulting creature. If Brundle "incorporates" enough normal people into himself, he could reduce his "fly" content to a minimum. Of course, scientists tell us humans that we are already only a few DNA toggles away from lower classes of the animal world.

Brundle-Fly's horrible plan to gene-splice himself with Veronica has a terrifying romantic aspect as well. Karloff's *The Mummy* felt he was doing Zita Johann a favor by granting her an eternal life – after knifing her to death. Brundle sees the melding of their separate bodies as the ultimate fulfillment of the romantic desire of lovers to "become one". If Veronica loves him, she would do anything to save him, right? And don't women claim to want their mating relationship to be permanent? Brundle can guarantee it.

The Fly also made news by bringing stomach-churning gore visuals into the movie mainstream. In addition to the horrid mid-metamorphosis Brundle-Fly, looking like one huge infected abscess, we're treated to the sight of a monkey turned inside out by a malfunctioning matter transmitter. Typical for Cronenberg, he expresses his cerebral concerns through direct imagery. Seth Brundle ends the picture hopelessly melded with a broken section of the transporter itself. Mad scientists traditionally transgress by taking their profane experiments where "man was not meant to go"; Seth Brundle arrives at the same destination by a wholly material path. Brundle's sad miscalculations turn him into a Darwinian casualty, caught between the biological past and the technological future. In the film's poetic final image, he has become fused both with an evolutionary competitor and his own futuristic invention.

Cronenberg and composer Howard Shore revisited *The Fly* in 2008, as an opera in two acts.

Fox's Blu-ray of **The Fly** is a fine presentation of of David Cronenberg's modern classic. The elegant special effects and disturbing makeup come across well in HD, particularly the delicate operation of Brundle's transporter pods, inspired by the motorcycle parts but suggesting metallic insect cocoons. Howard Shore's ominous music score has an even heavier impact on the DTS lossless audio track.

David Cronenberg provides the informative commentary; he speaks about his films in an articulate and unpretentious manner. A trivia track is also included, along with an extended documentary, deleted scenes, test footage and galleries of advertising art and trailers. The Blu-ray lacks a lengthy multi-part documentary included on the DVD Special Edition.

INNERSPACE

Warners Reviewed: July 11, 2002
1987 / Color / 1:85 widescreen / 120 min.
Cinematography Andrew Laszlo. Visual
Effects Supervisor James H. Spencer. Art
Direction Dennis Muren. Editor Kent Beyda.
Music Jerry Goldsmith. Written by Jeffrey
Boam, Chip Proser, story by Chip Proser.
Produced by Michael Finnell, Peter Guber,
Kathleen Kennedy, Frank Marshall, Jon Peters,
Chip Proser, Steven Spielberg.
Directed by Joe Dante

Joe Dante's most engaging comedy stems from a
love of fantasy films, science fiction and of course
Warner Bros. cartoons. Coming just at the sunset
of conventional optical special effects, *Innerspace*,
as described in its extremely entertaining and informative commentary track, is like a Jerry Lewis
– Dean Martin movie, if you shrunk Dino to the
size of a germ and injected him into Jerry's bloodstream. The main difference is that Dante's film is
funnier than any Martin-Lewis picture.

Troublemaking Astronaut Tuck Pendleton (Dennis Quaid) volunteers for a remarkable experiment. Both he and a mini-submarine are to be
miniaturized and injected into the bloodstream
of a rabbit. Unfortunately, spies intervene, and
Tuck is hypo'ed into the reluctant rump of hypochondriac supermarket cashier Jack Putter
(Martin Short). When Tuck starts communicating
with Jack from inside, Jack thinks he's going crazy. With the spies still in hot pursuit, Tuck has to
talk Jack into becoming a sci-fi secret agent, to set
things right and get Tuck out in time to be reunited with his fiancée, Lydia Maxwell (Meg Ryan).

It didn't sound very promising: *Fantastic Voyage*
(1966) was a glossy, thoroughly-hyped Fox film
that all of us Junior High School kids thought sophisticated until we grew up and saw it again.
When Hollywood revisits old material like this,
it's usually in the form of clunky remakes that
miss the whole point of the original, like *The Blob*
or *Invaders from Mars*. At their worst, they can
hopelessly befoul what were originally wonderful movies, as with *The Time Machine*.

Dante and writers Jeffrey Boam & Chip Proser
reinvent *Fantastic Voyage* as a wacky chase comedy. Dennis Quaid spends 9/10ths of the film
alone in the tiny submarine, floating inside
comedian Martin Short. Cashier Jack Putter is
a neurotic schlemiel helpless in a crunch and
hopeless with the women in his life, namely, the
amusing Wendy Schaal. If the fantasy concept
weren't so strong we'd think the whole show
was an excuse for comedy bits like Short's ridiculous dance. That it doesn't come off as gratuitous mugging is due to the actor's charm and
lack of pretension. This is indeed a Jerry Lewis
role, but done well.

Joe Dante excels at retelling old stories with
a quirky flair, as in *The 'burbs*. He also has a
knack for gleeful cynicism (*Gremlins*) and is
one of the few filmmakers of the 80's to get seriously sentimental with teenaged characters,

in *Explorers* and the later *Matinee*. The technically complicated *Innerspace* must be told in a straightforward manner, and the setup with Dennis Quaid and the miniaturization project takes a while to get going. Meg Ryan's charming smile tides us over.

Once Quaid is inside Short, Dante's storytelling skills get a workout as he establishes the ground rules for his premise. Quaid expects to be tooling around inside the bloodstream of a rabbit (according to the hilarious roadmap graphic on his control panel) and every part of their 'symbiotic' relationship needs to be explained: He taps into Short's inner ear to hear what Short hears, and finds he can talk to him. This results in a good gag where Short thinks he's possessed – only to have patient doctor William Schallert assure him that infernal demons talk *through* the people they possess, not *to* them. When Quaid clamps a video receiver onto Short's optic nerve, Short's pantomimed reaction to the sudden pain behind his eye is fall-down funny.

The complicated spy chase is mined for every iota of comedy potential. Kevin McCarthy and Fiona Lewis play ridiculous mad doctors, aided by stoic Vernon Wells and Middle Eastern 'cowboy' Robert Picardo. Nobody assembles a fun cast as well as Joe Dante, utilizing actors from his favorite old monster movies along with the more contemporary faces of his stock company: Dick Miller, Orson Bean, Archie Hahn, Henry Gibson, Kenneth Tobey, the wonderful Kathleen Freeman, Joe Flaherty and Andrea Martin. Frequent Dante DP John Hora does well in the straight-man role of a scientist. Robert Picardo is of course a standout, making an unpromising-sounding cowboy character into a riot. In a gratuitous but successful gag, an excuse is made to make Short look just like Picardo's character. For a few minutes that gives Picardo the opportunity to "step in" to the Martin Short role. Dante keeps the screwball antics at a high pitch.

Innerspace's running time is a bit long for a comedy. The movie is so tightly packed with incident, that something major would have to go if it were shortened. I'm glad it wasn't – Dante's recent *Small Soldiers* shows signs of compromise both in content and cutting, which doesn't augur well for his special kind of moviemaking.

Warner's DVD of **Innerspace** is a terrific 16:9 transfer that greatly improves on the handsome laserdisc. The clever ILM special effects for the interior of the human body are rich with detail, even in dark shots. ILM foundation brick Dennis Muren was one of four Oscar winners for effects on the movie, and participates in the disc's commentary track.

Always a funny host, Joe Dante guides the track with producer Michael Finnell and actors Kevin McCarthy and Robert Picardo. It's a great mix. Finnell and Dante have no problem digging equally into big ideas and details. Nobody could think up a better title, and Steven Spielberg got involved in the casting. They also point out dozens of in-gags that might slip by, like Dante's hero Chuck Jones as a supermarket patron, and a *Body Snatchers* seed pod in Kevin McCarthy's greenhouse-like meeting room.

McCarthy also joins in the commentary and is delighted to be there. Picardo arrives to talk about the ridiculous costume and the lengths he had to go to make the cowboy work as a character. He even slips in a sly joke about *Star Trek: the Next Generation*. The straight man of the piece is Dennis Muren, who starts off as the butt of jokes – "Oh look Dennis – is that another Fat Cell?" Muren deadpans his way through the effects explanations, sounding like an ILM corporate spokesman. By the end he manages a couple of clever remarks of his own.

The soundtrack is particularly well mixed, brightly billboarding all of the director's favorite Looney Tunes sound effects.

ROBOCOP

MGM Blu-ray Reviewed August 26, 2007
1987 / Color / 1:85 / 103 min.
Cinematography Sol Negrin, Jost Vacano.
Production Design William Sandell. Special
Effects and Makeup Rob Bottin, Peter Kuran,
Rocco Gioffre, Phil Tippett, Harry Walton,
Tom St. Amand, Robert Blalack. Editor Frank
J. Urioste. Original Music Basil Poledouris.
Written by Edward Neumeier and Michael
Miner. Produced by Jon Davison, Arne
Schmidt, Edward Neumeier.
Directed by Paul Verhoeven

RoboCop is both the best and the most important science fiction film of the 1980s. The violent
fantasy concept is material one might initially
think was better suited for children: a robot-
man serves as an incorruptible and heroic policeman. But the violence is far too adult for
kiddies and the emphasis is on wicked social
and political satire. Audiences thrill as Robo-
Cop prevails over criminals on the streets and
in the boardrooms, but laugh uneasily as they
realize that the joke is on them ... the American
dream of peace and plenty is grinding to a stop
as the U.S.A. becomes a corporate state. Overstated gore and dynamic comic-book action
make *RoboCop* both funny and disturbing, like
an exploitation film from fifteen years in the
future. Holding a mirror to present trends like
privatization is what science fiction does best.

Detroit is beset by a wave of brutal crimes. The
Omni Consumer Products Corporation steps into
the breach offering to privatize the police force.
OCP VP Dick Jones (Ronny Cox) has developed
an "urban pacification" robot called ED-209,
but it has serious malfunction issues. To fill the
gap while the bugs are worked out, OCP's CEO
"The Old Man" (Dan O'Herlihy) gives hotshot
junior executive Bob Morton (Miguel Ferrer) a
green light for his competing RoboCop prototype, which uses terminally-injured policeman
Alex Murphy (Peter Weller) as the basis for a
surgically-constructed part-man, part-machine
cyborg. Programmed to be the perfect patrol
officer, RoboCop's initial forays into the mean
streets of Detroit are a remarkable success for
OCP. Unforeseen complications ensue. Spurred
by contact with his former duty partner Officer
Anne Lewis (Nancy Allen), the 'dead' Murphy's
personality reasserts itself through memories of
his lost family. Robo's investigations eventually
lead him to suspect a connection between criminal gang leader Clarence Boddicker (Kurtwood
Smith) and OCP's own Dick Jones.

RoboCop is really an inside-out remake of Fritz
Lang's *Metropolis*: using high technology and
Reaganomics, a corporate elite is rebuilding
Detroit as a prototype for a future in which
big business can operate without limit or restraint. RoboCop is a super-weapon in The War
on Crime, a public relations stunt to help OCP
grab more power. OCP takes economic control

of Detroit by cutting funding to its police force and presenting itself as the better alternative. To frighten the citizenry into acquiescence, Dick Jones underwrites the criminal terror he's supposed to be eradicating.

Metropolis envisioned the ruler of its supercity as a financial Pharaoh, a one-man government making dozens of decisions a minute. Ed Neumeier and Michael Miner's script for *RoboCop* proposes a wickedly accurate corporate Old Boy's Club. With the stakes set so high, O'Herlihy's supposedly benign Old Man knows that his promotion-hungry underlings will murder each other to stay on top. *RoboCop* presents OCP as a criminal enterprise by contrasting it with real criminals and then erasing all distinctions. Clarence Boddicker's outrageously brutal and sadistic gang runs free because it has been granted license by Dick Jones; they're 'softening up' Detroit so the public will consider OCP's tyranny a welcome relief.

None of the overarching political satire in *RoboCop* would work if the show weren't so well constructed and directed. Paul Verhoeven had gone off the deep end with his pointlessly grotesque *Flesh + Blood* but the politics of *RoboCop* give him a constructive outlet for his violent fantasies – after coming from Europe he was shocked to see just how gun-crazy America is. Alex Murphy is an epic hero in that he 'dies' and is resurrected, a rite often portrayed in myth as a journey to and from the underworld. Verhoeven claims that Murphy is sort of a Yankee Christ, agonizing at the hands of the Devil (Boddicker) and returning to kick ass ... in the penultimate scene, RoboCop more or less walks on water. Thanks to Basil Pouledoris' dynamic music score, Robo is an intimidating metallic Golem in pursuit of criminals: *"Dead or alive, you're coming with me"*. Yet the score becomes very emotional when Robo uses the remaining bit of his brain to remember his idyllic life with his wife and son.

Paul Verhoeven's graphic style and Frank Urioste's slick editing drive Robo's steamroller momentum. Preprogrammed for any contingency, Robo confronts criminals and resolves problems without hesitation and with brutal efficiency. He offers rape counseling to a distraught woman, and gives sober advice on television to admiring kids: *"Stay out of trouble"*. RoboCop is a worthy original – perhaps the best fantasy character since the heyday of the Universal monsters – because he overcomes an agonizing death and personal tragedy to reassert himself as a human being. The crooks can't stop him and neither can the malfunctioning "Made in America" ED-sel of a robot.

Writer Ed Neumeier dotes on testosterone thrills (*"Guns, guns, GUNS!"*) and gross-out hyperbole, providing great material for every goon and gunsel in the script. Henchman Ray Wise foolishly tries to kick Robo in the crotch and the cocky Miguel Ferrer sneers in the face of poor police sergeant Robert DoQui. The hapless Paul McCrane gets a deliciously gross toxic-waste comeuppance, the picture's most perverse laugh. The film is interrupted by a number of highly prophetic video 'media breaks' with satirical TV commercials and cheerfully depressing news anchors. But Neumeier also knows how to drive home his political points. The big action finale takes place in a newly abandoned steel mill, a gigantic edifice that might as well be an Egyptian construction built for an unknown purpose. Corporate skyscrapers flourish in the city's center but grassroots America is collapsing all around.

Dick Jones' recorded video death message to Bob Morton plays on a CD-like video disc ... ten years before DVDs were introduced.

MGM and Fox's **RoboCop, 20th Anniversary Edition** presents both cuts of this modern classic. The enhanced transfers are excellent, although some scenes still look a tiny bit flat and contrasty. This two-disc set comes in an attractive metal box and recycles the extras from earlier MGM releases. The Extended Version is a cut of the film before its final MPAA approval and reinstates a number of 'overkill' moments of violence. On the commentary Verhoeven uses the Herschel Gordon Lewis argument to make the case that the extra gore is actually less disturbing: it's so exaggerated, it's funny. We can tell that these filmmakers believe in what they're doing, as *RoboCop* could have easily have earned ten times its money were it more family friendly. But then it wouldn't be the unique adult entertainment that it is.

The three new featurettes were produced by Laurel Parker. In *Villains of Old Detroit* actors Ray Wise, Kurtwood Smith, Ronny Cox and Miguel Ferrer discuss the joy of being on-set delinquents, and surviving the film's scary pyrotechnics. Paul Verhoeven, Michael Miner and Ed Neumeier add their comments as well. *Special Effects Then and Now* interviews production designer William Sandell, matte painter Rocco Gioffre, designer Craig Hayes, and animator Phil Tippett. Gioffre gives us a good rundown of matte techniques and Tippett shows the old ED-209 animation model, which keeps falling apart in his hands. In *RoboCop: Creating a Legend* Jon Davison, Peter Weller, Ed Neumeier, Paul Verhoeven, Kurtwood Smith, Ray Wise and Paul Sammon talk about the genesis of the Robo-suit, which was initially a big problem. Miguel Ferrer has some funny comments, and Michael Miner interestingly relates Robo to Dumas' *The Man in the Iron Mask*.

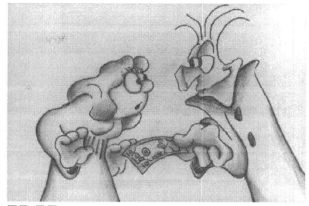

TO BE

Not on DVD Reviewed November 13, 2008
1990 / Color / 1:37 flat / 10 min.
Producer David Verrall.
Original Music, Written and directed by John Weldon.

*"There's a question haunting me
A problem in philosophy …"*

Thus begins John Weldon's intriguing Film Board of Canada short subject *To Be*, a light-hearted animated cartoon that utilizes a common science fiction concept to ponder the meaning of identity in an age where human cloning is surely only a few years in the future.

John Weldon, wrote, directed the animation and scored the music for this amazing little picture; he's responsible for a number of highly entertaining and often thoughtful Film Board of Canada animations, like *Special Delivery* (a Noir-ish tale involving mailman-icide) and *Spinnolio*, a wry parable about a woodcarver who only *thinks* his wooden puppet has come to life. *To Be* takes as its starting point the basic teleportation concept from George Langelaan's original *The Fly*, but discards horror in favor of a moral-philosophical investigation.

The perky, mischievous heroine (voiced and sung in fine form by Kim Handysides) attends a science exhibit in which a crackpot inventor (voice Howard Ryshpan) demonstrates his matter transmitter, which is nothing more than two refrigerator boxes topped with TV rabbit ears. When a volunteer enters fridge #1, the professor cycles the process. A loud bang comes from the first booth. The volunteer then emerges unchanged from the second booth, just as did Andre Delambre and Jeff Goldblum before.

Weldon animates this in a free form, fast moving style to match the Scientist's flaky, evasive sales pitch for his process, which he says makes people feel better too! The sketchy line drawings express more than the characters and the setting, as the heroine's eyes reflect first her awe and then her demonic intention to discover the flaw in the scientist's concept.

First, she forces the inventor to admit that his invention isn't strictly a teleportation device. The transportee doesn't actually go anywhere; the machine instead analyzes him, and transmits a blueprint by radio to the second booth. The receiver then builds an exact copy of the volunteer – it's actually a human duplicator. Because of the inconvenience and confusion of making a personal copy every time one wants to travel, the first booth automatically *disintegrates* the original.

The scientist argues that the identical copy is the equal of the original, so it's okay to destroy one of the redundant duplicates. After demonstrating the process with the refrigerator doors open – the inventor allows himself to be destroyed-duplicated several times – The heroine talks him into taking one more trip, but delaying by a few minutes the mechanism in booth one that destroys the original. As the twin inventors admire one another, the heroine announces that it's time for one of them to return to the machine to be annihilated. Naturally, issues of self-preservation immediately come to the fore. Each bickering twin now has reasons for the *other* duplicate to be destroyed.

Without having to be explicit, the wickedly funny *To Be* raises perplexing issues about identity and existence. Fables from earlier ages dealt with the idea on a religious basis, usually with the verdict that artificial life has no soul and therefore is inherently evil, as in the German silents *Homunculus* and *Alraune*. Mary Shelley's original *Frankenstein* subverts this notion, by blaming the creator and not the creation.

In *To Be* the invention is a clear case of convenience masking outright murder; anyone who goes through the teleportation is destroyed and replaced by an identical, but separate twin. Souls don't enter into the picture. If we could duplicate ourselves, as Edgar Allan Poe proposed in his horror tale *William Wilson*, each twin would be highly suspicious of the other. On a physical level, how many of our cells are replaced as we grow? How much of our bodies are not the same matter as when we were young? *To Be* ends with the happy heroine singing, knowing that, as a "guiltless copy", she's no longer responsible for the sins of the woman she once was. The teleportation invention aids the process of psychotic denial. How many criminals simply dissociate themselves from that "other person" who committed bad deeds?

To Be is a gem of a film, a philosophic wonder in miniature. I haven't seen anything like it, and it's not readily available save for occasional screenings on cable TV animation programs. In 1996 Harold Ramis made a feature called *Multiplicity*, a comedy about a busy man who makes numerous duplicates of himself to keep up with his responsibilities. It isn't as provocative or as funny as *To Be*: "Hello bird, on my head, aren't you glad my old one's dead?"

BIS ANS ENDE DER WELT

Long version on R2 PAL DVD Reviewed:
November 13, 2008
1991 Color / 2:66 / 158 min (U.S. theatrical), 181
min (International 1991), **280** min (1996 revised
3-film version) / *Until the End of the World*
Camera Robby Müller. Production Design Sally
Campbell, Thierry Flamand. Music Graeme
Revell. Written by Michael Almereyda, Peter
Carey, Solveig Dommartin, Wim Wenders.
Produced by Ulrich Felsberg, Jonathan T. Taplin.
Directed by Wim Wenders

Also referenced:

DEATHWATCH

Not on DVD
1980 / Color / 2:35 / 128 min. / *La mort en direct*
Camera Pierre William Glenn. Music Graeme
Revell. Written by David Rayfiel, Bertrand
Tavernier from the novel by David Compton.
Producers Elie Kfouri, Janine Rubeiz.
Directed by Bertrand Tavernier

Wim Wenders' 1991 *Until the End of the World*
premiered in Europe at three hours, and was
trimmed by twenty minutes before receiving
a half-hearted limited American release. Initial reaction was disappointing, especially after Wenders' previous international hit *Wings
of Desire*. Much of the negative reaction may
have stemmed from *Until*'s atypical structure.
It begins as an oddball thriller about a pair of
lover-fugitives pursuing one another across
four continents. For two hours it cannot decide
if its main subject is a bank robbery, a runaway
party girl or a nuclear crisis. Those themes are
left in the background when the movie finally
focuses on the meaning of a bizarre invention.
The film's action is brought to a halt by a technical and philosophical investigation.

This odd structure is coupled with a Wenders-
like refusal to dumb down his story or give it a
Hollywood pace. His film is almost completely
unpredictable.

Love it or not, *Until the End of the World* is truly unique. It boasts a charming and convincing glimpse of a near future that has already
passed – the millennium. We see cars that talk
and VidPhones. A hilarious detective computer
program called The Bounty Bear (*"I search them
here, I search them there"*) runs on "those superior Vietnamese chips". The film doesn't predict
the Internet, however. Beautiful imagery filmed
around the world is accompanied by well-cho-
sen alternative rock music.

In the year 1999 French playgirl Claire Tourneur
(the late Solveig Dommartin) is returning to Par-
is and her estranged boyfriend, writer Eugene
Patrick (Sam Neill) when her car collides with
another driven by bank robbers Chico Remy
(Chick Ortega) and Raymond Monnet (Eddy
Mitchell). Claire agrees to transport their loot to
Paris for a third of the take.

A threat from space throws Europe into a panic: a
radioactive satellite is due to fall into the Earth's

atmosphere. Against international protests, the United States has decided to shoot it down. Riots and protests have sprung up worldwide.

Claire picks up a hitchhiker, Trevor McPhee (William Hurt), who is being pursued by an Australian bounty hunter, Burt (Ernie Dingo). Claire is intrigued, so much so that after briefly stopping with Eugene, she follows Trevor to Berlin. Trevor slips away and Claire hires detective Phillip Winter (Rudiger Vogler) to help her trace him. They find and lose their quarry in Lisbon, but Phillip's computer detects Trevor in Moscow – and discovers that a huge reward has been put on his head for stealing Australian opals.

Funded by the stolen cash, Claire continues to pursue Trevor, whose real name is revealed as Sam Farber, across Asia and on to Japan. Phillip and Eugene follow for their private reasons. The chase continues to San Francisco before doubling back to Australia, where we discover the real reason for Sam Farber's mad race around the world: Sam is carrying the invention of his father, Henry (Max Von Sydow), back to Henry's secret lab in the Australian outback. The American intelligence community wants the device and to get it has framed the Farbers as thieves. Sam introduces Claire to his mother Edith (Jeanne Moreau) as their pursuers begin to straggle in – the Americans have shot down the rogue satellite with a nuclear missile, and the Electro-Magnetic Pulse effect has disrupted most transport and all communications. Has the world ended?

Wisely retaining control of his original film elements, Wim Wenders cut, mixed and had at least one answer print made of a third version of *Until the End of the World*: a three-movie, 4.5-hour tryptich. The director was hoping for studio interest in a second release but primarily wanted to see his film finished as he intended. He was foiled by legal considerations: Warners holds the U.S. rights to the 1991 version of the

film in the United States, and parallel distribution of a longer version would violate that agreement.

Starting in 1996, Wim Wenders began screening a special four-hour and forty-minute cut of *Bis ans Ende der Welt* at various museums and film societies. I caught an American Cinematheque showing on October 12 of that year – a screening I'll never forget. Wenders spoke after the marathon session, and told his rapt audience the following:

· Original compositions were solicited from Wenders' favorite musicians, including Peter Gabriel, U2, Elvis Costello and Nick Cage. He received so much good music that he decided to use it all. Wenders admitted without a hint of regret that this decision locked him into epic length ...

· Most plot elements were known ahead of time but, in accordance with Wenders' working methods, many details were improvised as filming went along. Wenders' core group of talent picked up crews and production aides in new locations as they traveled around the world. Hence the endless credits at the end with enough production personnel for four movies.

· When money ran thin, a China shoot became impossible. Actress Solveig Dommartin and one cameraperson surreptitiously taped the Chinese scenes (that Eugene watches on VideoFax in Paris) on their own.

· Wenders also confessed that his producers had to literally pull the plug to end the filming. He wanted to conclude the film in the African Congo. There, the Pygmy 'dream music' would bring his characters and themes full circle, and end his epic with a statement about the human community.

· Wenders cut the various versions of *Until the*

End of the World from successive inter-negative copies instead of letting his original negative be conformed to any particular version. He never surrendered control of his original elements. By doing so he avoided the kinds of disasters that occur when the negative falls into hostile editorial hands – witness *Greed*, *The Magnificent Ambersons*, etc.

THE ADDED CONTENT OF THE UNTIL THE END OF THE WORLD TRILOGY:

Viewers of the Warner Bros. U.S. cut of *Until the End of the World* will be curious about what has been added to comprise the 3-feature version now available on European DVD. Of what do the other two+ hours consist, exactly?

1.) Each of the three features has its own title sequence in German, distinguished by 'part one', 'two', & 'three' added to the title.

2) Claire Tourneur's party scene in Venice lasts several minutes longer as she gathers her belongings to exit her boyfriend's lavish digs. On her way Claire stumbles into a room where two children are playing with some hi-tech dinosaur and robot toys. We get a much better look at the jetsetters and party lizards hanging about.

3) Claire's journey includes a stop at the Italo-Franco border, and more wandering on those country roads not indexed on her car's computer guide map: *"You're on your own, Claire"*.

4) In Paris, we see a VidPhone view of Claire's friend Makiko (Adele Lutz). It is revealed that Claire's romance with Eugene was a committed relationship that collapsed after he and Makiko had an affair. Claire's fling with the wanted man Sam Farber now seems less of a caprice and more an expression of a wounded heart in search of something better.

5) In Lisbon, private detective Phillip Winter is referred to as a gentle soul who specializes in locating missing children. We see more news programs about the decaying orbit of the threatening Indian nuclear satellite.

6) Winter, Claire and Eugene walk to the Moscow office of the devious Krasikova (Elena Smirnova), who sells Eugene the fancy 'Bounty Bear' detective computer program. Here Claire explains why she calls Eugene by the pet name 'broken ladder': *"You're like a ladder with a missing rung – I can only climb so high and I get stuck."* Claire is at a romantic standstill because she cannot force her love for Eugene to develop any further. Eugene must watch as she drifts into an ironic relationship with Sam Farber, an outlaw who constantly deceives and betrays her.

7) The Siberian train ride is considerably longer. Claire waits for Sam outside his compartment door much longer and interacts a bit with some interesting Russians.

8) In Tokyo we see more of Claire and Eugene tracking down Sam and a tad more of Eugene and Detective Phillip Winter joining forces. Sam's herbal recovery at the rural Japanese inn is far longer, as is the introduction of the experimental vision-recording headset. Claire appears nude on the steps of the Japanese bungalow, a poetic scene reminiscent of *Wings of Desire*.

9) The San Francisco scenes are much more elaborate. The lovers hang out in a squatter's alley, awaiting monetary aid from Claire's French buddy Chico (Chick Ortega). The squalor on display makes America seem like the New Third World, the Superpower Without a Clue.

10) A brutal raid by plain-clothes police terrorizes Claire and her equally helpless neighbors. Claire is arrested.

11) Sam has little choice but to wait for Claire's release. She finds him in their favorite bar, a moment reminiscent of an encounter in *Wings of Desire*. This scene is used in the theatrical trailers.

12) A nervous man seen earlier in a tavern wailing amusingly about the threat of the nuclear satellite suddenly shows up on live television from Europe. Holding a hapless diplomat at gunpoint, he demands that the wayward satellite be dealt with, or else.

13) The regrouping of the principal players at the outback air hangar is longer. When the cops do an ID check on Sam, "bells ring" both with Krasikova's Bounty Bear program in Moscow and with bounty hunter Burt. This verifies Winter's explanation for the Yakuza problem in Tokyo and explains Burt's arrival at the outback laboratory. Also longer is Sam and Claire's trek across the wasteland.

14) Once the journey reaches the cave-laboratory, the pace slows down. Edith Farber's (Jeanne Moreau) Aboriginal 'sister' protests Edith's participation in the unnatural experiment. Much more elaboration of the little community develops while waiting for the world to end. Besides more and longer Aboriginal rituals, a group of scenes show the informal creation of a communal music-making group that slowly grows in size (Winter plays the harmonica, remember). The primitive 'society' born while waiting for the world to end thus musically relates to the primitive Pygmies. Claire dances, and sings her own cover of "Days" at a big party to mark the millennial New Year.

15) We are given far more dream images to study, so many that the film seems for a while to dissolve into abstract cinema. The 'disease of images' affects Sam more acutely, and Claire's withdrawal is longer and more harrowing.

16) The film ends in the year 2001. After the coda back in the states showing Sam visiting a grave, Eugene "tries out" a happy ending for *Dance Around the World*, his book about the experience. The ending is visualized as an affecting surreal bar scene. Sam sits at a barstool as a hauntingly beautiful Claire enters their favorite rendezvous one more time...

During his after-screening speech Mr. Wenders confided that his unique film was the result of ideas discussed and developed with director and friend Bertrand Tavernier back in the late 1970s. Based on Wenders' statement and the evidence of the films themselves, it would seem that in 1980 Bertrand Tavernier directed his own film from the same development discussions with Wenders. *La mort en direct* is also known by its English title *Deathwatch*. Based on the book *The Continuous Katherine Mortonhoe (U.S. title: The Unsleeping Eye)* by David Compton, *Deathwatch* is a visionary critique of the expanding Media Society:

In the near future death by illness has been all but eradicated. "Dying the old way" therefore carries such a morbid fascination for the public, that television entertainment is dominated by the hit show "Deathwatch". TV mogul Vincent Ferriman (Harry Dean Stanton) voyeuristically documents the slow deaths of those rare individuals struck down by disease. Ferriman has trouble securing a taping contract from the terminally diagnosed but privacy-minded Katherine Mortonhoe (a radiant Romy Schneider), who takes his initial down payment but goes on the run from Ferriman's barrage of network TV cameras.

Ferriman instead employs a new technological tool: Roddy (Harvey Keitel) has voluntarily had his eyes replaced with undetectable video cameras. Roddy's 'unsleeping eyes' transmit everything he sees and hears back to the *Deathwatch* TV studio, allowing TV recording without the giveaway presence of a camera. All Roddy need do is get close to the now-fugitive Katherine, and the *Deathwatch* show will make documentary history: a *Cinema* truly *Vérité*. Roddy befriends Katherine and accompanies her as she travels among undocumented transients and other "non-people" living below society's poverty line. Unaware that her every private moment is being broadcast to the public at large,

Katherine gravitates toward her ex-husband Gerald (Max von Sydow), who lives in a cottage at the far western end of the British Isles.

Deathwatch fully predicts the advent of Reality Programming, but might also be called "The Death of Privacy". The later Jim Carrey success *The Truman Show* is heavily in its debt. A science fiction thriller on a personal level, it has so many remarkable parallelisms with *Until the End of the World* that it's no surprise to discover that they had their genesis in the same creative brainstorm.

THE COMPARISON: DEATHWATCH / UNTIL THE END OF THE WORLD

Both *Deathwatch* and *Until the End of the World* are by continental directors dealing with a future society only slightly removed from our own. Both concern "vision-oriented" science fiction inventions. For clarity, the *Until* half of each of the following comparisons is in *italics*.

Katherine Mortonhoe of **Deathwatch** flees the cameras of a relentless media corporation. She has no conscious destination but ultimately heads for a former home in a place called "Land's End" to the West.

*In **Until the End of the World** Claire Tourneur flees her romantic past in the illogical pursuit of Sam Farber, ultimately heading to a remote part of Australia, "the end of the earth".*

The specter of certain death alters Katherine's values. She at first refuses to cooperate with Ferriman but then steals his money. To avoid his cameras she flees her home life for the uncertainty of a vagabond existence.

For Claire the specter of death is a potentially Earth-destroying nuclear satellite. She reacts with a series of value-bending, illogical actions. She becomes an accomplice in a robbery and abandons her lover for a vagabond existence pursuing wanted criminal Sam Farber.

Katherine's work as a writer of "computer books" is disrupted by the intrusion of Ferriman's voyeuristic TV network.

Eugene Fitzpatrick's (Sam Neill) laptop computer novel is erased by the EMP effect of nuclear detonations in outer space, and he must begin again.

As a disguise in her flight from the gaze of "Deathwatch", Katherine wears a full black wig.

To alter her identity and fool a bounty hunter, Claire sometimes employs a quite similar wig. Both heroines make a show of doffing their wigs with a headshake to reveal their natural, lighter hair underneath.

There seems to be a relationship between both of these movies and the 1943 noir horror drama *The Seventh Victim*. Both Katherine and Claire's wigs are reminiscent of the hairstyle worn by Jacqueline Gibson (Jean Brooks) in that classic horror film. The irrational, depressed and suicidal Jacqueline is described as "racing to her own death", an apt description of Katherine Mortonhoe, who threatens suicide and at one point pretends to have a fatal seizure.

Sam Farber's blind mother Edith, depressed by the visual world revealed by her husband's startling invention, becomes suicide-obsessed and desires to will herself to death.

Deathwatch is dedicated onscreen to director Jacques Tourneur, the prime directing talent associated with *The Seventh Victim*'s famous producer, Val Lewton. In *Until*, Claire's last name is Tourneur.

During their flight together, Roddy and Katherine share an odd discussion about Pygmies in Africa. The Pygmies asked a question of the first explorers to reach them: "Do you dream? We Pygmies thought that only we dreamed".

Sam Farber enchants Claire with his anthropologist mother's recordings of Pygmies singing 'dream songs'. Sam himself is later cured of the 'disease of images' by sleeping between two Australian Aborigines, who 'take his bad dreams away'. Director Wenders intimated that his un-filmed intention for Until was to bring the film full-circle back to the singing African Pygmies, whose harmonious communal culture represents a Utopian possibility.

Katherine's unconscious goal is to reunite briefly with her ex-husband Gerald (Max von Sydow) in his remote cottage at "Land's End". The helicopter-borne television magnate Ferriman finally corners her here, only to lose her services as a TV curiosity.

Claire discovers that the goal of her flight with Sam Farber is to reunite Sam with his scientist father Henry (also played by Max von Sydow) in one of the most remote places on Earth. Helicopter-borne American military intelligence agents finally converge on the rogue scientist's hidden cave laboratory, only to lose

the disputed invention they covet.

Vincent Ferriman's "visionary" invention is an undetectable camera that can enhance his televised reality shows. The mass audience prefers television's manufactured reality to the experience of real life seen through their own eyes, and "Deathwatch" is only too happy to dish up the illusions. The horror is that the media society demeans human values, turning individuals into passive consumer-voyeurs: *"Everything is interesting, but nothing matters"*. Respect for personal privacy is negated. Katherine flees the pitiless scrutiny of television because she wants to preserve her soul.

Henry Farber's "visionary" invention is a camera that records "the act of seeing" so that one person's vision can be transmitted directly into the brain of another – allowing a blind person to see, if only vicariously. The horror element has three manifestations. First, the blind already have their own sightless way of perceiving the world, a delicate psychic construction. A blessing becomes a curse when this personal security is replaced with the harsh reality sighted people take for granted. For the gift of a few miracle visions Edith Farber "loses her soul", just as her Aboriginal Sister warned.

Secondly, because Farber's camera retrieves visuals directly from the brain, it can also retrieve and display unconscious memories and dreams – un-interpreted and uncensored by our conscious minds. When a person views the contents of their own "soul", the fascination becomes a morbid obsession displacing all other concerns – in short, an addiction. The addict eventually becomes an uncommunicative zombie, incapable of relating to anything save the enigmatic visions. This is The Disease of Images.

The final horror is only alluded to: American Military Intelligence covets the invention because it can penetrate human minds in ways that inefficient brainwashing techniques cannot. Farber's invention promises limitless access to mental content regardless of the will of the individual. Because it can implant images in the brain, it can also be adapted to manipulate, deceive and torture victims with awful efficiency.

Katherine's instinctive demand to retain her cherished privacy is shunted aside by a Media World dismissive of the validity of such considerations.

The Aborigines' instinctive desire to guard the privacy and sanctity of the human psyche (their dreams) is dismissed as superstition by Dr. Henry Farber.

Roddy's implanted video eyes fail and threaten a permanent loss of vision, the fear of which causes him anguish and pain.

The Disease of Images causes Claire similar anguish and suffering, when she's threatened with even a momentary loss of visual access to her personal "dream images."

Deathwatch and *Until the End of the World* go beyond Cold War arguments about bigger and better bombs and robots, to demonstrate how technology in The Information Age might threaten basic human values. Both posit dangerous possibilities for the intrusive misuse of visual media, that go way beyond the two-way Telescreen monitors in George Orwell's *1984*.

Of course, neither film predicts the Internet, which has its own privacy issues. The Internet has revolutionized communication and democratized access to information, and has an enormous potential for positive social change. Still, Wenders' and Tavernier's revelatory concepts indicate that filmed sci-fi is still the ideal conduit for visionary messages. They've certainly thought the problem through and given it complementary, poetic screen interpretations. Reality producer Vincent Ferriman seems to understand the heritage of his profession – his office walls are decorated with posters from *The Incredible Shrinking Man*, *The Masque of the Red Death*, and, most appropriately, *"X", The Man With X-Ray Eyes*.

GATTACA

Sony Blu-Ray Reviewed November 13, 2008
1997 / Color / 2:35 / 106 min.
Cinematography Slawomir Idziak. Music Michael Nyman. Production Design Jan Roelfs. Producers Danny DeVito, Michael Shamberg, Stacey Sher.
Written and directed by Andrew Niccol.

From the beginning of the Industrial Age critics have warned about the effect of technology on human existence. Medical science was blamed for compromising the sanctity of life and political humanists imagined the workers of the future replaced by robots. Not much later, the writers of Utopian fiction seized on genetic discoveries to postulate societies of humans bred to be subservient to society's needs.

After the shift to escapist fantasy represented by *Star Wars*, science fiction thrillers only occasionally touched on social themes. New Zealand writer-director Andrew Niccol's 1997 debut feature **Gattaca** is perhaps the best movie to date that extrapolates trends in genetic research to their logical conclusion. The human genome is now completely mapped. Researchers are becoming skilled at altering species, and even creating customized microorganisms for specific purposes.

The possibilities seem endless for cautionary shockers about killer plagues and genetically engineered monsters, but Niccol chooses to address something much more basic. *Gattica* takes us to a near future in which parents with the financial resources can have their children 'fine tuned' in the womb. For a hefty fee, employees of genetic optimizing salons can sample the DNA of a fetus and identify DNA markers for physical flaws, inherited predispositions to disease, etc. Parents can pre-emptively eliminate those problems before birth. They can also pay to "upgrade" the fetus in other ways: intelligence, physical characteristics, etc.

Within only a generation or two, the populations of developed countries have already split into two classes, the "valids" and the "in-valids". Valids qualify for medical insurance and are vastly preferred for educational and employment opportunities. Why hire and train a man genetically predisposed to heart disease? The inferior in-valids cannot hide, as thumb-scanners are located everywhere and a tiny sample of hair or shed skin leads to immediate identification.

Gattica is organized as a detective thriller. In-valid Vincent Freeman (Ethan Hawke) is the son of parents morally opposed to genetic interference. Due to a minor but "flagged" heart defect, Vincent's only employment opportunity is janitorial work in an experimental space exploration complex. But he's initiated an extreme plan to impersonate a valid, and earn his place as an astronaut. Vincent arranges to buy the identity of Jerome Eugene Morrow (Jude Law), a crippled athlete. Vincent first undergoes months of suffering in a surgical procedure designed to lengthen his leg bones and give him more perfect proportions. Jerome lives with Vincent and stores away blood and skin samples for Vincent to use to pass daily identity checks at the space complex.

Everything works well. Vincent is only a few steps away from consideration for a major Jupiter mission, and has won the confidence of the mission director, Josef (Gore Vidal). He's even caught the eye of the beautiful space trainee Irene Cassini (Uma Thurman). Then a murder occurs at the space complex, and security measures are tightened. Vincent must be vigilant with his regimen of cleaning and ID substitution tricks, knowing that if the experts suddenly ask for a blood or urine sample, his real identity will be immediately revealed.

What's worse, one of the detectives assigned to the case is Anton Freeman (Loren Dean), Vincent's brother. The biased authorities assume that the murderer must be an in-valid, and random testing is sure to catch Vincent, just as his dreams are beginning to come true.

Gattica's space theme stays in the background. The settings are all quite futuristic but the only rockets we see are launching in the distance. The ability to do instant bio-scans has split society into classes by natural means, as opposed to regimentation based on politics, race or religion. Families unable to afford the benefits of genetic enhancement are marginalized. Valids control the purchasing power so the economy is naturally directed only at them. Meanwhile, society's narrow definition of beauty has produced a younger generation of aesthetic uniformity – everyone is pretty, tall and intelligent. The diversity of the race is threatened. And what happens to standards of taste? Do jaded "beautiful people" begin to admire individuals of unusual ugliness?

Meanwhile, the in-valids must do menial work and accept non-creative jobs where image does not matter. Vincent's brother Anton can become a policeman, but it's assumed that he might not be able to rise above a certain rank. H.G. Wells theorized that the labor / management split might divide humanity into two distinct races, effete Eloi and barbaric Morlocks. *Gattica* sees Aldous Huxley's *Brave New World* come to pass not by political dictatorship but through basic human nature. What parents don't want the very best for their children?

An expertly crafted drama, *Gattica* soon erases all doubts about its credibility. Already attuned to corporate lives without privacy or personal opinions, we readily accept Andrew Niccol's sleek future and the details of the high-tech detective work. The actors are uniformly fine, with strong input from the leads and expressive support in the smaller parts. In addition to Ernest Borgnine as a janitorial supervisor, Elias Koteas as Vincent's father and Alan Arkin as another detective, Elizabeth Dennehy, Tony Shalhoub and Xander Berkeley have standout roles. The movie is thoughtful, frightening and ultimately positive. The message is not that future technologies will change the world, but that they will change *us*.

Both the DVD and Blu-ray disc of *Gattica* are attractive discs with excellent image and audio. The special edition DVD contains a featurette that discusses gene manipulation, and a collection of deleted and blooper scenes. When people are asked to name the sci-fi film with a genuine connection to reality, the answer is often *Gattica*.

STARSHIP TROOPERS

Sony Blu-Ray Reviewed August 18, 2008
1997 / Color / 1:85 / 103 min.
Cinematography Jost Vacano. Production Design Allan Cameron. Written by Edward Neumeier from the book by Robert Heinlein. Produced by Jon Davison.
Directed by Paul Verhoeven

Today's science fiction movies must compete with action thrillers and comic book films, which makes Robert Heinlein's 1959 novel *Starship Troopers* sound like a natural. Action-packed and light on characterization, Heinlein's story of soldiers vs. monsters on distant planets was noted for its endorsement of a one-world rule positioned somewhere between ancient Sparta and Nazi Germany. The authoritarian society maintains a perpetual war footing, and military service is required for citizenship.

Starship Troopers fulfills the visual promise of older sci-fi thrillers limited by conventional special effects. A massive space armada cruises in tight orbital formation. Glowing plasma projectiles slam into a giant space cruiser, ripping it in two. Dozens of airmen spill into the inky vacuum of space.

Producer Jon Davison reunited the talent that had hit a bulls-eye ten years earlier with *Robo-Cop*: writer Ed Neumeier, special effects animator Phil Tippet and director Paul Verhoeven. The filmmakers were after more than spectacular visuals of galactic combat, which had already been exploited in James Cameron's 1986 *Aliens*. Audiences had loved *RoboCop*'s combination of pulp mythology and biting political satire. What might Davison's crew do with Heinlein's story about interplanetary infantrymen in a war of extermination against an alien species?

In a future Buenos Aires, high school seniors anticipate military service, by which they can become full citizens of the Federation. Rich boy Johnny Rico (Casper Van Dien) eagerly volunteers, to be near his sweetheart Carmen Ibanez (Denise Richards). Carmen's high math scores allow her to train as a spaceship pilot. The telepathic Carl Jenkins (Neil Patrick Harris) enters the intelligence corps. Johnny's poor grades put him in the Mobile Infantry, a planet-hopping force with a staggeringly high casualty rate. Beautiful Dizzy (Dina Meyer) loves Johnny and follows him into the infantry. While Johnny, Dizzy and new pal Ace Levy (Jake Busey) toughen up under their drill instructor Sergeant Zim (Clancy Brown), Carmen proves herself a star wing cadet, and becomes attracted to fellow pilot Zander Barcalow (Patrick Muldoon). Johnny feels he's signed up for nothing, and after making a deadly mistake in combat practice decides to resign. But the Federation's war with the insect civilization on the distant planet Klendathu jumps into high gear when

a Bug meteor strike wipes out the recruits' home town. It's all-out war as the Federation's armadas take the fight to the Bug planets.

Starship Troopers is a milestone film, if only because it shakes sci-fi free from the limp mythology of the *Star Wars* series, with its hand-me-down swashbuckling and wholesale borrowings from authors like Robert Heinlein and Frank Herbert. *Troopers* goes in for violent gore and grotesque images straight from old horror comics, as when a "Brain Bug" pierces a man's skull and sucks his brain matter out through a siphon. Audiences shocked by jolts like that one resented other aspects of the film as well. As in *RoboCop* the main object is political satire, but the dark ironies also sailed over the heads of disgruntled critics, some of whom decided that the film glorified fascism.

The film's space combat is *Sgt. Rock* on steroids. The pumped-up troopers charge onto the bug planet as if hitting the beach in a John Wayne battle epic. Colorful roughneck jargon abounds: *"This place crawls!"* … *"What's your malfunction?"* Phil Tippet's CGI insect monsters, wicked horrors with legs resembling African Assegais, overwhelm the troopers' massed machine gun defenses like the warriors of Cy Endfield's *Zulu*; the alien bug monsters attack by the thousands. Verhoeven gets plenty of shocks from the sight of troopers speared like fish and ripped to pieces – in the very first scene.

Starship Troopers' stylized future world conforms to no previous genre style. The high school kids look like teen fashion models and are as earnest and thoughtless as the characters of an *Archie* comic. Beautiful teen queens Carmen and Dizzy compete for the affections of the dumb but sincere Johnny Rico. Dizzy pines for Rico but Carmen has him dazzled with her killer smile.

The film's petty soap opera romance plot is modeled after old recruitment films promoting the armed services. The difference is that *Troopers* examines its future society's philosophy in full detail. Only the elite (like the wealthy Ricos) can afford to opt out of military service. Rico and his friends enthusiastically submit their SAT scores to the military and are placed according to their individual aptitudes. The swearing-in ceremony has a built-in Stop-Loss codicil. Enlistees serve for a minimum of two years – or as long as the army wants them to.

RoboCop had a strong sentimental angle as well as its cynical satire, and the lack of a hero to identify with is probably what hurt *Starship Troopers*. Audiences will eagerly accept the blatant pro-war, pro-aggression fare like *Rambo* and *Top Gun* if they have a hero to root for. In *Troopers* the audience is told that they are stupid pawns in a society that already resembles the fascist future, a strategy bound to generate resentment. With few exceptions movie audiences consistently misinterpret irony and reject political messages of any kind.

The world of *Starship Troopers* isn't an extrapolation of the Third Reich, it's a critique of today's war- driven society. The world has been unified under an all-powerful Federation that restricts democratic input. The government controls all media. Minority cultures and languages have been eliminated: Carmen's last name is Ibanez, not Ibañez. Buenos Aires is as American as Beverly Hills. High School indoctrinations preach a kinder, gentler form of fascism: all political power stems from military power, in short, brute violence.

The FedNet media breaks dispense orchestrated Federation lies. Shown the gory aftermath of a Mormon outpost butchered by Bugs, we suspect that the colonization of the Bug-adjacent planet was encouraged so that their massacre could serve to motivate Earth's retaliation. It also seems logical that the Bug Meteors aimed at Earth are the Insects' *response* to the Federation's invasion of their faraway planetary system. Another FedNet report is a sickening "uplift" segment in which schoolchildren are encouraged to stomp cockroaches, to foster hatred for the insect enemy. [1]

But what really sent the wrong signals were the film's Nazi uniforms. Audiences resented Neil Patrick Harris appearing in a leather SS getup for the final scenes. Critic Manohla Dargis accused the movie of celebrating Nazi iconography – even though the troopers' "Death From Above" tattoos copy a Vietnam-era Army slogan patterned after morbid Nazi insignia.

Filmgoers didn't like the filmmakers' bold message that we are already very much like Nazis. Couple that resentment with the general distaste for Verhoeven's gross-out gore, and *Troopers* was denied the success of a breakout hit. [2]

Starship Troopers is beautifully photographed by Jost Vacano. The casting is excellent, with personnel like Rue McClanahan, Jake Busey, and Clancy Brown making very strong contributions. Michael Ironside convinces as a fascist zealot, telling Johnny Rico that he's free to choose his destiny, albeit within the Federation's narrow limits. Dina Meyer and Neil Patrick Harris peg their characters perfectly. Despite negative assessments of their acting ability, it is clear that director Verhoeven gets exactly what he wants from Denise Richards and Casper Van Dien.

Sony's **Blu-ray** of *Starship Troopers* captures the full impact of the film's theatrical presentation. The added resolution lends much more detail to the dazzling space vistas and makes the young actors' complexions look too flawless to be real.

The extras come at the viewer like an onslaught on Klendathu. "FedNet Mode" is a trivia track on the film's politics enhanced with graphics and opinions from filmmakers & actors. Paul Verhoeven is alone on one commentary track of his own and joins his cast on another. Other extras include a rundown on the film's various Bug types and spaceship designs: comparisons of early special effects and storyboards to the final product, deleted scenes and screen tests.

In the newer making-of docu *Death From Above* Verhoeven, Davison and Neumeier are not bitter about the disappointing reception of their space epic. But remember the old Hollywood proverb: make a retro-futuristic faux-fascist propaganda piece that tells the audience that they're all budding Nazis, and you might encounter some resistance! *Starship Troopers* will become a classic precisely because of its cultural audacity.

1. *Starship Troopers* has taken on a new life post- 9/11, with the extremist claim that a secret government conspiracy purposely made the World Trade Center Towers fall. That irrational notion is prefigured in *Troopers* by the suspicion that the Bugs really can't shoot meteors all the way to Earth, and that the meteor that destroys Buenos Aires was actually launched by the Federation to justify its all-out assault on the Bugs. No outright evidence in the movie supports this, although the vast distance between here and Klendathu makes Bug-launched meteors seem impossible: Federation ships go into hyperspace to make the trip. With writer Ed Neumeier involved, there's little doubt that the suggestion of a faked Bug attack was intentional. The Brain Bugs treat their millions of Bug warriors as expendable, a philosophy shared by our own corporate powers with their "human resources" policies.

2. I attended an October 1997 press screening of *Starship Troopers* at Westwood's Village Theater. In time-honored Hollywood fashion producer Jon Davison spent the entire show pacing the lobby, alone. Both that audience and the opening weekend crowds at the Cinerama Dome gasped in disbelief at Verhoeven's extreme violence, and laughed uncomfortably at the co-ed shower scene and the jingoistic dialogue. All were clearly impressed by the space scenes and frightening effects – but they plain didn't "get" *Starship Troopers'* pose as a propaganda film from the future.

Republished by arrangement with Film.com.

WAR OF THE WORLDS

Paramount Blu-Ray Reviewed May 24, 2010
2005 / Color / 1:85 / 116 min.
Cinematography Janusz Kaminski. Film editor Michael Kahn. Written by Josh Friedman, David Koepp from the book by H.G. Wells.
Produced by Kathleen Kennedy, Paula Wagner, Colin Wilson.
Directed by Steven Spielberg

Steven Spielberg's 2005 version of *The War of the Worlds* is an intelligent and engrossing updating of the original H.G. Wells book, delivered with an intensity seen in few recent science fiction movies. It seems to have been produced because of the timeliness of its war theme – the new script makes numerous references to the idea of a technologically advanced society attempting to militarily occupy another country and take its natural resources.

The parallels with the then-hot war in Iraq are fairly obvious.

It's always good news when Hollywood remakes a sci-fi classic and avoids disaster. The new **War of the Worlds** shows Spielberg doing what he does best, pumping new energy into an established genre. When we first heard of the remake our initial response was that this particular fantasy had already been tapped out by the splashy but ultimately empty spectacle *Independence Day*. Spielberg goes in an opposite direction, embracing the events and atmosphere of the 1898 book. H.G. Wells' diary-like account of life under the heel of Martian invaders can be interpreted as the author's anticipation of 20th century wars fought with terrible technological weapons. This *War of the Worlds* is less about monsters from space than our 'complacent and secure' homeland suddenly experiencing a terror routinely suffered by much of the rest of the world.

> The action begins in a New Jersey shipping yard. Divorced dad Ray Ferrier (Tom Cruise) resents being parked with his unhappy children Rachel and Robbie (Dakota Fanning & Justin Chatwin) while his ex-wife Mary Ann (Miranda Otto) and her new husband go on vacation. Then an overwhelmingly powerful alien force attacks, and Ferrier is forced to take full responsibility for two kids who don't really trust him. Fleeing in a stolen car, they join a tide of humanity being swept before the onslaught of colossal walking tripods armed with unopposable heat rays. After narrowly surviving a number of close encounters with the conquerors, Ray and Rachel are separated from Robbie and hole up in a basement with an emotionally unstable survivalist, Harlan Ogilvy (Tim Robbins). They're surrounded by an invader encampment and must lay low while alien surveillance probes investigate their basement hideout.

Independence Day is a carnival ride next to Spielberg's film. The 1996 Fourth of July blockbuster borrows ideas from other films as is convenient. The biggest lift is the conception of giant space-ships parked over major cities from Arthur C. Clarke's unfilmed book *Childhood's End*, but almost everything else in the show is purloined from the George Pal 1953 version, including the specific staging of an attempted atom-bombing of an alien ship. "Bigger is Better" visual effects dominate *Independence Day* and remain its only lasting thrill. For a dramatic ending we get lame computer virus hacking and jingoistic last-stand speeches from a warrior President.

War of the Worlds takes most of its inspiration from H.G. Wells' source novel. The 1898 book is a first-person account of one Englishman's struggle to stay alive and rejoin his wife during a devastating alien attack. We know only what our narrator knows and share his fear of what he doesn't. Only infrequently does the book discuss the scope of the Martian invasion. As if that one narrator shouldn't be present at too many cataclysmic events, Wells includes a sequence the narrator hears about only later. A ferryboat attempts to reach the hoped-for security of France, only to be cut off by a Martian fighting machine that wades into the offshore shallows. Before it can turn its heat ray on the ferry, the tripod is challenged by the day's most formidable Earth weapon, an iron dreadnaught. The alien machine regards the charging battleship for a moment, wondering if it has been outmatched.

Josh Friedman and David Koepp's screenplay reworks this episode and many others into a storyline that adheres closely to Ray Ferrier's personal experience. Ferrier never really gets the big picture and a large part of his burden is avoiding panic over doubt and uncertainty. A full day after the first attacks he is is still unaware that hundreds of alien fighting machines are sweeping the nation, and not just the one he has seen. In other words, average American Ray is subjected to the terror routinely perpetrated on entire populations elsewhere in the world – instability, insecurity and the possibility of random slaughter without warning.

Spielberg's aliens come from underground, from alien machines buried perhaps thousands of years ago. This ancient invasion idea smacks somewhat of Nigel Kneale and *Quatermass and the Pit*. It also evokes the 'deep cover' paranoia associated with the 9/11 attack of 2001. The aliens were here before us, perhaps even before the Native Americans came. To them, humanity is merely a problem of pest extermination. The writers hint at the fear that terrorists are behind the invasion – while comparing the alien invaders to an army of occupation. Not only does the insane Harlan Ogilvy harp on this issue, Ray's son Robbie is introduced ignoring a school assignment on the French occupation of Algeria. Occupations never work, the film intones, a debatable issue that depends on where one draws the line between aggressive occupation and colonial husbandry. In any case, *War of the Worlds* presents a complex picture that avoids immediate interpretation in regard to the present world unrest.

Spielberg never shows an all-out pitched battle between Earth forces and the aliens. We see only the alien rampage and glimpses of ineffective armed resistance. This was surely an important issue in the film's conception. Some fans were disappointed when the movie didn't deliver an exhilarating battle sequence of the kind seen in *Independence Day*. Spielberg must have decided that if he included such a scene audiences would tune out the less spectacular content. He instead opts to maintain his focus on the Ferriers' personal ordeal.

The book's channel ferryboat becomes the movie's Hudson River Ferry, and combines with a book passage in which the narrator finds himself on a lonely road caught between war machines standing silhouetted like titans against the night sky. Wells' ferry passengers escape thanks to the suicidal attack of the battleship, but not so Spielberg's helpless refugees, who are drowned, harvested for blood and driven to their deaths by the aliens' heat rays. [1]

The book's narrator must hide in a wrecked house when one of the Martian cylinders lands above. The octopus-like aliens bury him alive while digging a nest. This scene is split in two for the movie. Ray's wife's house is partially wiped out when a jet plane (presumably shot down) crashes into it. Surprisingly few corpses are on board, which seems odd as no evidence is shown of human-harvesting tripods in the area. Later, Ray and Rachel voluntarily go into hiding with an addled survivalist who cracks up and threatens to reveal their presence to the invaders. The book's narrator spends a week or so in hiding with a similarly unhinged curate, who finally dies on his own. The cellar is explored by a metallic Martian tentacle, which in both film versions becomes a remote spy probe. The curate (and an earlier artilleryman) predicts that the Martians will eventually keep some humans as pets, and enslave some of them as Kapo-like agents to help track down stubborn human survivors.

Spielberg retains the old H.G. Wells premise of victory through bacteria. Although God is still mentioned in Morgan Freeman's bookend narration, the tone at the end of this film is simple Thanksgiving instead of divine intervention. The aliens just didn't do their research, is all, and pay the price of negligence. The germ deliverance of the original novel has been an unfortunate legacy for much of bad Sci Fi, where insoluble monster problems are routinely reversed through insultingly illogical means (see *The Day of the Triffids*). Nigel Kneale borrowed the *bacilli ex machina* ending for his updating of Wells' own fascinating *First Men in the Moon*.

Spielberg's movie also expands on Wells' concept of the Red Weeds, evidence of the aliens' desire to re-form Earth for their own needs. The fast-growing vines are filled with a fluid resembling blood. Wells' tentacled Martians were also vampires that sucked human blood, and Spielberg has them collecting victims in going-to-market baskets similar to the robot-roundup scene in *Artificial Intelligence A.I.*. The book's aliens also employed poison gas, something not touched upon here. The use of gas reached awful levels in WW1, lending more weight to the notion of H.G. Wells as a forecaster of Brave New Wars.

What Savant dreaded most about seeing *War of the Worlds* came from misleading reports that it was going to be yet another Spielberg 'family' film soaked in platitude-heavy sentimentality. Some Spielberg dramas are overburdened with simplistic ploys for audience sympathy. To take one example, the basically good *Catch Me If You Can* almost ruins itself with a staring-in-a-Christmas-window scene that would put Charles Dickens off his feed. The last thing I wanted to see was a Feel-Good invasion where The Family rebuffs those nasty critters from space, so they can play Goofy Golf and eat at McDonald's in peace.

So it was big surprise to see family concerns (and Tom Cruise movie vehicle issues) subordinated to the story. Cruise spends most of the film running in terror and cowering. Yes, there are vestiges of the old way of doing things. Cruise dodges heat rays, flying cars and exploding buildings, and the highways crowded with immobile cars leave a convenient pathway for his fleeing stolen mini-van. But with the exception of the rather gung-ho 'hand grenade up the alien tookus' scene, most of what Cruise's Ray Ferrier does is an exercise in frustration, as it would be for most of us. Ray, Rachel and Robbie survive because they're good at keeping their heads down and not getting caught up in the mass stampede around them. All of the performances are very good, especially Dakota Fanning's miraculously detailed Rachel. She conjures up a dozen different kinds of scared, from simple shock to exhausted desperation. And she convinces as a kid who wants to hear her favorite lullabye from *Chitty Chitty Bang Bang*. You know, from when she was *little*.

The anachronistic tripod fighting machines are a unique creation. They're so big that they tower into the sky; if they have a weakness it's that they seem to be made of sheet metal and jet turbine parts. The aliens themselves are unlikely tripod creatures lacking in interest. Spielberg does borrow visual ideas from earlier movies. The fighting machine cruising underwater alongside the ferry boat reminds us of the attacking Nautilus from *20,000 Leagues Under the Sea*, while the corkscrew motion of the pavement in Hoboken (and the vortex in the river) evoke both the unscrewing meteor hatch from the book, and the preferred tunneling method of *The Mysterians*. Remember the piece of landscape that revolves like a record turntable under an unlucky Japanese tank?

Spielberg gives the invaders force-field defenses that no longer need explanation, although we secretly imagine that if the aliens invaded Iraq, an average weeks' deployment of roadside IEDs and suicide bombers might be pretty effective against them. *War of the Worlds* does the military no favors by showing repeated attacks with tactics already proven ineffective. Army strategists surely have 1001 fallback weapons ideas that our valiant soldiers would be perfectly willing to test, no matter how risky the combat. If it were the only way, I'm sure our soldiers would volunteer as suicide bombers, too.

War of the Worlds' convincing scenes of panic and terror end up far in the plus column. Some people didn't see the film because its menace was too close to uncomfortable feelings about 9/11. I believe the film is a responsible and useful fantasy. Other doomsday scenarios stress the need for ruthless action to survive (*Panic in Year Zero!, No Blade of Grass*); this movie says that compassion and sticking together are important too.

Paramount's **Blu-ray** of *War of the Worlds* is a revisit of the 2-disc Limited DVD Edition from five years ago. The added resolution makes sense of Spielberg's chosen "look" for the film – everything has a certain grain and highlights are often burned-out. The purposeful visual degradation takes the term 'gritty realism' literally. The Blu-ray is much closer to the theatrical experience, with the beefy DTS master audio capable of blasting out the same way the theatrical track did. The Dolby 5.1 mix is available in English, French, Spanish and Portuguese.

The Blu-ray disc contains all of the extras from the earlier special edition, including the lengthy production docus by Laurent Bouzereau. It's all done in a promotional style. We learn that the show is a miracle of cooperation and harmony. There are regular infusions of Tom Cruise, Spielberg and little Dakota Fanning being charming, along with harmonious producer-director confabs that might well be staged. As is usual with these shows, the best content addresses the methodology behind the effects. We learn that the street that cracks and crumbles under the bystanders at the first alien encounter was completely added in post-production. That should have been obvious, but I was surprised to learn about it anyway.

1. By the way, the new heat ray is an unnerving electronic zapper that freeze-dries victims with concentrated microwaves – unlucky targets grimace in pain and then explode into powder, leaving their clothing flapping in the heat-draft. It's pretty chilling, almost as sanitary a device as the "electro-defragmentizer" from *Our Man Flint*. Instant traumatic cremation: Ray Ferrier becomes thoroughly dusted with powdered humanity. By avoiding showing a single bloody corpse, Spielberg also circumvents the censorship vigilance of the MPAA. As Lt. Colonel Kilgore might say, somebody got a case of beer for dreaming up that ratings dodge.

CHILDREN OF MEN

Universal Blu-Ray Reviewed May 11, 2009
2006 / Color / 1:85 / 110 min.
Cinematography Emmanuel Lubezki. Production Design Jim Clay, Geoffrey Kirkland. Film Editors Alfonso Cuarón, Alex Rodríguez. Original Music John Tavener. Written by Alfonso Cuarón, Timothy J. Sexton, David Arata, Mark Fergus, Hawk Ostby from the novel by P.D. James. Directed by Alfonso Cuarón

The new Millenium's most meaningful science fiction film to date is from Alfonso Cuarón, the versatile director of romantic comedies (*Sólo con tu pareja*) and blockbusters (*Harry Potter and the Prisoner of Azkaban*); he even made an exemplary film of the old children's chestnut *A Little Princess*.

Cuarón outdoes himself in **Children of Men**, a timely tale that shows the civilization of 2027 (reference: *Metropolis*) entangled in an apocalyptic nightmare. P.D. James's novel wades through a societal breakdown only a little more extreme than today's headlines: the world's governments have collapsed into chaos, anarchy and violence, and "Only Britain Soldiers On". The England that prevails is an authoritarian nightmare that scapegoats immigrants as terrorists and stages its own terror bombings to ensure public approval for its drastic methods. Immigrants are caged in public and forcibly deported to certain death on the continent. Newspaper headlines and TV bulletins announce nuclear bombings overseas, starvation in refugee camps and torture scandals; lethal pills are dispensed for free and cults have arisen that embrace mass suicide.

Following the lead of John Wyndham's *Day of the Triffids*, an additional fantastic (or not so fantastic) event has shaken the world to its foundations. Women have become infertile, and no babies have been born for seventeen years. The specter of extinction has undermined humanity's hope for a future, and with it the foundation of civilization.

The tightly scripted *Children of Men* follows ordinary guy Theo Faron (Clive Owen) into a desperate adventure. Narrowly escaping a café bomb blast (reference: *The Battle of Algiers*), Theo is contacted by his ex-wife Julian (Julianne Moore), now a leader in the resistance group called The Fishes. He volunteers to help the activist fugitives when Julian introduces him to Kee (Clare-Hope Ashitey), a black refugee who, to Theo's amazement, *is pregnant*. Julian wants to help smuggle Kee out of the country and into the hands of The Human Project, an independent group of environmental radicals. It's implied that if the government captures Kee, it will kill her and propagandize the baby as the offspring of a "posh London woman".

Unfortunately, a rebel faction within Julian's group has betrayed her; they want to exploit Kee as a rallying point for their planned uprising. Theo takes personal responsibility for getting Kee to an offshore rendezvous with The Human Project. Helping him are Miriam (Pam Ferris), an experienced midwife who talks too much, and Jasper (Michael Caine), a retired political cartoonist caring for his wife Janice (Philippa Urquhart), a reporter made catatonic by government torture.

Children of Men references all manner of political and post-apocalyptic sci-fi. The proposed rendezvous with the mysterious Human Project boat clicks with the film version of *Day of the Triffids*, as does the moment when Kee disrobes to display her pregnancy: Theo at first thinks she's trying to buy his loyalty with sex. *The Road Warrior* and other post-apocalyptic tales are echoed in the fortified farm used by Julian's rebels and the gangs that raid the countryside. The closest thing the movie has to a 'road warrior' character is Syd (Peter Mullan), a ruthless, mercenary security guard in an appalling ghetto-prison for deportees. Most importantly, *Children of Men* equates Britain's state of siege with the political madness of *It Happened Here*: the government utilizes Nazi hate & fear tactics to extort cooperation from its own citizens.

No Blade of Grass staged a harrowing live-birth sequence merely for exploitative shock value. *Children of Men* uses a 'miraculous birth' to represent the renewal of hope for humanity, accompanied by a strong Christian theme. Our concern for the welfare of Kee and her baby lends Cuarón's film the positive energy lacking in most post-apocalyptic films. The screen teems with evidence of decay and destruction – the streets are crowded with the hungry and homeless and fields are piled high with burned livestock. Life stumbles forward for those with the correct passport and a good job, and the rich can still enjoy a day at the dog races. A special museum has been set aside to safeguard famous works of art "rescued" from other countries; Theo regards Rembrandt's self-portrait and asks why it's being saved at all, considering the fertility crisis. In seventy years nobody will be alive to appreciate it.

The movie's humanist aims are clearly anti-everything associated with the War on Terror. The film also predicts a 2008 flu pandemic that claimed millions of lives, including the son of Julian and Theo. Key to Cuarón's politics is Michael Caine's Jasper character, a superannuated hippie modeled after John Lennon. Jasper has retreated to nurse his torture-victim wife, listen to rock music and smoke dope provided by a corrupt policeman. The entertaining, endearing and loyal Jasper would seem to represent the failure of his generation, but Julian's outlaw rebels aren't much of an improvement. Split between flaky altruism and ruthless pragmatism, The Fishes are too easily betrayed from within.

Children of Men comes together in a powerful sequence of a kind not attempted since silent film days. More than one sentimental anti-Great War picture showed soldiers dropping their weapons as the sky opens up over a battlefield, and heavenly hosts descend from on high. Cuarón achieves a similar 'miraculous' effect in the middle of an ugly military assault on the immigrant ghetto. The emotional uplift is one of the few moments in which science fiction and traditional faith seem wholly compatible: humanity yearns for hope.

Alfonso Cuarón's technique is as sophisticated as his politics. Shot on film but heavily manipulated in digital post, *Children of Men*'s design is cluttered with artifacts. The background teems with posters, graffiti and barely-glimpsed details of the roundup of thousands of illegals. Cuarón films most of this in lengthy master tracking shots. The movie has unbroken takes that last for several minutes, including a battle scene and a scene inside a moving car that makes impressive use of a remote-controlled camera. The effect is a feeling of scenes happening in real time, covered by an "expressive" documentary camera.

The show belongs to Clive Owen. The sympathetic everyman Theo Faron never picks up a gun and finds purpose and meaning in taking responsibility for Kee. Chiwetel Ejiofor plays Julianne Moore's more militant comrade in The Fishes. Pam Ferris' amusing midwife-activist is just the most visible of at least a dozen distinctive and eccentric characters struggling in this Anxious New World.

Universal's Blu-ray of *Children of Men* is a fine presentation appended with good extras. The HD transfer is sharp enough to read the text in newspaper bulletins and to pick out relevant details such as the hooded detainee assuming an Abu Ghraib pose in the background of one shot. DTS and Dolby 5.1 tracks serve the film's music particularly well. The older rock cues are classics that might be Jasper's favorites, like King Crimson's *"In the Court of the Crimson King"*.

The extras are headed up by Alfonso Cuarón's *The Possibility of Hope*, a stand-alone interview docu that presents a realistic assessment of the future of civilization overtaxed by overpopulation and global inequity. It assesses the issues from a radical viewpoint yet ends on a positive note. *Theo and Julian* is an okay character discussion by Clive Owen and Julianne Moore, while *Futuristic Design* and *Under Attack* investigate the look of the film's near-future and the difficulties of staging complex action in director Cuarón's extended takes. A picture-in-picture extra features a pop-up parade of media ads and commercials designed for *Children of Men*, at their full uninterrupted length. A couple of unused *Deleted Scenes* appear as well.

Also impressive is a demo showing exactly how Kee's baby was created with CGI enhancements. It's interesting to see advanced technology used to fashion something familiar and positive, instead of the usual monsters.

WALL-E

Disney Blu-Ray Reviewed November 15, 2008
2008 / Color / 2.39 / 98 min.
Production Design Ralph Eggleston. Film
Editor Stephen Schaffer. Original Music Thomas
Newman. Written by Andrew Stanton, Jim
Reardon, Pete Docter. Produced by Jim Morris.
Directed by Andrew Stanton

Just 25 years ago feature animation had almost
disappeared from American screens. The Pixar
studio has left the rest of the industry far behind by fashioning feature entertainments superior to Hollywood's live action alternatives.
Like *Ratatouille* before it, *WALL-E* surprises the
viewer with a bright new visual style, in this
case a fanciful blend of realistic and idealistic
futurism. A full half-hour transpires before any
serious dialogue is heard, yet we're held fast by
fascinating character concepts and breathtaking animation.

WALL-E makes child's play of concepts normally found in unappetizing atomic aftermath movies. The fate of its world is plenty
sobering, particularly when our worldwide
economy is weathering such hard times. Yet
the movie has an optimistic soul and a big
heart. It's a feast for the eyes and ears as well.

The title character is called WALL-E, which
stands for "Waste Allocation Load Lifter-
Earth-class." He's a personable little robot on
tank treads, with a trash compactor for a body
and a pair of binocular lenses for eyes. Earth
has been abandoned for 700 years while robots
like WALL-E stay behind to "clean things up".
Unfortunately, Terra Firma remains a parched
ruin of wrecked cities and dust storms; WALL-
E appears to be the last surviving clean-up
unit in operation. He dutifully collects metal
scrap, crushing it into cubes and stacking the
cubes into towers taller than skyscrapers. One
day he finds something that's been extinct for
seven centuries, a little green plant sprout.
The robot adds it to his collection of oddities –
which includes a videotape of *Hello Dolly!* that
has taught him to sing, dance, and develop romantic desires.

That's when a giant spaceship arrives and
disgorges EVE, a polished white robot droid
several centuries more advanced than WALL-
E. Like a porcelain hummingbird, EVE flits
about scanning random objects in a search for
living flora – EVE stands for "Extraterrestial
Vegetation Evaluator". WALL-E immediately
falls in love with the shapely new-generation
robot, but cannot distract her from her mission. When EVE finds WALL-E's lone seed-
ling, she snaps into mission mode and goes
into hibernation, waiting for the spaceship to
return for the green sprout that proves that
Earth is on the mend. Refusing to part with
EVE, WALL-E hitches a ride into outer space
... to parts unknown.

WALL-E begins like a silent comedy, with the

adorable robot scuttling about on his little tread feet. He can really race but is also capable of tiptoeing motions and little ice-skater's pirouettes. When frightened he retracts into his basic cube shape, like a turtle. Superb character animation allows WALL-E to perform his share of slapstick, and also to generate strong emotions. His pal is a little mutant cockroach, the only organic species to survive on Earth. WALL-E is a friendly guy with a good attitude, and EVE provides all the inspiration he needs to accomplish great things. As an in-joke for Apple lovers, WALL-E's solar charge sessions finish with the noise of a Mac computer rebooting.

The post-apocalyptic wasteland of Earth is littered with huge abandoned Buy N Large stores, an obvious pejorative placeholder for Wal-Mart. As it turns out, the Buy N Large Corporation governed the entire planet, and was responsible for encouraging humanity to bury itself in toxic garbage. This calamity takes place only a hundred years in our future.

WALL-E riffs on many Science-Fiction movies but most resembles Douglas Trumbull's 1972 Silent Running. In that film Earth ships off its last remaining plants to be preserved in space domes tended by a trio of cute robots. WALL-E instead displaces the entire human population to the Axiom, an enormous interplanetary vehicle with all the amenities of a luxury cruise ship. It's sort of a space ark, as in When Worlds Collide. Pampered for centuries, the inhabitants have atrophied into blobby doll-people incapable of standing on their own feet. Not only that, they've forgotten their origin or even what they're living for. Happily for the species, the Axiom's Captain educates himself, and re-discovers the ship's intended mission to re-colonize Earth.

WALL-E samples bits of sci-fi lore to fashion a scenario requiring very little exposition – by now everyone knows what an airlock is. A live-action Fred Willard appears in recorded sound bites, urging humanity to board the space ships. The film is peppered with little in-jokes and references to 2001: A Space Odyssey. WALL-E often looks like the CGI animation used to augment live-action films, only more "real" because it can set its own standard of reality. This frees us to enjoy the flow rather than analyze every new situation and object for concept flaws.

WALL-E took some political flak last summer from anti-environmentalist humbugs that declared it Green Propaganda. As the film's message and ideas are almost universally accepted, the complaints were largely ignored. WALL-E indeed is anti- the big corporation mindset – the drill-drill, clear-cut, strip-mine, rip-off, Wal-Mart, trash-the-joint attitude. And that's fine by me.

The humans of WALL-E may have atrophied into talking beanbags but they are still the stuff of heroes. The Captain fulfills his role by inspiring his charges with the challenge of reclaiming their home planet: "I don't want to survive, I want to live!" That line echoes back seventy years to Oswald Cabal in H.G. Wells' Things to Come: "Our revolution didn't abolish death and danger, it just made death and danger worthwhile!" After thirty years of futuristic movies shoving post-nuke horrors in our faces, WALL-E puts hope and humanism back on science fiction's agenda.

WALL-E on Blu-ray is sheer wonderment. Strong, purposeful design must be its secret, because its vastly complicated action scenes never generate the visual overload headaches produced by many another CGI film. The colors and textures are precise and the image razor sharp.

Also exclusive to the Blu-ray editions is a "Geek Track" pop-up commentary, a game section called the *Axiom Arcade*, 3D set fly-throughs and a feature with director Andrew Stanton called *Cine-Explore*.

Also present are a long list of the usual added value suspects – deleted scenes, Buy N Large short films, making-of featurettes. Two docus focus on the film's sound design (recommended) and the history of Pixar, the Animation Company That Seemingly Can Do No Wrong.

Singing animals and comic book comedy are known sure things, but environmentally oriented sci-fi has been a filmic pitfall for forty years – anyone remember *No Blade of Grass*? Pixar's *WALL-E* hasn't a single stump speech about saving the planet, yet it's sure to inspire millions of children – and enthusiastic adults – about the importance of the mission. When are they going to start giving out Pulitzers and Nobels for noble movies?

AVATAR

Fox Blu-Ray Reviewed: May 15, 2010
2009 / Color / 1:78 / 162 min.
Cinematography: Mauro Fiore. Music James Horner. Produced by James Cameron, Jon Landau.
Written and directed by James Cameron

When discussing *Avatar*, the most successful movie of all time, one is obliged to acknowledge that James Cameron has no present-day equal when it comes to technical innovation and a keen awareness of the mass audience. The director earned the enmity of film scholars everywhere thirteen years ago when he publicly took critic Kenneth Turan to task for daring to assert that his billion-dollar hit *Titanic* was anything less than superlative. In Cameron's opinion he was King and the critics' duty was to respect the taste of the ticket-paying public (no matter how rancid).

Cameron is a canny businessman-filmmaker well aware that he has nothing to lose by swinging his weight around. He's actually far less hubristic than the average filmic self-promoter. Cameron can back up his arrogance with impressive accomplishments, and not just the box-office kind. While the rest of the industry noodles along waiting for others to bankroll new technology, Cameron puts his career on the line. When he spends vast millions it's because he's already calculated that his film will return the investment tenfold. *Avatar* took eight years to get going, some of which was spent waiting for digital technology to catch up with Cameron's technical needs. Cameron and Fox knew when the digital 3D trend (craze? revolution?) would have just enough theaters in operation to make *Avatar* available to a wide audience. He was ready with "something the public had never seen before" – a description that has only come along three or four times in the short history of the movies: sound, color, big-format widescreen.

Audiences amused by Pixar's 3D animation films were bowled over by Cameron's masterful 3D illusions. Not only does the filmmaker know how to put together exciting sequences, he uses digital cinema's "directing in post-production" capability to maximize every shot. We're told that only about 30% of the film is live-action footage more or less as it came out of a camera. Almost every scene set in the wilds of the planet Pandora is a full digital creation in three dimensions, a virtual stage on which Cameron can choose (and change) his camera angles long after the performances have been recorded. The director can stick with simple over-the shoulder dialogue scenes or launch into whatever fanciful camera movements he wishes. His characters sprint through fantastic forests or ride on flying dragons through bizarre sky-scapes where islands of rock float like clouds. Cameron is an experienced visual master. The film doesn't contain a single dumb shot, nor any that work against his intended mood. When he films a flying monster his camera reframes the shot on the fly, as if the impossible beast were being filmed by a documentary cameraman. Cameron knows which buttons to push to suggest that his fantastic visuals are *real*.

James Cameron's onslaught of technical wonders compensates for his overly familiar storyline. Our ever-questing Earth consortiums have decided that they must possess an element called Unobtanimum (not a dumb name at all, as it turns out) found only on the planet Pandora. The problem is that indigenous "savages" called Na'vi are in the way. The Na'vi are ten-foot blue cat-like humanoids with prodigious physical strength. Their religion and their physical bodies are bound up in a globe-embracing natural web formed by intelligent plant life. Any outside disturbance to their planetary biosphere would threaten their physical and spiritual welfare.

While "Sgt. Rock"-style space marines led by the guts 'n' gristle Colonel Quaritch (Stephen Lang) prepare a massive weapons armada to forcibly evict the Na'vi from their most sacred places, scientist Grace Augustine (Sigourney Weaver) has been charged with researching a diplomatic solution. Because the Na'vi shun outsiders, Grace's bio labs have engineered amazingly perfect Nav'i clone bodies, using a mix of Na'vi and human DNA. A perfected "Avatar" process allows human researchers to remotely control / inhabit these lab-grown bodies. Paraplegic soldier Jake Scully (Sam Worthington, in a finely tuned performance) is put into a sleep trance and his mental consciousness is projected into his personal "blank" Na'vi clone. While Jake sleeps, his Na'vi self is awake, and vice versa. Jake 'becomes' a Na'vi to learn the aliens' ways and communicate to them the imperative to allow the Earth monopoly to peacefully mine Unobtanium.

Slimy bureaucrat Parker Selfridge (Giovanni Ribisi) knows that the Avatar Program is public relations BS intended to fail. Colonel Quaritch uses Jake as a military spy. In exchange for strategic info to be used against the Na'vi, Quaritch will reward Jake with the medical funding to repair his useless legs. Jake thinks this is fine until he falls in love with his Na'vi companion Neytiri (Zoe Saldana). Their idyllic life in the nurturing forest seems a far better alternative than Jake's servitude to his military masters. When the Corporation decides to shut down the Avatar program and take Pandora by force, Jake switches allegiances and prepares to help the Na'vi defend their turf.

James Cameron's storytelling competence is undeniable. He establishes his complex central concept with ease. Whereas the average big-budget movie dumbs down technology, the Avatar- transference idea challenges audiences to fill in the gaps. Yes, there's plenty of lame expository dialogue – Cameron's dialogue skills are weak – but once the film's Big Idea is established, audiences have no trouble leaping to new ideas on their own. For instance, when Colonel Quaritch threatens to smash Jake Scully in his sleep-pod, viewers from Thailand to Santiago immediately understand that Jake's Na'vi clone will be rendered insensible as well.

Although the Avatar idea initially sounds like a cheap way to transport the audience into an alien experience (as in, say, *Tron*, where video game players become immersed in their computer games), it's a clever expression of a basic human longing. None of us know where we go when we dream. That riddle has been the subject of storytelling art in all cultures.

Avatar's intoxicating visuals knocked viewers for a loop. More than just eye candy, the in-depth flora and fauna on the fantastic world of Pandora enchant at every turn. The film's look has been likened to the cover illustrations of dreamy classic sci-fi pocketbooks, only ren-

dered in minute detail and (for theatrical viewers) in 3D depth. The "you are there" quality of good 3D transported millions of viewers to a "new place", no mean achievement in an entertainment landscape where nothing seems to impress anybody anymore. Screenwriter Cameron puts his audience into highly desired fantasies, whether fighting six-legged, four-eyed monsters or swooping through the skies on the backs of bat-winged aerial steeds. Pandora's exotic plants empathize with the Na'vi. Little bugs fly like helicopters.

Some critics wasted no time going after Cameron's less-than-original concept of the noble Na'vi. It's funny that they should reference their story comparisons to Kevin Costner's *Dances with Wolves*, because *Avatar* swallows whole the entire noble savage subgenre of adventure films, from *Bird of Paradise* to *A Man Called Horse*. *Dances with Wolves* is itself a re-run of Sam Fuller's *Run of the Arrow*, and nobody complained. Newer movies assert that native cultures, especially the Native American culture, are superior because they are tied to the rhythms of nature, and abhor the artificial and destructive societies of Western civilization. Although there's plenty of truth to the destructive nature of advanced cultures (smallpox-infected blankets, anyone?), this approach ignores the barbarism, pointless bloody wars and fixed social rules of primitive cultures.

Cameron's Na'vi are sleek, squeaky-clean creatures living more or less in Peter Pan's Never Never Land, a place where all creatures live in harmony under a planet-wide deity residing in an enormous ecological Internet. The sacred trees are sentient because their myriad botanical connections form an enormous nervous system. Of course, the anointed Na'vi are at the top of the spiritual chain, and are allowed to slay for food as long as they dedicate their kills to the Great Spirit; six-legged horses and flying dragons are their natural servants. Neytiri's tribe is the usual theocracy, with four or five chiefs and innumerable followers. Neytiri isn't called a princess but she's definitely a Na'vi VIP – just like (sigh) Debra Paget back in the break-through Indians-are-swell western *Broken Arrow* (yet another western precursor to *Avatar*).

The westerns accepted native pantheism at face value – James Stewart, Rod Steiger and Kevin Costner found Indian ways an admirable alternative to the White Man's value system. Come the post- *Wounded Knee* minority empowerment movement of the 1970s, the Indians were transformed into helpless victims of American aggression. Some film directors were eager to be first with social revelations (mostly all revealed twenty years before in less pushy western fare) and some wanted to equate the historical Native American genocide with Vietnam. Audiences were wary about this politicizing, even when an auteur showed a sense of humor, as in Arthur Penn's *Little Big Man*. After an hour of hearing about Great Spirits and the like, we were amused when *Little Big Man's* big chief sighs, "Well, some times the magic works and some times it doesn't".

Audiences are no longer as sophisticated and James Cameron knows it. *Avatar* takes itself very seriously. The planet constantly affirms the reality of its magic. There's nothing spiritual about hot-wiring one's nervous system with one's ride for the day (jokes abounded about Jake having a USB connection in his hair-tentacle). The giant tree of life and grotto of souls or whatever are 100% functional. Jake can listen to the actual voices of the dead in a sparkly corridor of self-illuminated moss, and watch as hundreds of sacred Tinkerbelle air-jellyfish tickle his skin to welcome him to the Na'vi neighborhood. At its most trite, the film makes the super-duper tree of life accompany the Na'vi chants by flashing light to a disco beat. Who wouldn't believe in God, if God made a personal appearance every week in church? The Na'vi's religion isn't a religion, really, as faith in the unknowable is not a factor.

Cameron's Na'vi are a highly attractive fantasy. I'll bet that kids watching the Na'vi warriors sprint through the jungle and climb insane vine-cables to floating islands, get the same charge I got watching James MacArthur's Mohawk'ed white warrior race through the New England woods in Walt Disney's *The Light in the Forest*. Everybody wants to be Tarzan – Cameron is tapping into primal fantasies.

The militaristic future world of *Avatar* could be the same 'world' of Cameron's *Aliens*, where space marines conquer new planets for expansionist earth corporations. The older westerns that Cameron references often used their "military bad guys" to comment on Civil Rights or the Vietnam War. *Avatar* leaps whole hog into anti- Neo-con mode, pegging its story on the current assumption that the American presence in the Middle East is a cynical geo-strategy to control oil. Depending on one's political slant this is either liberal gospel or vicious propaganda; the truth is presumably much more complicated than either extreme. But to Cameron and *Avatar* there's no question that indigenous cultures are threatened by the greed of developed nations, and that the natives have the right to fight back. *Avatar* is therefore pro- Third World Rights; the folks back home would label its heroes "terrorists".

When Paul Verhoeven had the nerve to suggest nearly this exact same thing thirteen years before in his ironic, misunderstood *Starship Troopers*, he was considered crazy and his film incoherent. The only protest against Cameron's apparent endorsement of "evil terrorism" comes from a few right-wing pundits powerless to make headway against the multitudes that ignore politics when there's such a great thrill ride to appreciate. Just the same, I'd love to see *Avatar* with an audience in a Third World country, where the locals might identify the 'bad guys' as any outsider nation seeking to dominate them economically or militarily.

Avatar's most disturbing sight is the destruction of an enormous Na'vi tree, a growth a mile or two in height. This main action sequence is very much like the horrible 9/11 attack, only the other way around. James Cameron's idiotic plot turns in *Titanic* really griped this reviewer, but for this particular subversive move he wins the the grand prize. *Avatar's* story may be a superficial re-tread of older movies, but I find this nose-thumb to the global 'war on terror' to be daring in the extreme.

Cameron knows how to get his military rocks off. He avoids the path of his underperforming *The Abyss*, that ended with a non-violent message of Peace & Love. *Avatar's* last third is the all-out battle that every action blockbuster needs to win over an audience these days. Cameron trots out the oldest trick in the book, taken right from the classic *Tarzan* movies. Since the ecosystem of Pandora is all one happy symbiotic alliance (do Pandoran germs sing in harmony, too?), the Mother Nature deity unleashes an armada of alien pterodactyls and giant hammerhead monsters to stomp Colonel Quaritch's mechanical horde into the dust. I didn't need the extended "let's get personal" knife fight that follows, but the combat in *Avatar* is never repetitive or boring.

Perhaps the sinister pods of *Invasion of the Body Snatchers* came from Pandora, as the spiritual transference by which Jake Sully migrates from his crippled human body to his new Na'vi body looks a lot like the same kind of process: fall asleep, and you wake up twice as big, with blue skin and yellow cat's eyes. Got $500 million dollars to spend? No doubt James Cameron's *Avatar* sequel will involve some new technical wonder. Now that everybody's saying that the future of movies is all 3D – a statement surely inspired by inflated admission prices – we're bound to see more of these high-ticket super-dupercolossal extravaganzas. Come to the matinee! Financing available!

The bait 'n' switch experts of the movie industry have already trotted out cheapie fake 3D to justify big-ticket prices for *Clash of the Titans*. But, put out a genuine gee-whiz show like *Avatar* and the theater seats will magically fill up. Personally, I enjoyed the visuals and was somewhat bored by the lightweight storyline. But there's no denying that the film delivers on its promises, big-time.

Fox's Blu-ray of **Avatar** looks great in HD, even without the dimension of depth – which I'm not sure I even want as a regular diet at home. The movie's designs and imagery are just as impressive in 2D: there's nothing to complain about. The images are so detailed that we readily believe the publicity claims of intensive man-hours expended on each frame of this show – nothing in the picture looks like a visual or technical compromise. The release comes with a selection of audio track configurations, but no extras. I'll choose some other movie if I want dramatic depth, historical relevance or emotional uplift. And for a true science fiction experience, I'll watch *Metropolis* again. But there remains a definite place for knock-me-down visual fireworks, and *Avatar* is a major wonder movie.

SCIENCE FICTION AT THE BOXOFFICE

Compiled and annotated by **John McElwee**

(note: I've included John's figures and observations as they make the point that classic-era science fiction was in general not a huge moneymaker for Hollywood, and that many of our favorites were barely profitable. GE)

Big money was seldom spent on science fiction prior to the late sixties. Producers, and presumably mainstream audiences, associated the genre with lurid comic books and serials made for children. Fantastic films would for years be consigned to low-budget bins. The few exceptions were not notably successful. In fact, rentals for some of them would seem to have justified prejudices held toward the genre. What follows are sample numbers representing negative costs (NC), domestic rentals (DR), foreign rentals (FR), and profit/loss on science fiction features released in the fifties and sixties.

The Thing
NC --- 1.2 million
DR --- 2.0 million
FR --- $750,000
Profit --- $35,000

The Day The Earth Stood Still
NC --- $994,000
DR --- 1.6 million
FR --- 1.0 million
Profit --- $453,000

When Worlds Collide
NC --- $971,000
DR --- 1.5 million

War Of The Worlds
NC --- 1.7 million
DR --- 2.1 million

Them!
NC --- 1.2 million
DR --- 1.6 million
FR --- $890,000
Profit --- $685,000

Forbidden Planet
NC --- 1.9 million
DR --- 1.6 million
FR --- 1.8 million
Loss --- $16,000

Here are some rental figures for low-budget science fiction films released by United Artists and American-International Pictures.

Gog
DR --- $278,388
FR --- $190,000

The Monster That Challenged The World
DR --- $286,442
FR --- $272,439

Invisible Invaders
DR --- $138,385
FR --- $118,000

It Conquered The World
DR --- $284,000

Invasion Of The Saucer Men
DR --- $341,000

War Of The Colossal Beast
DR --- $185,000

Low-budget sci-fi way outnumbered major studio output throughout this period. As with series westerns and serials, it was possible to make money with these pictures as long as you didn›t spend much. MGM discovered the perils of over-investing in sci-fi with *Forbidden Planet*. By 1957, Warners was competing with cheap monster shows with its minimal negative cost of $250,000 in *The Black Scorpion*, which was still more than most independents were spending. By the end of the fifties, major distributors were doing business with the independents by way of negative pick-ups and distributing deals for things like *Teenagers From Outer Space* (domestic rentals --- $215,000) and even Japanese imports (*Gigantis, The Fire Monster*, which yielded $467,000 in domestic rentals).

The sixties represented a downturn in that many pictures released but a few years before were already being shown on television in sci-fi programming formats. There was little reason to pay admission for the privilege of watching spacemen and monsters in black-and-white. Still it was possible to ring the bell with kid-aimed features heavily saturated with TV advertising. Universal got it right with *King Kong vs. Godzilla*, a 1963 hit with 1.219 in domestic rentals. As before, however, studios could get snake-bit when too much was splurged --- MGM's *The Power* had a negative cost of 1.7 million, and only $352,000 in domestic rentals, $468,000 foreign, and an eventual loss of $822,000. Even the highly regarded *2001: A Space Odyssey* lost money on its initial go-round. With an astronomical negative cost of 10.3 million (you could have made *five seasons* of 50's sci-fi on this kind of money), the domestic rentals return (through 1970) was 16.3 million, with 5.5 million foreign. The loss would be $802,000.

Fantastic Voyage
DR --- 4.9 million (but still lost $191,000 because negative costs were 5.0 million)

First Men In The Moon
DR --- $887,000

Robinson Crusoe On Mars
DR --- $834,000

Wild, Wild Planet
DR --- $749,000 (final profit of $10,000!)

Crack In The World
DR --- $573,000

The Power
DR --- $352,000 (final loss of $822,000)

The Time Travelers
DR --- $282,000

Voyage To The End Of The Universe
DR --- $126,000

The Earth Dies Screaming
DR --- $93,000

ACKNOWLEDGEMENTS

This book has been encouraged and influenced by Gary Teetzel, an amazing resource for film research in general and the fantastic film in particular. I would also like to thank the following people for material and other support for the writing process. They're equally split between longtime associates and DVD Savant readers with like-minded interests.

Aitam Bar-Sagi for his research on *Metropolis*. Michael Bjortvedt for seeing the Star Child in *Ikarie XB 1*. Jon Bloom for inside filming information on *The Andromeda Strain*. Mark Bourne for his excellent Sci-Fi reviews and advice. Robin Brunet for details on cut scenes in *The Thing from Another World*. Randy Cook for calling my UCLA Project 2 a "Mexican Science Fiction Film". Dick Dinman for information about *Conquest of Space*. Kip Doto for providing a look at the Danish version of *Reptilicus*. Maria Erickson for translating the Italian subtitles of *La fin du monde*. Stuart Galbraith IV for his expertise on Japanese fantasy films. Glen Grant for the loan of *F. P. 1 Doesn't Answer*. Giancarlo Cairella of The International Movie Data Base for being such a helpful resource. Darren Gross for sharing his research into lost film materials. Michael Hyatt for his work on *The Day of the Triffids* and for screening a fine-quality print of *Invaders from Mars*. Andreas Kortmann for his help & corrections on German and Czech space movies, and for finding *Der große Verhau*. Tim Lucas for inviting me to write for Video Watchdog. Marek Mateja in Czechoslovakia for help on *Ikarie XB 1*. John McElwee for his insightful box office report. Claude Mettavant in France for his research into *Kosmitcheskiy Reys* and other lost Euro sci-fi. Steve Nielson for inspiring half of the insights (such as they are) in these reviews. Jim Peavy and others at the Classic Horror Board for corrections on *This Island Earth*. Kevin Pyrtle for making the original *La fin du monde* available. Wayne Schmidt for making the uncut *These are the Damned* available back in 1998. Bill Shaffer with info about Wade Williams' print of *Them!* Jeff Stafford for his continuing support and encouragement. Joel Stein for access to the short English version of *These Are the Damned*. Todd Stribich for guiding me to many obscure tape sources. Gordon Thomas for welcome research assists on *Metropolis* and *The War of the Worlds*. Thomas Treasure for information on *Ikarie XB 1*. Bill Warren convinced me that it was unwise to conclude that Dalton Trumbo wrote *Rocketship X-M*. Tom Weaver for his insights on *4D Man*.

BIBLIOGRAPHY

Jerome Agel: *The Making of 2001: A Space Odyssey* Signet Film Series 1970.

John Baxter: *Science Fiction in the Cinema* The Book Service Ltd. 1970

John Brosnan: *Future Tense* St. Martin's Press 1978

Lotte Eisner: *Fritz Lang* New York, Oxford University Press, 1977

Phil Hardy (editor): *The Overlook Film Encyclopedia: Science Fiction* Overlook TP, 1995.

Peter Hutchings: *Hammer and Beyond, The British Horror Film* Manchester University Press, 1993

Robert Skotak: *Ib Melchoir: Man of Imagination* Midnight Marquee, 2000.

Robert Skotak and Scot Molton: Liner notes from the 1992 Image Laserdisc of *Invaders from Mars*, itself referenced to an article in *Fantascene* magazine #4, written by.

Susan Sontag: The Imagination of Disaster: *Against Interpretation* New York: Farrar, Strauss & Giroux 1966.

Bill Warren: *Keep Watching the Skies! American Science Fiction Movies of the Fifties, The 21st Century Edition* McFarland 2009. This remains the primary resource on sci-fi cinema of the classic period, and provides much of the hard research that makes secondary essay books like this one possible.

Donald Willis, Editor: *Variety's Science Fiction Reviews* Garland, 1985. An essential read to understand the industry's attitude toward genre fare. Until the middle 1960s, *Variety* shows a distinct bias against foreign-produced "product".

15480510R00166

Made in the USA
Lexington, KY
30 May 2012